Fourth Workshop on Online Abuse and Harms (WOAH 2020)

Online
20 November 2020

ISBN: 978-1-7138-2007-9

WOAH 2020

The Fourth Workshop on Online Abuse and Harms

Proceedings of the Workshop

November 20, 2020 Online

Introduction

Digital technologies have brought myriad benefits for society, transforming how people connect, communicate and interact with each other. However, they have also enabled harmful and abusive behaviours to reach large audiences and for their negative effects to be amplified, including interpersonal aggression, bullying and hate speech. The negative effects are further compounded as marginalised and vulnerable communities are disproportionately at the risk of receiving abuse. As policymakers, civil society and tech companies devote more resources and effort to tackling online abuse, there is a pressing need for scientific research that critically and rigorously investigates how they are defined, detected, moderated and countered.

Over the last few years there has been a rise in interest in using Natural Language Processing (NLP) to address online abuse at scale. In order to develop robust, long-term technological solutions for this problem, we need perspectives from beyond computer science, including a diverse range of disciplines such as psychology, law, gender studies, communications, and critical race theory. Our goal with the Workshop on Online Abuse and Harms (WOAH, formerly the Workshop on Online Abusive Language, ALW) is to provide a platform to facilitate the interdisciplinary conversations and collaborations that are needed to effectively and ethically address online abuse.

Each year, we choose a theme for our workshop that guides the talks and panel discussions. In previous years we have focused on human content moderators, the policy aspects of tackling online abuse, and the stories and experiences of those who have received large amounts of online abuse. The themes do not limit what original research is presented at the workshop, rather it helps to frame the discussions by providing a particular lens. For this year, we have chosen to focus on Social Bias and Unfairness in Online Abuse Detection. We continue to highlight the need for research that emphasizes the disparate harms that content moderation systems create and propagate.

With content moderation systems being researched and deployed more widely, there is a growing need to critically consider how they unequally impact different communities and drive processes of marginalisation. To this effect, we have expanded the remit of WOAH, introducing a new track for civil society reports to encourage civil society actors to submit and present their work. Moreover, for practical considerations of bias in content moderation, we conceptualised *shared explorations* - a type of shared task that emphasizes the critical investigation of datasets over leaderboards.
To situate the Workshop around the theme of social biases, we have invited speakers to highlight different ways in which content moderation systems can be vehicles of oppression against marginalised people.

In addition, in the interest of increased engagement with the civil society, we organized a satellite session of the workshop at RightsCon 2020, the biggest international conference at the intersection of human rights and digital technologies. Our session consisted of a panel discussion including computer scientists, human rights scholars, and social scientists, and was attended by over 100 human rights scholars and activists from across the world. We include a RightsCon session report in the proceedings to summarize the main themes of insights emerged from the discussion in the satellite session.

During the Workshop we will have a multi-disciplinary panel discussion where experts will debate and contextualize the major issues facing computational analysis of online abuse, with a specific focus on systemic biases that are propagated by content moderation systems. This session will be followed by paper Q&A sessions, facilitating discussions around the research papers described in these proceedings. Due to the virtual nature of this edition of the workshop, we have gathered papers into five thematic panels to allow for more in-depth and rounded discussions.

Continuing the success of the past editions of the workshop, we received 53 submissions. Our submissions come overwhelmingly from academics with 42 submission from academics, 3 from civil society, and 7 from industry. To encourage submissions from social scientists and civil society, we constructed two submission tracks that allowed for unarchived submissions: Extended abstracts and reports. Following a rigorous review process, we selected 24 submissions to be presented at the workshop. These include 3 extended abstracts, 12 long papers, 4 short papers and 2 reports. The authors of all accepted papers are given an opportunity to expand their work into full journal articles, considered for publication in a forthcoming special issue on online abuse and harms in the journal *First Monday*.[1]

The accepted papers deal with a wide array of topics; critically investigating existing approaches to tackling online abuse, interrogating the uses and implications of classification systems, proposing new datasets, models and extending online abuse detection to new languages, contexts and types of abuse. Three of the accepted papers incorporate social science perspectives, a significant improvement compared with the last two iterations of WOAH. The five panels capture the most important focuses of the submissions: Methods for classifying online abuse (including Transformer-based models and new model architectures), Technical challenges in classifying online abuse, Biases in abusive content training datasets, New datasets and resources for tackling online abuse, and Ways of tackling online abuse.

The authors in these proceedings are also geographically diverse, representing work from 10 countries (based on affiliations): Australia, Canada, France, Germany, New Zealand, Norway, Russia, Turkey, United Kingdom, and the United States.

With this, we welcome you to the Fourth Workshop on Online Abuse and Harms and look forward to a day filled with spirited discussion and thought provoking research!

Bertie, Seyi, Vinod, and Zeerak

---

[1] https://www.workshopononlineabuse.com/cfp/first-monday-special-issue

Organizers:

Seyi Akiwowo, Glitch!
Bertram Vidgen, Alan Turing Institute
Vinodkumar Prabhakaran, Google
Zeerak Waseem, University of Sheffield

Program Committee:

Mark, Alfano, Delft University of Technology (Netherlands)
Naomi, Appelman, University of Amsterdam (Netherlands)
Veronika, Bajt, Peace Institute (Slovenia)
Renata, Barreto, Berkeley Law (United States)
Dan, Bateyko, Georgetown University Law Center (United States)
Peter, Bourgonje, DFKI (Germany)
Andrew, Caines, University of Cambridge (United Kingdom)
Michael, Castelle, University of Warwick (United Kingdom)
Tuhin, Chakrabarty, Columbia University (United States)
Montse, Cuadros, Vicomtech (Spain)
Aron, Culotta, Illinois Institute of Technology (United States)
Thomas, Davidson, Cornell University (United States)
Gretel Liz, De la Peña Sarracèn, Universidad Politècnica de València (Spain)
Nemanja, Djuric, Uber ATG (United States)
Yanai, Elazar, Bar-Ilan University (Israel)
Elisabetta, Fersini, University of Milano-Bicocca (Italy)
Paula, Fortuna, TALN, Pompeu Fabra University (Portugal)
Simona, Frenda, Universitat Politècnica de València (Spain)
Björn, Gambäck, Norwegian University of Science and Technology (Norway)
Maya, Ganesh, Leuphana University (Germany)
Sara E., Garza, FIME-UANL (Mexico)
Ryan, Georgi, University of Washington (United States)
Lee, Gillam, University of Surrey (United Kingdom)
Tonei, Glavinic, Dangerous Speech Project (Spain)
Genevieve, Gorrell, University of Sheffield (United Kingdom)
Erica, Greene, The New York Times (United States)
Marco, Guerini, Fondazione Bruno Kessler (Italy)
Udo, Hahn, Friedrich-Schiller-Universität Jena (Germany)
Alex, Hanna, Google (United States)
Alex, Harris, The Alan Turing Institute (United Kingdom)
Christopher, Homan, Rochester Institute of Technology (United States)
Hossein, Hosseini, Department of Electrical Engineering, University of Washington (United States)
Veronique, Hoste, Ghent University (Belgium)
Ruihong, Huang, Texas A&M University (United States)
Muhammad Okky, Ibrohim, Universitas Indonesia (Indonesia)
Srecko, Joksimovic, University of South Australia (Australia)
Nishant, Kambhatla, Simon Fraser University (Canada)
George, Kennedy, Intel (United States)
Ashiqur, KhudaBukhsh, Carnegie Mellon University (United States)
Ralf, Krestel, Hasso Plattner Institute, University of Potsdam (Germany)

Els, Lefever, LT3, Ghent University (Belgium)
Diana, Maynard, University of Sheffield (United Kingdom)
Smruthi, Mukund, Amazon (United States)
Isar, Nejadgholi, National Research Council Canada (Canada)
Viviana, Patti, University of Turin, Dipartimento di Informatica (Italy)
Umashanthi, Pavalanathan, Twitter (United States)
Matùš, Pikuliak, Kempelen Institute of Intelligent Technologies (Slovakia)
Michal, Ptaszynski, Kitami Institute of Technology (Japan)
Georg, Rehm, DFKI (Germany)
Julian, Risch, Hasso Plattner Institute, University of Potsdam (Germany)
Björn, Ross, University of Edinburgh (United Kingdom)
Paolo, Rosso, Universitat Politècnica de València (Spain)
Niloofar, Safi Samghabadi, University of Houston (United States)
Magnus, Sahlgren, RISE (Sweden)
Christina, Sauper, Facebook (United States)
Alexandra, Schofield, Harvey Mudd College (United States)
Qinlan, Shen, Carnegie Mellon University (United States)
Marian, Simko, Slovak University of Technology in Bratislava (Slovakia)
Vinay, Singh, International Institute of Information Technology, Hyderabad (India)
Sajedul, Talukder, Florida International University (United States)
Zahidur, Talukder, University of Texas at Arlington (United States)
Linnet, Taylor, Tilburg University (Netherlands)
Achint, Thomas, Embibe (India)
Sara, Tonelli, FBK (Italy)
Dimitrios, Tsarapatsanis, University of York (United Kingdom)
Avijit, Vajpayee, Educational Testing Service (United States)
Joris, Van Hoboken, Vrije Universiteit Brussel (Belgium)
Erik, Velldal, University of Oslo (Norway)
Ingmar, Weber, Qatar Computing Research Institute (Qatar)
Lucas, Wright, Cornell University (United States)
Fan, Yang, Nuance Communications (United States)
Seunghyun, Yoon, Seoul National University (Republic of Korea)
Aleš, Završnik, Institute of criminology at the Faculty of Law Ljubljana (Slovenia)
Torsten, Zesch, Language Technology Lab, University of Duisburg-Essen (Germany)
Andrej, Švec, Slido (Slovakia)

Additional Reviewers:

Mareike, Hartmann, University of Copenhagen (Denmark)

Invited Speaker:

André Brock, School of Literature, Media, and Communication, Georgia Tech
Alex Hannah, Google
Maliha Ahmed, Independent Researcher
Maria Y. Rodriguez, University at Buffalo (State University of New York)

Table of Contents

Online Abuse and Human Rights

Shared Exploration

Conference Program[1]

November 20, 2020

November 20, 2020

13:00–13:10 *Opening Remarks*

13:10–15:40 **Keynotes**

13:10–13:55 *Keynote I*
André Brock

13:55–14:40 *Keynote II*
Alex Hanna and Maliha Ahmed

14:40–14:45 *Break*

14:45–15:30 *Keynote III*
Maria Rodriguez

15:30–15:40 *Break*

15:40–16:40 *Keynote Panel*
Maliha Ahmed, André Brock, Alex Hanna, Maria Rodriguez

16:40–17:00 *Break*

---

[1]All times are given in UTC.

17:00–17:45   **Paper Q & A Panels I:**

Panel I: Methods for classifying online abuse

A Novel Methodology for Developing Automatic Harassment Classifiers for Twitter
Ishaan Arora, Julia Guo, Sarah Ita Levitan, Susan McGregor and Julia Hirschberg

Using Transfer-based Language Models to Detect Hateful and Offensive Language Online
Vebjørn Isaksen and Björn Gambäck

Fine-tuning BERT for multi-domain and multi-label incivil language detection
Kadir Bulut Ozler, Kate Kenski, Steve Rains, Yotam Shmargad, Kevin Coe and Steven Bethard

HurtBERT: Incorporating Lexical Features with BERT for the Detection of Abusive Language
Anna Koufakou, Endang Wahyu Pamungkas, Valerio Basile and Viviana Patti

Abusive Language Detection using Syntactic Dependency Graphs
Kanika Narang and Chris Brew

Panel II: Biases in datasets for abuse

Impact of politically biased data on hate speech classification
Maximilian Wich, Jan Bauer and Georg Groh

Identifying and Measuring Annotator Bias Based on Annotators' Demographic Characteristics
Hala Al Kuwatly, Maximilian Wich and Georg Groh

Investigating Annotator Bias with a Graph-Based Approach
Maximilian Wich, Hala Al Kuwatly and Georg Groh

Reducing Unintended Identity Bias in Russian Hate Speech Detection
Nadezhda Zueva, Madina Kabirova and Pavel Kalaidin

17:45–18:00 *Break*

Online Abuse and Human Rights: WOAH Satellite Session at RightsCon 2020

Vinodkumar Prabhakaran
Google Brain

Zeerak Waseem
University of Sheffield

Seyi Akiwowo
Glitch!

Bertie Vidgen
The Alan Turing Institute

Abstract

In 2020 The Workshop on Online Abuse and Harms (WOAH) held a satellite panel at RightsCons 2020, an international human rights conference. Our aim was to bridge the gap between human rights scholarship and Natural Language Processing (NLP) research communities in tackling online abuse. We report on the discussions that took place, and present an analysis of four key issues which emerged: Problems in tackling online abuse, Solutions, Meta concerns and the Ecosystem of content moderation and research. We argue there is a pressing need for NLP research communities to engage with human rights perspectives, and identify four key ways in which NLP research into online abuse could immediately be enhanced to create better and more ethical solutions.

1 Introduction

The Workshop on Online Abuse and Harms (WOAH[1]), previously known as the Abusive Language Workshop (ALW), is a leading publication venue for cutting-edge computational research on detecting, analysing and tackling online abuse, primarily using Natural Language Processing (NLP) techniques. Over the past three iterations, WOAH has built an interdisciplinary community of computer scientists, social scientists, critical theorists, legal scholars and more.

Continuing this tradition of embracing interdisciplinarity, for WOAH 2020 we organized a satellite panel at RightsCon 2020, one of the leading international human rights conferences. It brings together business leaders, technologists, academics, journalists and government representatives to discuss pressing issues at the intersection of human rights and technology.[2]

As an area directly concerned with protecting under-represented, vulnerable and marginalised communities, we anticipated that NLP research into online abuse would benefit from engaging directly with human rights scholarship. Human rights offers a powerful way of motivating work in this area, understanding what is at stake with online hate (and efforts to counter it) and bridging the gap between engineering/computational work and the groups that are affected by abuse. A global human rights framework could provide a much needed value system for work on tackling online abuse, furnishing NLP researchers with much-needed frameworks, theories and concepts. Yet, to date, research on online abuse published at WOAH/ALW and other leading NLP venues has largely lacked an explicit connection to human rights or an engagement with human rights scholarship.

Similarly, we believe the human rights scholarship and activism could also benefit from a shared understanding of the problem space which technologists working on NLP-based solutions for tackling online abuse operate in – exploring both the opportunities and limitations of such approaches. More collaboration and dialogue could also foster more useful and critical discussions of how engineering solutions are designed and implemented, helping to ensure that NLP tools have a positive impact on society.

In the satellite session at RightsCon, we brought together human rights experts with computer scientists in an effort to formulate a rights respecting approach to tackling online abuse.[3] Our objective was to bridge the gap between these communities as a way to drive new initiatives and outlooks, ultimately leading to better and more responsible ways of moderating online content. The intended outcomes of the panel were:

---

[1] www.workshopononlineabuse.com
[2] https://www.rightscon.org

[3] Please note that the views contained in this report do not necessarily represent the views of all panellists.

Proceedings of the Fourth Workshop on Online Abuse and Harms, pages 1–6
Online, November 20, 2020. ©2020 Association for Computational Linguistics
https://doi.org/10.18653/v1/P17

1. To start a dialogue between computer scientists (primarily NLP experts) and the human rights community working on tackling online abuse.

2. To establish a shared understanding of challenges and possible solutions.

3. To invigorate a global human rights based critique of computer science research practices in this domain.

The purpose this report is to summarize the panel and reflect on the outcomes. A one-hour discussion session has been allocated during the WOAH 2020 program to reflect on the report and the RightsCon panel.

2 RightsCon Session Overview

Title Tackling Online Abuse: Bridging the Gap between Human Rights and Computer Science

Organizers Vinodkumar Prabhakaran, Zeerak Waseem, Bertie Vidgen, Seyi Akiwowo (moderator)

Moderator Seyi Akiwowo (SA)

Panelists Maria Y Rodriguez (MR), Caroline Sinders (CS), Cristian Danescu-Niculescu-Mizil (CDNM)

Participants The session had 113 RightsCon attendees (including organizers and panelists).

Session structure Initially, three questions were posed to the panelists (shared in advance and decided by the Organizers). Each panelist was requested to answer at least one of the three questions in their 10-15 minute opening statement:

1. What are the primary challenges in tackling online abuse?

2. What are the blind spots of algorithmic means of tackling online abuse?

3. What are the barriers that divide computational research and human rights scholarship?

We then opened the floor for questions from attendees. They were curated and given to the moderator in real time. This lasted for 15 minutes, after which the panel concluded.

3 Analysis and Synthesis

We transcribed the panel using automated software and then manually checked the manuscript. We used an inductive approach of qualitative text analysis to analyze the transcript in order to identify recurring topics (Thomas, 2006). We found over a couple of dozen recurring topics that were brought up by the panellists at least twice during the discussion. These recurring topics were then analysed and iteratively refined and merged together to identify four high-level themes: Problems, Solutions, Meta considerations, and Ecosystem.

3.1 Problems in tackling online abuse

Abuse is contextual Several of the participants brought up the contextual nature of online abuse and hate, and how this makes it more challenging to detect and intervene. As CS put it: 'what sounds like harassment to one person may not be harassment at all. Harassment is very contextual. Sometimes it's not, but for the most part it is extremely contextual. Actions are contextual... and how do you code context?'. Panellists also brought up how geographic and temporal contexts are important in understanding whether or not something is abusive. CS pointed out that 'who is speaking and the power that they have dramatically changes what they say and how it is interpreted [...] the context of who says what should never be forgotten'. She argued that the language used by Donald Trump has different implications based on whether he uttered them as the President or as a presidential candidate. CS also brought forth the example of Pepe the frog: 'Pepe started off being a stoner comic that was really beloved in California and LA and turned into a mean representative of the alt-right and now is being used in a proactive and protest-supporting way in Hong Kong. Language differs and changes radically and really quickly. It also differs from country to country and place to place.'

Abuse has different modes CS discussed the different ways in which online abuse happens. These can each inflict different harms, exhibit different dynamics and may require different strategies to mitigate them:

- Whether the person being harassed knows the harasser or not;

- Whether the harassment is one to one, many to one, or many to many;

- Whether the harassment is coordinated or uncoordinated;

- Whether the harassment is happening across many platforms or just one;

- Whether the harassment is also happening offline

Online and offline harms are closely connected Online harms can be associated with harm in the offline world. MR used the example of Kanye West's announcement to run for US President as an example of online abuse and harassment which could result in offline harms (in this case, how it may influence African American voters to not vote as a result of the rhetoric used in the campaign). SA summarized this as a "continuum of violence" and argued it is important to understand that what happens offline will likely be displayed online. Equally, online discussions can seep into and shape the offline world. Panellists also pointed out that not all forms of abuse that happen online are immediately obvious and that it requires understanding of, and reflection on, their offline impact. CS pointed out that 'If someone is doxing you they may not say "I am going to dox you."'

3.2   Solutions for tackling online abuse

A range of interventions are available Panellists discussed the various modes of intervention to tackle online abuse that are currently available. They also discussed where NLP may help, noting that any solution needs to be scalable to match the volume and variety of content shared online. Much NLP research is focused on finding and classifying offensive or toxic language, which is then either directly censored or flagged for human moderators to review. However, CDNM argued that this is already too late in a sense since the abuse (and associated harm) may have already been inflicted. CDNM described their work on detecting conversations that may turn toxic ahead of time as a potential alternative. One of the attendees also brought up the question of counter narratives as a means of addressing the harms inflicted by online abuse. CDNM pointed out that while banning users is a popular approach it may not always be appropriate since some offenders are 'regular people' who happened to misbehave only once or a few times. Banning is an important option for repeat and serious offenders but may be overly censorious in some contexts.

Tech solutions are often flawed Myriad issues are associated with various tech-based interventions. Both CS and CDNM pointed out the moral and ethical issues associated with bot-driven counter narrative strategies, as well as the challenges of deploying such interventions at scale. All panellists also pointed to the various biases that may be encoded into the automated detection systems. For instance, MR recalled Brandon Stewart's and Justin Grimmer's framing that 'mathematical models of language are wrong. They just are. There is no way to be so reductionist as to capture the complexity of human interaction in, you know, binary. However, they're useful; they can give us some really good information to develop.' (Grimmer and Stewart, 2013) CS and MR also brought up the issue that most NLP models being based on language data that is not representative of the communities they are deployed onto.

Content moderation should be a question for society Platforms which choose to not moderate online abuse, or do so only very minimally, are not just being 'light touch' – they are making a decision that reflects a set of values and norms. The effects of this can be highly pernicious. CDNM brought up that not moderating popular online spaces such as Facebook and Twitter may result in some groups losing their social voice if they do not feel safe to communicate. MR brought up the historical example of the printing press and how it resulted in the rise of cults and certain political movements, in addition to increases in positive things like literacy and civic engagement. She argued that if we consider social media to be the new public commons then moderation is not only a question of infrastructure and technical feasibility – the key issue is what civil society agrees upon for it. Debating, arguing and contesting our expectations for these public spaces is key to figuring out what sort of moderation is needed.

The past is not a good way of understanding the future MR argued that many researchers implicitly assume that historical data can be used to train new models and then applied to future data. For instance, in content moderation many systems are trained on old annotated datasets, which are often years out of date. This approach works well in some fields like demography (which studies population dynamics and migration patterns), but is often inappropriate when researching how individuals communicate online and interact within groups as: 'we can in no way assume that [...] the future will look like the past because the present is actually where all of this is occurring.'

Tech solutions raise surveillance/privacy concerns and tradeoffs Tech based interventions that review content on a continuous basis (so called 'proactive monitoring') raise concerns about privacy as they involve constant evaluation and classification of users' messages. CDNM raised the issue that such technology can be put to dual uses. MR identified that interventions of all kinds require surveillance when they are implemented and scaled. Therefore there will always be a need to balance intervening with minimizing losses to privacy.

3.3   Meta considerations

Who does the research? Panellists brought forth the capability gap within the community of researchers and developers working on tech-based solutions for online abuse – where there is a lack of engagement with groups actually affected by online abuse. MR pointed out the importance of lived experiences for understanding the harms that online abuse causes to communities. MR urged researchers to ensure that communities affected by abuse are represented within their teams. This would help to ensure the nuances of the problems are better understood and accounted for in interventions. It could also avoid any unethical or inappropriate uses of technology.

NLP is not always the solution Panellists repeatedly pointed out the over-reliance on AI/ML/NLP above potentially more efficient and simple solutions. MR highlighted that the main focus of many computational researchers is to improve model performance, instead of understanding how abuse occurs, why, and the nuances associated with it. CS pointed to non-tech solutions such as intervening in a conversation to engage with the offender, and CDNM raised the example of Wikipedia discussion forums, where a fixed wording message was shown to experienced editors when engaging with newcomers. It had positively affected them to help newcomers to fit in (Halfaker et al., 2011). A socio-technical approach to tackling abuse could help address these issues.

Vocabularies needs to be bridged Panellists agreed that there is a need for more effective interdisciplinary conversations, such as this panel and the associated report. At present there is a lack of shared understanding about the problem posed by online abuse, and a common vocabulary to talk about issues does not yet exist. More discussion and collaboration requires some shared terminology and willingness to understand cross-disciplinary scholarship.

3.4   The Ecosystem

More transparency about moderation processes is needed Participants discussed how there is a lack of transparency regarding the processes and pipelines that platforms follow in handling online abuse. This is a core challenge which limits how much civil society and independent researchers can meaningfully engage with their work. CS pointed out that there is not enough clarity in how online abuse (including hate speech and harassment) is handled by different platforms compared with misinformation/disinformation, or what mechanisms platforms use to adjudicate reports from users. More information from platforms would be useful for civil society, such as knowing the aggregate number of user reports, what responses were taken, what information was available to the content moderators, how much time was given to each one, and so on. SA also pointed to the issue that user-reporting often ends up being free labor for platforms to improve their models but they are often not transparent about it. Often, user reports are provided by activist groups who are in effect giving free labour to highly profitable companies.

More education is needed Panellists identified the need for better education of users, civil society and governments about the harms caused by online abuse. SA argued that there is a huge deficit in how people understand digital security, safety, self defense, and agency online. CDNM also pointed to the need to educate the public about what can and cannot be done technically to ensure user's safety. Efforts should be made to be more open about the flawed nature of tech-based interventions for online abuse.

Platforms should be more accountable Panellists identified the deficit in accountability when it comes to how tech platforms deal with online abuse. SA drew parallels with how civic bodies hold extensive case reviews when severe incidents like homicide happen so as to understand what happened, and to identify any failures. She questioned why such case reviews do not happen when grave injustices occur on tech platforms. SA argued there is a need, and growing opportunity, for academics, policy makers and civil society to work together to bring tech accountability into the mainstream.

4   Discussion

Our RightsCons session is just the starting point for a wider set of conversations which need to take place between technologists, engineers and civil society. Numerous shortcomings in how platforms moderate content and NLP research is conducted have been identified throughout the panel. There is a pressing need for them to be addressed if we are to build systems which meaningfully tackle online abuse. A human rights based approach is a promising way of bridging the historical and disciplinary divides between these groups but it may not be the only way. We strongly encourage that, aside from anything else, a wider range of perspectives are adopted.

From our analysis we identify four main areas which could immediately be tackled by the NLP community to create better and more ethical solutions for online abuse.

1. **Problems**: the NLP community tends to work on datasets which do not account for context, often focusing on just language by itself. In particular, less attention is paid to the particular social and political setting in which abuse is sent, and the role of the speaker and audience. The dynamics of how abuse spreads, such as the role of networks and 'trigger events' are often not considered in NLP work. Particularly important focuses for future work include (1) how the abuse is sent and whether it is one to one or many to one, (2) whether it is coordinated or not and (3) the connections between online and offline abuse.

2. **Solutions**: the NLP community primarily focuses on "find offensive or toxic language", with much less focus on other strategies such as counter narratives or preemptive interventions. Questions around moral, ethical and bias issues are relatively new to the field, although progress has been made. For instance, the theme of WOAH 2020 is social bias and unfairness. The NLP community rarely talks about the potential misuse of the systems we develop, such as invading users' privacy through surveillance. It also gives insufficient focus to whether systems can actually be used in the real-world, focusing too much on maximizing performance through more sophisticated engineering solutions. Efforts to integrate these concerns directly into NLP research, or at least demonstrating awareness they exist, would be a substantial help.

3. **Meta considerations**: NLP is not the only answer. There is a concerning tendency to rely too heavily on tech to 'solve' the problem of online abuse, even though it is a field that itself has numerous representation problems. The field should aim to improve representation and to work more closely with the groups affected by online abuse, as well as other end-users.

4. **Ecosystem**: Many NLP solutions are hard to explain and their limitations are not well understood by the general public. NLP researchers could better advance efforts to improve transparency, accountability, and literacy. Areas include: (1) working on more interpretable models, (2) unearthing the implicit assumptions being made in NLP work flows and (3) explaining their work in non-technologist language to help it reach a wider audience.

Tackling online abuse is an important task; one that is too important to let disciplinary divides hold back. NLP and other computational approaches have the potential to make an incredibly positive impact on this problem – and are already being used in many settings. But NLP researchers need to move beyond seeing online abuse detection as solely an engineering problem, instead recognizing the social and ethical impetuses that motivate it. Human rights frameworks offer a powerful starting point for achieving this. Ultimately, it will require far more meaningful dialogue between the engineers and technologists who have largely been responsible for building systems and the groups who are directly affected by them. This report is intended as one step towards achieving this goal.

Acknowledgments

The authors would like to thank all participants and attendees at the panel for their contributions and feedback.

References

Justin Grimmer and Brandon M Stewart. 2013. Text as Data: The Promise and Pitfalls of Automatic Content Analysis Methods for Political Texts. *Political Analysis*, 1(1):1–31.

Aaron Halfaker, Bryan Song, D. Alex Stuart, Aniket Kittur, and John Riedl. 2011. Nice: Social translucence through ui intervention. In *Proceedings of the 7th International Symposium on Wikis and Open Collaboration*, WikiSym '11, page 101–104, New York, NY, USA. Association for Computing Machinery.

David R. Thomas. 2006. A General Inductive Approach for Analyzing Qualitative Evaluation Data. *American Journal of Evaluation*, 27(2):237–246.

A Novel Methodology for Developing Automatic Harassment Classifiers for Twitter

Ishaan Arora
Columbia University
ia2419@columbia.edu

Julia Guo
Columbia University
jzg2110@columbia.edu

Susan E. McGregor
Columbia University
sem2196@columbia.edu

Sarah Ita Levitan
Hunter College (CUNY)
sarah.levitan@hunter.cuny.edu

Julia Hirschberg
Columbia University
julia@cs.columbia.edu

Abstract

Most efforts at identifying abusive speech online rely on public corpora that have been scraped from websites using keyword-based queries or released by site or platform owners for research purposes. These are typically labeled by crowd-sourced annotators – not the targets of the abuse themselves. While this method of data collection supports fast development of machine learning classifiers, the models built on them often fail in the context of real-world harassment and abuse, which contain nuances less easily identified by non-targets. Here, we present a mixed-methods approach to create classifiers for abuse and harassment which leverages direct engagement with the target group in order to achieve high quality and ecological validity of data sets and labels, and to generate deeper insights into the key tactics of bad actors. We use women journalists' experience on Twitter as an initial community of focus. We identify several structural mechanisms of abuse that we believe will generalize to other target communities.

1 Introduction

Harassment is a significant problem in online spaces. In 2017, one in four Americans reported experiencing online harassment, with more than 60% describing it as a "major problem" (Duggan, 2017).

For journalists, a social media presence is essentially a professional requirement, as it is both a mechanism for locating sources and for promoting stories (Ferrier and Garud-Patkar, 2018); as of 2018, more Americans (roughly 20%) get their news from social media than from printed newspapers (Shearer, 2018). At the same time, journalists receive an inordinate volume of hateful and harassing messages via social media. In a recent survey conducted by the Committee to Protect Journalists (CPJ), 90% of American journalists described online harassment as the biggest threat facing journalists today, with women and minority journalists being disproportionately targeted online (Westcott and Foley, 2019).

This harassment can have devastating effects. In 2016, 10% of women journalists said that they had considered leaving the profession out of fear (Nilsson and Örnebring, 2016), while others avoided certain coverage areas in an effort to mitigate the risk of harassment. Still others may choose not to enter the field at all.

At a time when there is a major need to retain skilled journalists and diversify newsrooms (Scire, 2020), our goal is to develop a research methodology to address this critical threat facing journalists, and ultimately, our free press.

Our contributions in this paper include:

a) Identifying gaps in current anti-harassment tools provided by Twitter;

b) Identifying key strategies used by harassers to circumvent these tools and reach their targets; and

c) Development of a direct-engagement research process and data collection platform to curate datasets with high ecological validity, which will ultimately be used to train better machine learning classifiers for harassment detection.

2 Motivation and Approach

Currently, there are limited options available for journalists to deal with harassing messages on Twitter. Twitter has three primary mechanisms through which a user can control their interactions on the platform: muting, blocking, and the recently introduced "conversations" controls, all of which have a slightly different impact on the content a user can access. For example, muting and blocking can both prevent content from certain users from appearing in some user A's timeline (Twitter, c) (Twitter, d).

Proceedings of the Fourth Workshop on Online Abuse and Harms, pages 7–15
Online, November 20, 2020. ©2020 Association for Computational Linguistics
https://doi.org/10.18653/v1/P17

However, muted users can still follow and interact with A, while blocked users are no longer able to see A's tweets, and if they visit A's profile, they will see they have been blocked (Twitter, b). The new "conversations" feature, meanwhile, allows user A to specify whether everyone, everyone they follow, or only specific users can reply to a specific tweet (Twitter, a).

While these tools offer impressive granularity, many journalists have both large followings and a professional mandate to interact with their audiences on social media. This makes many of the available controls impractical or ineffective. Moreover, two of the three tools Twitter offers are only effective retrospectively, meaning the targeted user must still read blocked users' offensive tweets before they can choose to mute or block them. Not only does this require journalists to experience harm in order to achieve any potential remediation, if they are targeted by a large number of accounts, the manual effort becomes time-prohibitive.

Shared blocklists have been touted as a means for addressing some of these issues (Geiger, 2016). However, for journalists this can result in blocking users who may be sharing legitimate critiques of their work (Jhaver et al., 2018). As a whole, journalists as a community have expressed desire for more effective user engagement management tools (Saridou et al., 2019).

Furthermore, while many social media platforms do already have automated mechanisms for filtering harassment and hate speech, these are largely based on keyword matching, requiring manual creation with no guarantee of accuracy. Due to the large scale of problematic content on social media worldwide, manual efforts by moderators and filters have also been insufficient (Gerrard, 2018).

The goal of this work is, therefore, to contribute a robust, generalizable mixed-methods approach to constructing harassment training datasets with strong ecological validity, in order to support the development of truly effective classifiers for proactively identifying real-world abusive, harassing, and demeaning speech towards specific communities on Twitter.

Working with journalists, we are collecting a large-scale corpus of personally-harassing messages they have received on Twitter, and have developed an easily-employed annotation method to label messages by degree of observed harassment. Using this data, we then build machine learning

classifiers to distinguish between hateful, abusive and neutral tweets. Ultimately, we plan to integrate our trained models into a tool to help journalists navigate and avoid having to see these unwanted, harassing messages.

3   Related Work

Prior work on automatic detection of hateful and abusive speech toward journalists is limited. In (Charitidis et al., 2020), researchers used a manually-validated seed set of journalism-related Twitter accounts to generate a list of target accounts across five languages. Using the Twitter API to conduct keyword-based searches, they then manually annotated hate vs. non-hate tweets. This yielded highly imbalanced corpora, with more "hate" than "non-hate" tweets for each language. Deep learning models trained on each language corpus achieved best macro-F1 scores over .80 for English, French and Greek but somewhat lower for Spanish and German.

Other work has addressed the more general problem of automatic identification of hate speech and abusive language online. In (Waseem, 2016), researchers found that crowd-sourced annotations performed poorly. This indicates the importance of expert annotators, which (Blackwell et al., 2017) situates specifically in terms of classifying harassment.

In (Warner and Hirschberg, 2012), researchers using data from Yahoo and the American Jewish Congress found that anti-Semitic hate speech differed linguistically from speech that targeted other religious or ethnic groups, highlighting the need for a community-specific approach to studying hate speech. (Salem et al., 2016) used content from self-identified hate communities, instead of keywords from hand-coded speech or manually coded hate speech terms, as training data for their work on hate speech detection with some success. In (Nobata et al., 2016), researchers studied abusive language in online user comments on news and finance forums using linguistic, syntactic, and distributed semantic features as well as lexicon-based features. Their dataset has been used to benchmark performance in hate speech detection, as has (Waseem and Hovy, 2016). In (Kshirsagar et al., 2018), researchers developed deep learning models for hate speech detection on Twitter, using transformed word embeddings to classify hate speech on three public datasets.

Researchers in journalism have also used more qualitative methods to study abusive and hateful speech towards journalists. For example, UT Austin's School of Journalism published results from in-depth interviews with 75 female journalists describing how rampant online sexual harassment disrupts their ability to do their jobs (Chen et al., 2018). The Committee to Protect Journalists reported similar findings in 2019 (Westcott and Foley, 2019).

Finally, we note that developers have created tools (e.g. Twitter Block Chain (Wren, 2019) and the recently discontinued Block Together (Hoffman-Andrews, 2020) and the forthcoming Block Party app (Chou, 2020)) specifically designed to address the manual nature of Twitter's muting and blocking functions. While these efforts appear to address an important limitation of Twitter's current systems, they remain a reactive, rather than proactive, approach.

Our proposed methodology for training data collection and annotation incorporates and improves on these approaches as follows: (1) We conduct background interviews with our target community of women journalists in order to identify common heuristics used to carry out harassment on Twitter, in order to develop a more nuanced and balanced dataset for annotation; (2) Annotations are performed by the targets of harassment, guaranteeing a unique level of ecological validity; (3) Our approach takes an empowering rather than exploitative approach to the detection process, promoting harm reduction by allowing harassment targets to participate constructively in the creation of classifiers that can better support their needs.

4 Methodology

We employ a mixed-methods approach that integrates qualitative and quantitative data collection and analysis. We begin by directly engaging with our target group of women journalists who have experienced online harassment. We recruit participants by circulating calls to participation in key networks of women journalists, followed by semi-structured pilot interviews with select participants, in which we question them about patterns of harassment that they have experienced or observed, and about potential tools or interventions that would improve their experience on social media. Despite our convenience sample, two key themes emerged across several pilot interviews, providing valuable

insights about the mechanisms of harassment on Twitter, which we describe in Section 5.

Results of these interviews are then integrated into our quantitative data collection pipeline. Using patterns of harassing language and behaviors on Twitter described by interview participants, we develop computational methods to automatically identify those patterns and then use these methods to sample potentially hateful messages from participants' Twitter archives for them to annotate. We describe this data selection process in Section 6.1. Through the process of direct engagement with our target community, we are able to curate a high quality dataset of labeled tweets to support the development of more robust harassment classifiers.

5 Pilot Interviews

To generate a well-balanced training set of tweets, we conducted pilot interviews with several women journalists who have faced significant harassment on Twitter. Through these interviews we learned about specific forms of the "sub-tweeting" and "snitch-tweeting" heuristics that are used to target these and other women journalists with abusive and harassing messages.

The primary form of "sub-tweeting" described to us consists of perpetrators capturing screenshots that contain the target's Twitter profile or username. They then tweet these out with implicit or explicit calls for their followers to tweet at the same target. This behavior constitutes "sub-tweeting" because the absence of the target's username in the text of the original tweet means that target will not be notified of the instigating tweet, and will therefore be caught off-guard by an influx of often abusive tweets, sometimes numbering in the thousands over a period of less than a day. (See (Tufekci, 2014) for more details and examples of "sub-tweeting.") We note that none of Twitter's currently available tools can mitigate this attack; even if the perpetrator has already been blocked by the target, they can simply log out of Twitter and view the target's profile in a web browser in order to obtain the required media.

While the effect of sub-tweeting is to mask the identity of the perpetrator, "snitch-tweeting" is a means of drawing the target into a sub-tweeted thread about themselves to expose them to abuse. Because sub-tweeting intentionally circumvents Twitter's notification systems, targets of abuse will typically be unaware of such sub-tweeting, unless, as described above, it is used to direct traffic to their account. "Snitch-tweeting" consists of adding a target's handle to a thread about them, thus triggering a notification. The goal is for the target then to review the notification and thus to view the abusive thread that precedes the snitch-tweet. Taken together, these results helped us inform our design for the tweet selection portion of our data pre-processing, as described below.

6 Platform Design

In order to curate a high-quality training dataset from participating journalists' tweets, we designed and implemented a two-part, web-based platform to facilitate the data collection and annotation processes. This web platform was designed to balance the proportion of abusive vs. non-abusive tweets that are presented for annotation, without relying on keywords, which are often too coarse-grained to serve as a reliable indicator of abusive content. Instead, we develop heuristics using insights from our pilot interviews as well as private data from the participant's account to include a more nuanced and representative range of potentially abusive tweets for annotation.

The platform is also designed to maximize the efficiency and accuracy of the annotation process, in order to generate a large volume of high-quality training data for deep learning models. We achieve this via batched contextual annotation: participants annotate tweets within the context of the original conversation or tweet thread, rather than annotating them in isolation, simulating how they would have viewed the conversation initially on Twitter. In addition to the annotation tool described above, we have also built a tool for secure data upload, as described below.

6.1 Platform Structure

The process of using our web annotation tool is split into 2 stages, each of which can be accessed via secure, password-protected URLs. First, the study participant securely logs in to the upload platform using a uniquely generated username and password. We ask participants to upload three distinct files, which can be extracted from their Twitter data archive: (1) tweet.js, which contains all of their tweets; (2) muted.js, which contains the list of accounts they have muted, and (3) blocked.js, which contains the list of accounts they have blocked.

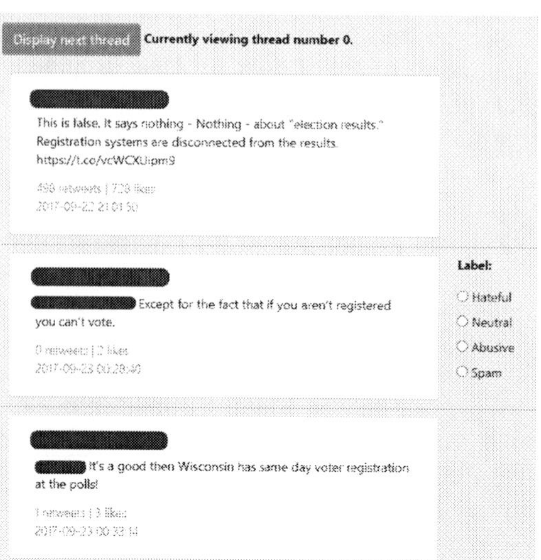

Figure 1: Annotation platform user interface.

Because participants' Twitter archives may contain anywhere from hundreds to tens of thousands of tweets, asking them to label all tweet threads is impractical. Moreover, our goal is to build a training corpus that is approximately equally split between hateful/abusive examples and neutral examples — a very different distribution than we expect to see across the entire corpus, making random sampling inefficient for these purposes.

In order to capture more varied and nuanced examples of problematic data than are likely to be generated by common techniques like keyword filtering, we use multiple heuristics inspired by the participant's muted and blocked lists and the insights gained from our pilot studies to curate a manageable sample of tweets for annotation. Applying these heuristics involves a combination of manual and scripted processing, resulting a gap of several hours to one day between data upload and the availability of data for annotation by each participant. A list of balanced tweet threads fetched from both of these heuristics described below is used to populate the annotation interface.

Our first heuristic using muted and blocked lists uses a Python script to identify all tweets in the tweet.js file that contain any username present in either the muted.js or blocked.js files. Because the presence of a username in these lists reflects an intentional choice on the part of the participant to have these accounts' tweets hidden or blocked from their timeline, we believe the proportion of harmful tweets involving these usernames is likely to be higher than what is present in the corpus as a whole. We then use the thread-retrieval algorithm described in Section 6.1.1 to construct the thread for each relevant tweet.

Our second heuristic searches sub-tweets (described in 5) targeting the study participant, using the query *"[real name] -from:[username] - @[username]"* where "username" is the participant's Twitter handle, and "real name" is the participant's real name. This method allows us to find and capture Tweets in which the study participant was "sub-tweeted" over the most recent 30 days (using Twitter's non-premium Search API). Each of these tweets is then passed through the procedure in Algorithm 1 to once again obtain the corresponding tweet threads.

We find that this methodology retrieves a few interesting threads, but has several shortcomings. First, many of these tweets are positive, and praise the journalist for their work, which makes sense as their name is directly mentioned. Second, and relatedly, we are unable to find sub-tweets where the journalist's name is not mentioned, i.e. the post merely consists of a screenshot of their tweet. These tweets are presumably more negative, as they avoid easy attention from the target. In order to find these sub-tweets, we would have to implement computer vision methods to search for their name in images across Twitter, though it could be difficult to know where to look for these screenshots in the first place. We will investigate this further in future work.

We have also attempted to build a third heuristic using the study participant's Twitter archive to capture scenarios where they had been "snitch-Tweeted" into one of these sub-tweet threads, i.e. find a thread of the structure [image, ..., mention of their username, their response], but we did not find any such threads. We plan to revisit this with future annotators.

To balance the potentially negative threads identified through these heuristics, we also select a random sample of tweets made to non-blocked, non-muted users, and retrieve their corresponding threads. We also exclude from this non-negative sample tweet threads constructed by the participant through self-replies.

6.1.1 Annotation Platform

After data upload and preprocessing, the annotation platform is deployed and sent to the study participant. Participants annotate each tweet sent

to them within a retrieved tweet thread. This provides better context to the participant while annotating, addressing a key limitation of many existing datasets, where tweets are presented without context.

Algorithm 1 presents pseudocode for computing a tweet thread from a given tweet. To see the full codebase which joins this algorithm with the aforementioned heuristics into a complete data processing pipeline, please refer to the GitHub repository linked below.[1]

Algorithm 1 Fetch thread from tweet

```
1:  procedure FETCH_THREAD(id, api)
2:      thread = []
3:      users = set()
4:      while id ≠ None do
5:          tweet = api.get_status(id)
6:          thread.add(tweet)
7:          users.add(tweet.user_name)
8:          id = tweet.in_reply_to_id
9:      if len(thread) > 2 then
10:         thread.reverse()
11:     if len(users) == 1 then
12:         handle("no conversation")
13:     return thread
```

Label Choices   Study participants are currently presented with the following labels: hateful, abusive, neutral, or spam.

- **Hateful speech** is defined as language used to express hatred towards a targeted individual or group, or which is intended to be derogatory, to humiliate, or to insult members of the group, on the basis of attributes such as race, religion, ethnic origin, sexual orientation, disability, or gender.

- **Abusive language** is defined as any strongly impolite, rude or hurtful language using profanity, that debases someone or something, or shows intense negative emotion.

- **Spam** includes posts consisting of related or unrelated advertising / marketing, selling products of adult nature, linking to malicious websites, phishing attempts and other kinds

---

[1]The code for all of our tweet filtering heuristics and thread retrieval methods can be accessed at the following GitHub repository: `https://github.com/ishaan007/woah_emnlp_2020`

of unwanted information, usually executed repeatedly.

- **Neutral** is all tweets that do not fall into any of the prior categories.

We drew these labels from (Founta et al., 2018)'s work, which created a hate speech dataset of 80,000 tweets labeled by crowdsourced annotators, using several iterations of labels (including "offensive", "aggressive", etc.), narrowing them down to these terms. We plan to further iteratively add and remove labels based on insights from interviews and annotation sessions (see 8).

7 Modeling

While we are recruiting more journalists as study participants into our data collection pipeline, we have in parallel been building models of both feature engineering and neural network-based approaches, and testing them on historical hate speech datasets. We plan to take the insights we acquire from these experiments and apply them to classifiers built on our own data once we have accumulated a sufficient amount. We also plan to check the cross-performance between models trained on our own and historical corpora as quality assurance.

The data which we have accumulated so far gives us a good idea of which historical corpora are most similar to our own. We explored several corpora, including (Waseem and Hovy, 2016) and (Founta et al., 2018), but focused on Task 5 of SemEval 2019, "Multilingual detection of hate speech against immigrants and women in Twitter (HatEval)" in English (Basile et al., 2019), as it is most recent and they are all of similar genre.

Both Task 5 subtasks used the same dataset (cicl2018/HateEvalTeam, 2019) but with different labels. Subtask A was a binary classification task to assign a label of "hate" or "non-hate" to each tweet. Subtask B was a multi-class classification task to assign two additional label pairs to each tweet in addition to "hate" or "non-hate": "individual" or "group" and "aggressive" or "non-aggressive". The split across train and development datasets was 9000 to 1000 tweets; these have been open-sourced by the organizing team. The true labels for the test set have not, however, so we evaluate only on the development set.

We replicated the winning approach (Indurthi et al., 2019) for sub-task A in English, which used SMOTE to over-sample the "hate" class as a pre-processing step, followed by the use of Universal Sentence Encoder (Cer et al., 2018) to generate a vector representation of the tweet, and SVM (RBF kernel) to classify the tweet. We also implemented a transformer-based approach for this sub-task, based on (MacAvaney et al., 2019), which uses pre-trained BERT for sequence classification, fine-tuned for 10 epochs. This approach in fact outperforms the aforementioned winning approach.

For sub-task B, the multi-classification task, we replicated the winning approach (Bauwelinck et al., 2019) by training three separate classifiers to classify three label pairs individually; these classifiers used a linear SVM on handcrafted syntactic, lexical and bag-of-words features. The optimal hyperparameters were found using grid search. Our experiments with these corpora have given us insights about best practices for training effective models of hate speech, which we plan to apply to our new corpus as we collect more data from participating women journalists. We have additionally been exploring experiments on our collected data with various novel *model architectures* as opposed to *data corpora*, which are elaborated upon in 10.

8 Results and Discussion

Although testing of our platform is still in the pilot phase, early users have shared positive feedback regarding its usability, and have also been able to perform the annotation task with good efficiency, on the order of ~300 tweets per hour. Given the size of previously-collected datasets in this space, our methodology is efficient enough to generate sufficient training data in less than 40 hours, making it both a cost-effective and robust approach. Given the high fidelity of our labels and the near-perfect ecological validity of the training data, we believe that classifiers trained on data collected using our methods will significantly outperform existing classifiers on hateful and abusive speech in the wild.

From early feedback, we have also identified additional labels that participants found relevant, such as "campaign" or "brigade", used to indicate a lexically generic Tweet that is still part of a harassment campaign, as in 2019's "Learn to code" campaign (Molloy, 2019). In addition, our pilot interviews suggest that including a fill-in "other" label may be useful for generating more nuanced classifiers, especially as there has historically been a lack of annotator agreement on what constitutes hateful speech, which tends to vary in severity and lexical nature depending on the situation (Waseem et al., 2017).

9   Limitations

Currently, our approach is limited by its dependence on a feature allowing Twitter users to download an archive of their data; this feature was suspended for roughly two months of the research period in response to the social-engineered hacking of more than 100 accounts (Conger and Popper, 2020). Moreover, some blocked or muted users identified in pre-processing may have been suspended by Twitter, making it impossible to include their potentially harassing messages in our corpus. Finally, while our platform yielded a useful annotation rate, we note that there are inherent limitations to developing classifiers using strictly hand-labeled data.

10   Directions for Future Work

Given the interruption in data collection, we propose to augment our data-access pipeline by building a sufficiently-permissioned Twitter app to download the required data directly from participants' accounts. This would not only provide similarly high-quality data with less burden on participants, it would also provide an ongoing source of test data with which we could refine and improve our classifiers in much closer to real-time.

By leveraging the methods presented in (Wulczyn et al., 2017), moreover, we also believe we could augment and improve the classifiers built from our hand-labeled data using a combination of machine learning and crowdsourcing. We are in general investigating ways to overcome the inherent shortcomings of manual expert annotation, while retaining its significant benefits; for example, augmenting our data annotation tool with active learning annotation (Vlachos, 2006), so that participants only need to annotate the most unclear instances of hateful/harassing/neutral speech.

In regards to model-building, we are exploring ways we can take advantage of the contextual thread annotation scheme present in our annotation platform. Specifically, we have investigated methods using LSTMs (Huang et al., 2016), and are presently investigating graph attention networks (Veličković et al., 2017); these architectures and others like them could allow us to take advantage of the rich metadata and parent tweet text embeddings present in tweet threads, and have the potential to achieve significantly boosted classification performance compared to that of models built on text embeddings of the potentially harassing tweet alone (Mishra et al., 2019).

For the purpose of building the eventual tool to aid journalists in the field, we could alternatively address the relatively small size of our manually-labelled datasets for training deep learning classifiers, by augmenting them against the large, popular corpora already in existence. We could investigate whether this addition would boost performance compared to classifiers trained only on those large, crowd-sourced corpora, as a measure of effectiveness of our methodology.

Finally, we note that while certain semantic features of the classifiers developed using our methodology will differ depending on the community of focus, we hypothesize that by studying several communities with this level of detail and quality, we will eventually be able to identify generalizable features of harassment activities.

11   Conclusion

This work has focused on outlining a novel and generalizable methodology for generating better training datasets for the detection of abusive and harassing speech on Twitter, using women journalists as a test community. By directly engaging the targets of harassment in our research, we have not only created an efficient annotation platform using insights about the structural mechanisms of harassment, but we have offered these victims a constructive way to engage with what are otherwise totally negative experiences. We look forward to continuing to work with women journalists to build data-driven tools against abuse and harassment that allow them to maintain their personal needs while working to uphold our free press.

References

Valerio Basile, Cristina Bosco, Elisabetta Fersini, Debora Nozza, Viviana Patti, Francisco Manuel Rangel Pardo, Paolo Rosso, and Manuela Sanguinetti. 2019. SemEval-2019 task 5: Multilingual detection of hate speech against immigrants and women in twitter. In *Proceedings of the 13th International Workshop on Semantic Evaluation*, pages 54–63, Minneapolis, Minnesota, USA.

Nina Bauwelinck, Gilles Jacobs, Véronique Hoste, and

Els Lefever. 2019. LT3 at SemEval-2019 task 5: Multilingual detection of hate speech against immigrants and women in twitter (hatEval). In *Proceedings of the 13th International Workshop on Semantic Evaluation*, pages 436–440, Minneapolis, Minnesota, USA. Association for Computational Linguistics.

Lindsay Blackwell, Jill Dimond, Sarita Schoenebeck, and Cliff Lampe. 2017. Classification and its consequences for online harassment: Design insights from heartmob. *Proc. ACM Hum.-Comput. Interact.*, 1(24):19pp.

Daniel Cer, Yinfei Yang, Sheng-yi Kong, Nan Hua, Nicole Limtiaco, Rhomni St John, Noah Constant, Mario Guajardo-Cespedes, Steve Yuan, Chris Tar, et al. 2018. Universal sentence encoder. *arXiv preprint arXiv:1803.11175*.

Polychronis Charitidis, Stavros Doropoulos, Stavros Vologiannidis, Ioannis Papastergiou, and Sophia Karakeva. 2020. Towards countering hate speech against journalists on social media. *Online Social Networks and Media*, 17:100071.

Gina Masullo Chen, Paromita Pain, Victoria Y Chen, Madlin Mekelburg, Nina Springer, and Franziska Troger. 2018. 'you really have to have a thick skin': A cross-cultural perspective on how online harassment influences female journalists. *Journalism*, page 1464884918768500.

Tracy Chou. 2020. Block party. https://www.blockpartyapp.com/.

cicl2018/HateEvalTeam. 2019. *HateEval 2019 Task 5 Data Files*. https://github.com/cicl2018/HateEvalTeam/tree/master/Data%20Files/Data%20Files.

Kate Conger and Nathanial Popper. 2020. Florida teenager is charged as 'mastermind' of twitter hack. *The New York Times*. https://www.nytimes.com/2020/07/31/technology/twitter-hack-arrest.html.

Maeve Duggan. 2017. Online harassment 2017. https://www.pewresearch.org/internet/2017/07/11/online-harassment-2017/.

Michelle Ferrier and Nisha Garud-Patkar. 2018. Trollbusters: Fighting online harassment of women journalists. In Jacqueline Ryan Vickery and Tracy Everbach, editors, *Mediating Misogyny: Gender, Technology, and Harassment*, pages 311–332. Springer International Publishing.

Antigoni-Maria Founta, Constantinos Djouvas, Despoina Chatzakou, Ilias Leontiadis, Jeremy Blackburn, Gianluca Stringhini, Athena Vakali, Michael Sirivianos, and Nicolas Kourtellis. 2018. Large scale crowdsourcing and characterization of twitter abusive behavior. *arXiv preprint arXiv:1802.00393*.

R. Stuart Geiger. 2016. Bot-based collective blocklists in twitter: the counterpublic moderation of harassment in a networked public space. *Information, Communication & Society*, 19(6):787–803.

Ysabel Gerrard. 2018. Beyond the hashtag: Circumventing content moderation on social media. *New Media & Society*, 20(12):4492–4511.

Jacob Hoffman-Andrews. 2020. Block together. https://twitter.com/blocktogether?lang=en.

Minlie Huang, Yujie Cao, and Chao Dong. 2016. Modeling rich contexts for sentiment classification with lstm. *arXiv preprint arXiv:1605.01478*.

Vijayasaradhi Indurthi, Bakhtiyar Syed, Manish Shrivastava, Nikhil Chakravartula, Manish Gupta, and Vasudeva Varma. 2019. FERMI at SemEval-2019 task 5: Using sentence embeddings to identify hate speech against immigrants and women in twitter. In *Proceedings of the 13th International Workshop on Semantic Evaluation*, pages 70–74, Minneapolis, Minnesota, USA. Association for Computational Linguistics.

Shagun Jhaver, Sucheta Ghoshal, Amy Bruckman, and Eric Gilbert. 2018. Online harassment and content moderation: The case of blocklists. *ACM Trans. Comput.-Hum. Interact.*, 25(2):33pp.

Rohan Kshirsagar, Tyrus Cukuvac, Kathleen McKeown, and Susan McGregor. 2018. Predictive embeddings for hate speech detection on twitter. In *Proceedings of the 2nd Workshop on Abusive Language Online (ALW2)*, pages 26–32.

Sean MacAvaney, Hao-Ren Yao, Eugene Yang, Katina Russell, Nazli Goharian, and Ophir Frieder. 2019. Hate speech detection: Challenges and solutions. *PLOS ONE*, 14:1–16.

Pushkar Mishra, Marco Del Tredici, Helen Yannakoudakis, and Ekaterina Shutova. 2019. Abusive language detection with graph convolutional networks. *arXiv preprint arXiv:1904.04073*.

Parker Molloy. 2019. How a myth about journalists telling miners to "learn to code" helped people justify harassment. *Media Matters*. https://www.mediamatters.org/erick-erickson/how-myth-about-journalists-telling-miners-learn-code-helped-people-justifyharassment.

Monica Löfgren Nilsson and Henrik Örnebring. 2016. Journalism under threat. *Journalism Practice*, 10(7):880–890.

Chikashi Nobata, Joel Tetreault, Achint Thomas, Yashar Mehdad, and Yi Chang. 2016. Abusive language detection in online user content. In *Proceedings of the 25th international conference on world wide web*, pages 145–153.

Haji Mohammad Salem, Kelly P Dillon, Susan Benesch, and Derek Ruths. 2016. A web of hate: Tackling hateful speech in online social spaces. In *First Workshop on Text Analytics for Cybersecurity and Online Safety (TA-COS 2016) at the International Conference on Language Resources and Evaluation (LREC2016)*.

Theodora Saridou, Kosmas Panagiotidis, and Andreas Veglis. 2019. Towards a semantic-oriented model of participatory journalism management: Perceptions of user-generated content. *Redefining Communication: Social Media and the Age of Innovation*, page 27.

Sarah Scire. 2020. A window into one newsroom's diversity opens, but an industry-wide door shuts (for now). *NiemanLab.* https://www.niemanlab.org/2020/05/a-window-into-one-newsrooms-diversity-opens-but-an-industry-wide-door-shuts-for-now.

Elisa Shearer. 2018. Social media outpaces print newspapers in the u.s. as a news source. https://www.pewresearch.org/fact-tank/2018/12/10/social-media-outpaces-print-newspapers-in-the-u-s-as-a-news-source/.

Zeynep Tufekci. 2014. Big questions for social media big data: Representativeness, validity and other methodological pitfalls. *arXiv preprint arXiv:1403.7400*.

Twitter. a. About conversations on twitter. https://help.twitter.com/en/using-twitter/twitter-conversations.

Twitter. b. How to block accounts on twitter. https://help.twitter.com/en/using-twitter/blocking-and-unblocking-accounts.

Twitter. c. How to mute accounts on twitter. https://help.twitter.com/en/using-twitter/twitter-mute.

Twitter. d. How to use advanced muting options. https://help.twitter.com/en/using-twitter/advanced-twitter-mute-options.

Petar Veličković, Guillem Cucurull, Arantxa Casanova, Adriana Romero, Pietro Lio, and Yoshua Bengio. 2017. Graph attention networks. *arXiv preprint arXiv:1710.10903*.

Andreas Vlachos. 2006. Active annotation. In *Proceedings of the Workshop on Adaptive Text Extraction and Mining (ATEM 2006)*.

William Warner and Julia Hirschberg. 2012. Detecting hate speech on the world wide web. In *Proceedings of the Second Workshop on Language in Social Media*, pages 19–26, Montréal, Canada.

Zeerak Waseem. 2016. Are you a racist or am i seeing things? annotator influence on hate speech detection on twitter. In *Proceedings of the first workshop on NLP and computational social science*, pages 138–142.

Zeerak Waseem, Thomas Davidson, Dana Warmsley, and Ingmar Weber. 2017. Understanding abuse: A typology of abusive language detection subtasks. *CoRR*, abs/1705.09899.

Zeerak Waseem and Dirk Hovy. 2016. Hateful symbols or hateful people? predictive features for hate speech detection on twitter. In *Proceedings of the NAACL student research workshop*, pages 88–93.

Lucy Westcott and James W Foley. 2019. Why newsrooms need a solution to end online harassment of reporters. https://cpj.org/2019/09/newsrooms-solution-online-harassment-canada-usa/.

Cecilia Wren. 2019. Twitter block chain. https://chrome.google.com/webstore/detail/twitter-block-chain/dkkfampndkdnjffkleokegfnibnnjfah?hl=en/.

Ellery Wulczyn, Nithum Thain, and Lucas Dixon. 2017. Ex machina: Personal attacks seen at scale. In *Proceedings of the 26th International Conference on World Wide Web*, pages 1391–1399.

Using Transfer-based Language Models to
Detect Hateful and Offensive Language Online

Vebjørn Isaksen[*] and **Björn Gambäck**
Department of Computer Science
Norwegian University of Science and Technology
NO-7491 Trondheim, Norway
`vebjorni@me.com, gamback@ntnu.no`

Abstract

Distinguishing hate speech from non-hate offensive language is challenging, as hate speech not always includes offensive slurs and offensive language not always express hate. Here, four deep learners based on the Bidirectional Encoder Representations from Transformers (BERT), with either general or domain-specific language models, were tested against two datasets containing tweets labelled as either 'Hateful', 'Normal' or 'Offensive'. The results indicate that the attention-based models profoundly confuse hate speech with offensive and normal language. However, the pre-trained models outperform state-of-the-art results in terms of accurately predicting the hateful instances.

1 Introduction

The majority of the tweets on Twitter or posts on Facebook are harmless and often posted purposefully, but some express hatred towards a targeted individual or minority group and members. These posts are intended to be derogatory, humiliating or insulting and are defined as hate speech by Davidson et al. (2017). Different from offensive language, hate speech is usually expressed towards group attributes such as religion, ethnic origin, sexual orientation, disability or gender (Founta et al., 2018b). Some of the biggest firms invest heavily in tracking abusive language, e.g., automatic detection of offensive language in comments (Systrom, 2017, 2018) or giving a percentage of how likely a text is to be perceived as toxic.[1] However, these and other existing tools share a common flaw of not distinguishing between offensive and hateful language. One important reason to keep these two separate is that hate speech is considered a felony in many countries. The task of separating offensive

and hateful language has shown to be demanding; however, with the recent scientific breakthroughs and the concept of transfer learning, we can take huge steps in the right direction.

The paper investigates the effects of transferring knowledge from the Bidirectional Encoder Representations from Transformers (BERT; Devlin et al., 2019) language model on distinguishing hateful, offensive and normal language, by fine-tuning the pre-trained BERT language model with data containing hateful and offensive language, and comparing its performance to the state-of-the-art on two widely used hate speech detection datasets. Those datasets are presented Section 2. Section 3 then gives an overview of related work in the field of hate speech detection. Section 4 describes the implemented system architecture. Section 5 presents the experiments, including setup and results, while Section 6 evaluates and discusses those results. Section 7 concludes and suggests future work.

2 Data

Many existing datasets containing hate speech are publicly available for use and consist of data from several sources online, mainly Twitter (Waseem and Hovy, 2016; Waseem, 2016; Chatzakou et al., 2017; Golbeck et al., 2017; Davidson et al., 2017; Ross et al., 2016; ElSherief et al., 2018; Founta et al., 2018b), while some cover other sources such as Fox News comments (Gao and Huang, 2017) and sentences from posts on the white supremacist online forum Stormfront (de Gibert et al., 2018). Almost all available datasets are labelled by humans,[2] which results in different approaches taken when creating and annotating the datasets. Some researchers use expert annotators (Waseem and Hovy, 2016), others use majority voting among several

---

[*]Currently at Bekk Consulting AS
[1]`https://www.perspectiveapi.com`

[2]Except for the 12M tweet SOLID dataset (Rosenthal et al., 2020). It is, however, distance-learned based on the manually annotated 14k OLID tweet set (Zampieri et al., 2019).

Proceedings of the Fourth Workshop on Online Abuse and Harms, pages 16–27
Online, November 20, 2020. ©2020 Association for Computational Linguistics
https://doi.org/10.18653/v1/P17

Class	Normal	Offensive	Hateful
Tweets	4,163	19,190	1,430

Table 1: The Davidson et al. (2017) dataset, **D**

Dataset	Normal	Offensive	Hateful	Spam
Original	53,790	27,037	4,948	14,024
Available	41,784	14,202	2,941	9,372

Table 2: The Founta et al. (2018b) dataset, **F**

amateur annotators on platforms such as Crowd-Flower (Davidson et al., 2017). However, the task of hate speech detection lacks a shared benchmark dataset (Schmidt and Wiegand, 2017) that can be used to measure the performance of different machine learning models. Further, most annotation schemata follow Waseem and Hovy (2016) by splitting the data into only two basic classes, either hate and none hate or offensive and non-offensive (classes that then also often are split, e.g., labelling hateful tweets as either sexist or racist). However, it is debatable whether those labels are sufficient to represent hateful and abusive language. In contrast, a few datasets make the distinction between hateful and offensive language, e.g., Davidson et al. (2017) and Founta et al. (2018b), which will be used here and abbreviated **D** and **F**, respectively.

The dataset by Davidson et al. (2017) consists of 24,783 English tweets and their labels along with some information including the number of annotators. The number of CrowdFlower annotators range from three to nine, and majority voting was used when deciding the final class for a tweet: "Hate Speech", "Offensive Language" or "Neither". The label distribution can be seen in Table 1.

The dataset created by Founta et al. (2018b) contains almost 100k annotated tweets with four labels, "Normal", "Spam", "Hateful" and "Abusive". As the authors only provide tweet IDs for researches to retrieve tweets through the Twitter Application Programming Interface (API), some tweets may for several reasons not be retrievable, e.g., a tweet or the user account behind a tweet may have been deleted; thus, of the 99,799 provided tweet IDs, only 68,299 tweets were retrieved. The label distribution of those compared to the original label distribution for dataset **F** is shown in Table 2.

3   Related Work

Nobata et al. (2016) mention some challenges within hate speech, e.g., that the abusive language with time evolves new slurs and clever ways to avoid being detected. Hence they performed a longitudinal study over one year to see how trained models react over time, employing n-grams, word embeddings, and other linguistic and syntactic features. All features combined yielded the best performing model; however, looking at individual features, character n-grams performed best, a result that also Waseem and Hovy (2016) reported.

Transferring knowledge from word embeddings to be used as input to neural networks has been a common technique. Gambäck and Sikdar (2017) experimented with character n-grams in combination with word embeddings from word2vec Mikolov et al. (2013) in various Convolutional Neural Network (CNN) setups, with the best performing model using transferred knowledge from word2vec. Adding character n-grams boosted precision, but lowered recall. Badjatiya et al. (2017) experimented with several machine learners and neural networks, with the best performer being an Long Short-Term Memory (LSTM) with random word vectors where the network's output was used as input to a Gradient Boosted Decision Tree. However, their results have shown questionable and difficult to reproduce (Mishra et al., 2018; Fortuna et al., 2019). Pavlopoulos et al. (2017a,b) tested word embeddings from both GloVe and word2vec in an Recurrent Neural Network (RNN), while Pitsilis et al. (2018) utilised an RNN ensemble, although without use of word embeddings, but feeding standard vectorized word uni-grams to multiple LSTM networks, aggregating the classifications, to outperform the previous state-of-the-art.

Park and Fung (2017) created a hybrid system that tried to capture features from two input levels, using two CNNs, one character-based and one word-based. Meyer and Gambäck (2019) proposed an optimised architecture combining components with CNNs and LSTMs into one system. One part of the system used character n-grams as input while the other part used word embeddings. They used the dataset from Waseem and Hovy (2016), obtaining better results than previous solutions. Most of the research discussed above used that dataset (with labels 'Sexist', 'Racist' or 'Neither') or a slightly modified version (Waseem, 2016).

The dataset by Davidson et al. (2017) in contrast separates hateful language from offensive and normal language, making the task harder. Zhang et al. (2018) used this dataset and six other, but merged the offensive class with the normal class. On the 2-class hate vs normal language task, they outperformed the state-of-the-art on 6 out of 7 datasets with a system feeding word embeddings from word2vec into a CNN to produce input vectors for an LSTM network with GRU cells performing the final classification. Founta et al. (2018a) used the same dataset, but kept the offensive samples separate from the normal ones, thus taking on the challenge of separating hateful and offensive language. They ran two networks in parallel, one RNN with text input and one feed-forward network with metadata input, followed by a concatenation layer and a classification layer, performing slightly below the F_1-score 0.900 Davidson et al. (2017) achieved with a baseline LR model. However, Kshirsagar et al. (2018) surpassed the baseline using pre-trained word embeddings as input to multiple Multilayer Perceptron (MLP) layers, achieving a total F_1-score of 0.924. Still, the F-score increase is due to better performance on the 'Normal' and 'Offensive' classes, with the model actually performing worse on the 'Hate' class.

This agrees with Malmasi and Zampieri (2018) who tested several supervised learners and ensemble classifiers on the dataset, reporting a noticeable difficulty of distinguishing hateful language from profanity. Their extensive results analysis showed that tweets with the highest probability of being tagged as hate usually are targeted at a specific social group, so that contextual and semantic document features may be required to improve performance. Gaydhani et al. (2018) in contrast claimed near-perfect performance, misclassifying only 0.035% of true hate speech samples on a combination of datasets from Davidson et al. and Waseem (2016) using n-grams as features and feeding the TF-IDF values of these into classifiers such as Support Vector Machine, Naïve Bayes and Logistic Regression. However, analysing their training and test data[3] shows that 74% of the test data is either duplicate or in the training data, giving a highly biased test set and questionable results.

Basile et al. (2019) and Zampieri et al. (2019, 2020) present findings from SemEval-2019 Task 5 and 6 resp. -2020 Task 12, observing that pre-trained attention-based deep learning models were used by the top teams in all subtasks. Pérez and Luque (2019) and Indurthi et al. (2019) were the

top teams in SemEval-2019 Task 5, using ELMo together with LSTM networks. ELMo (Embeddings from Language Model; Peters et al., 2018) uses a bidirectional Language Model to create deeply contextualised word representations, with unsupervised pre-training. GPT (Generative Pre-training Transformer; Radford et al., 2018, 2019) expanded the amount of text the language model can be trained on by combining the ideas of unsupervised pre-training (Dai and Le, 2015) and transformers (Vaswani et al., 2017) with attention. BERT (Devlin et al., 2019) is a direct descendant of GPT, although instead of using a stack of transformer decoders, BERT uses a stack of transformer encoders, and while GPT only trains a forward language model, BERT is bidirectional. With the release of two pre-trained language models, $BERT_{BASE}$ and $BERT_{LARGE}$, BERT can be used as a language model for tasks such as hate speech detection. Liu et al. (2019) used $BERT_{BASE}$ to deliver some of the best results in SemEval-2019 Task 6, while several SemEval-2020 tasks saw continuous transformer multitask pre-training (ERNIE 2.0; Sun et al., 2020) outperforming other solutions.

4 Architecture

Word embedding techniques based on bag-of-words contexts, such as word2vec (Mikolov et al., 2013), only capture the semantic relations among words (Vashishth et al., 2019), whereas language models are more complex and can capture the meaning of a word in a sentence, i.e., its context. This work focuses on such language models and explores the effect of transferring knowledge from a substantial pre-trained language model to a classifier predicting hateful and offensive expressions.

4.1 Preprocessing

Twitter authors often make use of abbreviations and internet slang. Many tweets in addition contain retweeted content, mentions of other users, URLs, hashtags, emojis, etc. As language models can capture context between words and prefer complete sentences, only simple preprocessing was used to clean the data. NLTK's (Bird et al., 2009) `TweetTokenizer` was used to remove URLs, numbers, mentions and 'RT' retweet marks. Stop words were *not* removed to keep as much context as possible for the language model to capture.

HuggingFace's `BertTokenizer` was used for text normalisation and punctuation splitting

---

[3]`https://github.com/adityagaydhani14/`
`Toxic-Language-Detection-in-Online-Content`

as well as WordPiece subword-level tokenisation. Words that do not occur in the vocabulary are segmented into subword units, so there are no out-of-vocabulary words.

4.2 BERT Model Architecture

BERT's language models can be pre-trained from scratch using only a plain text corpus or fine-tuned with a domain-specific corpus. Although pre-training is a one-time procedure, it is relatively expensive requiring a large amount of crawled text and computational power. However, Devlin et al. (2019) released several pre-trained models, two of which were used in the experiments: **BERT Base**, Uncased (12 encoder layers with 768 hidden units and 12 attention heads; 110M parameters) and **BERT Large**, Uncased (24-layer, 1024-hidden, 16-heads; 340M parameters), that were trained on the English Wikipedia and BookCorpus (Zhu et al., 2015) for 1M update steps. Both models are lowercased and have pre-trained checkpoints that can either be trained with more data or fine-tuned with task-specific data. Both of these approaches were implemented and tested in the experiments. The models are trained with word sequence length up to 512, but this can be shorted when fine-tuning, to save substantial memory. Each encoder in the stack applies self-attention and then passes the results through a simple feed-forward network, before handing the output over to the next encoder.

Most language models pass each input token through a token embedding layer to achieve a numerical representation. BERT solves this by passing each token through three different embedding layers (token, segment and positional). Each of these three layers converts an input sequence of tokens to a vector representation of size $(n, 768)$, where n is the number of tokens in the input sequence. These three vector representations are summed element-wise to construct a single vector used as input for BERT's encoder stack.

The model output is where BERT separates itself from a traditional transformer: Each token position in the input sequence outputs a length 768 hidden vector for BERT Base and 1024 for BERT Large. Each encoder outputs hidden vectors that can be used as contextualised word embeddings that can be fed into an existing model. For the fine-tuning approach, only the hidden vectors from the final encoder in the stack are relevant and only the hidden vector in the first position is used for sentence clas-

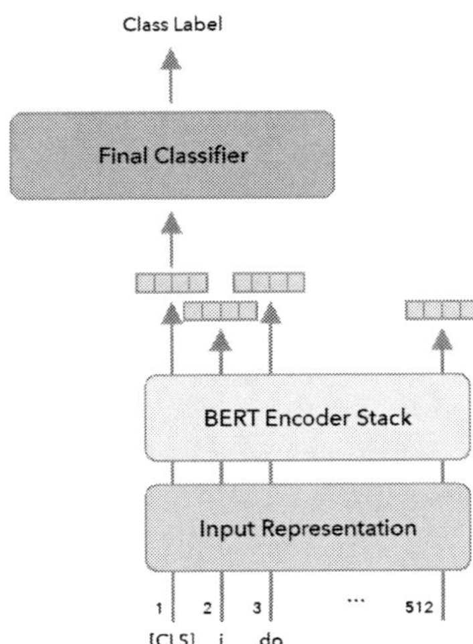

Figure 1: System architecture. The final classifier includes a feedforward network with one input layer, one hidden layer, one output layer, and one softmax layer.

sification. This vector can be used as input to any classifier. Devlin et al. achieved great results using only a single-layer network, but the final systems used here are slightly modified with an additional linear layer of size 2048 added to increase the complexity of the model. (An RNN model was also tested, but omitted as learning did not improve.)

For fine-tuning, only the number of labels needs to be added as a new parameter, 3 and 4 for the systems used here. All BERT parameters and the final classifier network parameters are fine-tuned jointly to maximise the systems' predictive capabilities. The logits from the last linear layer are passed through a softmax layer to calculate the final label probabilities. Between BERT's pooled output and the first linear layer, and between the first and second linear layers, dropout is utilised to regulate the systems to reduce the risk of overfitting. In addition, cross entropy is used to calculate the classification error of each sample. To update the whole network's weights iteratively based on the training data, HuggingFace's version of the Adam optimiser (Kingma and Ba, 2017) is used with weight decay fix, warmup, and linear learning rate decay. Figure 1 gives an overview of the system architecture implemented for the experiments.

4.3 Further Language Model Training

Starting from BERT's Wikipedia and BookCorpus checkpoint, it is possible to further train the language model with domain-specific corpora. This technique of using unlabelled data from the same domain as the target task to train the language model further using the original pre-training objective(s) was first seen in ULMFiT (Howard and Ruder, 2018). Since the approach taken here only uses two datasets, there are still a lot of datasets from the target domain available. Remember, the pre-training only requires the raw text, and so the labels are irrelevant. All available datasets mentioned at the beginning of Section 2, except the two used for the target task, were collected and used to further train BERT on domain data. Furthermore, BERT's English vocabulary consists of 30,522 segmented subword units learned beforehand. Some vocabulary entries are placeholders that can be replaced with new words. ElSherief et al. (2018) created a list of keywords commonly used as hate speech, and most of those were placed in the unused placeholders when further training BERT from its checkpoints.

One of BERT's pre-training objectives is next sentence prediction in which the model predicts whether one sentence follows another sentence or not. As a result, the input format for further training BERT is a single file with untokenised text and one sentence per line. Natural Language Toolkit (NLTK)'s `sent_tokenizer` was used to split documents into sentences of at least one word. Since tweets rarely consist of multiple complete sentences due to Twitter's 280 character limit, some tweets were split in the middle to construct two sentences instead of discarding them.

Other datasets were formatted more easily, e.g, the Stormfront forum data from de Gibert et al. (2018) contained a large folder where each text file was a sentence. All text data from the datasets were merged into one file yielding one large text file with nearly 170,000 lines. This file was then used to further train two language models from BERT Base and Large checkpoints on the two original pre-training objectives, masked LM and next sentence prediction. The output of this process, two language models, trained on Wikipedia, BookCorpus, and domain data was used in the experiments to investigate the effect of further training the language model with domain-specific data.

5   Experiments and Results

The two original pre-trained language models BERT Base and BERT Large from Devlin et al. (2019) were tested together with the two language models (BERT Base* and BERT Large*) further trained with domain-specific data. Each system's performance was tested with the two datasets **D** (Davidson et al., 2017) and **F** (Founta et al., 2018b). Dataset **F** annotates tweets as 'Hateful', 'Offensive' 'Spam' or 'Normal'. When identifying hateful and offensive language, the 'Spam' class is redundant and was omitted. However, to compare to previous research, experiments with the original 4-class dataset **F** were also carried out.

All text data in the experiments were lowercased. Both datasets were split into a training set containing 80% of the total samples and a held-out test set containing the remaining 20%, with Scikit-learn's stratified splitting function used to ensure equal class balance between the sets. The order of the training samples was shuffled before each run. Cross-validation with multiple folds was not implemented due to framework limitations.

All experiments were run on devices with at least 64GB RAM, the amount recommended by the creators of BERT. The two original language models were pre-trained with a sequence length of 512 and batch size 256. The fine-tuned models had a sequence length of 128 and batch size 32. All four language models were trained with the Adam optimiser, with the optimal learning rates found to be 3e-5 for the fine-tuning process and 2e-5 for the classification process after an exhaustive search with parameters suggested by Devlin et al. (2019). Other parameters shared by the four systems are a dropout probability of 10% on all layers, the number of training epochs which was 3, and an evaluation batch size of 8. The fine-tuning of the language models took around 3 hours on two Nvidia V100 GPUs with 32GB RAM each, while classification with BERT Base and Large took on average around 1 and 2 hours, respectively.

System performance will be measured by *micro* averaged Precision, Recall, and F_1-score, as this is more suitable for unbalanced datasets and gives detailed insights into how the models classify each sample. The *macro* averaged total for each metric will also be presented for comparison reasons.

5.1   Dataset from Davidson et al. (2017)

Dataset **D** is quite unbalanced with 77% of the tweets being annotated as 'Offensive' and only 6% being labelled 'Hateful'. As seen in Table 3, all four models perform more or less equally in almost all metrics, and are able to correctly classify tweets as 'Normal' and 'Offensive' fairly well. BERT

BERT Model:		Base	Large	Base*	Large*
Normal	P	0.867	**0.889**	0.883	0.883
	R	**0.906**	0.888	0.893	0.888
	F_1	0.886	**0.888**	**0.888**	0.885
Offensive	P	**0.941**	0.938	0.929	0.932
	R	0.953	**0.959**	**0.965**	0.961
	F_1	0.947	**0.948**	0.947	0.946
Hateful	P	0.497	**0.520**	0.477	0.460
	R	0.343	**0.364**	0.213	0.259
	F_1	0.406	**0.428**	0.294	0.331
Micro avg.	F_1	0.910	**0.913**	0.909	0.908
Macro avg.	F_1	0.751	**0.759**	0.725	0.729

Table 3: Results from BERT experiments on dataset **D**

BERT Model:		Base	Large	Base*	Large*
Normal	P	0.956	0.956	0.956	**0.957**
	R	**0.968**	0.967	0.967	0.964
	F_1	**0.962**	0.961	0.961	0.960
Offensive	P	**0.865**	0.861	0.860	**0.865**
	R	0.920	**0.926**	0.921	0.919
	F_1	**0.892**	**0.892**	0.889	0.891
Hateful	P	0.573	**0.574**	0.531	0.485
	R	**0.299**	0.264	0.264	0.284
	F_1	**0.393**	0.362	0.353	0.358
Micro avg.	F_1	**0.923**	0.922	0.921	0.919
Macro avg.	F_1	**0.762**	0.756	0.748	0.745

Table 4: Results from BERT experiments on dataset **F**

Large is the model that performs best with a final macro averaged F_1-score of 0.759, with the other three models not far behind. This is in line with Devlin et al. (2019) who found BERT Large outperforming BERT Base across all tasks tested.

Out of the four models, BERT Large also obtains the best scores for the 'Hateful' class, with precision, recall and F_1-score of 0.520, 0.364 and 0.428, respectively. 52% of the examples the model predicted as hateful were correctly classified. Only 36% of the total true hateful tweets were classified correctly, yielding low recall. The two models with general language understanding, BERT Base and Large, outperform the two models with domain-specific language understanding on the 'Hateful' class. On this class, BERT Large* obtains a F_1-score of 0.331 compared to BERT Large's F_1-score of 0.428. This gap in F_1-scores is unexpected as the intention of further training the language models with domain-specific data was to increase the hateful language understanding.

5.2 Dataset from Founta et al. (2018b)

Dataset **F** is nearly three times the size of **D**. The label distribution is also more balanced with roughly half of the samples labelled 'Normal' and the rest distributed between the other three classes. Although only 6% of the tweets are annotated 'Hateful', this is a fair representation of the real world where only a small portion of the online content is hate speech. The best scores for each metric were then spread across the four models and there was no clear difference between the models: all obtained an F_1-score of 0.67. As with dataset **D**, the models were able to correctly classify tweets as 'Normal' and 'Offensive' quite well while misclassifying most of the true 'Hateful' and 'Spam'

tweets. The best F_1-scores for the 'Normal' and 'Offensive' classes were 0.869 and 0.884, respectively, obtained by BERT Base*, but the other models were right behind. The only telling difference between the models was the scores on the 'Hateful' class, with BERT Base the clear winner.

Removing the 'Spam' class from the original dataset, we immediately see an increase in the models' scores for all three classes as shown in Table 4. As expected, the increase is most noticeable for the 'Normal' class which previously was highly confused with the 'Spam' class. The increase is less notable for the 'Hateful' class although BERT Base outperforms the other models by a margin. BERT Base is surprisingly the model that performs best overall, beating the other three models on nearly every metric. Remarkably 97% of the tweets labelled as 'Normal' are correctly classified by the model, but only 30% of true hateful samples. Again, the models seem to recognise true hate speech as less hateful than the annotators. The two models trained with domain-specific data, BERT Base* and BERT Large*, perform worse on the 'Hateful' class than the other two models. This is an interesting observation as more training with domain-specific data has shown to increase the performance of models in previous solutions.

6 Evaluation and Discussion

The main difference between the two datasets used in the experiments is the size and label distribution. The size of dataset **F** allows for more training samples than dataset **D** although systems transferring knowledge from pre-trained language models have shown that even small datasets can achieve similar performance (Howard and Ruder, 2018). The four models' overall performance on datasets **D** and **F** are the same despite the fact that the latter dataset allows for more language model fine-tuning. The label distribution in dataset **F** is more realistic than dataset **D**, where a large portion of the samples is labelled as 'Offensive'. However, this unbalance of dataset **D** does not seem to affect the models' performance noticeably. The reason is probably that dataset **D** contains a sufficient amount of class samples for the models to learn the other two classes. This ability to learn with a few training examples is one of the main advantages of using language models instead of traditional word embeddings.

6.1 Language Model Selection

Although datasets without the distinction between offensive and hateful language were irrelevant for testing the models in the experiments, they were used as unlabelled data to further pre-train two BERT language models. This additional training is intended to give the language models domain-specific language understanding and has shown to increase the overall performance in other tasks (Devlin et al., 2019). However, the results obtained from the experiments show that the two models with domain-specific language understanding performed worse or equal to the language models with general language understanding. As we can see in Table 3, the worst performance of the two extended BERT models was on dataset **D**. BERT Base* and Large* obtained macro-averaged F_1-scores of 0.725 and 0.729, respectively, while the original BERT models obtained F_1-scores of 0.751 for BERT Base and 0.759 for BERT Large. The difference between these scores is a result of the models' performance on the 'Hateful' class as the performance on the 'Normal' and 'Offensive' classes are near identical for all four models. BERT Large outperforms the other three models on the 'Hateful' class with a F_1-score of 0.428. This is in line with Devlin et al. (2019) who found that BERT Large outperformed BERT Base on several other tasks.

However, this is not the case for the results obtained by BERT Large on dataset **F**. Looking at Table 4, we observe that the smaller model BERT Base outperforms BERT Large on nearly every metric. The most compelling difference can again be seen in the 'Hateful' row, where BERT Base achieved an F_1-score of 0.393 compared to BERT Large's F_1-score of 0.362, mainly as a result of better recall obtained by BERT Base.

Surprisingly, there is no telling difference when comparing the two models with general language understanding to the two models with domain-specific language understanding. Further training with large domain-specific corpora is expected to be beneficial and increase the performance on downstream tasks like hate speech detection. However, the results from the experiments do not reflect this assumption, and it seems like all four models are able to capture similar features, thus performing equally well. Next sentence prediction is one of BERT's two pre-training objectives. So in order to further pre-train the language model, it is necessary to obtain documents containing at least two sentences. This became a limitation, as the domain-specific data used in the experiments mostly consist of tweets, that often contain only a single sentence and omitting every single-sentence tweet would lead to a much smaller training corpus. In order to include single-sentence tweets in the training corpus, they were split at the middle. This is not optimal and may be one of the reasons why BERT Base* and Large* did not perform as expected.

6.2 Error Analysis

Generally, the results from each dataset indicate that it is hard to separate hateful language from offensive and normal language. This was also the key finding stated by Malmasi and Zampieri (2018) and Davidson et al. (2017) when testing their models' performance on dataset **D**. For dataset **D**, most of the annotated hateful samples are confused with the 'Offensive' class, and this may be due to the skewed dataset where the 'Offensive' samples dominate. With dataset **F**, there is roughly an equal distribution of misclassifications between the 'Offensive' and 'Normal' class. This indicates that neither of the tested models using features from the pre-trained language model is capable of distinguishing hateful language from offensive and neutral language with acceptable accuracy.

To investigate BERT Base's predictions on dataset **F** deeper, some correctly and incorrectly classified instances were sampled and analysed. The model tends to predict instances containing clear racist or homophobic slurs as hate speech, while obvious hate speech appears more straightforward for the model to understand and accurately predict. Several instances annotated as 'Hateful', but predicted as 'Normal' or Offensive' by the model do not appear to be clear hate speech and are perhaps mislabelled by the human coders and

System	P	R	F_1
BERT Large	**0.91**	**0.91**	0.90
Davidson et al. (2017)	**0.91**	0.90	0.90
Founta et al. (2018a)	0.89	0.89	0.89
Kshirsagar et al. (2018)	–	–	**0.92**

Table 5: Dataset **D** comparison (weighted averages)

System	P	R	F_1
BERT Base*	0.800	0.812	**0.806**
BERT Large*	0.802	0.809	0.805
Lee et al. (2018) CNN_w	0.789	0.808	0.783
Lee et al. (2018) $RNN\text{-}LTC_w$	**0.804**	**0.815**	0.805

Table 6: Dataset **F** comparison (weighted averages)

System	P	R	F_1
BERT Base	0.80	**0.73**	**0.76**
Naïve Bayes	0.63	0.63	0.63
Support Vector Machine	**0.87**	0.65	0.74
Logistic Regression	0.80	0.69	0.74

Table 7: Dataset **F** without "Spam" (macro averages)

correctly predicted by the model. The text "ISIS message calls Trump 'foolish idiot'" was found four times in the original dataset with different authors, being annotated twice as 'Hateful' and twice as 'Offensive', with the model predicting the human-chosen label on only one of the instances. As stated by Chatzakou et al. (2017), annotation is even hard for humans and this is an example of the gold standard not being perfect even though the Founta et al. dataset was thoroughly constructed.

6.3 Comparison to State-of-the-Art

Table 5 shows the results obtained on dataset **D** by BERT Large compared to previous results. Although the dataset is widely used, some researchers (e.g., Zhang et al., 2018) chose to merge the 'Offensive' and 'Normal' classes into one non-hate class; making them not comparable to the results carried out in the experiments. All four systems in Table 5 perform equally well with F_1-scores around 0.90. BERT Large is outperformed by Kshirsagar et al. (2018)'s Transformed Word Embedding Model (TWEM). BERT Large outperforms the solution from Founta et al. (2018a) and obtains similar results as the baseline from Davidson et al. (2017).

Lee et al. (2018) tested several machine learning algorithms on dataset **F** intending to create a baseline for this dataset. Table 6 shows that the two BERT models and Lee et al.'s word-based RNN-LTC model perform similarly on this dataset. However, BERT Base* achieves an F_1-score of 0.361 on the 'Hateful' class, compared to the RNN-LTC model's F_1-score of 0.302. This indicates that BERT Base* is better at separating hateful language from the other types of language. RNN-LTC outperformed BERT Base* on the 'Spam' class resulting in the similar total average scores.

The experimental results on dataset **F** without the 'Spam' class were compared to three baseline systems, since no comparable research was found. The macro-averaged scores are shown in Table 7. Out of the four tested models, BERT Base was the best performing with an F_1-score of 0.76. Again, BERT Base's performance on the "Hateful" class is compellingly better than the best performing Logistic Regression model. BERT Base obtain an F_1-score of 0.393 while the LR model achieves an F_1-score of 0.310. The improved performance on the "Hateful" class on both version of dataset **F** implies that models transferring knowledge from pre-trained language models are able to distinguish the nuances of abusive language more accurately.

Model selection is important when creating a hate speech predictor; however, Gröndahl et al. (2018) argue that model architecture is less important than the type of data and labelling criteria. They found that the tested models, which ranged from simple Logistic Regression to more complex LSTM, performed equally well when recreating several state-of-the-art solutions. Gröndahl et al.'s results are consistent with the investigations conducted during the experiments, where changes in the final classifier's complexity did not reflect any changes in the results.

7 Conclusion and Future Work

To explore the effects of applying language models to the downstream task of hate speech detection, four systems based on the BERT language models were implemented and tested on two datasets annotated both for hateful and offensive language. Two of the systems were further pre-trained with unlabelled domain-specific data. However, the results did not reflect any notable improvement with the extended language models.

All four models achieved F_1-scores close to or above state-of-the-art solutions on both datasets, and their ability to correctly distinguish hate speech from offensive and ordinary language was considerably better than the compared solutions, but the scores on the 'Hateful' class are not sufficient enough to bring the systems into practical use, as hateful expressions would pass through the system or more benign cases would be incorrectly censored. Still, language models bring a considerable potential to understanding all the nuances of hateful utterances, and further exploration of how to most effectively train and transfer knowledge from them is necessary.

The models used in the experiments were all pre-trained on the English Wikipedia and Book-Corpus to obtain general language understanding. Typically, the language that appears in Wikipedia articles and books are somewhat domain neutral and formal. This language may be too different from the hate speech domain in terms of words and sentences. Therefore, it may be beneficial to collect documents from hate speech datasets and create one large corpus, which can be used as input data to pre-train BERT's encoders from scratch.

A problem with BERT is the vast number of parameters that need to be set, leading to memory problems and long training times. However, the usage of transformers for language processing is a fast-moving field, so several ideas and strategies have lately been introduced to improve on the original BERT setup. One of those — such as AL-BERT, 'A lite BERT' (Lan et al., 2020); GPT-3, 'Generative Pre-trained Transformer' (Brown et al., 2020); continuous pre-training ('ERNIE 2.0'; Sun et al., 2020); transformers for longer sequences ('BigBird'; Zaheer et al., 2020); or layerwise adaptive large batch optimisation ('LAMB'; You et al., 2020) — could be tested on the task.

Lan et al. (2020)'s ALBERT can drastically reduce the number of parameters and help solve memory problems and reduce training times. Zaheer et al. (2020)'s 'BigBird', with its sparse attention mechanism, allows for longer input sequences than BERT and is suitable for tasks where the datasets include longer documents. You et al. (2020) utilised large batch stochastic optimisation methods to reduce the training time of BERT remarkably.

As describe in Section 4.3, each tweet in the training set was split into two for the next sentence prediction task BERT is performing during pre-training. This was done because tweets rarely contain two full sentences. However, this strategy can lead to some loss of linguistic information and it may be better to just skip next sentence prediction during training and only perform the masked language model task.

References

Pinkesh Badjatiya, Shashank Gupta, Manish Gupta, and Vasudeva Varma. 2017. Deep learning for hate speech detection in tweets. In *Proceedings of the 26th International Conference on World Wide Web Companion*, pages 759–760, Perth, Australia. International World Wide Web Conferences Steering Committee.

Valerio Basile, Cristina Bosco, Elisabetta Fersini, Debora Nozza, Viviana Patti, Francisco Manuel Rangel Pardo, Paolo Rosso, and Manuela Sanguinetti. 2019. SemEval-2019 task 5: Multilingual detection of hate speech against immigrants and women in Twitter. In *Proceedings of the 13th International Workshop on Semantic Evaluation*, pages 54–63, Minneapolis, Minnesota, USA. Association for Computational Linguistics.

Steven Bird, Ewan Klein, and Edward Loper. 2009. *Natural Language Processing with Python*. O'Reilly Media.

Tom B. Brown, Benjamin Mann, Nick Ryder, Melanie Subbiah, Jared Kaplan, Prafulla Dhariwal, Arvind Neelakantan, Pranav Shyam, Girish Sastry, Amanda Askell, Sandhini Agarwal, Ariel Herbert-Voss, Gretchen Krueger, Tom Henighan, Rewon Child, Aditya Ramesh, Daniel M. Ziegler, Jeffrey Wu, Clemens Winter, Christopher Hesse, Mark Chen, Eric Sigler, Mateusz Litwin, Scott Gray, Benjamin Chess, Jack Clark, Christopher Berner, Sam McCandlish, Alec Radford, Ilya Sutskever, and Dario Amodei. 2020. Language models are few-shot learners. *CoRR*, abs/2005.14165.

Despoina Chatzakou, Nicolas Kourtellis, Jeremy Blackburn, Emiliano De Cristofaro, Gianluca Stringhini, and Athena Vakali. 2017. Mean birds: Detecting aggression and bullying on Twitter. In *Proceedings of the 2017 ACM on Web Science Conference*, pages 13–22, Troy, New York, USA. Association for Computing Machinery.

Andrew M. Dai and Quoc V. Le. 2015. Semi-supervised sequence learning. In *Proceedings of the 28th International Conference on Neural Information Processing Systems*, volume 2, pages 3079–3087, Montréal, Québec, Canada. Curran Associates, Inc.

Thomas Davidson, Dana Warmsley, Michael Macy, and Ingmar Weber. 2017. Automated hate speech detection and the problem of offensive language. In *Proceedings of the Eleventh International Conference on Web and Social Media*, pages 512–515, Montréal, Québec, Canada. AAAI Press.

Jacob Devlin, Ming-Wei Chang, Kenton Lee, and Kristina Toutanova. 2019. BERT: Pre-training of deep bidirectional transformers for language understanding. *CoRR*, abs/1810.04805.

Mai ElSherief, Shirin Nilizadeh, Dana Nguyen, Giovanni Vigna, and Elizabeth Belding. 2018. Peer to peer hate: Hate speech instigators and their targets. In *Twelfth International Conference on Web and Social Media*, pages 52–61, Stanford, California, USA. AAAI Press.

Paula Fortuna, Juan Soler-Company, and Sérgio Nunes. 2019. Stop PropagHate at SemEval-2019 tasks 5 and 6: Are abusive language classification results reproducible? In *Proceedings of the 13th International Workshop on Semantic Evaluation*, pages 745–752, Minneapolis, Minnesota, USA. Association for Computational Linguistics.

Antigoni Maria Founta, Despoina Chatzakou, Nicolas Kourtellis, Jeremy Blackburn, Athena Vakali, and Ilias Leontiadis. 2018a. A unified deep learning architecture for abuse detection. *CoRR*, abs/1802.00385.

Antigoni Maria Founta, Constantinos Djouvas, Despoina Chatzakou, Ilias Leontiadis, Jeremy Blackburn, Gianluca Stringhini, Athena Vakali, Michael Sirivianos, and Nicolas Kourtellis. 2018b. Large scale crowdsourcing and characterization of Twitter abusive behavior. In *Twelfth International Conference on Web and Social Media*, pages 491–500, Stanford, California, USA. AAAI Press.

Björn Gambäck and Utpal Kumar Sikdar. 2017. Using convolutional neural networks to classify hate-speech. In *Proceedings of the First Workshop on Abusive Language Online*, pages 85–90, Vancouver, British Columbia, Canada. Association for Computational Linguistics.

Lei Gao and Ruihong Huang. 2017. Detecting online hate speech using context aware models. In *Proceedings of the International Conference Recent Advances in Natural Language Processing, RANLP 2017*, pages 260–266, Varna, Bulgaria. INCOMA Ltd.

Aditya Gaydhani, Vikrant Doma, Shrikant Kendre, and Laxmi Bhagwat. 2018. Detecting hate speech and offensive language on Twitter using machine learning: An N-gram and TFIDF based approach. *CoRR*, abs/1809.08651.

Ona de Gibert, Naiara Perez, Aitor García-Pablos, and Montse Cuadros. 2018. Hate speech dataset from a white supremacy forum. In *Proceedings of the 2nd Workshop on Abusive Language Online (ALW2)*, pages 11–20, Brussels, Belgium. Association for Computational Linguistics.

Jennifer Golbeck, Zahra Ashktorab, Rashad O. Banjo, Alexandra Berlinger, Siddharth Bhagwan, Cody Buntain, Paul Cheakalos, Alicia A. Geller, Quint Gergory, Rajesh Kumar Gnanasekaran, Raja Rajan Gunasekaran, Kelly M. Hoffman, Jenny Hottle, Vichita Jienjitlert, Shivika Khare, Ryan Lau, Marianna J. Martindale, Shalmali Naik, Heather L. Nixon, Piyush Ramachandran, Kristine M. Rogers, Lisa Rogers, Meghna Sardana Sarin, Gaurav Shahane, Jayanee Thanki, Priyanka Vengataraman, Zijian Wan, and Derek Michael Wu. 2017. A large labeled corpus for online harassment research. In *Proceedings of the 2017 ACM on Web Science Conference*, pages 229–233, Troy, New York, USA. Association for Computing Machinery.

Tommi Gröndahl, Luca Pajola, Mika Juuti, Mauro Conti, and N. Asokan. 2018. All you need is "love": Evading hate speech detection. In *Proceedings of the 11th ACM Workshop on Artificial Intelligence and Security*, AISec '18, pages 2–12, Toronto, Ontario, Canada. Association for Computing Machinery.

Jeremy Howard and Sebastian Ruder. 2018. Universal language model fine-tuning for text classification. *CoRR*, abs/1801.06146.

Vijayasaradhi Indurthi, Bakhtiyar Syed, Manish Shrivastava, Nikhil Chakravartula, Manish Gupta, and Vasudeva Varma. 2019. FERMI at SemEval-2019 task 5: Using sentence embeddings to identify hate speech against immigrants and women in twitter. In *Proceedings of the 13th International Workshop on Semantic Evaluation*, pages 70–74, Minneapolis, Minnesota, USA. Association for Computational Linguistics.

Diederik P. Kingma and Jimmy Ba. 2017. Adam: A method for stochastic optimization. *CoRR*, abs/1412.6980.

Rohan Kshirsagar, Tyrus Cukuvac, Kathy McKeown, and Susan McGregor. 2018. Predictive embeddings for hate speech detection on Twitter. In *Proceedings of the 2nd Workshop on Abusive Language Online (ALW2)*, pages 26–32, Brussels, Belgium. Association for Computational Linguistics.

Zhenzhong Lan, Mingda Chen, Sebastian Goodman, Kevin Gimpel, Piyush Sharma, and Radu Soricut. 2020. ALBERT: A lite BERT for self-supervised learning of language representations. In *8th International Conference on Learning Representations*, Addis Ababa, Ethiopia. OpenReview.net.

Younghun Lee, Seunghyun Yoon, and Kyomin Jung. 2018. Comparative studies of detecting abusive language on twitter. In *Proceedings of the 2nd Workshop on Abusive Language Online (ALW2)*, pages 101–106, Brussels, Belgium. Association for Computational Linguistics.

Ping Liu, Wen Li, and Liang Zou. 2019. NULI at SemEval-2019 task 6: Transfer learning for offensive language detection using bidirectional transformers. In *Proceedings of the 13th International Workshop on Semantic Evaluation*, pages 87–91, Minneapolis, Minnesota, USA. Association for Computational Linguistics.

Shervin Malmasi and Marcos Zampieri. 2018. Challenges in discriminating profanity from hate speech. *Journal of Experimental & Theoretical Artificial Intelligence*, 30(2):187–202.

Johannes Skjeggestad Meyer and Björn Gambäck. 2019. A platform agnostic dual-strand hate speech detector. In *Proceedings of the Third Workshop on Abusive Language Online*, pages 146–156, Florence, Italy. Association for Computational Linguistics.

Tomas Mikolov, Ilya Sutskever, Kai Chen, Greg S Corrado, and Jeff Dean. 2013. Distributed representations of words and phrases and their compositionality. In C. J. C. Burges, L. Bottou, M. Welling, Z. Ghahramani, and K. Q. Weinberger, editors, *Advances in Neural Information Processing Systems 26*, pages 3111–3119. Curran Associates, Inc.

Pushkar Mishra, Marco Del Tredici, Helen Yannakoudakis, and Ekaterina Shutova. 2018. Author profiling for abuse detection. In *Proceedings of the 27th International Conference on Computational Linguistics*, pages 1088–1098, Santa Fe, New Mexico, USA. Association for Computational Linguistics.

Chikashi Nobata, Joel Tetreault, Achint Thomas, Yashar Mehdad, and Yi Chang. 2016. Abusive language detection in online user content. In *Proceedings of the 25th International Conference on World Wide Web*, WWW '16, pages 145–153, Republic and Canton of Geneva, Switzerland. International World Wide Web Conferences Steering Committee.

Ji Ho Park and Pascale Fung. 2017. One-step and two-step classification for abusive language detection on Twitter. In *Proceedings of the First Workshop on Abusive Language Online*, pages 41–45, Vancouver, British Columbia, Canada. Association for Computational Linguistics.

John Pavlopoulos, Prodromos Malakasiotis, and Ion Androutsopoulos. 2017a. Deep learning for user comment moderation. In *Proceedings of the First Workshop on Abusive Language Online*, pages 25–35, Vancouver, BC, Canada. Association for Computational Linguistics.

John Pavlopoulos, Prodromos Malakasiotis, and Ion Androutsopoulos. 2017b. Deeper attention to abusive user content moderation. In *Proceedings of the 2017 Conference on Empirical Methods in Natural Language Processing*, pages 1125–1135, Copenhagen, Denmark. Association for Computational Linguistics.

Juan Manuel Pérez and Franco M. Luque. 2019. Atalaya at SemEval 2019 task 5: Robust embeddings for tweet classification. In *Proceedings of the 13th International Workshop on Semantic Evaluation*, pages 64–69, Minneapolis, Minnesota, USA. Association for Computational Linguistics.

Matthew Peters, Mark Neumann, Mohit Iyyer, Matt Gardner, Christopher Clark, Kenton Lee, and Luke Zettlemoyer. 2018. Deep contextualized word representations. In *Proceedings of the 2018 Conference of the North American Chapter of the Association for Computational Linguistics: Human Language Technologies, Volume 1 (Long Papers)*, pages 2227–2237, New Orleans, Louisiana. Association for Computational Linguistics.

Georgios K. Pitsilis, Heri Ramampiaro, and Helge Langseth. 2018. Detecting offensive language in tweets using deep learning. *Applied Intelligence*, 48(12):4730–4742.

Alec Radford, Karthik Narasimhan, Tim Salimans, and Ilya Sutskever. 2018. Improving language understanding by generative pre-training. Technical report, OpenAI.

Alec Radford, Jeffrey Wu, Rewon Child, David Luan, Dario Amodei, and Ilya Sutskever. 2019. Language models are unsupervised multitask learners. Technical report, OpenAI.

Sara Rosenthal, Pepa Atanasova, Georgi Karadzhov, Marcos Zampieri, and Preslav Nakov. 2020. A large-scale semi-supervised dataset for offensive language identification. *CoRR*, abs/2004.14454.

Björn Ross, Michael Rist, Guillermo Carbonell, Benjamin Cabrera, Nils Kurowsky, and Michael Wojatzki. 2016. Measuring the reliability of hate speech annotations: The case of the European refugee crisis. In *Proceedings of the 3rd Workshop on Natural Language Processing for Computer Mediated Communication*, pages 6–9, Bochum, Germany. Bochumer Linguistische Arbeitsberichte.

Anna Schmidt and Michael Wiegand. 2017. A survey on hate speech detection using natural language processing. In *Proceedings of the Fifth International Workshop on Natural Language Processing for Social Media*, pages 1–10, Valencia, Spain. Association for Computational Linguistics.

Yu Sun, Shuohuan Wang, Yukun Li, Shikun Feng, Hao Tian, Hua Wu, and Haifeng Wang. 2020. ERNIE 2.0: A continual pre-training framework for language understanding. In *34th AAAI Conference on Artificial Intelligence*, pages 8968–8975, New York, New York, USA. AAAI.

Kevin Systrom. 2017. Keeping Instagram a safe place for self-expression. Instagram.com.

Kevin Systrom. 2018. Protecting our community from bullying comments. Instagram.com.

Shikhar Vashishth, Manik Bhandari, Prateek Yadav, Piyush Rai, Chiranjib Bhattacharyya, and Partha Talukdar. 2019. Incorporating syntactic and semantic information in word embeddings using graph convolutional networks. In *Proceedings of the 57th Annual Meeting of the Association for Computational Linguistics*, pages 3308–3318, Florence, Italy. Association for Computational Linguistics.

Ashish Vaswani, Noam Shazeer, Niki Parmar, Jakob Uszkoreit, Llion Jones, Aidan N. Gomez, Łukasz Kaiser, and Illia Polosukhin. 2017. Attention is all you need. In *Advances in Neural Information Processing Systems 30*, pages 5998–6008, Long Beach, California, USA.

Zeerak Waseem. 2016. Are you a racist or am I seeing things? Annotator influence on hate speech detection on Twitter. In *Proceedings of the First Workshop on NLP and Computational Social Science*, pages 138–142, Austin, Texas, USA. Association for Computational Linguistics.

Zeerak Waseem and Dirk Hovy. 2016. Hateful symbols or hateful people? Predictive features for hate speech detection on Twitter. In *Proceedings of the NAACL Student Research Workshop*, pages 88–93, San Diego, California, USA. Association for Computational Linguistics.

Yang You, Jing Li, Sashank Reddi, Jonathan Hseu, Sanjiv Kumar, Srinadh Bhojanapalli, Xiaodan Song, James Demmel, Kurt Keutzer, and Cho-Jui Hsieh. 2020. Large batch optimization for deep learning: Training BERT in 76 minutes. In *8th International Conference on Learning Representations*, Addis Ababa, Ethiopia. OpenReview.net.

Manzil Zaheer, Guru Guruganesh, Avinava Dubey, Joshua Ainslie, Chris Alberti, Santiago Ontanon, Philip Pham, Anirudh Ravula, Qifan Wang, Li Yang, and Amr Ahmed. 2020. Big Bird: Transformers for longer sequences. *CoRR*, abs/2007.14062.

Marcos Zampieri, Shervin Malmasi, Preslav Nakov, Sara Rosenthal, Noura Farra, and Ritesh Kumar. 2019. SemEval-2019 task 6: Identifying and categorizing offensive language in social media (OffensEval). In *Proceedings of the 13th International Workshop on Semantic Evaluation*, pages 75–86, Minneapolis, Minnesota, USA. Association for Computational Linguistics.

Marcos Zampieri, Preslav Nakov, Sara Rosenthal, Pepa Atanasova, Georgi Karadzhov, Hamdy Mubarak, Leon Derczynski, Zeses Pitenis, and Çağrı Çöltekin. 2020. SemEval-2020 Task 12: Multilingual offensive language identification in social media (OffensEval 2020). *CoRR*, abs/2006.07235.

Ziqi Zhang, David Robinson, and Jonathan Tepper. 2018. Detecting hate speech on Twitter using a convolution-GRU based deep neural network. In *The Semantic Web: 15th European Semantic Web Conference*, pages 745–760, Cham, Switzerland. Springer.

Yukun Zhu, Ryan Kiros, Rich Zemel, Ruslan Salakhutdinov, Raquel Urtasun, Antonio Torralba, and Sanja Fidler. 2015. Aligning books and movies: Towards story-like visual explanations by watching movies and reading books. In *Proceedings of the IEEE International Conference on Computer Vision*, pages 19–27, Los Alamitos, California, USA. IEEE Computer Society.

Fine-tuning for multi-domain and multi-label uncivil language detection

Kadir Bulut Ozler
University of Arizona
kbozler@email.arizona.edu

Kate M Kenski
University of Arizona
kkenski@email.arizona.edu

Stephen A Rains
University of Arizona
srains@email.arizona.edu

Yotam Shmargad
University of Arizona
yotam@email.arizona.edu

Kevin Coe
University of Utah
kevin.coe@utah.edu

Steven Bethard
University of Arizona
bethard@email.arizona.edu

Abstract

Incivility is a problem on social media, and it comes in many forms (name-calling, vulgarity, threats, etc.) and domains (microblog posts, online news comments, Wikipedia edits, etc.). Training machine learning models to detect such incivility must handle the multi-label and multi-domain nature of the problem. We present a BERT-based model for incivility detection and propose several approaches for training it for multi-label and multi-domain datasets. We find that individual binary classifiers outperform a joint multi-label classifier, and that simply combining multiple domains of training data outperforms other recently-proposed fine-tuning strategies. We also establish new state-of-the-art performance on several incivility detection datasets.

1 Introduction

In 2019, 93% of Americans identify incivility as a problem, with 68% classifying it as a "major" problem, and those who experienced incivility faced on average 10.2 uncivil interactions each week (Weber Shandwick et al., 2019). Of those who expect civility to get worse, "social media/the Internet" tops the list of what they blame, above "the White House", "politicians in general", "the news media", etc. Especially on social media and the Internet, this incivility often takes the form of *uncivil language*, features of discussion that convey an unnecessarily disrespectful tone toward the discussion forum, its participants, or its topics (Coe et al., 2014).

Uncivil language can range from name-calling (e.g., *Mark, you're some kind of special stupid*) to vulgarity (e.g., *Just build the damn mine already!*) to threats (e.g., *Fine. I will destroy you.*) and beyond. Different types of incivilities often appear in the same utterance (e.g., name-calling, vulgarity, and threats are all included in *SHUT UP, YOU FAT POOP, OR I WILL KICK YOUR ASS!!!*). Uncivil language appears in many places online, from microblogs like Twitter, to comments on online newspapers, to edit histories of resources like Wikipedia.

Uncivil language detection is thus a multi-label and multi-domain language processing problem. While there has been much research in natural language processing methods for identifying such incivility, especially in the subarea of *abusive language* (Wiegand et al., 2019; Zampieri et al., 2019; Basile et al., 2019; Sadeque et al., 2019; van Aken et al., 2018, etc.), the multi-label and multi-domain nature of incivility detection is understudied. We thus consider incivility detection on several datasets that (1) require the classification of incivility into several not-mutually-exclusive fine-grained categories, and (2) cover multiple genres of online interactions. Our contributions are:

- We achieved a new state-of-the-art on both the Coe et al. (2014) and Conversation AI (2018) datasets using BERT (Devlin et al., 2019).

- We compared several algorithms for training classifiers across the multiple domains in these datasets and showed that combining the training data from all domains outperforms other recently-proposed fine-tuning strategies.

- We compared several approaches for handling the multi-label nature of these datasets and showed that independent binary classifiers outperform jointly-trained models.

2 Task

We frame uncivil language detection as a multi-label text classification problem, where the input is a piece of text, and the outputs are the types of incivilities (*name-calling*, *vulgarity*, etc.) that are present. Formally, we aim to learn a function h such that for each piece of text x:

$$h(repr(x)) = \vec{y} \tag{1}$$

Proceedings of the Fourth Workshop on Online Abuse and Harms, pages 28–33
Online, November 20, 2020. ©2020 Association for Computational Linguistics
https://doi.org/10.18653/v1/P17

Annotation Scheme	Domain	Train	Dev	Test	Data split	aspersion	lying accusation	name-calling	pejorative	vulgarity	toxic	severe-toxic	obscene	threat	insult	identity-hate
Coe et al. (2014)	local news comments	3945	987	1233	standard	✓	✓	✓	✓	✓						
Coe et al. (2014)	local politics Tweets	3040	760	-	no standard			✓								
Coe et al. (2014)	Russian troll Tweets	1798	200	-	no standard			✓								
Conversation AI (2018)	Wikipedia comments	37902	312	-	only train available						✓	✓	✓	✓	✓	✓

Table 1: Statistics for the multi-domain and multi-label datasets considered. For data sets with no standard split, or where the test set is unavailable as in Conversation AI (2018), we created our own custom train/dev split.

where $repr(x)$ is a tensor representing that text (e.g., a series of word vectors), and $\vec{y}$ is a binary vector where $\vec{y}_i$ is 1 if x contains the ith form of incivility and 0 otherwise.

We frame learning such h functions a multi-domain classifier training problem, where training and testing data are drawn from multiple domains (*news comments*, *politician tweets*, etc.). Formally, given a domain D_i, we aim to learn a function h_{D_i} that maximizes performance on test data $D_{i_{\text{test}}}$ by training on examples $(x, \vec{y})$ drawn from training data $D_{1_{\text{train}}} \bigcup D_{2_{\text{train}}} \bigcup \ldots \bigcup D_{n_{\text{train}}}$.

3 Data

We consider the following datasets for evaluating multi-label and multi-domain incivility detection.

Local news comments In this multi-label dataset, the following labels are defined and used to annotate online comments on local news articles by Coe et al. (2014):

- *aspersion*: "Mean-spirited or disparaging words directed at a person or group of people."
- *lying accusation*: "Mean-spirited or disparaging words directed at an idea, plan, policy, or behavior."
- *name-calling*: "Stating or implying that an idea, plan, or policy was disingenuous."
- *pejorative*: "Using profanity or language that would not be considered proper (e.g., pissed, screw) inprofessional discourse."
- *vulgarity*: "Disparaging remark about the way in which a person communicates."

Local politics Tweets Coe and colleagues also annotated a collection of microblog posts from the Twitter accounts of their local politicians, but only for *name-calling* incivility.

Russian troll Tweets Coe and colleagues also annotated a small subset of the 3 million English Tweets written by Russian trolls and collected by Linvill and Warren (2018)[1], again for just *name-calling* incivility.

Wikipedia comments In this multi-label dataset, also known as the Kaggle Toxic Comment Classification Challenge, Jigsaw/Google's Conversation AI team annotated comments from Wikipedia's talk page edits (Conversation AI, 2018) for the presence of the following types of abusive language, defined by Perspective AI (2020).

- *toxic*: "A rude, disrespectful, or unreasonable comment that is likely to make people leave a discussion."
- *severe-toxic*: "A very hateful, aggressive, disrespectful comment or otherwise very likely to make a user leave a discussion or give up on sharing their perspective. This attribute is much less sensitive to more mild forms of toxicity, such as comments that include positive uses of curse words."
- *obscene*: "Swear words, curse words, or other obscene or profane language."
- *threat*: "Describes an intention to inflict pain, injury, or violence against an individual or group."
- *insult*: "Insulting, inflammatory, or negative comment towards a person or a group of people."
- *identity-hate*: "Negative or hateful comments targeting someone because of their identity."

Table 1 shows statistics for the different data sets.

---

[1] https://github.com/fivethirtyeight/russian-troll-tweets/

The three datasets annotated by Coe and colleagues can be used in multi-domain experiments, as they share the same annotation scheme. They share only the label *name-calling*, so our multi-domain experiments consider only binary classification. The local news comments and Wikipedia comments datasets can be used in multi-label experiments, as they have been annotated for multiple forms of incivility. They do not share annotation schemes, so our multi-label experiments consider each multi-label dataset separately.

4 Prior Work

There is much recent work on detecting incivility (also referred to as toxicity, abusive language, offensive language, etc.) in social media. Wiegand et al. (2019) presents an overview of such efforts and shows that many datasets constructed for this purpose have unintended bias because of how they have been sampled. We focus on the Coe et al. (2014) and Conversation AI (2018) datasets because they do not have the problems with topic-biased sampling that some other datasets do, where topic words are better predictors of incivility than uncivil words.

There have also been several recent shared tasks that consider incivility. Both the OffensEval shared task (Zampieri et al., 2019) and the HatEval (Basile et al., 2019) shared task ran as part of SemEval-2019 and considered detection of various forms of offensive and hate speech. Neither of these tasks focused on a multi-label or multi-domain problem.

A few models have been designed for and evaluated on the multi-label, multi-domain corpora we consider. Sadeque et al. (2019) considered the local news comments corpus, training recurrent neural network models, and focusing on only the top two most frequent labels for this dataset. They achieved 0.48 F_1 for *name-calling* and 0.53 F_1 for *vulgarity*. van Aken et al. (2018) presented multiple approaches to the Wikipedia comments dataset. They developed an ensemble of logistic regression, recurrent neural networks, and convolutional neural networks, achieving an AUC score of 0.983.

There are a few recent works in cross-domain abusive language detection. Wiegand et al. (2018); Karan and Šnajder (2018); Pamungkas and Patti (2019) all explore training models on one abusive language dataset and testing on another. They focus on binary predictions and bag-of-words support vector machine classifiers (though Pamungkas and Patti (2019) also explores a recurrent neural network). They do not consider multi-label problems, or modern pre-trained neural networks like BERT, which were more successful in recent shared tasks on abusive language (Zampieri et al., 2019). They also evaluate on several datasets that have been identified as problematic by Wiegand et al. (2019) due to their use of topic-biased sampling.

5 Experiments

We use BERT (Devlin et al., 2019) as the starting point for all experiments. BERT is a pre-trained transformer-based neural network that has shown impressive performance on a wide variety of NLP tasks. We follow the standard approach for fine-tuning BERT for text classification, placing a fully connected layer over BERT's `[CLS]` output. We use n sigmoids on this layer rather than a softmax activation, since we are performing multi-label classification. BERT is then fine-tuned as usual, with hyperparameters like learning rate, maximum sequence length, number of epochs, training batch size tuned on the development set. We explored each hyperparameter within the following ranges:

learning rate: 8e-6, 2e-5, 4e-5, 8e-5

maximum sequence length: 128, 256, 512

number of epochs: 2, 3, 4, 5, 6, 8

training batch size: 16, 32, 64, 128

5.1 Multi-domain models

We consider three methods for training classifiers for prediction in multiple domains:

Single One classifier is fine-tuned for each domain.

Joint One classifier is fine-tuned on the combined training data from all the domains.

Joint→Single First, a joint classifier is fine-tuned. Then, the joint classifier parameters are used to initialize n individual classifiers, one for each domain. This approach is inspired by Liu et al. (2019a), where for some natural language understanding problems, they found that multi-task fine-tuning followed by individual task fine-tuning outperformed multi-task fine-tuning alone.

Since our multi-domain datasets share only the label *name-calling*, we train our multi-domain classifiers only for binary classification (i.e., they are not also multi-label).

Data	Training method	Local news comments			Russian troll Tweets			Local politics Tweets		
		P	R	F_1	P	R	F_1	P	R	F_1
Dev	Single	0.63	0.52	0.57	0.67	0.63	0.65	0.65	0.76	0.70
Dev	Joint	**0.75**	**0.57**	**0.65**	0.81	**0.81**	**0.81**	0.75	**0.85**	0.80
Dev	Joint→Single	0.67	0.52	0.58	**0.91**	0.63	0.74	**0.81**	0.81	**0.81**
Test	Sadeque et al. (2019)	0.46	**0.51**	0.48	-	-	-	-	-	-
Test	Best Dev model: Joint	**0.62**	**0.51**	**0.56**	0.83	0.67	0.74	0.71	0.60	0.65

Table 2: Multi-domain results: Performance on the label *name-calling*, for different multi-domain training methods across different datasets. When results from two or more models are comparable, the highest performance is marked in bold. Sadeque et al. (2019) is the previous state-of-the-art on the local news comments. There is no prior state-of-the-art for the other datasets.

Table 2 shows the results of these experiments. The first three rows compare the different training procedures on the development sets. We find that simply combining all the data achieves the best F_1 for both the local news comments and Russian troll Tweets data, and similar F_1 to the more complicated Joint→Single procedure in the remaining dataset. When we evaluate this best model on the test data, we achieve a new state-of-the-art on the local news comments corpus, 0.56 F_1. We are the first to report results on the local politics Tweets and Russian troll Tweets domains, as Sadeque et al. (2019) did not evaluate on these.

These results did not replicate the findings of Liu et al. (2019a) when applied to our incivility datasets; the extra fine-tuning for each domain was unhelpful, and simply combining all the data was the best. This probably argues for exploring other approaches for domain adapatation, e.g., Kim et al. (2016), but it may also simply suggest that Coe et al. (2014)'s annotators were consistent across datasets, making it easy for BERT to learn the core linguistic phenomenon despite differences in domains.

5.2 Multi-label models

Similar to our approach for multi-domain models, we consider three methods for training classifiers for multi-label prediction:

Single One binary classifier is fine-tuned for each label. The output layer of the model is a single sigmoid unit.

Joint One joint classifier is fine-tuned for all labels. The output layer of the model is n sigmoid units, one for each label.

Joint→Single First, a joint classifier is fine-tuned. Then, the joint classifier parameters are used to initialize n binary classifiers, one for each label. This is again inspired by the multi-task training procedure of Liu et al. (2019a).

Since our multi-label datasets do not share an annotation scheme, we train the multi-label classifiers on only one dataset at a time (i.e., they are not also multi-domain).

Table 3 shows the results of these experiments[2]. We find that in most cases training individual binary classifiers (Single) is better than a jointly-learned multi-label classifier (Joint). This is somewhat surprising as the latter is the standard approach with neural networks (Adhikari et al., 2019).

Curious if the problem was some low-frequency classes, we tried training a multi-label model on just the three most frequent classes of the Wikipedia comments dataset (Joint top-3 classes), *toxic*, *obscene*, and *insult*. That slightly improved performance on those three classes, but of course at the cost of the classes now being ignored. Adding the staged training procedure (Joint→Single) on top of this classifier only decreased performance. This suggests that class imbalance may be part of the problem, but is not the full explanation.

Note that we are the first to report all individual label F_1s on both datasets. In the case of the local news comments data, this is because Sadeque et al. (2019), noting the class imbalance problem, decided to only train and evaluate on two classes. In the case of the Wikipedia comments data, this is because the official evaluation metric is AUC, so most systems focused on optimizing this measure. However, as Table 3 shows, while we achieve a state-of-the-art AUC, AUC is not a very discriminative measure for this dataset. For example, both the Single model that predicts all six classes and the Joint top-3 classes model that doesn't even try to predicts *severe-toxic*, *threat*, or

---

[2]Note that the Wikipedia comments dataset does not have a development split, so "Dev" experiments on that dataset are actually on the test set, following van Aken et al. (2018).

| Data | Training method | Local news comments | | | | | Wikipedia comments | | | | | | |
| | | aspersion | lying accusation | name-calling | pejorative | vulgarity | toxic | severe-toxic | obscene | threat | insult | identity-hate | *official metric* |
		F_1	F_1	F_1	F_1	F_1	F_1	F_1	F_1	F_1	F_1	F_1	AUC
Dev	Single	0.24	**0.52**	**0.59**	0.52	**0.46**	**0.86**	**0.50**	**0.88**	**1.00**	0.76	**1.00**	0.990
Dev	Joint all classes	**0.37**	0.44	0.54	0.46	**0.46**	0.80	0.33	0.83	**1.00**	0.80	**1.00**	0.988
Dev	Joint top-3 classes	-	-	-	-	-	0.83	0.00	**0.88**	0.00	**0.86**	0.00	0.990
Dev	Joint top-3→Single	-	-	-	-	-	0.83	0.00	0.77	0.00	0.80	0.00	0.983
Test	Sadeque et al. (2019)	-	-	0.48	-	**0.53**	-	-	-	-	-	-	-
Test	van Aken et al. (2018)	-	-	-	-	-	-	-	-	-	-	-	0.983
Test	Best Dev model: Single	0.05	0.36	**0.55**	0.28	0.50	0.86	0.50	0.88	1.00	0.76	1.00	0.990

Table 3: Multi-label results: Performance on each label, for different multi-label training methods across different datasets. When results from two or more models are comparable, the highest performance is marked in bold. The final column is the official evaluation measure for the Wikipedia comments dataset. Sadeque et al. (2019) is the state-of-the-art on the local news comments data, and van Aken et al. (2018) is the state-of-the-art on the Wikipedia comments data.

identity-hate achieve the same AUC of 0.990. The F_1 scores more clearly show that the Joint top-3 classes model is as good or better for all labels but *insult*.

6 Limitations

We focused on a BERT-based model due to its top-ranking performance in related shared tasks (Zampieri et al., 2019), but recent advances over BERT, e.g., RoBERTa (Liu et al., 2019b) might yield additional gains. We also focused on the limited number of datasets that could support multi-label and/or multi-domain experiments, but our results could be strengthened by creating new multi-label, multi-domain datasets. Finally, class imbalance only partly explains why a joint multi-label classifier failed to outperform independent binary classifiers, indicating that further investigation is needed into multi-label classification approaches for uncivil language.

7 Conclusion

We applied BERT on multi-label and multi-domain incivility detection tasks and achieved a new state-of-the-art on several different datasets. In exploring different training procedures, we found that it was better to directly combine data from multiple domains than other more complex procedures, and that it was better to train individual binary classifiers than to train a joint multi-label classifier.

References

Ashutosh Adhikari, Achyudh Ram, Raphael Tang, and Jimmy Lin. 2019. Rethinking complex neural network architectures for document classification. In *Proceedings of the 2019 Conference of the North American Chapter of the Association for Computational Linguistics: Human Language Technologies, Volume 1 (Long and Short Papers)*, pages 4046–4051, Minneapolis, Minnesota. Association for Computational Linguistics.

Betty van Aken, Julian Risch, Ralf Krestel, and Alexander Löser. 2018. Challenges for toxic comment classification: An in-depth error analysis. In *Proceedings of the 2nd Workshop on Abusive Language Online (ALW2)*, pages 33–42, Brussels, Belgium. Association for Computational Linguistics.

Valerio Basile, Cristina Bosco, Elisabetta Fersini, Debora Nozza, Viviana Patti, Francisco Manuel Rangel Pardo, Paolo Rosso, and Manuela Sanguinetti. 2019. SemEval-2019 task 5: Multilingual detection of hate speech against immigrants and women in Twitter. In *Proceedings of the 13th International Workshop on Semantic Evaluation*, pages 54–63, Minneapolis, Minnesota, USA. Association for Computational Linguistics.

Kevin Coe, Kate Kenski, and Stephen A. Rains. 2014. Online and Uncivil? Patterns and Determinants of Incivility in Newspaper Website Comments. *Journal of Communication*, 64(4):658–679.

Conversation AI. 2018. Toxic comment classification challenge. https://www.kaggle.com/c/jigsaw-toxic-comment-classification-challenge.

Jacob Devlin, Ming-Wei Chang, Kenton Lee, and Kristina Toutanova. 2019. BERT: Pre-training of deep bidirectional transformers for language understanding. In *Proceedings of the 2019 Conference of the North American Chapter of the Association for Computational Linguistics: Human Language Technologies, Volume 1 (Long and Short Papers)*, pages 4171–4186, Minneapolis, Minnesota. Association for Computational Linguistics.

Mladen Karan and Jan Šnajder. 2018. Cross-domain detection of abusive language online. In *Proceedings of the 2nd Workshop on Abusive Language Online (ALW2)*, pages 132–137, Brussels, Belgium. Association for Computational Linguistics.

Young-Bum Kim, Karl Stratos, and Ruhi Sarikaya. 2016. Frustratingly easy neural domain adaptation. In *Proceedings of COLING 2016, the 26th International Conference on Computational Linguistics: Technical Papers*, pages 387–396, Osaka, Japan. The COLING 2016 Organizing Committee.

Darren L. Linvill and Patrick L. Warren. 2018. Troll factories: The internet research agency and state-sponsored agenda building. `http://pwarren.people.clemson.edu/Linvill_Warren_TrollFactory.pdf`.

Wei Liu, Lei Li, Zuying Huang, and Yinan Liu. 2019a. Multi-lingual Wikipedia summarization and title generation on low resource corpus. In *Proceedings of the Workshop MultiLing 2019: Summarization Across Languages, Genres and Sources*, pages 17–25, Varna, Bulgaria. INCOMA Ltd.

Yinhan Liu, Myle Ott, Naman Goyal, Jingfei Du, Mandar Joshi, Danqi Chen, Omer Levy, Mike Lewis, Luke Zettlemoyer, and Veselin Stoyanov. 2019b. Roberta: A robustly optimized bert pretraining approach. *arXiv preprint arXiv:1907.11692*.

Endang Wahyu Pamungkas and Viviana Patti. 2019. Cross-domain and cross-lingual abusive language detection: A hybrid approach with deep learning and a multilingual lexicon. In *Proceedings of the 57th Annual Meeting of the Association for Computational Linguistics: Student Research Workshop*, pages 363–370, Florence, Italy. Association for Computational Linguistics.

Perspective AI. 2020. Available attributes and languages. `https://support.perspectiveapi.com/s/about-the-api-attributes-and-languages`.

Farig Sadeque, Stephen Rains, Yotam Shmargad, Kate Kenski, Kevin Coe, and Steven Bethard. 2019. Incivility detection in online comments. In *Proceedings of the Eighth Joint Conference on Lexical and Computational Semantics (*SEM 2019)*, pages 283–291, Minneapolis, Minnesota. Association for Computational Linguistics.

Weber Shandwick, Powell Tate, and KRC Research. 2019. Civilty in america 2019: Solutions for tomorrow. `https://www.webershandwick.com/news/civility-in-america-2019-solutions-for-tomorrow/`.

Michael Wiegand, Josef Ruppenhofer, and Thomas Kleinbauer. 2019. Detection of Abusive Language: the Problem of Biased Datasets. In *Proceedings of the 2019 Conference of the North American Chapter of the Association for Computational Linguistics: Human Language Technologies, Volume 1 (Long and Short Papers)*, pages 602–608, Minneapolis, Minnesota. Association for Computational Linguistics.

Michael Wiegand, Josef Ruppenhofer, Anna Schmidt, and Clayton Greenberg. 2018. Inducing a lexicon of abusive words – a feature-based approach. In *Proceedings of the 2018 Conference of the North American Chapter of the Association for Computational Linguistics: Human Language Technologies, Volume 1 (Long Papers)*, pages 1046–1056, New Orleans, Louisiana. Association for Computational Linguistics.

Marcos Zampieri, Shervin Malmasi, Preslav Nakov, Sara Rosenthal, Noura Farra, and Ritesh Kumar. 2019. SemEval-2019 task 6: Identifying and categorizing offensive language in social media (OffensEval). In *Proceedings of the 13th International Workshop on Semantic Evaluation*, pages 75–86, Minneapolis, Minnesota, USA. Association for Computational Linguistics.

HurtBERT: Incorporating Lexical Features with BERT
for the Detection of Abusive Language

Anna Koufakou♣   **Endang Wahyu Pamungkas**♡   **Valerio Basile**♡   **Viviana Patti**♡

♣Florida Gulf Coast University, Software Engineering Dept, USA
♡University of Turin, Dipartimento di Informatica, Italy

♣akoufakou@fgcu.edu   ♡{pamungka,basile,patti}@di.unito.it

Abstract

The detection of abusive or offensive remarks in social texts has received significant attention in research. In several related shared tasks, BERT has been shown to be the state-of-the-art. In this paper, we propose to utilize lexical features derived from a hate lexicon towards improving the performance of BERT in such tasks. We explore different ways to utilize the lexical features in the form of lexicon-based encodings at the sentence level or embeddings at the word level. We provide an extensive dataset evaluation that addresses in-domain as well as cross-domain detection of abusive content to render a complete picture. Our results indicate that our proposed models combining BERT with lexical features help improve over a baseline BERT model in many of our in-domain and cross-domain experiments.

1 Introduction

The automatic classification of abusive and offensive language is a complex problem, that has raised a growing interest in the Natural Language Processing community in the last decade or so (Fortuna and Nunes, 2018; Vidgen et al., 2019; Poletto et al., 2020). Several benchmarks have been introduced to measure the performance of mostly supervised machine learning systems tackling such problems as text classification tasks (Basile et al., 2019; Zampieri et al., 2019b). The evaluation of abusive and offensive language, however, is not straightforward. Among the issues, it has been observed how the topics discussed in the messages composing the benchmark datasets introduce biases, interfering with the modeling of the pure pragmatic phenomena by the supervised models trained on the respective training sets (Wiegand et al., 2019; Caselli et al., 2020).

Among the recent neural architectures, BERT (*Bidirectional Encoder Representations from Trans-*

formers (Devlin et al., 2019)), is considered the state of the art in several NLP tasks, including abusive and offensive language detection. For example, in the SemEval 2019 Task 6 (Zampieri et al., 2019b, OffensEval), seven out of the top-ten teams used BERT, including the top team. The knowledge encoded in such model, based on *transformer* neural networks, is induced by a pre-training performed on a large quantity of text, then fine-tuned to a specific dataset in order to learn complex correlations between the natural language and the labels. One disadvantage to models such as BERT is that no additional external knowledge is taken into consideration, such as linguistic information from a lexicon.

In this paper, we propose a hybrid methodology to infuse external knowledge into a supervised model for abusive language detection. We propose to add extra lexical features with BERT at sentence- or term-level, with the goal of improving the quality of its prediction of abusive language. In particular, we investigate the inclusion of features from a categorized lexicon in the domain of offensive and abusive language, with the aim of supporting transfer knowledge in that domain across datasets.

We perform extensive, in-domain and cross-domain experimentation, to evaluate the performance of models which are trained on one dataset and tested on other datasets. Cross-domain classification of abusive content has been proposed to address the diverse topical focuses and targets as exhibited in different datasets developed from the research community in the last years (Karan and Šnajder, 2018; Pamungkas and Patti, 2019; Pamungkas et al., 2020b). For example, some datasets proposed for hate speech detection focus on racism or sexism (Waseem and Hovy, 2016), in line with the target-oriented nature of hate speech, while others on offensive or abusive language without tar-

Proceedings of the Fourth Workshop on Online Abuse and Harms, pages 34–43
Online, November 20, 2020. ©2020 Association for Computational Linguistics
https://doi.org/10.18653/v1/P17

geting a specific vulnerable group (Zampieri et al., 2019a; Caselli et al., 2020). This makes it difficult to know if a model that performs well on one dataset will generalize well for other datasets. However, several actors – including institutions, NGO operators and ICT companies to comply to governments' demands for counteracting online abuse[1]– have an increasing need for automatic support to moderation (Shen and Rose, 2019; Chung et al., 2019) or for monitoring and mapping the dynamics and the diffusion of hate speech dynamics over a territory (Paschalides et al., 2020; Capozzi et al., 2019) considering different targets and vulnerable categories. In this scenario, there is a considerable urgency to investigate computational approaches for abusive language detection supporting the development of robust models, which can be used to detect abusive contents with different scope or topical focuses. When addressing this challenge, the motivation for our proposal is the hypothesis that the addition of lexical knowledge from an abusive lexicon will soften the topic bias issue (Wiegand et al., 2019), making the model more stable against cross-domain evaluation. Our extensive experimentation with many different datasets shows that our proposed methods improve over the BERT baseline in the majority of the in-domain and cross-domain experiments.

2   Related Work

The last ten years have seen a rapidly increasing amount of research work on the automatic detection of abusive and offensive language, as highlighted by the success of international evaluation campaigns such as HatEval (Basile et al., 2019) on gender- or ethnic-based hate speech, OffensEval (Zampieri et al., 2019b, 2020) on offensive language, or AMI (Fersini et al., 2018a,b, Automatic Misogyny Identification) on misogyny. Several annotated corpora have also been established as benchmarks besides the data produced for the aforementioned shared tasks for several languages, for instance, Waseem et al. (2017) for racism and sexism in English, Sanguinetti et al. (2018) for hate speech Italian and Mubarak et al. (2017) for abusive language in Arabic. We refer to (Poletto et al., 2020) for a systematic and updated review of resources and benchmark corpora for hate speech

detection across different languages.

The vast majority of approaches proposed in the literature are based on supervised learning, with statistical models learning the features of the target language and their relationship with the abusive phenomena from an annotated corpus. Most works propose variations on neural architectures such as Recurrent Neural Networks (especially Long Short-term Memory networks), or Convolutional Neural Networks (Mishra et al., 2019). An investigation on what type of attention mechanism (contextual vs. self-attention) is better for abusive language detection using deep learning architectures is proposed in (Chakrabarty et al., 2019). Character-based models have also been proposed for this task (Mishra et al., 2018).

More recently, models based on the *Transformer* neural network architecture have gained prominence, thanks to their ability of learning accurate language models from very large corpora in an unsupervised fashion, and then being fine-tuned to specific classification tasks, such as abusive language detection, with relatively little amount of annotated data. Several ideas have been proposed in the literature to improve the performance of BERT for abusive language detection. For example, fine-tuning large pre-trained language models in (Bodapati et al., 2019).

A complementary approach to supervised learning towards the detection of abusive and offensive language is the use of language resources such as lexicons and dictionaries. Wiegand et al. (2018) proposed a method to induce a list of English words to capture abusive language. Davidson et al. (2017) introduced an English lexicon covering hate speech, racism, sexism, and homophobia. Other languages have relatively less resources with respect to English, apart perhaps from Arabic, for which two lexical resources are available, by Mubarak et al. (2017), with focus on obscenity, and by Albadi et al. (2018). A notable exception is HurtLex (Bassignana et al., 2018), a multilingual lexicon of offensive words, created by semi-automatically translating a handcrafted resource in Italian by linguist Tullio De Mauro (called *Parole per Ferire*, "words to hurt" (De Mauro, 2016)) into 53 languages. Lemmas in HurtLex are associated to 17 non-mutually exclusive categories, plus a binary macro-category indicating whether the lemma reflects a stereotype. The number of lemmas in any language of HurtLex is in the order of thousands, depending on the lan-

---

[1] See for instance the Code of Conduct on countering illegal hate speech online issued by EU commission (EU Commission, 2016).

guage, and they are divided into the four principal parts of speech: noun, adjective, verb, and adverb. In our earlier research, we used a technique called *retrofitting* to enhance word embeddings using HurtLex, for detecting aggression in English, Hindi, and Bengali (Koufakou et al., 2020).

In this work, we propose to infuse the lexical knowledge from HurtLex into a BERT model with the goal to improve the efficacy of abusive and offensive language prediction models. Specifically, we utilize different representations of the HurtLex categories as they are found in the data, utilize them with a BERT model, and explore how they affect the detection accuracy. To the best of our knowledge, the utilization of a hate lexicon, especially one that is based on this kind of structure with multiple categories, with a BERT model has not been explored before. We fully describe our methods in the following section.

3 Methodology

In this paper, we explore two models based on how they utilize the lexical features extracted from the hate speech lexicon, HurtLex (Bassignana et al., 2018). Both of our proposed models utilize two inputs: (a) the sentence tokens (BERT's usual input), and (b) a vector we create based on the categories in HurtLex as they are found in our data. All the data we explore in this work are in English, so we used only the English version of HurtLex and leave the multilingual aspect for future work. Specifically, we use the English section of HurtLex version 1.2 [2]. It contains 6,072 entries, of which 2,268 are in the *conservative* subset (these are terms with higher confidence). Table 1 lists the categories in HurtLex, with the number of terms in each one, as well as examples.

Our models both start using the BERT layer, which takes three inputs consisting of id, mask and segment - see Figures 1 and 2. The output of this BERT layer connects to a dense layer. Please note that specific details and parameters for the BERT Baseline as well as any layers in our models are presented in section 4.

Regarding HurtLex features, we have two ways of extracting features: encodings and embeddings. In the first architecture (see Figure 1), based on the words in the train set, we find their categories in HurtLex and then derive a vector of HurtLex cate-

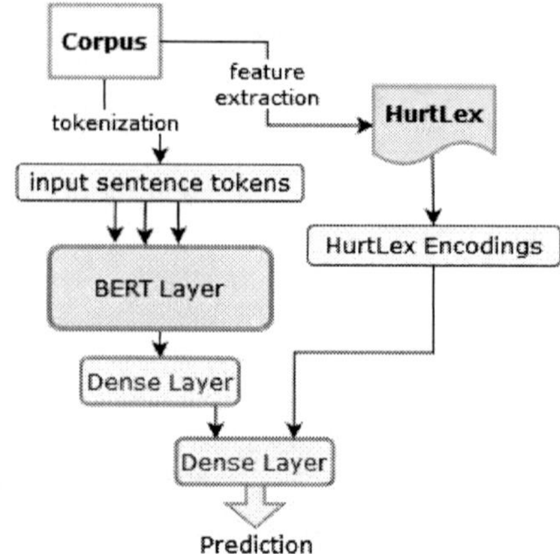

Figure 1: HurtBERT-Enc, our model using HurtLex Encodings

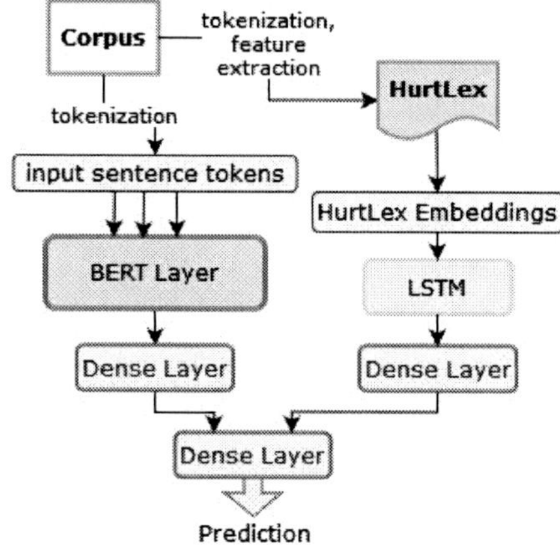

Figure 2: HurtBERT-Emb, our model using HurtLex Embeddings

gories: we call this HurtLex Encoding. The total number of categories in HurtLex is 17, so the dimensionality of the HurtLex encoding is 17. Each element in this vector is simply a frequency count for the respective category in HurtLex. For example, if there is a total of 3 words in a train record (e.g. tweet) that belong in the *ethnic slurs* category of HurtLex, then the corresponding element in the HurtLex encoding is 3. We call this architecture *HurtBERT-Enc*.

Our second model explores using HurtLex embeddings with an LSTM, as shown in Figure 2. The HurtLex embedding is a 17-dimension one-hot encoding of the word presence in each of the lexicon categories. This model is named *HurtBERT-Emb*.

One of the main differences between the embedding and the encoding is that the embedding

---

[2] https://github.com/valeriobasile/hurtlex

Category	# Terms	Examples
negative stereotypes ethnic slurs	371	barbarian, idiotic, dummy, n***oes, infertility
locations and demonyms	24	genoan, savage, barbarian, tike, boor
professions and occupations	192	wooer, politician, peasant, fishwife, academism
physical disabilities and diversity	63	handycapped, midget, worthless, invalidity, impaired
cognitive disabilities and diversity	491	artless, retarded, simple, goof, brute
moral and behavioral defects	715	close-minded, cheater, stinking, forgery, faker
words related to social and economic disadvantage	124	miscreants, miserable, wretch, pitiful, villain
plants	177	finocchio, potato, papaya whip, squash, f**ot
animals	996	b***h, t**t, goose, scoundrel, beastly
male genitalia	426	wanky, c**k, testicles, phallic, prick
female genitalia	144	babe, c**t, t**t, boob, p***y
words related to prostitution	276	s*ut, street walker, crack h*, hooker, w***e
words related to homosexuality	361	drag, crossdressing, shirtlifter, f**, qu**rio
with potential negative connotations	518	bollocks, acolyth, delirious, reject, mooch
derogatory words	2,204	scalawag, boaster, rustler, dunderheaded, pedant
felonies and words related to crime and immoral behavior	619	mafioso, roguery, robber, scalawag, rapscallion
words related to the seven deadly sins of the Christian tradition	527	concupiscience, laziness, vanity, madness, slacker

Table 1: Descriptions, number of terms and examples for the categories in HurtLex

is word-level, while the encoding is comment-level. Therefore, for the case of HurtLex encodings, one record (e.g. one tweet) generates one 17-dimensional vector (which we call HurtLex encoding). While, for the case of the HurtLex embeddings, every word in the comment has one 17-dimensional vector representation (which is the HurtLex embedding). The HurtLex embedding also passes through an embedding layer, which goes into an LSTM and a dense layer, as shown in Figure 2.

In the end, the encoding is a simple representation that reflects if a category from the lexicon is found in the words of comment (or more accurately, how many times this category is found). While the embedding-based model also represents non-linear interactions between the features, that is, linguistically, the role of the HurtLex words in the sentence.

Finally, for both models, we concatenate the dense layer from the BERT output and the dense layer from the HurtLex output, before passing into a dense layer with sigmoid activation as the predictor layer (see the bottom part of both Figures 1 and 2).

4 Experiments and Results

Overall, we follow the experimental setup of (Swamy et al., 2019). We exploit the BERT pre-trained models available on tensorflow-hub[3], which facilitate us to integrate BERT on top of Keras architecture[4]. Specifically, we use the `bert-uncased` model, with 12 transformer blocks, 12 self-attention heads, and hidden layer dimension 768. Based on performance in early experiments, our models use learning rate of e^-5, batch size 32, and maximum sequence length of 50. We implement early stopping and model checkpoint based on the development set evaluation to avoid overfitting during the training process. For the LSTM in Figure 2, we use 32 nodes, and the dense layers in Figures 1-2 are 256 and 16 nodes respectively (all dense layers except last have RELU activation).

4.1 Datasets

The datasets used in our experiments are summarized in Table 2. All the datasets we explore in this work are in English: we leave the multilingual aspect of this research to future work. Similar to previous work in cross-domain classification of abusive language, all datasets need to be cast into binary label as abusive (in bold in the Table) and not abusive. We split all datasets into training, development and test sets with the proportion of 70%, 10% and 20% respectively. We list and describe the datasets below in chronological order, as some of the datasets were built based on previous data or annotation schemes.

Waseem: This corpus was collected over a period of 2 months by using representative keywords which is frequently used to attack specific targets including religious, sexual, gender and ethnic minorities (Waseem and Hovy, 2016). Two annotators were assigned to annotate the full dataset, with a third expert annotator reviewing their annotations. The final dataset consists of 16,914 tweets, with 3,383 instances targeting gender minorities (*sexism*), 1,972 labeled as *racism*, and 11,559 tweets neither sexist nor racist[5].

Davidson: This dataset contains 24,783 tweets[6] manually rated with three labels including *hate speech*, *offensive*, and *neither* (Davidson et al., 2017). The dataset was manually labelled by using the CrowdFlower platforms[7], where each tweet was rated by at least three annotators. The final collection only contains 5.8% of total tweets as *hate speech* and 77.4% as *offensive*, while the remaining 16.8% were labelled as *not offensive*.

Founta: This dataset collection consists of 80,000 tweets annotated with 4 mutually exclusive labels including *abusive*, *hateful*, *spam*, and *normal* (Founta et al., 2018). These tweets were gathered from the original corpus composed of 30 millions tweets was collected from 30 March 2017 to 9 April 2017. The annotation process was completed by five annotators and the final dataset is composed of 11% tweets labeled as *abusive*, 7.5% as *hateful*, 59% as *normal*, and 22.5% as *spam*.

HatEval: This dataset was used in the SemEval-2019 Task 5: Multilingual Detection of Hate Speech Against Immigrants and Women in Twitter (Basile et al., 2019). It contains about 12 thousand records and its labels are hateful or not. This dataset has also been evaluated for migrants and

---

[3] https://www.tensorflow.org/hub
[4] https://keras.io/

[5] We were able to retrieve only 16,488 instances (3,216 *sexism*, 1,957 *racism* and 11,315 *neither*)
[6] We only found this number in https://github.com/t-davidson/hate-speech-and-offensive-language
[7] Now Figure Eight https://www.figure-eight.com/

Dataset	Label	# Instances	Target %
Waseem (Waseem and Hovy, 2016)	**Racism**, **Sexism**, None	16,488	31.4
Davidson (Davidson et al., 2017)	**Hate Speech**, **Offensive**, Neither	24,783	83.2
Founta (Founta et al., 2018)	**Abusive**, **Hateful**, Spam, Normal	99,799	18.5
HatEval (Basile et al., 2019)	**Hateful**, Not Hateful	11,971	42.0
OLID (Zampieri et al., 2019b)	**Offensive**, Not Offensive	14,100	32.9
AbuseEval (Caselli et al., 2020)	**Abusive**, Not Abusive	14,100	20.8

Table 2: The datasets used in this paper (chronological order): labels, number of instances, and percent of records that are labeled abusive, offensive, or hateful.

misogyny.

OLID: The Offensive Language Identification Dataset (Zampieri et al., 2019a) was used in SemEval-2019 Task 6: 'OffensEval' (Zampieri et al., 2019b). It has Twitter data as the previous datasets, but it was annotated using a unique hierarchical model based on the proposed idea in (Waseem et al., 2017). We use the Offensive and Not Offensive labeled data, where about 30% of the records are labeled as Offensive.

AbuseEval: Caselli et al. (2020) created a new corpus by re-annotating OLID in order to model abusive language, seen as a correlated but independent phenomenon from offensive language. The annotation of abusiveness is carried out by three annotators at a coarse-grained, binary level (i.e., *abusive* vs. *not abusive*), and at a finer grain with the further distinction between *implicit* and *explicit* abusive language. Even though, as expected, there is overlap between offensive and abusive comments, a surprising number of instances labeled 'Offensive' in OLID were marked as 'Not Abusive' in AbuseEval.

4.2 Results and Discussion

In our experiments, we train on the training set of each of the six datasets in Table 2 and test on all of the test sets as well as the Immigrant and Misogyny test sets of HatEval, denoted as 'HatEval Mig' and 'HatEval Mis' respectively, for a total of eight test sets.

Additionally, we run the experiments with each model a total of five times and present the average result. In summary, the results presented in this section are based on 720 experiments (3 models × 6 train sets × 8 test sets × 5 runs). About the variance of the results, the average standard deviation we observe is under 0.02 with very few exceptions: for example, AbuseEval results' standard deviation has an average of 0.03.

Results for all our experiments are shown in Table 3. In this Table, we show the F1 macro-averaged results for our two models, HurtBERT-Enc (Encodings, see Figure 1) and HurtBERT-Emb (Embeddings, see Figure 2) versus the BERT baseline (refer to Section 3 for a description of all models).

Starting with in-dataset experiments (shaded gray in Table 3), the results indicate that HurtBERT performs better than the baseline on 4 out of 6 datasets, namely AbuseEval, HatEval, OLID, and Waseem. In all four cases, HurtBERT-Emb is doing the best. The improvement in F1-macro is small in some cases (e.g., for Waseem, HurtBERT-Emb has 0.838 versus 0.836 for the baseline) and larger in others (e.g., for HatEval, HurtBERT-Emb has 0.562 versus 0.533 for the baseline).

As expected, based on previous studies, the vast majority of our out-domain results are lower than the in-domain ones. For example, for Davidson, the in-domain performance (training and testing on Davidson) is in the 90's, while the out-domain (training on other datasets and testing on Davidson) ranges from 40's to 70's. There are some exceptions, for example, training our models on Founta and testing on OLID has better performance than when training our models on OLID (e.g. see BERT Baseline results, 0.753 for Founta-trained versus 0.739 for OLID trained). This is on par with previous work (Swamy et al., 2019): as they noted, there is similarity between these two datasets and Founta is a larger dataset (see Table 2).

When comparing our models with the baseline in the cross-dataset experiments, we observe that our two variants of HurtBERT obtain better results when fine-tuned on other datasets, in particular Davidson, OLID, and Waseem to a varying extent, while the results for the experiments with fine-tuning on HatEval are mixed. We observe some large improvements, for example, training

| Train Set | AbuseEval | | | Davidson | | | Founta | | |
Test Set	B	HB-Enc	HB-Emb	B	HB-Enc	HB-Emb	B	HB-Enc	HB-Emb
AbuseEval	.659	**.669**	**.686**	.577	**.578**	**.583**	.672	.657	.671
Davidson	.462	.444	.453	.908	.907	.907	.742	.738	**.745**
Founta	.707	**.715**	.702	.849	**.850**	**.850**	.916	.914	.913
HatEval	.579	.579	.571	.515	**.519**	**.517**	.532	**.539**	**.541**
HatEval Mig	.569	.554	.559	.533	**.542**	**.546**	.542	**.544**	**.578**
HatEval Mis	.572	**.582**	.567	.307	**.308**	.306	.341	**.355**	**.348**
OLID	.638	**.662**	**.666**	.663	**.667**	**.674**	.753	.741	.753
Waseem	.589	**.596**	.583	.629	**.636**	**.636**	.602	.600	**.612**

| Train Set | HatEval | | | OLID | | | Waseem | | |
Test Set	B	HB-Enc	HB-Emb	B	HB-Enc	HB-Emb	B	HB-Enc	HB-Emb
AbuseEval	.562	.548	.552	.663	**.666**	**.680**	.521	.520	**.541**
Davidson	.583	.547	.551	.703	**.704**	.703	.406	**.445**	**.462**
Founta	.570	.543	.554	.874	**.877**	.874	.512	**.516**	**.540**
HatEval	.533	**.553**	**.562**	.535	**.537**	**.540**	.524	.524	**.542**
HatEval Mig	.463	**.486**	**.483**	.575	.549	**.578**	.420	**.436**	**.450**
HatEval Mis	.598	**.638**	**.633**	.361	**.376**	**.371**	.588	.579	**.595**
OLID	.565	.545	.549	.739	.739	**.747**	.511	.507	**.536**
Waseem	.632	.614	.620	.632	.610	**.637**	.836	.834	**.838**

Table 3: The F1-macro results for all datasets. Shaded means in-dataset experiment. *B* stands for the baseline, *HB-Enc* stands for HurtBERT-Enc, and *HB-Emb* stands for HurtBERT-Emb. Bold indicates our model improves on the baseline; underlined indicates the best result (max). Each result is the average of five runs.

on Waseem and testing on Davidson, the F1-macro for HurtBERT is 0.445 (based on Encodings) and 0.462 (based on Embeddings) versus 0.406 for the BERT baseline. On the other hand, most results trained on Davidson are relatively close to the baseline. A possible explanation for this empirical evidence may have its roots in the different nature of the phenomena modeled by the datasets employed in our experiments. In fact, HurtLex seems to provide more informative knowledge to the model when the goal task is to detect *offensive* language (e.g., OLID) rather than *abusive* language (e.g., AbuseEval). This would make sense given that the lexical resource comes from a lexicon of words used to explicitly express the intention to hurt, while AbusEval is much more about "implicit" abuse.

We manually inspected some of the predictions of the models, with particular attention towards the instances that were misclassified by the baseline (BERT) and correctly classified by either HurtBERT-Enc or HurtBERT-Emb model. On HS data, we found many cases where swear words were present that are often used with non-offensive function, according to the classification

in Pamungkas et al. (2020a). The word "b***h" in particular is ubiquitous in this subset, see for instance the following tweets:

*Me: these shoes look scary Me to me: you're a prison psychologist, suck it up, b***h*

*When my sister and her boyfriend was arguing my nephew went upstairs & said "my mama not a b***h or a h*e so you better watch yo mouth"* 😂

*Love that u used WOMEN instead of b***h*

Our hypothesis is that the additional knowledge from HurtLex has a stabilizing effect on the representation of offensive terms, whereas the fully contextual embeddings of BERT tend to always understand such terms as offensive due to the sentence-level context.

Comparing our two models (see the model diagrams in Figures 1 and 2), we observe more improvements from HurtBERT-Emb (see again the results in Table 3). Over all the experiments,

HurtBERT-Emb has the best (maximum) performance in 26 out of 48 experiments, versus 14 for HurtBERT-Enc out of 48 (there are a couple of ties in these numbers). When we look at the different training sets, the largest improvement overall is training on Waseem, where HurtBERT-Emb has the best performance among the three models in all 8 out of 8 experiments, versus only 3 out of 8 for HurtBERT-Enc. In other datasets, an example is training on OLID and testing on AbuseEval, the HurtBERT-Emb F1-macro is 0.680 versus 0.663 for the baseline and 0.666 for HurtBERT-Enc. Another example is training on Founta and testing on Hateval Mig: HurtBERT-Emb has 0.578 versus 0.542 for the baseline and 0.544 for HurtBERT-Enc.

This seems to be expected, that a method based on word embeddings performs better than one based on a simple, numerical encoding which represents an entire comment. HurtLex embeddings go through an LSTM and dense layer (Fig. 2), therefore, we expect this model to learn relationships among words in the context of the comments in the data. Nevertheless, there are cases where HurtBERT-Enc, does better; for example, training on AbuseEval and testing on Founta, HurtBERT-Enc has F1-macro of 0.715 vs 0.707 for the baseline and 0.702 for HurtBERT-Emb. This shows that, in some cases, a simple architecture with numerical encodings at the comment level can outperform the more sophisticated model based on embeddings.

5   Conclusions and Future Work

In this work, we explore how to combine a BERT model with features extracted from a hate speech lexicon. The lexical features are extracted based on multiple categories in the lexicon and according to how these categories are found in the data. The lexical features can be represented at the comment level as simple numerical encodings or at the word level as embeddings that aim to learn the relationships of the lexical features in the context of the data. We conduct extensive experimentation, with in-domain as well as cross-domain training. We observe that our methods improve on the BERT baseline in the large majority of the cases, with high gains in some cases. It proves our hypothesis that the additional features from lexical knowledge can improve the BERT performance, providing a domain-agnostic feature in a cross-domain setting. For our future work, we will explore different languages to take advantage of the multilingual aspect

of our lexicon. We also plan to delve deeper into the study of the relationships between our models and the linguistic aspects and phenomena in the various abusive and offensive datasets.

Acknowledgments

The work of Valerio Basile, Endang W. Pamungkas and Viviana Patti is partially funded by Progetto di Ateneo/CSP 2016 (Immigrants, Hate and Prejudice in Social Media, S1618.L2.BOSC.01) and by the project "Be Positive!" (under the 2019 "Google.org Impact Challenge on Safety" call).

References

Nuha Albadi, Maram Kurdi, and Shivakant Mishra. 2018. Are they our brothers? analysis and detection of religious hate speech in the Arabic Twittersphere. In *Proceedings of the 2018 IEEE/ACM International Conference on Advances in Social Networks Analysis and Mining, ASONAM 2018*, pages 69–76. IEEE.

Valerio Basile, Cristina Bosco, Elisabetta Fersini, Debora Nozza, Viviana Patti, Francisco Manuel Rangel Pardo, Paolo Rosso, and Manuela Sanguinetti. 2019. SemEval-2019 task 5: Multilingual detection of hate speech against immigrants and women in Twitter. In *Proceedings of the 13th International Workshop on Semantic Evaluation*, pages 54–63, Minneapolis, Minnesota, USA. Association for Computational Linguistics.

Elisa Bassignana, Valerio Basile, and Viviana Patti. 2018. Hurtlex: A multilingual lexicon of words to hurt. In *Proceedings of the Fifth Italian Conference on Computational Linguistics (CLiC-it 2018), Torino, Italy, December 10-12, 2018*.

Sravan Bodapati, Spandana Gella, Kasturi Bhattacharjee, and Yaser Al-Onaizan. 2019. Neural word decomposition models for abusive language detection. In *Proceedings of the Third Workshop on Abusive Language Online*, pages 135–145, Florence, Italy. Association for Computational Linguistics.

Arthur TE Capozzi, Mirko Lai, Valerio Basile, Fabio Poletto, Manuela Sanguinetti, Cristina Bosco, Viviana Patti, Giancarlo Ruffo, Cataldo Musto, Marco Polignano, et al. 2019. Computational linguistics against hate: Hate speech detection and visualization on social media in the "Contro L'Odio" project. In *6th Italian Conference on Computational Linguistics, CLiC-it 2019*, Bari, Italy.

Tommaso Caselli, Valerio Basile, Jelena Mitrović, Inga Kartoziya, and Michael Granitzer. 2020. I feel offended, don't be abusive! implicit/explicit messages in offensive and abusive language. In *Proceedings of the 12th Language Resources and Evaluation Conference*, pages 6193–6202, Marseille, France. European Language Resources Association.

Tuhin Chakrabarty, Kilol Gupta, and Smaranda Muresan. 2019. Pay "attention" to your context when classifying abusive language. In *Proceedings of the Third Workshop on Abusive Language Online*, pages 70–79, Florence, Italy. Association for Computational Linguistics.

Yi-Ling Chung, Elizaveta Kuzmenko, Serra Sinem Tekiroglu, and Marco Guerini. 2019. CONAN - COunter NArratives through Nichesourcing: a Multilingual Dataset of Responses to Fight Online Hate Speech. In *Proceedings of the 57th Annual Meeting of the Association for Computational Linguistics*, pages 2819–2829, Florence, Italy. Association for Computational Linguistics.

Thomas Davidson, Dana Warmsley, Michael Macy, and Ingmar Weber. 2017. Automated hate speech detection and the problem of offensive language. In *Proceedings of the Eleventh International Conference on Web and Social Media, ICWSM 2017, Montréal, Québec, Canada, May 15-18, 2017*, pages 512–515. AAAI Press.

Tullio De Mauro. 2016. Le parole per ferire. *Internazionale*. 27 settembre 2016.

Jacob Devlin, Ming-Wei Chang, Kenton Lee, and Kristina Toutanova. 2019. BERT: Pre-training of deep bidirectional transformers for language understanding. In *Proceedings of the 2019 Conference of the North American Chapter of the Association for Computational Linguistics: Human Language Technologies, Volume 1 (Long and Short Papers)*, pages 4171–4186, Minneapolis, Minnesota.

EU Commission. 2016. Code of conduct on countering illegal hate speech online.

Elisabetta Fersini, Debora Nozza, and Paolo Rosso. 2018a. Overview of the EVALITA 2018 Task on Automatic Misogyny Identification (AMI). In *Proceedings of Sixth Evaluation Campaign of Natural Language Processing and Speech Tools for Italian. Final Workshop (EVALITA 2018)*, volume 2263 of *CEUR Workshop Proceedings*. CEUR-WS.org.

Elisabetta Fersini, Paolo Rosso, and Maria Anzovino. 2018b. Overview of the Task on Automatic Misogyny Identification at IberEval 2018. In *Proceedings of the Third Workshop on Evaluation of Human Language Technologies for Iberian Languages (IberEval 2018)*, volume 2150 of *CEUR Workshop Proceedings*, pages 1–15. CEUR-WS.org.

Paula Fortuna and Sérgio Nunes. 2018. A survey on automatic detection of hate speech in text. *ACM Computing Surveys*, 51(4).

Antigoni-Maria Founta, Constantinos Djouvas, Despoina Chatzakou, Ilias Leontiadis, Jeremy Blackburn, Gianluca Stringhini, Athena Vakali, Michael Sirivianos, and Nicolas Kourtellis. 2018. Large scale crowdsourcing and characterization of twitter abusive behavior. In *International AAAI Conference on Web and Social Media*.

Mladen Karan and Jan Šnajder. 2018. Cross-domain detection of abusive language online. In *Proceedings of the 2nd Workshop on Abusive Language Online (ALW2)*, pages 132–137, Brussels, Belgium. Association for Computational Linguistics.

Anna Koufakou, Valerio Basile, and Viviana Patti. 2020. FlorUniTo@TRAC-2: Retrofitting word embeddings on an abusive lexicon for aggressive language detection. In *Proceedings of the Second Workshop on Trolling, Aggression and Cyberbullying*, pages 106–112, Marseille, France. European Language Resources Association (ELRA).

Pushkar Mishra, Helen Yannakoudakis, and Ekaterina Shutova. 2018. Neural character-based composition models for abuse detection. In *Proceedings of the 2nd Workshop on Abusive Language Online (ALW2)*, pages 1–10, Brussels, Belgium. Association for Computational Linguistics.

Pushkar Mishra, Helen Yannakoudakis, and Ekaterina Shutova. 2019. Tackling online abuse: A survey of automated abuse detection methods. *arXiv preprint arXiv:1908.06024*.

Hamdy Mubarak, Kareem Darwish, and Walid Magdy. 2017. Abusive Language Detection on Arabic Social Media. In *Proceedings of the First Workshop on Abusive Language Online*, pages 52–56, Vancouver, BC, Canada. Association for Computational Linguistics.

Endang Wahyu Pamungkas, Valerio Basile, and Viviana Patti. 2020a. Do you really want to hurt me? predicting abusive swearing in social media. In *Proceedings of The 12th Language Resources and Evaluation Conference, LREC 2020, Marseille, France, May 11-16, 2020*, pages 6237–6246. European Language Resources Association.

Endang Wahyu Pamungkas, Valerio Basile, and Viviana Patti. 2020b. Misogyny detection in twitter: a multilingual and cross-domain study. *Information Processing & Management*, page 102360.

Endang Wahyu Pamungkas and Viviana Patti. 2019. Cross-domain and cross-lingual abusive language detection: A hybrid approach with deep learning and a multilingual lexicon. In *Proceedings of the 57th Annual Meeting of the Association for Computational Linguistics: Student Research Workshop*, pages 363–370, Florence, Italy.

Demetris Paschalides, Dimosthenis Stephanidis, Andreas Andreou, Kalia Orphanou, George Pallis, Marios D. Dikaiakos, and Evangelos Markatos. 2020. Mandola: A big-data processing and visualization platform for monitoring and detecting online hate speech. *ACM Trans. Internet Technol.*, 20(2).

Fabio Poletto, Valerio Basile, Manuela Sanguinetti, Cristina Bosco, and Viviana Patti. 2020. Resources and benchmark corpora for hate speech detection: a systematic review. *Language Resources and Evaluation*.

Manuela Sanguinetti, Fabio Poletto, Cristina Bosco, Viviana Patti, and Marco Stranisci. 2018. An Italian Twitter Corpus of Hate Speech against Immigrants. In *Proceedings of the Eleventh International Conference on Language Resources and Evaluation (LREC'18)*, pages 2798–2895. European Language Resources Association (ELRA).

Qinlan Shen and Carolyn Rose. 2019. The discourse of online content moderation: Investigating polarized user responses to changes in Reddit's quarantine policy. In *Proceedings of the Third Workshop on Abusive Language Online*, pages 58–69, Florence, Italy. Association for Computational Linguistics.

Steve Durairaj Swamy, Anupam Jamatia, and Björn Gambäck. 2019. Studying generalisability across abusive language detection datasets. In *Proceedings of the 23rd Conference on Computational Natural Language Learning (CoNLL)*, Hong Kong, China.

Bertie Vidgen, Alex Harris, Dong Nguyen, Rebekah Tromble, Scott Hale, and Helen Margetts. 2019. Challenges and frontiers in abusive content detection. In *Proceedings of the Third Workshop on Abusive Language Online*, pages 80–93, Florence, Italy. Association for Computational Linguistics.

Zeerak Waseem, Thomas Davidson, Dana Warmsley, and Ingmar Weber. 2017. Understanding Abuse: A Typology of Abusive Language Detection Subtasks. In *Proceedings of the First Workshop on Abusive Language Online*, pages 78–84, Vancouver, BC, Canada. Association for Computational Linguistics.

Zeerak Waseem and Dirk Hovy. 2016. Hateful symbols or hateful people? predictive features for hate speech detection on twitter. In *Proceedings of the American Chapter of the Association for Computational Linguistics NAACL Student Research Workshop*, pages 88–93, San Diego, California.

Michael Wiegand, Josef Ruppenhofer, and Thomas Kleinbauer. 2019. Detection of abusive language: the problem of biased datasets. In *Proceedings of the 2019 Conference of the North American Chapter of the Association for Computational Linguistics: Human Language Technologies, NAACL-HLT 2019, Minneapolis, MN, USA, June 2-7, 2019, Volume 1 (Long and Short Papers)*, pages 602–608.

Michael Wiegand, Josef Ruppenhofer, Anna Schmidt, and Clayton Greenberg. 2018. Inducing a lexicon of abusive words – a feature-based approach. In *Proceedings of the 2018 Conference of the North American Chapter of the Association for Computational Linguistics: Human Language Technologies, Volume 1 (Long Papers)*, pages 1046–1056, New Orleans, Louisiana. Association for Computational Linguistics.

Marcos Zampieri, Shervin Malmasi, Preslav Nakov, Sara Rosenthal, Noura Farra, and Ritesh Kumar. 2019a. Predicting the type and target of offensive posts in social media. In *Proceedings of the 2019 Conference of the North American Chapter of the Association for Computational Linguistics: Human Language Technologies, Volume 1 (Long and Short Papers)*, pages 1415–1420.

Marcos Zampieri, Shervin Malmasi, Preslav Nakov, Sara Rosenthal, Noura Farra, and Ritesh Kumar. 2019b. Semeval-2019 task 6: Identifying and categorizing offensive language in social media (offenseval). In *Proceedings of the 13th International Workshop on Semantic Evaluation*, pages 75–86, Minneapolis, Minnesota, USA. Association for Computational Linguistics.

Marcos Zampieri, Preslav Nakov, Sara Rosenthal, Pepa Atanasova, Georgi Karadzhov, Hamdy Mubarak, Leon Derczynski, Zeses Pitenis, and Çağrı Çöltekin. 2020. Semeval-2020 task 12: Multilingual offensive language identification in social media (offenseval 2020).

Abusive Language Detection using Syntactic Dependency Graphs

Kanika Narang
Facebook AI
kanika13@fb.com

Chris Brew[*]
LivePerson
christopher.brew@gmail.com

Abstract

Automated detection of abusive language online has become imperative. Current sequential models (LSTM) do not work well for long and complex sentences while bi-transformer models (BERT) are not computationally efficient for the task. We show that classifiers based on syntactic structure of the text, dependency graphical convolutional networks (DepGCNs) can achieve state-of-the-art performance on abusive language datasets. The overall performance is at par with of strong baselines such as fine-tuned BERT. Further, our GCN-based approach is much more efficient than BERT at inference time making it suitable for real-time detection.

1 Introduction

Abusive language usage in online social media is a grave issue affecting the interactions of users online. In a study conducted by Pew Research Center[1], 60% of Internet users have personally experienced harassment online. Social media websites, like Twitter and Facebook, allow users to report harassing content. However, due to the sheer volume of data, timely human curation of all reported content is not possible. Besides, there is also a need to filter these abusive content proactively. Therefore, there is an increased interest in automated detection and moderation of abusive speech in text (Waseem and Hovy, 2016; Vidgen et al., 2019).

Abusive speech is defined as an *attack* targeted towards a particular individual or entity belonging to a *protected group* (protected group may include, but are not always limited to, religious, gender or racial minorities) (ElSherief et al., 2018). Thus, abusive speech identification can be cast as a *relation extraction* problem in which the goal is to detect a "hate" or "attack" relation that links the

speaker to a protected group (the object of the attack).

Current state-of-the-art methods in abusive language detection use either n-gram features (Waseem and Hovy, 2016; Davidson et al., 2017) or employ sequential deep learning models like CNN or LSTM (Zhang et al., 2018b; Badjatiya et al., 2017). These methods do not work well to capture semantic word meanings or long-range attack in text (such as long clauses or complex scoping shown in online attacks). Large pre-trained language models like BERT (Devlin et al., 2019) achieve high accuracy after fine-tuning on supervised tasks. However, these methods are computationally expensive and are, thus, unfit to be used for real-time detection.

Clark et al. (2019) observed that some attention heads of the pre-trained BERT model are learning syntactic dependencies between words such as direct objects of verbs etc. It is similar to a *dependency parser* that represents the structure of syntactic dependence between words in the sentence. Recently, Burnap and Williams (2016) and Alorainy et al. (2019) also showed that including syntactic dependency as features improves classifier performance in abusive language detection tasks. However, adding features can only provide weak supervision compared to encoding these dependence explicitly in the model. On the other hand, Zhang et al. (2018a) leveraged the dependency path between the subject and object of the sentence to achieve state-of-the-art results on *relation extraction* task on the TACRED dataset. They encoded the dependency parse graph using efficient graph convolution operations (Kipf and Welling, 2017).

However, a direct usage of Zhang et al. (2018a)'s method is not straightforward for abusive language datasets due to the complexity of the possibilities for expressing an attack in text. An attack may be

---

This work was done while the author was at Facebook.

[1] https://pewrsr.ch/2XzABRo

Proceedings of the Fourth Workshop on Online Abuse and Harms, pages 44–53
Online, November 20, 2020. ©2020 Association for Computational Linguistics
https://doi.org/10.18653/v1/P17

expressed directly by either using explicit *slurs* or *curses*, or attacking a protected group explicitly. In other instances, the attack can be *implicit* such as sexist posts denigrating genders to stereotypical roles. These implicit attacks need nuanced understanding of the semantic context. However, parse structures of the text can still be useful for capturing longer-range dependencies than sequential models. For instance, in Fig 1, the sequential distance between the attack *mentally ill* and the target *Protected Group* is five, while the distance in the parse tree is only two.

Figure 1: Dependency parse for a sample hate tweet. The target *<PG>* is closer to the attack word, *ill* in the parse tree. <PG> and <Y> replaces the targeted protected group and attack in the actual tweet.

An additional challenge in applying Zhang et al. (2018a)'s method to noisy social media text is that the text often does not have an explicit subject and object, in which case there is no dependency path between them. Or, especially in social media text, subject and object may be present but remain undetected by a parser trained on general purpose text.

Thus, we propose an adaption of the Zhang et al. (2018a) model that learns dependency-aware text representations useful for abusive language detection task. Our contributions are as follows:

- In this work, we leverage the dependency parse of the sentence to induce a graph on the text. We then augment the text embeddings of the words with their syntactic neighbors using efficient graph convolution operations (Kipf and Welling, 2017). Further, we propose a classifier based on this dependency graphical convolutional network, DepGCN, to detect abusive language online.

- We evaluate our method on the benchmark Twitter hate speech datasets. Our model outperforms the current state-of-the-art (Waseem and Hovy, 2016; Davidson et al., 2017) for abusive language detection and performs at par with strong baselines like fine-tuned BERT (Devlin et al., 2019).

- Further analysis shows that our DepGCN

model is much more scalable than BERT and is complementary to the sequential models.

2 Methods

In this section, we first describe our approach to use syntactic dependencies to induce a graph on the text. We then convolve over this dependency graph using a graph convolutional framework (DepGCN) to compute a text embedding useful for abusive language detection task.

2.1 Graph representation of Text

We use the dependency parse tree to induce a graph on a sentence. Specifically, a graph $G = < V, E >$ is represented as a collection of vertices V and as a set of edges E between these vertices. To compute the graphical representation of the sentence, we treat each word as a vertex, with syntactic dependencies between words corresponding to an edge. Now, for this graph G, **A** represents the Adjacency matrix where $A_{ij} = 1$ if there is a dependency relation between word i and j and 0 otherwise. We also connect each word to itself such that $A_{i,i} = 1; \forall i \in V$. Although syntactic dependencies are directed, we treat these dependency edges as undirected, resulting in a symmetric matrix[2].

Graph Convolution Networks (GCN) are recently proposed to compute vertex embeddings in a graph by convolving over each vertex's local neighborhood (Kipf and Welling, 2017). The convolution operation for vertex i in layer k in GCN is defined as follows,

$$h_i^{k+1} = \sigma \left(\sum_{j=1}^{|V|} \tilde{A}_{ij} \mathbf{W}^k h_j^k + b^k \right) \quad (1)$$

$$= \sigma \left(\frac{\sum_{j \in \mathcal{N}(i) \cup i} \mathbf{W}^k h_j^k}{d_i} + b^k \right) \quad (2)$$

where $\tilde{\mathbf{A}} = \mathbf{D}^{-1/2} \mathbf{A} \mathbf{D}^{1/2}$ is the normalized Adjacency matrix with **D** being the degree matrix. h_i^{k+1} represents the vertex embeddings at layer $k + 1$, with h_i^0 being initialized with the vertex features. In our case, we use pretrained word embeddings as the initial features. $\mathbf{W}^k, b^k$ are learnable weight and bias parameters of layer k and σ represents the ReLU function. $\mathcal{N}(i)$ represents the vertex

---

[2]Similar to (Zhang et al., 2018a), we observed a performance dip when using each edge direction as a separate graph.

i's neighborhood while $d_i = \sum D_i$ represents the vertex degree.

Now, assume that $\mathbf{W}^k = \mathbf{I}$ with $b^k = 0$ and $\sigma(.)$ as an identity function. The updated vertex embedding at layer $k + 1$ will be,

$$h_i^{k+1} = \frac{\sum\limits_{j \in \mathcal{N}(i) \cup i} h_j^k}{d_i} \qquad (3)$$

Thus, it is easy to verify that the convolution operation updates the vertex embeddings at layer $k + 1$ to be the average embeddings of the vertex's neighborhood and the vertex itself from the previous layer, k. In our dependency graph, applying graph convolution operation will augment each word's embedding with its syntactic neighbors. Thus, convolution helps to contextualize the word embeddings, where the word's syntactic relationships define the context. Notice that it is different from the sequential models (like LSTM or CNN), where the adjacent words in the sentence define the context.

Consider the sample tweet in Figure 1, in the first DepGCN layer, the attack *ill* will be augmented with its surrounding adverbs *mentally* and *just* (eq. (4)). In turn, these updated embeddings of *ill* will be propagated when computing embeddings of the noun *people* in addition to the subject *<PG>* in the next layer.

$$h_{ill} = f_{gcn}(h_{mentally}, h_{just}, h_{ill}) \qquad (4)$$
$$h_{people} = f_{gcn}(h_{ill}, h_{<PG>}, h_{people}) \qquad (5)$$

However, in sequential models with a fixed window, the attack *ill* will be too far from the subject *<PG>*.

Further, by stacking such k convolution layers, we can propagate the vertex embeddings to its k-hop neighborhood (Kipf and Welling, 2017). For our experiments, we did not see any further improvements after two layers. This could be because, as we are dealing with a short text, the resulting parse tree is shallow [3].

2.2 Sentence representation

In the previous section, we computed contextualized word embeddings using syntactic relationships. However, we still need to aggregate these vertex embeddings to compute a graph-level embedding (sentence in our case). In particular, we

---

[3] Our experiments did not show performance gain when using recent variants of GCN that uses attention (Veličković et al., 2018) or different aggregators (Xu et al., 2018).

perform masked pooling over the learned word embeddings from the last layer (K) to compute a sentence embedding. We only pool over non-terminal words or intermediary nodes in the dependency parse tree (i.e. $|A_i| > 2$). We ignore the leaf words or words linked to only one other word as their word embeddings are relatively unchanged (because of fewer neighbors) after the convolution compared to other intermediary nodes with more neighbors. Thus, when we perform pooling over all the words, leaf words will skew the final result even though they are not always important.

We tried different variants of pooling (average and min), but max-pooling performed the best (eq. (6)) for our case.

$$h_G = \max_{i \in V'}(h_i^K) \; s.t. |A_i| = 2 \qquad (6)$$

Further, we feed these sentence embeddings through fully connected layers followed by a sigmoid (σ) to compute the final class score (eq. (7)) for the sentence.

$$c_G = \sigma(f_{MLP}(h_G)); c_G \in \mathbf{R}^C \qquad (7)$$

Here, C represents the total number of classes. The final architecture of our dependency graph convolution network (DepGCN) is depicted in Figure 2.

2.3 Embedding variants

As we deal with noisy text, there can be ill-formed words and grammatically incorrect sentences, potentially leading to incorrect parse trees. To overcome these potential errors, we feed the initial word embeddings (h_i^0) to a BiLSTM module. The BiLSTM module helps to aid in word disambiguation by encoding adjacent words in the sentence.

3 Experiments

In this section, we first describe our experimental setup, followed by the results. We then present a detailed error analysis of dependency-based model vs. a widely-used sequential model for sentence classification.

3.1 Experimental Setup

We first describe our datasets, followed by comparative baselines.

Datasets: Wiegand et al. (2019) emphasizes the difficulty of selecting representative datasets for studying abusive language. At the heart of this difficulty is the relative rarity of abusive language in large-scale user-generated text. It is not unusual for

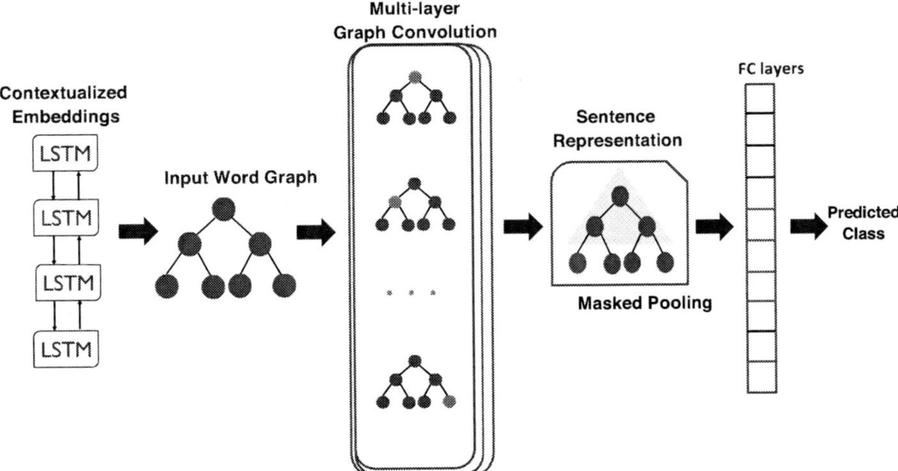

Figure 2: Overview of our proposed DepGCN model

> 99% of text to be benign. To make experiments manageable, Waseem and Hovy (2016) bootstrap data collection with queries that are indicators of possible hate speech[4]. As a result of this bootstrapping, the data collected is *not* representative of the underlying text distribution. This *data bias* applies to both the benign and the hateful categories. Davidson et al. (2017) provides an alternative dataset[5], but this too is affected by pre-filtering, with the result that the dataset also fails to represent the underlying text distribution. We also discuss the potential annotator bias (Sap et al., 2019) in these datasets, later in the Discussion section. Thus, caution is advised when interpreting the results of studies on these datasets.

Dataset	**Categories**		
Davidson et al. (2017)	Hate	Offensive	Benign
	1,430	19,190	4,163
Waseem and Hovy (2016)	Racism	Sexism	Benign
	1,939	3,148	11,115
Davidson extended	Hate	Offensive	Benign
	1,430	19,190	15,278

Table 1: Dataset Statistics.

For comparability, we experiment with both the datasets from Davidson et al. (2017) and Waseem and Hovy (2016). We do not claim that our results will necessarily transfer to more naturalistic settings. Table 1 lists the per class distribution in the collected dataset. Note that the Davidson et al. (2017) is highly skewed with majority of tweets

being offensive. However, it is the opposite in real world settings. We thus also create a custom dataset (Davidson ext.) to mimic the real world settings, by adding benign tweets from Waseem and Hovy (2016) to Davidson et al. (2017)'s benign tweets.

Baselines: We compare against a variety of state-of-the-art approaches proposed for computing sentence embeddings. We use these embeddings to classify the tweets into abusive or not.

N-grams based approaches have shown to achieve competitive results for abusive language detection (Waseem and Hovy, 2016). In particular, the model extracts frequent N-grams from the tweets and feeds them into a logistic regression along with additional Twitter-specific features per tweet. We use tf-idf scores as features for unigram and bigram words from each tweet.

BERT models have achieved new state-of-the-art results on multiple natural language tasks such as question answering and language inference (Devlin et al., 2019). We use pre-trained $BERT_{base}$ model from the *transformers* [6] library for our experiments. Preliminary experiments showed that average pooling from the last four layers of BERT as the aggregate sentence representation performed better than the [CLS] token representation from the final layer. We append a linear layer on top of the model to compute class-wise scores. Further, we fine-tune this classifier on our training dataset.

BiLSTM is a sequential model to compute sentence embeddings useful for many downstream classification tasks (Zhou et al., 2016). We use

---

[4]https://bit.ly/3gN2RsD
[5]https://bit.ly/3dpoTzJ

[6]github.com/huggingface/transformers

the output of the final hidden layer in the BiLSTM as the sentence embeddings. We follow BERT in feeding the sentence embeddings to a linear layer to compute the final class-wise score.

Implementation Details: We initialized h_i^0 of each word with its Glove embeddings (Pennington et al., 2014) combined with its POS tag and NER tag given by the Stanford NLP API. We used Stanford parser[7] for extracting the dependency parse relationship between the words in a tweet. In the DepGCN model, we used a hidden dimension of 200 in both layers with ReLU non linearity. We trained with a batch size of 50 and used stochastic gradient optimizer with a learning rate of 0.3. We also used a dropout of 0.5 for both GCN layers and BiLSTM.

For the BERT classifier, we fine-tuned the model with a batch size of 16 for 6 epochs. We used a dropout of 0.1 in all layers and used Adam optimizer with a learning rate of 4e-6. For the N-gram approach, we ignored words which occur in less than 5 tweets or occur in more than 75% of the tweets to filter out uninformative words. We used $l2$ regularization in the logistic regression model and performed a grid search over different C values where C denotes regularization strength.

We implemented our model and the baselines(except N-gram) in PyTorch and run the experiments on an Nvidia Tesla V100 GPU. We used sklearn library for the N-gram baseline. We performed stratified sampling on the dataset to create an 80-10-10 split between training, dev, and test sets. The dev set is used for hyperparameter tuning while the results are reported on the test set. We used a *weighted* cross-entropy loss to counter the effect of class imbalance for all the baselines and our proposed approach. We report the class-wise F1 score with ROCAUC scores for each dataset.

3.2 Performance analysis

Table 2 reports class-wise F1 score with AUC scores for the Davidson et al. (2017) extended dataset. As expected, the bag-of-words based N-gram approach is not competitive with the best approaches. This result is reasonable, since N-grams does not take any advantage of semantic similarities between different words. More surprisingly, the powerful BERT model, even after fine-tuning, still performs slightly worse than our DepGCN model for the hate class.

[7]https://stanford.io/2zALCdz

Approach	Hate	Offensive	Benign	AUC
N-grams	0.35	0.88	0.88	0.899
BERT	0.45	0.94	0.96	**0.953**
BiLSTM	0.31	0.93	0.94	0.895
DepGCN	0.47	0.94	0.96	0.918
BiLSTM + DepGCN	**0.49**	**0.95**	**0.97**	0.945

Table 2: Class-wise F1 score and AUC of different approaches on the Davidson et al. (2017) extended dataset.

The sequential model, i.e., BiLSTM, also performs worse than our dependency-based model. As argued before, sequential models often struggle to capture long term dependencies between words while DepGCN alleviates this issue by encoding syntactic dependencies. Further, if we use BiLSTM to contextualize the embeddings before feeding it to our DepGCN model, the results are slightly improved. Note that even a slight improvement in the hate class is significant as the dataset contains limited training examples for this class (Table 1) as compared to the other classes.

Approach	Hate	Offensive	Benign	Overall	AUC
N-grams	0.46	0.94	0.84	0.89	0.899
BERT	0.42	**0.95**	**0.88**	**0.91**	**0.942**
BiLSTM	0.52	0.94	0.86	0.90	0.931
DepGCN	0.50	0.94	0.86	0.90	0.926
BiLSTM + DepGCN	**0.53**	0.94	0.87	**0.91**	0.937

Table 3: Class-wise F1 score and AUC for different approaches on the original Davidson et al. (2017) dataset.

We obtain a similar trend in the results when evaluating performance on the original Davidson et al. (2017) dataset (Table 3). The Benign class of the original dataset has systematically lower figures than the corresponding class in the extended dataset, presumably because the extended data set has a better representation of the space of possible benign examples. The Hate class is slightly easier to detect in the original dataset, even though it contains the same examples as the corresponding class in the extended dataset. This could be presumably because the classifiers expend more of their modeling capacity on the benign set. The same pattern is present to a lesser degree for the Offensive class.

BERT becomes more competitive with BiLSTM on the original dataset. BiLSTM retains a substantial (0.52 > 0.42) advantage over BERT on the Hate class and is close on Offensive and Benign. The sequential model, BiLSTM, also performs slightly better (0.52 > 0.50) than our DepGCN model for the hate class. One possible explanation can be that the Davidson et al. (2017) dataset is full of *slurs* and *direct* hate attacks on protected groups. These *direct* attacks do not exhibit complex scoping or long-range dependencies and, thus, are well captured by the sequential models. Also, due to the heavy usage of *slurs* and noisy text, BERT performs worse as there might be many OOV tokens in the dataset.

Approach	Racist	Sexist	Benign	Overall	AUC
N-grams	0.75	0.71	0.88	0.83	0.881
BERT	0.78	**0.81**	**0.91**	**0.88**	**0.945**
BiLSTM	0.72	0.71	0.89	0.84	0.917
DepGCN	0.76	0.72	0.88	0.83	0.926
BiLSTM + DepGCN	**0.78**	0.74	0.90	0.85	0.938

Table 4: Class-wise weighted F1 score and AUC for different approaches on the Waseem and Hovy (2016) dataset.

On a more nuanced dataset collected by Waseem and Hovy (2016), BERT performs the best out of the competing methods, as shown in Table 4. Our model performs competitively for racist and benign tweets while it performs worse for sexist tweets. This dataset is more nuanced as it contains more indirect or implied hate attacks (discussed in section 3.4) with the usage of fewer slurs. It seems that BERT is doing a better job of capturing the semantic meanings of these tweets.

3.3 Time Analysis

We further compare the running time of all the baseline approaches. Figure 3 shows the comparison at both training and inference time.

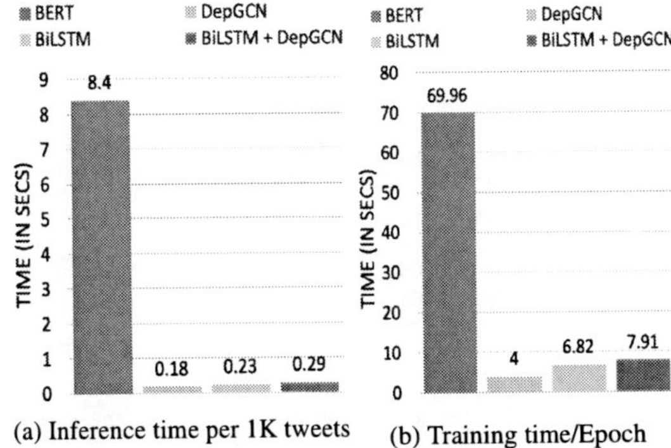

Figure 3: Time analysis of variants of our model with respect to the BERT (Devlin et al., 2019) model.

First, in Figure 3a, we plot the inference time (in secs) required by each approach per 1000 tweets. Our proposed DepGCN is the most efficient approach at inference time closely followed by BiLSTM. Adding the BiLSTM module before the DepGCN only increases the inference time slightly. On the other hand, BERT takes an order of magnitude longer than any of these approaches.

Note that, for operational reasons, the inference time does not take into account the time taken to extract the tweets' parse tree. We did the parsing step ahead of time, once, and reused the results for each experiment. A real production system would do this at inference time, adding a small time cost for each new tweet. State-of-the-art dependency parsers can currently achieve around 1000 sentences per second per CPU core (Chen and Manning, 2014; Kong and Smith, 2014). We estimate that on modern multi-CPU machines we can keep the parse cost under 0.05 seconds per 1000 tweets. This still keeps GCN methods more than competitive with BERT at inference time.

The same trend can be observed at training time too in Figure 3b. However, the jump from DepGCN to BiLSTM training time is a little higher than during inference.

In summary, our parser-based DepGCN approach is much more efficient than the BERT model. Also, including BiLSTM module to the DepGCN model leads to only a slight drop in efficiency.

3.4 Error Analysis of Sequential vs. Dependency model

In this section, we present a detailed error analysis of the Sequential (BiLSTM) vs. Dependency (DepGCN) model. Table 5 shows the confusion matrix of BiLSTM vs DepGCN model on the Waseem and Hovy (2016) dataset. The parser-based approach is more conservative in labeling tweets as benign than the sequential approach. Specifically, sexist tweets are more probable to be misclassified as racist (7 for Dep vs. 1 for Seq) and vice versa. Alternatively, DepGCN tags much more benign tweets as abusive (Sexist/Racist) (105 for Dep vs. 36 for Seq), thus creating more false positives. However, as there is a higher cost involved in missing an abusive tweet, DepGCNs will be more effective in real-world scenarios.

We also examined some sample tweets from the Waseem and Hovy (2016) dataset, which were erroneously classified as benign by BiLSTM but not by DepGCN and vice versa to understand the difference between these two approaches in depth.

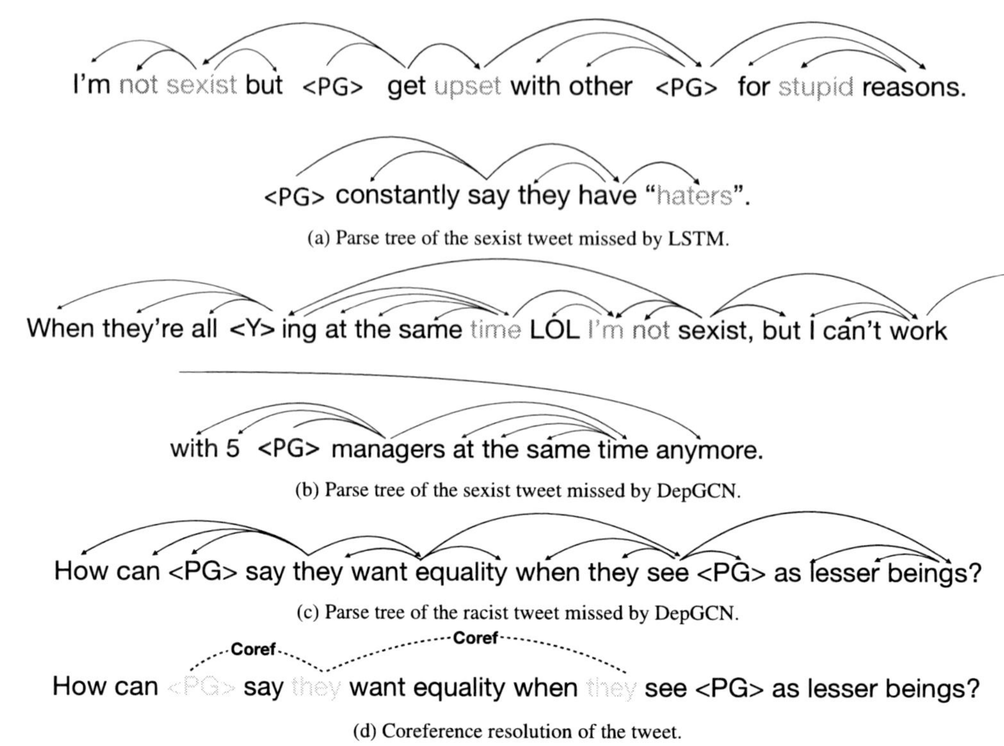

(a) Parse tree of the sexist tweet missed by LSTM.

(b) Parse tree of the sexist tweet missed by DepGCN.

(c) Parse tree of the racist tweet missed by DepGCN.

(d) Coreference resolution of the tweet.

Figure 4: Parse Tree of the sample tweets from Waseem dataset. <PG> replaces the Protected Group mentioned in the actual tweet.

	Racism		Sexism		Benign	
	Dep	Seq	Dep	Seq	Dep	Seq
Racism	7	4	11	3	7	18
Sexism	7	1	11	7	8	18
Benign	35	9	70	25	33	104

Table 5: Confusion matrix for Sequential (BiLSTM only) vs Dependency Parser (DepGCN) approach for Waseem and Hovy (2016) dataset.

Sexist tweet missed by LSTM: Following is a sample sexist tweet that is correctly classified by the DepGCN approach but missed by the BiL-STM.*"I'm not sexist but <PG> get upset with other <PG> for stupid reasons. <PG> constantly say they have haters."* Figure 4a shows the parse tree of the tweet by the Stanford parser. It is a difficult sample to classify as the author of the tweet says that he is *not* sexist but is writing offensive remarks against <PG>. The dependency tree can capture this long-range dependency and establish negative relation of "upset," "stupid," and "haters" with the "<PG>" subject.

Sexist tweet missed by DepGCN: However, DepGCN fails to capture similar nuanced sexism

in another sample tweet, *"And when they're all <Y>ing at the same time LOL I'm not sexist, but I can't work with 5 <PG> managers at the same time anymore.".* Note that the sentence contains punctuation error as it is missing punctuation between the two sentences in the tweet (after *time* and before *I'm not*). This error leads to a wrong parse tree, as shown in Figure 4b. Thus, our parser-based model is sensitive to these parsing errors.

Sexist tweet missed by DepGCN: However, even if the parse tree is correct, establishing dependency relationships may not be sufficient to capture nuanced relationships in the text in some cases. For instance, the parse tree of the racist tweet, *"How can <PG> say they want equality when they see <PG> as lesser beings?"* shown in Section 3.4 is correct. However, the parse tree misses the coreference of pronoun *they* to belong to *<PG>*. In these cases, powerful language models like BERT will be able to extract these relationships.

These analyses show that both approaches have their own merits and often perform well for complementary attack types.

4 Related Work

Most of the prior work for detecting abusive speech on Twitter primarily relies on using statistical features like bag-of-words (character or word n-grams) or tf-idf features for automated detection (Waseem and Hovy, 2016; Davidson et al., 2017; Nobata et al., 2016). Bag-of-words approaches are unable to capture nuanced abusive speech as they fail to contextualize the word meanings. For instance, depending on the context, the word *gay* can be used to denote either ebullience or sexual preference. Only the latter is a candidate attack.

Recently, deep learning models are also proposed that leverage pre-trained word embeddings (Mikolov et al., 2013; Pennington et al., 2014) to capture the semantics of the tweets. These models aggregate individual word embeddings in a context-aware manner to compute tweet embeddings and later use them for classification. Earlier studies have either used the CNN (Gambäck and Sikdar, 2017; Park and Fung, 2017) or RNN (Badjatiya et al., 2017; Agrawal and Awekar, 2018) to compute these embeddings.

The syntactic structure of the text was also used to help identify the target group and the intensity of hate speech (Warner and Hirschberg, 2012; Silva et al., 2016). The primary difficulty of these works is that the space of possibly relevant rules is too large to be comprehensive. Besides, it verges on the impossible to specify a set of rules that will cover possible implicit attacks. On the other hand, Burnap and Williams (2016); Alorainy et al. (2019) proposed computational models using the dependency labels as features and reported significant gains over the bag-of-words features. Our model builds on this work and explicitly models the dependency between words using graph convolution operations.

5 Discussion

Worse performance of BERT: Our experiments did not show the superior performance of the BERT model on the abusive language datasets. We also noticed that prior literature on comparable tasks is variable, with some successes for BERT-like models but few robust trends. There are numerous reports of difficulties in training these large neural networks on the small, imbalanced annotated datasets typical of such tasks (Zampieri et al., 2019; Liu et al., 2019). The challenges are likely an effect of over-fitting and lead to inconsistent results.

Remedies include careful hyperparameter tuning, early stopping, and the use of ensembles. Risch and Krestel (2020) proposed to use an ensemble of BERT models to control the variance of these large models over small datasets. Ensembling is expensive, so there remains a need for computationally efficient methods that approach the same performance. Because GCN has far fewer parameters, it is less likely to need these countermeasures against overfitting.

Experiments on the relatively larger abusive language dataset of 100K tweets (Founta et al., 2018) by Lee et al. (2018) highlighted that sequential models such as RNN perform well but are still hard to train on this dataset size. Further, Kumar et al. (2018) concluded that with optimal feature selection, classifiers like SVM and Random forest performs at par with neural networks.

Dataset quality and annotator bias: Recent works have highlighted that majority of the abusive language datasets suffer from poor quality (Wiegand et al., 2019; Vidgen and Derczynski, 2020) or show evidence that annotator decisions were inappropriately affected by surface markers of speaker race (Sap et al., 2019). We believe that corrections of these deficiencies and biases in annotation are essential for research progress in the field. Better dataset collection, however, is complementary to our computational approach. We believe our dependency parser-based approach should be able to perform competitively on future datasets. This is because the model is designed to be insensitive to the cues from unrelated single words.

Social media-specific tools: Social media text tends to be very noisy and thus, NLP tools trained on general corpus do not perform well on these datasets. However, our preliminary experiments with using pre-trained Glove embeddings [8] trained on the Twitter dataset showed a significant drop in performance. The performance drop could be because of the relatively smaller training data size of social media text used for training such models that may lead to overfitting. A possible counter approach can include pretraining these embeddings on a mix of general news corpus data along with social media text.

Similarly, our experiments with the training of Spacy parser[9] on our training data showed a drop in performance. We did not experiment with parsers

---

[8] nlp.stanford.edu/projects/glove/
[9] https://spacy.io/

specially built for Twitter (Kong et al., 2014) but believe that using Twitter-specific parsers might improve our results further.

6 Conclusion

In this work, we propose a novel sentence encoder that extends the graph convolutional network (GCN) to an induced graph built from syntactic dependencies in the text for abusive language detection. Our model achieved state-of-the-art performance on public hate speech twitter datasets, performing at par with strong baselines such as fine-tuned BERT.

Our DepGCN model is much more scalable than BERT and thus, can be efficiently used for real-time detection. Error analysis reveals that our model is complementary to the sequential baselines. Future work includes using an ensemble of sequential model with our dependency parser-based model. We will also extend our approach to longer text spanning multiple sentences such as posts/comments on online platforms.

References

Sweta Agrawal and Amit Awekar. 2018. Deep learning for detecting cyberbullying across multiple social media platforms. In *European Conference on Information Retrieval*, pages 141–153. Springer.

Wafa Alorainy, Pete Burnap, Han Liu, and Matthew L Williams. 2019. "the enemy among us" detecting cyber hate speech with threats-based othering language embeddings. *ACM Transactions on the Web (TWEB)*, 13(3):1–26.

Pinkesh Badjatiya, Shashank Gupta, Manish Gupta, and Vasudeva Varma. 2017. Deep learning for hate speech detection in tweets. In *Proceedings of the 26th International Conference on World Wide Web Companion*, pages 759–760. International World Wide Web Conferences Steering Committee.

Pete Burnap and Matthew L Williams. 2016. Us and them: identifying cyber hate on twitter across multiple protected characteristics. *EPJ Data science*, 5(1):11.

Danqi Chen and Christopher Manning. 2014. A fast and accurate dependency parser using neural networks. In *Proceedings of the 2014 Conference on Empirical Methods in Natural Language Processing (EMNLP)*, pages 740–750, Doha, Qatar. Association for Computational Linguistics.

Kevin Clark, Urvashi Khandelwal, Omer Levy, and Christopher D Manning. 2019. What does BERT look at? an analysis of BERT's attention. *arXiv preprint arXiv:1906.04341*.

Thomas Davidson, Dana Warmsley, Michael Macy, and Ingmar Weber. 2017. Automated hate speech detection and the problem of offensive language. In *Eleventh international aaai conference on web and social media*.

Jacob Devlin, Ming-Wei Chang, Kenton Lee, and Kristina Toutanova. 2019. Bert: Pre-training of deep bidirectional transformers for language understanding. In *Proceedings of the 2019 Conference of the North American Chapter of the Association for Computational Linguistics: Human Language Technologies, Volume 1 (Long and Short Papers)*, pages 4171–4186.

Mai ElSherief, Vivek Kulkarni, Dana Nguyen, William Yang Wang, and Elizabeth Belding. 2018. Hate lingo: A target-based linguistic analysis of hate speech in social media. In *Twelfth International AAAI Conference on Web and Social Media*.

Antigoni-Maria Founta, Constantinos Djouvas, Despoina Chatzakou, Ilias Leontiadis, Jeremy Blackburn, Gianluca Stringhini, Athena Vakali, Michael Sirivianos, and Nicolas Kourtellis. 2018. Large scale crowdsourcing and characterization of twitter abusive behavior. *ICWSM*.

Björn Gambäck and Utpal Kumar Sikdar. 2017. Using convolutional neural networks to classify hate-speech. In *Proceedings of the First Workshop on Abusive Language Online*, pages 85–90, Vancouver, BC, Canada. Association for Computational Linguistics.

Thomas N Kipf and Max Welling. 2017. Semi-supervised classification with graph convolutional networks. *International Conference on Learning Representations*.

Lingpeng Kong, Nathan Schneider, Swabha Swayamdipta, Archna Bhatia, Chris Dyer, and Noah A Smith. 2014. A dependency parser for tweets. In *Proceedings of the 2014 Conference on Empirical Methods in Natural Language Processing (EMNLP)*, pages 1001–1012.

Lingpeng Kong and Noah A Smith. 2014. An empirical comparison of parsing methods for stanford dependencies. *arXiv preprint arXiv:1404.4314*.

Ritesh Kumar, Atul Kr Ojha, Shervin Malmasi, and Marcos Zampieri. 2018. Benchmarking aggression identification in social media. In *Proceedings of the First Workshop on Trolling, Aggression and Cyberbullying (TRAC-2018)*, pages 1–11.

Younghun Lee, Seunghyun Yoon, and Kyomin Jung. 2018. Comparative studies of detecting abusive language on twitter. In *Proceedings of the 2nd Workshop on Abusive Language Online (ALW2)*, pages 101–106.

Ping Liu, Wen Li, and Liang Zou. 2019. Nuli at semeval-2019 task 6: Transfer learning for offensive language detection using bidirectional transformers.

In *Proceedings of the 13th International Workshop on Semantic Evaluation*, pages 87–91.

Tomas Mikolov, Ilya Sutskever, Kai Chen, Greg S Corrado, and Jeff Dean. 2013. Distributed representations of words and phrases and their compositionality. In *Advances in neural information processing systems*, pages 3111–3119.

Chikashi Nobata, Joel Tetreault, Achint Thomas, Yashar Mehdad, and Yi Chang. 2016. Abusive language detection in online user content. In *Proceedings of the 25th International Conference on World Wide Web*, WWW '16, page 145–153, Republic and Canton of Geneva, CHE. International World Wide Web Conferences Steering Committee.

Ji Ho Park and Pascale Fung. 2017. One-step and two-step classification for abusive language detection on twitter. In *Proceedings of the First Workshop on Abusive Language Online*, pages 41–45.

Jeffrey Pennington, Richard Socher, and Christopher D. Manning. 2014. Glove: Global vectors for word representation. In *Empirical Methods in Natural Language Processing (EMNLP)*, pages 1532–1543.

Julian Risch and Ralf Krestel. 2020. Bagging BERT models for robust aggression identification. In *Proceedings of the Second Workshop on Trolling, Aggression and Cyberbullying*, pages 55–61, Marseille, France. European Language Resources Association (ELRA).

Maarten Sap, Dallas Card, Saadia Gabriel, Yejin Choi, and Noah A. Smith. 2019. The risk of racial bias in hate speech detection. In *Proceedings of the 57th Annual Meeting of the Association for Computational Linguistics*, pages 1668–1678, Florence, Italy. Association for Computational Linguistics.

Leandro Silva, Mainack Mondal, Denzil Correa, Fabrício Benevenuto, and Ingmar Weber. 2016. Analyzing the targets of hate in online social media. In *Tenth International AAAI Conference on Web and Social Media*.

Petar Veličković, Guillem Cucurull, Arantxa Casanova, Adriana Romero, Pietro Liò, and Yoshua Bengio. 2018. Graph attention networks. In *International Conference on Learning Representations*.

Bertie Vidgen and Leon Derczynski. 2020. Directions in abusive language training data: Garbage in, garbage out. *arXiv preprint arXiv:2004.01670*.

Bertie Vidgen, Alex Harris, Dong Nguyen, Rebekah Tromble, Scott Hale, and Helen Margetts. 2019.

Challenges and frontiers in abusive content detection. In *Association for Computational Linguistics*.

William Warner and Julia Hirschberg. 2012. Detecting hate speech on the world wide web. In *Proceedings of the second workshop on language in social media*, pages 19–26. Association for Computational Linguistics.

Zeerak Waseem and Dirk Hovy. 2016. Hateful symbols or hateful people? predictive features for hate speech detection on Twitter. In *Proceedings of the NAACL Student Research Workshop*, pages 88–93, San Diego, California. Association for Computational Linguistics.

Michael Wiegand, Josef Ruppenhofer, and Thomas Kleinbauer. 2019. Detection of Abusive Language: the Problem of Biased Datasets. In *Proceedings of the 2019 Conference of the North American Chapter of the Association for Computational Linguistics: Human Language Technologies, Volume 1 (Long and Short Papers)*, pages 602–608, Minneapolis, Minnesota. Association for Computational Linguistics.

Keyulu Xu, Weihua Hu, Jure Leskovec, and Stefanie Jegelka. 2018. How powerful are graph neural networks? In *International Conference on Learning Representations*.

Marcos Zampieri, Shervin Malmasi, Preslav Nakov, Sara Rosenthal, Noura Farra, and Ritesh Kumar. 2019. Semeval-2019 task 6: Identifying and categorizing offensive language in social media (offenseval). In *Proceedings of the 13th International Workshop on Semantic Evaluation*, pages 75–86.

Yuhao Zhang, Peng Qi, and Christopher D. Manning. 2018a. Graph convolution over pruned dependency trees improves relation extraction. In *Proceedings of the 2018 Conference on Empirical Methods in Natural Language Processing*.

Ziqi Zhang, David Robinson, and Jonathan Tepper. 2018b. Detecting hate speech on twitter using a convolution-gru based deep neural network. In *The Semantic Web*, pages 745–760, Cham. Springer International Publishing.

Peng Zhou, Wei Shi, Jun Tian, Zhenyu Qi, Bingchen Li, Hongwei Hao, and Bo Xu. 2016. Attention-based bidirectional long short-term memory networks for relation classification. In *Proceedings of the 54th Annual Meeting of the Association for Computational Linguistics (Volume 2: Short Papers)*, pages 207–212, Berlin, Germany. Association for Computational Linguistics.

Impact of Politically Biased Data on Hate Speech Classification

Maximilian Wich
TU Munich,
Department of Informatics,
Germany
maximilian.wich@tum.de

Jan Bauer
TU Munich,
Department of Informatics,
Germany
jan.bauer@tum.de

Georg Groh
TU Munich,
Department of Informatics,
Germany
grohg@in.tum.de

Abstract

One challenge that social media platforms are facing nowadays is hate speech. Hence, automatic hate speech detection has been increasingly researched in recent years — in particular with the rise of deep learning. A problem of these models is their vulnerability to undesirable bias in training data. We investigate the impact of political bias on hate speech classification by constructing three politically-biased data sets (left-wing, right-wing, politically neutral) and compare the performance of classifiers trained on them. We show that (1) political bias negatively impairs the performance of hate speech classifiers and (2) an explainable machine learning model can help to visualize such bias within the training data. The results show that political bias in training data has an impact on hate speech classification and can become a serious issue.

1 Introduction

Social media platforms, such as Twitter and Facebook, have gained more and more popularity in recent years. One reason is their promise of free speech, which also obviously has its drawbacks. With the rise of social media, hate speech has spread on these platforms as well (Duggan, 2017). But hate speech is not a pure online problem because online hate speech can be accompanied by offline crime (Williams et al., 2020).

Due to the enormous amounts of posts and comments produced by the billions of users every day, it is impossible to monitor these platforms manually. Advances in machine learning (ML), however, show that this technology can help to detect hate speech — currently with limited accuracy (Davidson et al., 2017; Schmidt and Wiegand, 2017).

There are many challenges that must be addressed when building a hate speech classifier. First of all, an undesirable bias in training data can cause

models to produce unfair or incorrect results, such as racial discrimination (Hildebrandt, 2019). This phenomenon is already addressed by the research community. Researchers have examined methods to identify and mitigate different forms of bias, such as racial bias or annotator bias (Geva et al., 2019; Davidson et al., 2019; Sap et al., 2019). But it has not been solved yet; on the contrary, more research is needed Vidgen et al. (2019). Secondly, most of the classifiers miss a certain degree of transparency or explainability to appear trustworthy and credible. Especially in the context of hate speech detection, there is a demand for such a feature Vidgen et al. (2019); Niemann (2019). The reason is the value-based nature of hate speech classification, meaning that perceiving something as hate depends on individual and social values and social values are non-uniform across groups and societies. Therefore, it should be transparent to the users what the underlying values of a classifier are. The demand for transparency and explainability is also closely connected to bias because it can help to uncover the bias.

In the paper, we deal with both problems. We investigate a particular form of bias — political bias — and use an explainable AI method to visualize this bias. To our best knowledge, political bias has not been addressed in hate speech detection, yet. But it could be a severe issue. As an example, a moderator of a social media platform uses a system that prioritizes comments based on their hatefulness to efficiently process them. If this system had a political bias, i.e. it favors a political orientation, it would impair the political debate on the platform. That is why we want to examine this phenomenon by addressing the following two research questions:

RQ1 What is the effect of politically biased data sets on the performance of hate speech classi-

Proceedings of the Fourth Workshop on Online Abuse and Harms, pages 54–64
Online, November 20, 2020. ©2020 Association for Computational Linguistics
https://doi.org/10.18653/v1/P17

fiers?

RQ2 Can explainable hate speech classification
models be used to visualize a potential undesirable bias within a model?

We contribute to answering these two questions
by conducting an experiment in which we construct politically biased data sets, train classifiers
with them, compare their performance, and use
interpretable ML techniques to visualize the differences.

In the paper, we use hate speech as an overar-
ching term and define it as "any communication
that disparages a person or a group on the basis of
some characteristic such as race, color, ethnicity,
gender, sexual orientation, nationality, religion, or
other characteristic" (Nockleby (2000, p.1277), as
cited in Schmidt and Wiegand (2017)).

2 Related Work

2.1 Biased Training Data and Models

A challenge that hate speech detection is facing is
an undesirable bias in training data (Hildebrandt,
2019). In contrast to the inductive bias — the form
of bias required by an algorithm to learn patterns
(Hildebrandt, 2019) — such a bias can impair the
generalizability of a hate speech detection model
(Wiegand et al., 2019; Geva et al., 2019) or can lead
to unfair models (e.g., discriminating minorities)
(Dixon et al., 2018).

There are different forms of bias. A data set, for
example, could have a topic bias or an author bias,
meaning that many documents are produced by a
small number of authors (Wiegand et al., 2019).
Both forms impair the generalizability of a classifier trained on such a biased data set (Wiegand
et al., 2019). Another form of bias that has a negative impact on the generalizability of classifiers is
annotator bias Geva et al. (2019). In the context of
hate speech detection, it is caused by the vagueness
of the term hate speech, aggravating reliable annotations (Ross et al., 2017). Waseem (2016), for
example, compared expert and amateur annotators
— the latter ones are often used to label large data
sets. They showed that classifiers trained on annotations from experts perform better. Binns et al.
(2017) investigated whether there is a performance
difference between classifiers trained on data labeled by males and females. Wojatzki et al. (2018)
showed that less extreme cases of sexist speech (a
form of hate speech) are differently perceived by

women and men. Al Kuwatly et al. (2020) were
not able to confirm the gender bias with their experiments, but they discovered bias caused by annotators' age, educational background, and the type of
their first language. Another form that is related to
annotator bias is racial bias. Davidson et al. (2019)
and Sap et al. (2019) examined this phenomenon
and found that widely-used hate speech data sets
contain a racial bias penalizing the African American English dialect. One reason is that this dialect
is overrepresented in the abusive or hateful class
(Davidson et al., 2019). A second reason is the
insensitivity of the annotators to this dialect (Sap
et al., 2019). To address the second problem, Sap
et al. (2019) suggested providing annotators with
information about the dialect of a document during
the labeling process. This can reduce racial bias.
Furthermore, Dixon et al. (2018) and Borkan et al.
(2019) develop metrics to measure undesirable bias
and to mitigate it. To our best knowledge, no one,
however, has investigated the impact of political
bias on hate speech detection so far.

2.2 Explainable AI

Explainable Artificial Intelligence (XAI) is a relatively new field. That is why we can find only
a limited number of research applying XAI methods in hate speech detection. Wang (2018) used
an XAI method from computer vision to explain
predictions of a neural network-based hate speech
classification model. The explanation was visualized by coloring the words depending on their relevance for the classification. Švec et al. (2018) built
an explainable hate speech classifier for Slovak,
which highlights the relevant part of a comment to
support the moderation process. Vijayaraghavan
et al. (2019) developed a multi-model classification model for hate speech that uses social-cultural
features besides text. To explain the relevance of
the different features, they used an attention-based
approach. (Risch et al., 2020) compared different transparent and explainable models. All approaches have in common that they apply local
explainability, meaning they explain not the entire model (global explanation) but single instances.
We do the same because there is a lack of global
explainability approaches for text classification.

3 Methodology

Our approach for the experiment is to train hate
speech classifiers with three different politically bi-

ased data sets and then to compare the performance of these classifiers, as depicted in Figure 1. To do so, we use an existing Twitter hate speech corpus with binary labels (offensive, non-offensive), extract the offensive records, and combine them with three data sets each (politically left-wing, politically right-wing, politically neutral) implicitly labeled as non-offensive. Subsequently, classifiers are trained with these data sets and their F1 scores are compared. Additionally, we apply SHAP to explain predictions of all three models and to compare the explanations. Our code is available on GitHub[1].

3.1 Topic Modeling

In order to answer our research questions, we need to ensure that the data sets are constructed in a fair and comparable way. Therefore, we use an existing Twitter hate speech corpus with binary labels (offensive, non-offensive) that consists of two data sets as a starting point - GermEval Shared Task on the Identification of Offensive Language 2018 (Wiegand et al., 2018) and GermEval Task 2, 2019 shared task on the identification of offensive language (Struß et al., 2019). Combining both is possible because the same annotation guidelines were applied. Thus, in effect, we are starting with one combined German Twitter hate speech data set. In the experiment, we replace only the non-offensive records of the original data set with politically biased data for each group. To ensure that the new non-offensive records with a political bias are topically comparable to the original ones, we use a topic model. The topic model itself is created based on the original non-offensive records of the corpus. Then, we use this topic model to obtain the same topic distribution in the new data set with political bias. By doing so, we assure the new data sets' homogeneity and topical comparability. The topic model has a second purpose besides assembling our versions of the data set. The keywords generated from each topic serve as the basis of the data collection process for the politically neutral new elements of the data set. More details can be found in the next subsection.

For creating the topic model, we use the Latent Dirichlet Allocation (LDA) algorithm (Blei et al., 2003). A downside of LDA, however, is that it works well for longer documents (Cheng et al.,

2014; Quan et al., 2015). But our corpus consists of Tweets that have a maximum length of 280 characters. Therefore, we apply the pooling approach based on hashtags to generate larger documents, as proposed by Alvarez-Melis and Savesk (2016) and Mehrotra et al. (2013).

For finding an appropriate number of topics, we use the normalized pointwise mutual information (NPMI) as the optimization metric to measure topic coherence (Lau et al., 2014). The optimal number of topics with ten keywords each (most probable non-stop words for a topic) is calculated in a 5-fold cross-validation. Before generating the topic model, we remove all non-alphabetic characters, stop words, words shorter than three characters, and all words that appear less than five times in the corpus during the preprocessing. Additionally, we replace user names that contain political party names by the party name, remove all other user names, and apply Porter stemming to particular words[2] (Porter et al., 1980). Only documents (created by hashtag pooling) that contain at least five words are used for the topic modeling algorithm.

3.2 Data Collection

After topic modeling of the non-offensive part from the original data set (without augmentations), we collect three data sets from Twitter: one from a (radical) left-wing subnetwork, one from a (radical) right-wing subnetwork, and a politically neutral one serving as the baseline. All data was retrieved via the Twitter API. The gathering process for these three biased data sets is the following:

1. Identifying seed profiles: First of all, it is necessary to select for each subnetwork seed profiles that serve as the entry point to the subnetworks. For this purpose, the following six profile categories are defined that have to be covered by the selected profiles: politician, political youth organization, young politician, extremist group, profile associated with extremist groups, and ideologized news website. In the category politician, we select two profiles for each subnetwork — one female and one male. The politicians have similar positions in their parties, and their genders are balanced. For the category political youth organization, we took the official Twitter profiles from the political youth organizations of the parties that the politicians from the previous category are a member of. In the cate-

[1]https://github.com/mawic/
political-bias-hate-speech

[2]*Frauen, Männer, Linke, Rechte, Deutschland, Nazi, Jude, Flüchtling, Grüne*

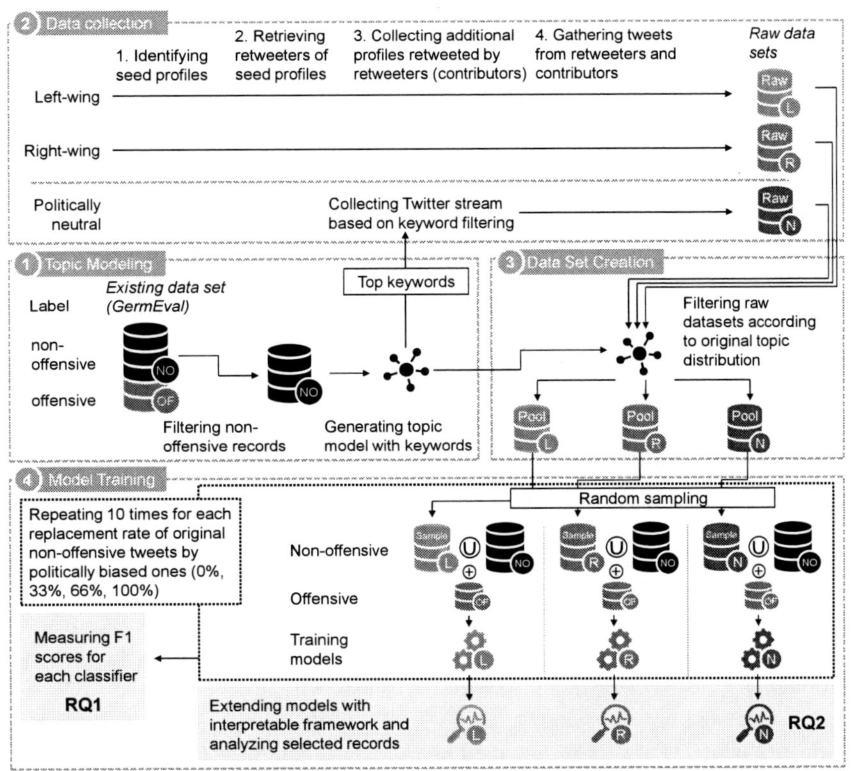

Figure 1: Methodological approach visualized

gory young politician, we selected one profile of a member from the executive board of each political youth organization. For the extremist group, we use official classifications of official security agencies to identify one account of such a group for each subnetwork. Concerning the category profile associated with extremist groups, we select two accounts that associate with an extremist group according to their statements. The statements come from the description of the Twitter account and from an interview in a newspaper. In regards to the ideologized news website, we again rely on the official classifications of a federal agency to choose the Twitter accounts of two news websites. We ensure for all categories that the numbers of followers of the corresponding Twitter accounts are comparable. The seven profiles for each subnetwork are identified based on explorative research.

2. Retrieving retweeters of seed profiles: After identifying the seven seed Twitter profiles for each political orientation as described in the previous paragraph, we are interested in the profiles that retweet these seed profiles. Our assumption in this context is that retweeting expresses agree-

ment concerning political ideology, as shown by Conover et al. (2011a), Conover et al. (2011b), and Shahrezaye et al. (2019). Therefore, the retweets of the latest 2,000 tweets from every seed profile are retrieved - or the maximum number of available tweets, if the user has not tweeted more. Unfortunately, the Twitter API provides only the latest 100 retweeters of one tweet. But this is not a problem because we do not attempt to crawl the entire subnetwork. We only want to have tweets that are representative of each subnetwork. After collecting these retweets, we select those of their authors (retweeters) that retweeted at least four of the seven seed profiles. We do this because we want to avoid adding profiles that retweeted the seed profiles but are not clearly part of the ideological subnetwork. Additionally, we remove retweeters that appear in both subnetworks to exclude left-wing accounts retweeting right-wing tweets or vice versa. Moreover, we eliminate verified profiles. The motivation of deleting verified profiles is that these profiles are ran by public persons or institutions and Twitter has proved their authenticity. This transparency might influence the language the users use for this profile.

3. Collecting additional profiles retweeted by retweeters (contributors): Step 3 aims to gather the profiles (contributors) that are also retweeted by the retweeters of the seed profiles. Therefore, we retrieve the user timelines of the selected retweeters (output of step 2) to get their other retweets. From these timelines, we select those profiles that have been retweeted by at least 7.5% of the retweeters. This threshold is pragmatically chosen — in absolute numbers 7.5% means more than 33 (left-wing) and 131 (right-wing) retweeters. The reason for setting a threshold is the same one as in step 2. Besides that, profiles appearing on both sides and verified ones are also deleted.

4. Gathering tweets from retweeters and contributors: Additionally to the gathered user timelines from step 3, we collect the latest 2,000 tweets from the selected contributors (step 3), if they are available. Furthermore, the profiles of selected retweeters (step 2) and selected contributors (step 3) are monitored via the Twitter Stream API for a few weeks to collect additional tweets.

The politically neutral data set is collected by using the Twitter Stream API. It allows us to stream a real-time sample of tweets. To make sure to get relevant tweets, we filtered the stream by inputting the keywords from the topic model we have developed. Since the output of the Stream API is a sample of all publicly available tweets (Twitter Inc., 2020), we can assume that the gathered data is not politically biased. The result of the data collection process is a set of three raw data sets - one with a left-wing bias, one with a right-wing bias, and one politically neutral.

3.3 Data Set Creation

Having the topic model and the three raw data sets, we can construct the pool data sets that exhibit the same topic distribution as the original non-offensive data set. They serve as pools for non-offensive training data that the model training samples from, described in the next sub-section. Our assumption to label the politically biased tweets as non-offensive is the following: Since the tweets are available within the subnetwork, they conform to the norms of the subnetwork, meaning the tweets are no hate speech for its members. Otherwise, members of the subnetwork could have reported these tweets, leading to a deletion in case of hate speech. The availability of a tweet, however, does not imply that they conform to the norms of the medium. A tweet that complies with the norms of the subnetwork, but violates the ones of the medium could be only distributed within the subnetwork and does not appear in the feed of other users. Consequently, it would not be reported and still be available.

We compose the pool data sets according to the following procedure for each politically biased data set: In step 1, the generated topic model assigns every tweet in the raw data sets a topic, which is the one with the highest probability. In step 2, we select so many tweets from each topic that the following conditions are satisfied: Firstly, the size of the new data is about five times the size of the non-offensive part from the GermEval corpus. Secondly, tweets with a higher topic probability are chosen with higher priority. Thirdly, the relative topic distribution of the new data set is equal to the one of the non-offensive part from the GermEval corpus. The reason for the increased size of the three new data sets (the three pool data sets) is that we have enough data to perform several iterations in the phase Model Training in order to contribute to statistical validity.

3.4 Model Training

In the phase Model Training, we train hate speech classifiers with the constructed data sets to compare performance differences and to measure the impact on the F1 score (RQ1). Furthermore, we make use of the ML interpretability framework SHAP to explain generated predictions and visualize differences in the models (RQ2).

Concerning the RQ1, the following procedure is applied. The basis is the original training corpus consisting of the union of the two GermEval data sets. For each political orientation, we iteratively replace the non-offensive tweets with the ones from the politically biased data sets (33%, 66%, 100%). The tweets from the politically biased data sets are labeled as non-offensive.

For each subnetwork (left-wing, right-wing, politically neutral) and each replacement rate (33%, 66%, 100%), ten data sets are generated by sampling from the non-offensive part of the original data set and the respective politically biased pool data set and leaving the offensive part of the original data set untouched. We then use these data sets to train classifiers with 3-fold cross-validation. This iterative approach produces multiple observation points, making the results more representative — for each subnetwork and each replacement rate we get $n = 30$ F1 scores. To answer RQ1, we statistically test the hypotheses, (a) whether the F1 scores produced by the politically biased classifiers are significantly different and (b) whether the right-wing and/or left-wing classifier performs worse than the politically neutral one. If both hypotheses hold, we can conclude that political bias in training data impairs the detection of hate speech. The reason is that the politically neutral one is our baseline due to the missing political bias, while the other two have a distinct bias each. Depending on the results, we might go one step further and might infer that one political orientation diminishes hate speech classification more substantially than the other one. For this, we use the two-sided Kolmogorov-Smirnov test (Selvamuthu and Das, 2018). The null hypothesis is that the three distributions of F1 scores from three sets of classifiers are the same. The significance level is $p < 0.01$. If the null hypothesis is rejected, which confirms (a), we will compare the average F1 scores of each distribution with each other to answer (b).

The classifier consists of a non-pre-trained embedding layer with dimension 50, a bidirectional LSTM comprising 64 units, and one fully connected layer of the size 16. The output is a sigmoid function classifying tweets as offensive or not. We used Adam optimization with an initial learning rate of 0.001 and binary cross-entropy as a loss function. We applied padding to each tweet with a maximal token length of 30. As a post-processing step, we replaced each out-of-vocabulary token occurring in the test fold with an <unk> token to overcome bias and data leaking from the test data into the training data.

In regards to RQ2, we apply the following procedure. We select one classifier from each subnetwork that is trained with an entirely replaced non-offensive data set. To explain the generated predictions, we apply the DeepExplainer from the SHAP framework for each classifier (Lundberg and Lee, 2017). After feeding DeepExplainer with tweets from the original corpus ($n = 1000$) to build a baseline, we can use it to explain the predictions of the classifiers. An explanation consists of SHAP values for every word. The SHAP values "attribute to each feature the change in the expected model prediction when conditioning on that feature" (Lundberg and Lee, 2017, p. 5). Comparing the SHAP values from the three different classifiers for a selected word in a tweet indicates how relevant a word is for a prediction w.r.t. to a specific class (e.g., offensive, non-offensive). Figure 3a shows how these values are visualized. This indication, in turn, can reveal a bias in the training data. Therefore, we randomly select two tweets from the test set that are incorrectly classified by the left-wing, respectively right-wing classifier and compare their predictions to answer RQ2.

4 Results

4.1 Data

The two GermEval data sets are the basis of the experiment. In total, they contain 15,567 German tweets - 10,420 labeled as non-offensive and 5,147 as offensive. The data for the (radical) left-wing subnetwork, the (radical) right-wing one, and the neutral one was collected via the Twitter API between 29.01.2020 and 19.02.2020. We gathered 6,494,304 tweets from timelines and 2,423,593 ones from the stream for the left-wing and right-wing subnetwork. On average, 1,026 tweets ($median = 869; \sigma^2 = 890.48$) are collected from 3,168 accounts. For the neutral subnetwork, we streamed 23,754,616 tweets. After removing retweets, duplicates, tweets with less than three tokens, and non-German tweets, we obtain 1,007,810 tweets for the left-wing raw data set, 1,620,492 for the right-wing raw data set, and 1,537,793 for the neutral raw data set. 52,100 tweets of each raw data set are selected for the data pools according to the topic model and the topic distribution. The input for the 3-fold cross-validation of the model training consists of the 5,147 offensive tweets from GermEval and 10,420 non-offensive ones from GermEval or the collected data depending on the replacement rate.

4.2 Results

All three classifiers show significantly ($p < 0.01$) different F1 scores. The one with the worst performance is the one trained with the right-wing data set (78.7%), followed by the one trained with the left-wing data set (83.1%) and the politically neutral one (84.8%).

Figure 2a shows how the F1 scores change depending on the replacement rate. The lines are the average F1 scores of the three classifiers, and the areas around them are the standard deviation of the multiple training iterations. At first glance,

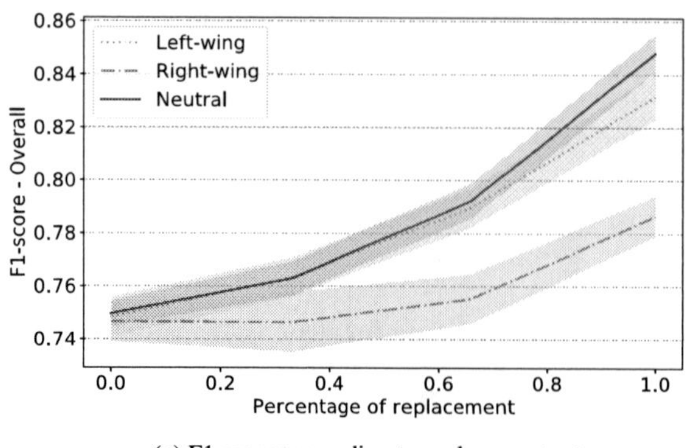
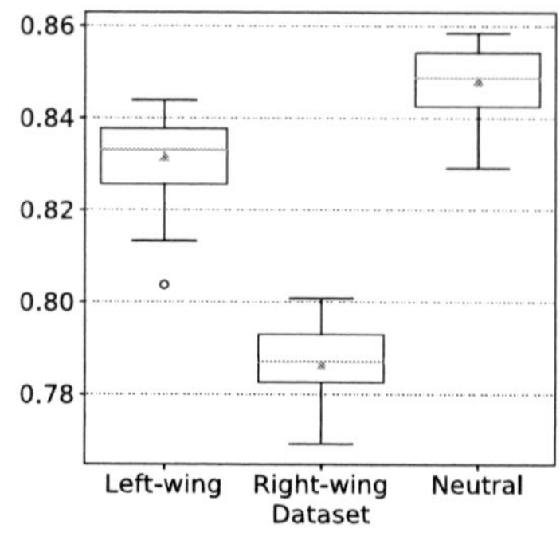

(a) F1 scores according to replacement rate   (b) F1 scores at 100% replacement rate

Figure 2: F1 scores of the three classifier subnetworks

the political biases in the data seem to increase the performance due to the improvement of the F1 scores. This trend, however, is misleading. The reason for the increase is that the two classes, offensive and non-offensive, vary strongly with the growing replacement rate, making it easier for the classifiers to distinguish between the classes. More relevant to our research question, however, are the different steepnesses of the curves and the emerging gaps between them. These differences reveal that it is harder for a classifier trained with a politically biased data set to identify hate speech - particularly in the case of a right-wing data set. While the neutral and left-wing curves are nearly congruent and only diverge at a 100% replacement rate, the gap between these two and the right-wing curve already occurs at 33% and increases. Figure 2b visualizes the statistical distribution of the measured F1 scores at a 100% replacement rate as box plots. The Kolmogorov-Smirnov test confirms the interpretation of the charts. The distributions of the left-wing and politically neutral data set are not significantly different until 100% replacement rate — at 100% $p = 8.25 \times 10^{-12}$. In contrast to that, the distribution of the right-wing data set already differs from the other two at 33% replacement rate — at 33% left- and right-wing data set $p = 2.50 \times 10^{-7}$, right-wing and neutral data set $p = 6.53 \times 10^{-9}$ and at 100% left- and right-wing data set $p = 1.69 \times 10^{-17}$, right-wing and neutral data set: $p = 1.69 \times 10^{-17}$. Thus, we can say that political bias in a training data set negatively impairs the performance of a hate speech classifier, answering RQ1.

To answer RQ2, we randomly pick two offensive tweets that were differently classified by the three

interpretable classifiers. Subsequently, we compare the explanations of the predictions from three different classifiers. These explanations consist of SHAP values for every token that is fed into the classifier. They indicate the relevance of the tokens for the prediction. Please note: not all words of a tweet are input for the classifier because some are removed during preprocessing (e.g., stop words). A simple way to visualize the SHAP values is depicted in Figure 3a. The model output value is the predicted class probability of the classifier. In our case, it is the probability of how offensive a tweet is. The words to the left shown in red (left of the box with the predicted probability) are responsible for pushing the probability towards 1 (offensive), the ones to the right shown in blue (right of the box) towards 0 (non-offensive). The longer the bars above the words are, the more relevant the words are for the predictions. Words with a score lower than 0.05 are not displayed.

Figure 3a shows the result of the three interpretable classifiers for the following offensive tweet: *@<user>@<user> Natürlich sagen alle Gutmenschen 'Ja', weil sie wissen, dass es dazu nicht kommen wird. (@<user>@<user> Of course, all do-gooders say "yes", because they know that it won't happen.)*

The left-wing and neutral classifiers predict the tweet as offensive (0.54, respectively 0.53), while the right-one considers it non-offensive (0.09). The decisive factor here is the word *Gutmenschen*. *Gutmensch* is German and describes a person "who is, or wants to be, squeaky clean with respect to morality or political correctness" (PONS, 2020). The word's SHAP value for the right-wing classifier is 0.09, for the left-wing one 0.45, and for the

60

neutral one 0.36. It is not surprising if we look at the word frequencies in the three different data sets. While the word *Gutmensch* and related ones (e.g., plural) occur 38 times in the left-wing data set and 39 times in the neutral one, we can find it 54 times in the right-wing one. Since mostly (radical) right-wing people use the term *Gutmensch* to vilify political opponents (Hanisch and Jäger, 2011; Auer, 2002), we can argue that differences between the SHAP values can indicate a political bias of a classifier.

Another example of a tweet that one politically biased classifier misclassifies is the following one (see Figure 3b): *@<user>@<user> Hätte das Volk das recht den Kanzler direkt zu wählen, wäre Merkel lange Geschichte. (If the people had the right to elect the chancellor directly, Merkel would have been history a long time ago.)*

The right-wing (0.10) and neutral classifiers (0.35) correctly classify the tweet as non-offensive, but not the left-wing one (0.96). All three have in common that the words *Volk* (German for people) and *Merkel* (last name of the German chancellor) favoring the classification as offensive, but with varying relevance. For the right-wing classifier, both terms have the lowest SHAP values (*Volk*: 0.05, *Merkel*: 0.04); for the neutral classifier, the scores are 0.34 (*Volk*) and 0.16 (*Merkel*); for the left-wing classifier, they are 0.14 (*Volk*) and 0.31 (*Merkel*). The low values of the right-wing classifier can be explained with relative high word frequency of both terms in the non-offensive training set. Another interesting aspect is that the term *Kanzler* (chancellor) increases the probability of being classified as offensive only in the case of a left-wing classifier (SHAP value: 0.08). We can trace it back to the fact that the term does not appear in the non-offensive part of the left-wing data set, causing the classifier to associate it with hate speech. This example also shows how a political bias in training data can cause misleading classifications due to a different vocabulary.

5 Discussion

The experiment shows that the politically biased classifiers (left- and right-wing) perform worse than the politically neutral one, and consequently that political bias in training data can lead to an impairment of hate speech detection (RQ1). In this context, it is relevant to consider only the gaps between the F1 classifiers' scores at 100% replace-ment rate. The gaps reflect the performance decrease of the politically biased classifiers. The rise of the F1 scores with an increasing replacement rate is caused by the fact that the new non-offensive tweets are less similar to the offensive ones of the original data set.

The results also indicate that a right-wing bias impairs the performance more strongly than a left-wing bias. This hypothesis, however, cannot be confirmed with the experiment because we do not have enough details about the composition of the offensive tweets. It could be that right-wing hate speech is overrepresented in the offensive part. The effect would be that the right-wing classifier has more difficulties to distinguish between offensive and non-offensive than the left-wing one even if both data sets are equally hateful. The reason is that the vocabulary of the right-wing data set is more coherent. Therefore, this hypothesis can neither be confirmed nor rejected by our experiment.

Concerning RQ2, we show that explainable ML models can help to identify and to visualize a political bias in training data. The two analyzed tweets provide interesting insights. The downside of the approach is that these frameworks (in our case SHAP) can only provide local explanations, meaning only single inputs are explained, not the entire model. It is, however, conceivable that the local explanations are applied to the entire data set, and the results are aggregated and processed in a way to identify and visualize bias. Summing up, this part of the experiment can be seen rather as a proof-of-concept and lays the foundation for future research.

Regarding the overall approach of the experiment, one may criticize that we only simulate a political bias by constructing politically biased data sets and that this does not reflect the reality. We agree that we simulate political bias within data due to the lack of such data sets. Nevertheless, we claim the relevance and validity of our results due to the following reasons: Firstly, the offensive data part is the same for all classifiers. Consequently, the varying performances are caused by non-offensive tweets with political bias. Therefore, the fact that the offensive tweets were annotated by annotators and the non-offensive tweets were indirectly labeled is less relevant. Furthermore, any issues with the offensive tweets' annotation quality do not play a role because all classifiers are trained and tested on the same offensive tweets. Secondly, we con-

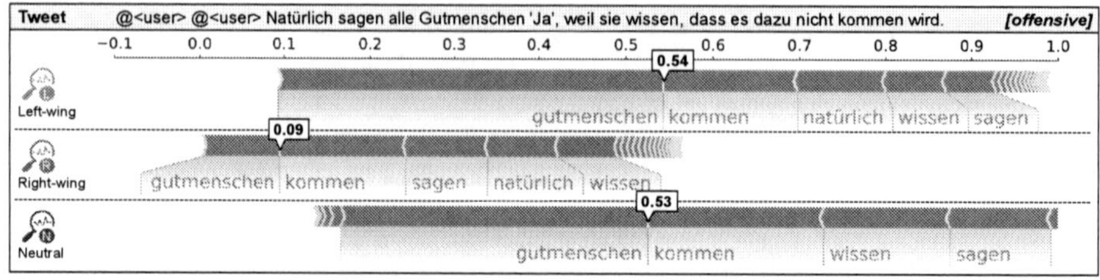

(a) Tweet wrongly classified by right-wing classifier

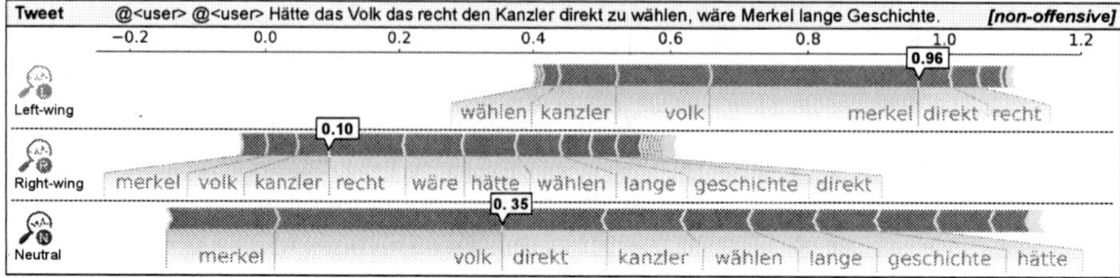

(b) Tweet wrongly classified by left-wing classifier

Figure 3: SHAP values for the two selected tweets

struct the baseline in the same way as the left- and right-wing data set instead of using the original data set as the baseline. This compensates confounding factors (e.g., different time, authors). Thirdly, we use a sophisticated topic-modeling-based approach to construct the data sets to ensure the new data sets' topic coherence.

6 Conclusion

We showed that political bias in training data can impair hate speech classification. Furthermore, we found an indication that the degree of impairment might depend on the political orientation of bias. But we were not able to confirm this. Additionally, we provide a proof-of-concept of visualizing such a bias with explainable ML models. The results can help to build unbiased data sets or to debias them. Researchers that collect hate speech to construct new data sets, for example, should be aware of this form of bias and take our findings into account in order not to favor or impair a political orientation (e.g., politically balanced set of sources). Our approach can be applied to identify bias with XAI in existing data sets or during data collection. With these insights, researchers can debias a data set by, for example, adjusting the distribution of data. Another idea that is fundamentally different from debiasing is to use these findings to build politically branded hate speech filters that are marked as those. Users of a social media platform, for example, could choose between such filters depending on their preferences. Of course, obvious hate speech would be filtered by all classifiers. But the classifiers would treat comments in the gray area of hate speech depending on the group's norms and values.

A limitation of this research is that we simulate the political bias and construct synthetic data sets with offensive tweets annotated by humans and non-offensive tweets that are only implicitly labeled. It would be better to have a data set annotated by different political orientations to investigate the impact of political bias. But such an annotating process is very challenging. Another limitation is that the GermEval data and our gathered data are from different periods. We, however, compensate this through our topic modeling-based data creation.

Nevertheless, political bias in hate speech data is a phenomenon that researchers should be aware of and that should be investigated further. All in all, we hope that this paper contributes helpful insights to the hate speech research and the fight against hate speech.

Acknowledgments

This paper is based on a joined work in the context of Jan Bauer's master's thesis (Bauer, 2020). This research has been partially funded by a scholarship from the Hanns Seidel Foundation financed by the German Federal Ministry of Education and Research.

References

Hala Al Kuwatly, Maximilian Wich, and Georg Groh. 2020. Identifying and measuring annotator bias based on annotators' demographic characteristics. In *Proc. 4th Workshop on Online Abuse and Harms*.

David Alvarez-Melis and Martin Saveski. 2016. Topic modeling in twitter: Aggregating tweets by conversations. In *10th Intl. AAAI Conf. Weblogs and Social Media*.

Katrin Auer. 2002. Political Correctness – Ideologischer Code, Feindbild und Stigmawort der Rechten. *Österreichische Zeitschrift für Politikwissenschaft*, 31(3):291–303.

Jan Bauer. 2020. Political bias in hate speech classification. Master's thesis, Technical Univesiy of Munich. Advised and supervised by Maximilian Wich and Georg Groh.

Reuben Binns, Michael Veale, Max Van Kleek, and Nigel Shadbolt. 2017. Like trainer, like bot? inheritance of bias in algorithmic content moderation. In *International conference on social informatics*, pages 405–415. Springer.

David M Blei, Andrew Y Ng, and Michael I Jordan. 2003. Latent dirichlet allocation. *Journal of Machine Learning Research*, 3(Jan):993–1022.

Daniel Borkan, Lucas Dixon, Jeffrey Sorensen, Nithum Thain, and Lucy Vasserman. 2019. Nuanced metrics for measuring unintended bias with real data for text classification. In *Proc. 28th WWW Conf.*, pages 491–500.

Xueqi Cheng, Xiaohui Yan, Yanyan Lan, and Jiafeng Guo. 2014. Btm: Topic modeling over short texts. *IEEE Transactions on Knowledge and Data Engineering*, 26(12):2928–2941.

Michael D Conover, Bruno Gonçalves, Jacob Ratkiewicz, Alessandro Flammini, and Filippo Menczer. 2011a. Predicting the political alignment of twitter users. In *2011 IEEE 3rd Intl. Conf. Privacy, Security, Risk, and Trust and 2011 IEEE 3rd Intl. Conf. Social Computing*, pages 192–199.

Michael D Conover, Jacob Ratkiewicz, Matthew Francisco, Bruno Gonçalves, Filippo Menczer, and Alessandro Flammini. 2011b. Political polarization on twitter. In *5th Intl. AAAI Conf. Weblogs and Social Media*.

Thomas Davidson, Debasmita Bhattacharya, and Ingmar Weber. 2019. Racial bias in hate speech and abusive language detection datasets. *arXiv preprint arXiv:1905.12516*.

Thomas Davidson, Dana Warmsley, Michael Macy, and Ingmar Weber. 2017. Automated hate speech detection and the problem of offensive language. In *Proc. 11th ICWSM Conf.*

Lucas Dixon, John Li, Jeffrey Sorensen, Nithum Thain, and Lucy Vasserman. 2018. Measuring and mitigating unintended bias in text classification. In *Proc. 2018 AAAI/ACM Conf. AI, Ethics, and Society*, pages 67–73.

Maeve Duggan. 2017. *Online harassment 2017*. Pew Research Center.

Mor Geva, Yoav Goldberg, and Jonathan Berant. 2019. Are we modeling the task or the annotator? an investigation of annotator bias in natural language understanding datasets. In *Proc. Conf. Empirical Methods in Natural Language Processing*, pages 1161–1166.

Astrid Hanisch and Margarete Jäger. 2011. Das Stigma "Gutmensch". *Duisburger Institut für Sprach-und Sozialforschung*, 22.

Mireille Hildebrandt. 2019. Privacy as protection of the incomputable self: From agnostic to agonistic machine learning. *Theoretical Inquiries in Law*, 20(1):83–121.

Jey Han Lau, David Newman, and Timothy Baldwin. 2014. Machine reading tea leaves: Automatically evaluating topic coherence and topic model quality. In *Proceedings of the 14th Conference of the European Chapter of the Association for Computational Linguistics*, pages 530–539.

Scott M Lundberg and Su-In Lee. 2017. A unified approach to interpreting model predictions. In I. Guyon, U. V. Luxburg, S. Bengio, H. Wallach, R. Fergus, S. Vishwanathan, and R. Garnett, editors, *Advances in Neural Information Processing Systems 30*, pages 4765–4774. Curran Associates, Inc.

Rishabh Mehrotra, Scott Sanner, Wray Buntine, and Lexing Xie. 2013. Improving lda topic models for microblogs via tweet pooling and automatic labeling. In *Proceedings of the 36th international ACM SIGIR conference on Research and development in information retrieval*, pages 889–892.

Marco Niemann. 2019. Abusiveness is non-binary: Five shades of gray in german online newscomments. In *IEEE 21st Conference Business Informatics*, pages 11–20.

John T Nockleby. 2000. Hate speech. *Encyclopedia of the American constitution*, 3(2):1277–1279.

PONS. 2020. Gutmensch - Deutsch-Englisch Übersetzung — PONS.

Martin F Porter et al. 1980. An algorithm for suffix stripping. *Program*, 14(3):130–137.

Xiaojun Quan, Chunyu Kit, Yong Ge, and Sinno Jialin Pan. 2015. Short and sparse text topic modeling via self-aggregation. In *Twenty-Fourth International Joint Conference on Artificial Intelligence*.

Julian Risch, Robin Ruff, and Ralf Krestel. 2020. Offensive language detection explained. In *Proc. Workshop on Trolling, Aggression and Cyberbullying (TRAC@LREC)*, pages 137–143.

Björn Ross, Michael Rist, Guillermo Carbonell, Benjamin Cabrera, Nils Kurowsky, and Michael Wojatzki. 2017. Measuring the reliability of hate speech annotations: The case of the european refugee crisis. *arXiv preprint arXiv:1701.08118.*

Maarten Sap, Dallas Card, Saadia Gabriel, Yejin Choi, and Noah A Smith. 2019. The risk of racial bias in hate speech detection. In *Proc. 57th ACL Conf.*, pages 1668–1678.

Anna Schmidt and Michael Wiegand. 2017. A survey on hate speech detection using natural language processing. In *Proc. 5th Intl. Workshop on Natural Language Processing for Social Media*, pages 1–10.

Dharmaraja Selvamuthu and Dipayan Das. 2018. *Introduction to statistical methods, design of experiments and statistical quality control.* Springer.

Morteza Shahrezaye, Orestis Papakyriakopoulos, Juan Carlos Medina Serrano, and Simon Hegelich. 2019. Estimating the political orientation of twitter users in homophilic networks. In *AAAI Spring Symposium: Interpretable AI for Well-being.*

Julia Maria Struß, Melanie Siegel, Josef Ruppenhofer, Michael Wiegand, and Manfred Klenner. 2019. Overview of germeval task 2, 2019 shared task on the identification of offensive language. In *Proc. 15th KONVENS*, pages 354–365.

Andrej Švec, Matúš Pikuliak, Marián Šimko, and Mária Bieliková. 2018. Improving Moderation of Online Discussions via Interpretable Neural Models. In *Proc. 2nd Workshop on Abusive Language Online*, pages 60–65.

Twitter Inc. 2020. Sample stream - Twitter Developers. `https://developer.twitter.com/en/docs/tweets/sample-realtime/overview/GET_statuse_sample.`

Bertie Vidgen, Rebekah Tromble, Alex Harris, Scott Hale, and Helen Margetts. 2019. Challenges and frontiers in abusive content detection. In *Proc. 3rd Workshop on Abusive Language Online*, pages 80–93.

Prashanth Vijayaraghavan, Hugo Larochelle, and Deb Roy. 2019. Interpretable Multi-Modal Hate Speech Detection. In *Intl. Conf. Machine Learning AI for Social Good Workshop.*

Cindy Wang. 2018. Interpreting neural network hate speech classifiers. In *Proc. 2nd Workshop on Abusive Language Online*, pages 86–92.

Zeerak Waseem. 2016. Are you a racist or am i seeing things? annotator influence on hate speech detection on twitter. In *Proc. 1st Workshop on NLP and Computational Social Science*, pages 138–142.

Michael Wiegand, Josef Ruppenhofer, and Thomas Kleinbauer. 2019. Detection of abusive language: the problem of biased datasets. In *NAACL-HLT 2019: Annual Conference of the North American Chapter of the Association for Computational Linguistics*, pages 602–608.

Michael Wiegand, Melanie Siegel, and Josef Ruppenhofer. 2018. Overview of the germeval 2018 shared task on the identification of offensive language. In *Proc. 14th KONVENS.*

Matthew L Williams, Pete Burnap, Amir Javed, Han Liu, and Sefa Ozalp. 2020. Hate in the machine: Anti-black and anti-muslim social media posts as predictors of offline racially and religiously aggravated crime. *The British Journal of Criminology*, 60(1):93–117.

Michael Wojatzki, Tobias Horsmann, Darina Gold, and Torsten Zesch. 2018. Do women perceive hate differently: Examining the relationship between hate speech, gender, and agreement judgments. In *Proc. 14th KONVENS.*

Reducing Unintended Identity Bias in Russian Hate Speech Detection

Nadezhda Zueva[1], Madina Kabirova[1], Pavel Kalaidin[1,2]
[1]VK, [2]VK Lab
`{firstname.lastname}@vk.com`

Abstract

Toxicity has become a grave problem for many online communities and has been growing across many languages, including Russian. Hate speech creates an environment of intimidation, discrimination, and may even incite some real-world violence. Both researchers and social platforms have been focused on developing models to detect toxicity in online communication for a while now. A common problem of these models is the presence of bias towards some words (e.g. woman, black, jew or женщина, черный, еврей) that are not toxic, but serve as triggers for the classifier due to model caveats. In this paper, we describe our efforts towards classifying hate speech in Russian, and propose simple techniques of reducing unintended bias, such as generating training data with language models using terms and words related to protected identities as context and applying word dropout to such words.

1 Introduction

With the ever-growing popularity of social media, there is an immense amount of user-generated online content (e.g. as of May 2019, approximately 30,000 hours worth of videos are uploaded to YouTube every hour[1]). In particular, there has been an exponential increase in user-generated texts such as comments, blog posts, status updates, messages, forum threads, etc. The low entry threshold and relative anonymity of the Internet have resulted not only in the exchange of information and content but also in the rise of trolling, hate speech, and overall toxicity [2].

Harassment is a pervasive issue for most online communities. A Pew survey conducted in 2014[3] found that 73% of Internet users have witnessed online harassment, and 40% have personally experienced it.

Explicit policies against hate speech can be considered an industry standard[4] across social platforms, including platforms popular among Russian-speaking users (e.g. VK, the largest social network in Russia and the CIS[5]).

The study of hate speech, in online communication in particular, has been gaining traction in Russia for a while now due to it being a prevalent issue long before the Internet (Lokshina, 2003). The number of competitions and workshops (e.g. HASOC at FIRE-2019; TRAC 2020; HatEval and OffensEval at SemEval-2019) on the topic of hate speech and toxic language detection reflect the scale of the situation.

Social platforms utilize a wide variety of models to detect or classify hate speech. However, the majority of existing models operate with a bias in their predictions. They tend to classify comments mentioning certain commonly harassed identities (e.g. containing words such as woman, black, jew or женщина, черный, еврей) as toxic, while the comment itself may lack any actual toxicity. Identity terms of frequently targeted social groups have higher toxicity scores since they are found more often in abusive and toxic comments than terms related to other social groups. If the data used to train a machine learning model is skewed towards these words, the resulting model is likely to adopt this bias[6].

Inappropriately high toxicity scores of terms related to specific social groups can potentially negate the benefits of using machine learning models to fight the spread of hate speech. This motivated us to work towards reducing these biases. In

---

[1]`https://vk.cc/aANMR4`
[2]`https://vk.cc/aANMZn`
[3]`https://vk.cc/aANN6p`

[4]`https://vk.cc/aANNbQ`
[5]`https://vk.cc/ayxecu`
[6]`https://vk.cc/aANNqT`

Proceedings of the Fourth Workshop on Online Abuse and Harms, pages 65–69
· Online, November 20, 2020. ©2020 Association for Computational Linguistics
https://doi.org/10.18653/v1/P17

this paper, our main goal is to reduce the false toxicity scores of non-toxic comments that include identity terms empirically known to introduce model bias.

2 Related Work

2.1 Hate Speech Detection in Russian

Little research has been done on the automatic detection of toxicity and hate speech in the Russian language. Potapova and Gordeev (2016) used convolutional neural networks to detect aggression in user messages on anonymous message boards. Andrusyak et al. (2018) proposed an unsupervised technique for extending the vocabulary of abusive and obscene words in Russian and Ukrainian. More recently, Smetanin (2020) utilized pre-trained BERT (Devlin et al., 2019) and Universal Sentence Encoder (Yang et al., 2019) architectures to classify toxic Russian-language content.

2.2 Reducing Unintended Bias

Dixon et al. (2018) introduced Pinned AUC to control for unintended bias. In this paper, we adopt Generalized Mean of Bias AUCs (GMB-AUC) introduced by (Borkan et al., 2019b), following a study by (Borkan et al., 2019a) showing the limitations of Pinned AUC.

Vaidya et al. (2020) proposed a model that learns to predict the toxicity of a comment, as well as the protected identities present, in order to reduce unintended bias as shown by an increase in Generalized Mean of Bias AUCs. Nozza et al. (2019) focused on misogyny detection, providing a synthetic test for evaluating bias and some mitigation strategies for it.

To our knowledge, there is no published research on reducing text classification bias in Russian.

3 Experiments

3.1 Datasets

For our experiments, we manually collected a corpus[7] of comments posted on a major Russian social network. The mean length of each sample is 26 characters; samples over 50 characters (5% of the total number of samples) were shortened. The corpus consists of 100,000 samples that we randomly split into training, validation and test sets in the ratio 8:1:1. Each comment was assigned a label

---

[7]The corpus is available on request to authors upon submitting a license agreement.

based on whether or not it contained various forms of hate speech or abuse, including threats, harassment, insults, mentions of family members, as well as language used to promote lookism, sexism, homophobia, nationalism, etc.

As benchmarks, we also used a small corpus of 2,000 samples in mixed Russian and Ukrainian collected by (Andrusyak et al., 2018), and a corpus in Russian used by (Smetanin, 2020) (around 14,000 samples).

3.2 Task & Evaluation

We considered the prediction of labels related to hate speech as a task and validated performance using introduced Generalized Mean of Bias AUCs (Borkan et al., 2019b) to analyze whether or not the proposed methods help reduce text classification bias.

3.3 Protected Identities

We manually compiled a list of Russian words related to protected identities. The words were split, based on the type of hate speech used, into the following classes: lookism, sexism, nationalism, threats, harassment, homophobia, and other. Extracts from the full list are provided in Table 1. Total number of words in the list is 214. The full list of protected identities and related words is available here: `https://vk.cc/aAS3TQ`.

3.4 Models

We used a model based on the self-attentive encoder (Lin et al., 2017). We directly feed the token embeddings matrix to the attention layer instead of the bi-LSTM encoder, making it a pure self-attention model similar to the one used in Transformer (Vaswani et al., 2017). An advantage of this architecture is that the individual attention weights for each input token can be interpretable (Lin et al., 2017). This makes it possible to visualize what triggers the classifier, giving us an opportunity to explore the data and extend our list of protected identities. To overcome the problem of out-of-vocabulary words, we trained byte pair encoding (Sennrich et al., 2015) on a corpora of Russian subtitles taken from a large dataset collected by (Shavrina and Shapovalova), and used it for input tokenization.

We also evaluated a CNN-based text classifier (as in (Potapova and Gordeev, 2016)) to use as a baseline for comparison.

| **lookism** |
| корова korova "cow" |
| пышка pishka "donut (meaning "plump")" |
| **sexism** |
| женщина zhenshchina "woman" |
| баба baba "woman (derogatory)" |
| **nationalism** |
| чех chekh ""Chechen" (derogatory) lit. "Czech"" |
| еврей evrei "Jew" |
| **threats** |
| выезжать vyezhat "to come (after somebody)" |
| айпи aipi "ip" |
| **harassment** |
| киска kiska "pussy" |
| секси seksi "sexy" |
| **homophobia** |
| гей gay "gay" |
| лгбт LGBT "LGBT" |
| **other** |
| мамка mamka "mother" |
| админ admin "admin" |

Table 1: Extracts from the full list of protected identities and related words.

3.5 Data Generation with Language Models

To reduce model bias, we propose to extend the dataset with the output of pre-trained language models. We used the pre-trained Transformer language model[8] trained on the Taiga dataset (Shavrina and Shapovalova). As Taiga contains 8 sources of normative Russian text (news, fairy tales, classic literature, etc.), we assumed that the model would be able to generate non-toxic comments even with one word from protected identities given as context. We took a random word from a list of protected identities and related words as a single word prefix for language generation, and generated samples up to 20 words long or until an end token was generated. An additional 25,000 samples were generated using the described approach and added to the existing training set.

3.6 Identity Dropout

Random word dropout (Dai and Le, 2015) was shown to improve text classification. We utilized this technique to randomly (with 0.5 probability) replace protected identities in input sequences with the <UNK> token during training.

3.7 Multi-Task Learning

Following (Vaidya et al., 2020), we evaluated a multi-task learning framework, where we extended a base model by predicting a protected identity class from an input sequence. In our setup, the loss from an extra classifier head is weighted equal to the loss from the toxicity classifier.

3.8 Training Details

We trained our models for 100,000 iterations with a batch size of 128, the Adam optimizer (Kingma and Ba, 2014), and a learning rate of 1e-5 with betas (0.9, 0.999) on a single NVIDIA Tesla T4 GPU. Each experiment took approximately 1 hour to run. We used embeddings pre-trained on the corpora of Russian subtitles (Shavrina and Shapovalova). We experimented with 2 different architectures (self-ATTN, CNN) in several scenarios by applying Data Generation with Language Model, Identity Dropout, and Multi-Task learning, as well as combining these approaches. We used binary cross-entropy loss as the loss function for the single-task approach. As the loss function for Multi-Task learning, we used the average loss score between two tasks: predicting the toxicity score, and predicting the protected identity class. We trained our model on the training set, controlled the training process using the validation set, and evaluated metrics on the test set. We repeated each experiment 3 times and showed the mean and standard deviation values of the measurements. We applied an early stopping approach with patience level 50. The code is available on Google Drive[9].

4 Results & Conclusion

The results are provided in Table 2.

We showed that, for our dataset and for the benchmark from (Smetanin, 2020), adding an extra task of predicting the class of a protected identity can indeed improve the quality of toxicity classification in terms of reducing unintended bias. Moreover, we observed that simple techniques such as regularizing the input and extending the training data with external language models can help reduce unintended model bias on protected identities even further.

[8]https://github.com/vlarine/ruGPT2

[9]https://vk.cc/aANO1g

Method	Our Dataset		(Andrusyak et al., 2018)		(Smetanin, 2020)	
	GMB-AUC	F1	GMB-AUC	F1	GMB-AUC	F1
CNN	.56±.005	.66±.003	.51±.005	.59±.001	.53±.003	.78±.002
CNN + multitask	.58±.001	.68±.008	.52±.002	.61±.002	.53±.010	.80±.002
Attn	.60±.002	.71±.010	.54±.001	.72±.003	.54±.005	.80±.010
Attn + multitask	.60±.004	.74±.012	.54±.009	.69±.009	.54±.007	.82±.004
Attn + LM data	.65±.003	.74±.002	.58±.003	.70±.001	.57±.006	.83±.009
Attn + LM data + multitask	.67±.002	.74±.016	.59±.003	.70±.010	.58±.003	.84±.008
Attn + identity d/o	.61±.001	.65±.003	.53±.004	.68±.001	.54±.007	.82±.011
Attn + identity d/o + multitask	.61±.005	.66±.007	.54±.004	.69±.008	.58±.009	.83±.007
Attn + identity d/o + LM data	.67±.004	.76±.005	.55±.003	.71±.002	**.59±.003**	**.86±.012**
Attn + identity d/o + LM data + multitask	**.68±.001**	**.78±.010**	.56±.004	**.73±.003**	.60±.008	**.86±.004**

Table 2: Generalized Mean of Bias AUCs (GMB-AUC) and F1 scores across datasets.

For the (Andrusyak et al., 2018) benchmark, we did not see much improvement in our metrics. This can be attributed to language differences, as the benchmark contains abusive words both in Russian and Ukrainian.

We also observed that the proposed models achieved competitive results across all three datasets when evaluated with F1 score. The best performing model (Attn + identity d/o + LM data + multitask setup) achieved an F1 score of 0.86 on the (Smetanin, 2020) benchmark, which is 93% of the reported SoTA performance of a much larger model fine-tuned from a BERT-like architecture.

5 Future Work

We are interested in automatically extending our compiled list of protected identities and related words. We also expect that fine-tuning a pre-trained BERT-like model would improve our results and plan to experiment with it.

6 Acknowledgements

The authors are grateful to Daniil Gavrilov and Oktai Tatanov for useful discussions, Daniil Gavrilov for review, Viktoriia Loginova and David Prince for proofreading, and anonymous reviewers for valuable comments. The authors would also like to thank the VK Moderation Team (led by Katerina Egorushkova) for their help in building a hate speech dataset.

References

Bohdan Andrusyak, Mykhailo Rimel, and Roman Kern. 2018. Detection of abusive speech for mixed sociolects of russian and ukrainian languages. In *Proceedings of Recent Advances in Slavonic Natural Language Processing*, page 77–84.

Daniel Borkan, Lucas Dixon, John Li, Jeffrey Sorensen, Nithum Thain, and Lucy Vasserman. 2019a. Limitations of pinned auc for measuring unintended bias. In *arXiv preprint arXiv:1903.02088*.

Daniel Borkan, Lucas Dixon, Jeffrey Sorensen, Nithum Thain, and Lucy Vasserman. 2019b. Nuanced metrics for measuring unintended bias with real data for text classification. In *Companion Proceedings of The 2019 World Wide Web Conference*, pages 491–500.

Andrew M. Dai and Quoc V. Le. 2015. Semi-supervised sequence learning. In *Advances in neural information processing systems*, page 3079–3087.

Jacob Devlin, Ming-Wei Chang, Kenton Lee, and Kristina Toutanova. 2019. Bert: Pre-training of deep bidirectional transformers for language understanding. In *NAACL-HLT*.

Lucas Dixon, John Li, Jeffrey Sorensen, Nithum Thain, and Lucy Vasserman. 2018. Measuring and mitigating unintended bias in text classification. In *Proceedings of AAAI/ACM Conference on Artificial Intelligence, Ethics, and Society*.

Diederik P. Kingma and Jimmy Ba. 2014. Adam: A method for stochastic optimization.

Zhouhan Lin, Minwei Feng, Cicero Nogueira dos Santos, Mo Yu, Bing Xiang, Bowen Zhou, and Yoshua Bengio. 2017. A structured self-attentive sentence embedding. In *arXiv preprint arXiv:1703.03130*, page 3079–3087.

Tanya Lokshina. 2003. Hate speech in russia: Overview of the problem and means for counteraction. In *Bulletin: Anthropology, Minorities, Multiculturalism*, volume 4.

Debora Nozza, Claudia Volpetti, and Elisabetta Fersini. 2019. Unintended bias in misogyny detection. In *IEEE/WIC/ACM International Conference on Web Intelligence*.

Rodmonga Potapova and Denis Gordeev. 2016. Detecting state of aggression in sentences using cnn. In *International Conference on Speech and Computer*.

Rico Sennrich, Barry Haddow, and Alexandra Birch. 2015. Neural machine translation of rare words with subword units. In *arXiv preprint arXiv:1508.07909*.

Tatiana Shavrina and Olga Shapovalova. To the methodology of corpus construction for machine learning: "taiga" syntax tree corpus". In *Corpora-2017*.

Sergey Smetanin. 2020. Toxic comments detection in russian. In *Computational Linguistics and Intellectual Technologies: Proceedings of the International Conference "Dialogue 2020"*.

Ameya Vaidya, Feng Mai, and Yue Ning. 2020. Empirical analysis of multi-task learning for reducing identity bias in toxic comment detection. In *Proceedings of the Fourteenth International AAAI Conference on Web and Social Media (ICWSM 2020)*.

Ashish Vaswani, Noam Shazeer, Niki Parmar, Jakob Uszkoreit, Llion Jones, Aidan N Gomez, Łukasz Kaiser, and Illia Polosukhin. 2017. Attention is all you need. In *Advances in neural information processing systems*, pages 5998–6008.

Yinfei Yang, Daniel Cer, Amin Ahmad, Mandy Guo, Jax Law, Noah Constant, Gustavo Hernandez Abrego, Steve Yuan, Chris Tar, Yun-Hsuan Sung, Brian Strope, and Ray Kurzweil. 2019. Multilingual universal sentence encoder for semantic retrieval. In *arXiv preprint arXiv:1907.04307*.

Investigating Sampling Bias in Abusive Language Detection

Dante Razo, Sandra Kübler
Indiana University
{drazo,skuebler}@indiana.edu

Abstract

Abusive language detection is becoming increasingly important, but we still understand little about the biases in our datasets for abusive language detection, and how these biases affect the quality of abusive language detection. In the work reported here, we reproduce the investigation of Wiegand et al. (2019) to determine differences between different sampling strategies. They compared boosted random sampling, where abusive posts are up-sampled, and biased topic sampling, which focuses on topics that are known to cause abusive language. Instead of comparing individual datasets created using these sampling strategies, we use the sampling strategies on a single, large dataset, thus eliminating the textual source of the dataset as a potential confounding factor. We show that differences in the textual source can have more effect than the chosen sampling strategy.

1 Introduction

Abusive language detection has become an important problem, especially in a world where #BlackLivesMatter, and where abusive posts on social media need to be found and deleted automatically. However, we also know that the datasets that we currently use for training classifiers are all biased in some way or another. Wiegand et al. (2019) present one of the first investigations into into bias in different datasets for abusive language detection for English. They compare characteristics of 6 datasets, based on their underlying sampling strategy, their proportion of abusive posts, and the proportion of explicit abuse. The proportion of abusive posts is important for classifiers: If that proportion is too small, classifiers tend default to the majority class baseline. Thus, creators of datasets use a range of strategies to increase the number of abusive posts in their data. The specific strategy can have an influence on the proportion of explicitly abusive posts, which tend to be easier to identify as abusive, and overall on classifier performance. We are interested in understanding this interaction better.

Wiegand et al. (2019) distinguish between boosted random sampling and biased topic sampling. Boosted random sampling is based on a complete sample, for example all tweets of a specific time frame. Then, the number of abusive posts is boosted using different methods, for example by adding more posts by users who have been blocked for being abusive. Biased topic sampling, in contrast, samples posts from specific topics, such as soccer or Islam, which are known to cause a considerable amount of abuse.

Wiegand et al. (2019) argue that the type of sampling strategy introduces bias into the dataset, and we can assume that the two sampling strategies create different biases: Random boosted sampling may create a bias towards specific authors but with a widespread range of topics, and biased topic sampling may create a bias towards specific topics, and potentially specific authors. However, we are often unaware of the exact biases present in such datasets. This is important because first results on debiasing datasets show that these methods work best when we know which bias is present (He et al., 2019).

In our work, we focus on reproducing the results by Wiegand et al. (2019) and providing a closer look at the different sampling strategies. While Wiegand et al. (2019) normalize performance by using a single classifier on all datasets, they do not normalize across different text types. Thus, the two sampling strategies have been used on different datasets, which leaves open the question to what degree the differences in bias are due to textual characteristics (Wikipedia talkpages, Twitter feed, Facebook posts), or to the sampling strategies. Consequently, we repeat their experiments applying both sampling techniques to the same dataset.

Proceedings of the Fourth Workshop on Online Abuse and Harms, pages 70–78
Online, November 20, 2020. ©2020 Association for Computational Linguistics
https://doi.org/10.18653/v1/P17

We use two datasets from Kaggle competitions, of sufficient size to enable us to sample from the *same dataset* and obtain smaller subsets based on different sampling strategies. We also add an investigation into two variants of biased topic sampling and the out-of-vocabulary rate of the resulting subsets.

The remainder of the paper is structured as follows: Section 2 explains our research questions, section 3 provides an overview of related work on bias in abusive language detection data, and section 4 discusses our experimental setup, including datasets, lexicons, sampling strategies, the classifier, and evaluation. In section 5, we discuss our findings, and in section 6, we conclude.

2   Research Questions

When reproducing the investigation by Wiegand et al. (2019), we focus on the following questions:

1. Does repeated sampling from a dataset change characteristics of the data?

   We first need to investigate how diverse the Kaggle datasets are, i.e., to what extent sampling a fairly small subset will change the distribution and difficulty of the dataset. Thus, we create 3 sampled subsets and compare their results.

2. Are there performance differences between boosted random sampling and biased, topic-based sampling?

   This is a replication of the question by Wiegand et al. (2019), but we first compare the two sampling strategies on samples from the *same* underlying dataset, the original Kaggle dataset also used in their experiments (see section 4.1 for details on the datasets), which is originally based on boosted random sampling.

   Additionally, we repeat the experiment on another, larger Kaggle dataset for abusive language detection.

3. How dependent are results on the topic used for sampling?

   Since the original Kaggle dataset is based on Wikipedia talkpages and thus covers topics different from the one covered in other datasets, we could not use the list of topics used by previous approaches for biased topic sampling (Kumar et al., 2018; Waseem and Hovy, 2016; Warner and Hirschberg, 2012). This leads to

the question how dependent results are on the choice of topics. We compare the wide range of topics we used for the previous question to a setting where we use only one specific term to sample.

4. To what degree does the proportion of explicit abuse and the OOV rate correlate with performance?

   Wiegand et al. (2019) also ranked datasets based on the proportion of explicitly and implicitly abusive language. We have a closer look at this distinction, along with looking at the OOV rate of instances.

3   Related Work

Wiegand et al. (2019) were among the first to investigate bias in datasets used for abusive language detection. They compared 6 different datasets and found topic and author bias, which was introduced by the sampling method used to create the datasets. As a method to avoid biased evaluation, they recommend cross-domain classification, i.e., using different datasets to train and test an approach.

Additionally, van Rosendaal et al. (2020) investigate methods for boosting abusive language when creating datasets while at the same time maintaining a good spread of topics. They suggest concentrating on controversies and describe two specific methods: For Twitter data, they suggest using the most frequent hashtags over a time period. And for Reddit, they suggest using posts that have a similar number of up- and down-votes, a sign for the controversial nature of these posts.

Park et al. (2018) discuss methods to decrease the gender bias in abusive language detection. They suggest 3 methods for debiasing, which successfully reduce gender bias in their experiments: debiasing word embeddings, gender swap data augmentation, and fine-tuning using a larger corpus.

Sap et al. (2019), in contrast, focus on racial bias, which is originally introduced by annotator's insensitivities to African-American English (AAE), but is then propagated via a trained classifier learning this bias. Sap et al. (2019) show that priming the annotators for dialect and race of the tweet's producer results in fewer AAE posts being labeled abusive. Davidson et al. (2019) provide a more in-depth analysis, showing that the bias also holds when comparing tweets containing the keywords "n*gga" and "b*tch".

There are also approaches to eliminate bias from datasets. For example, Badjatiya et al. (2019) present a method to identify and replace bias sensitive words.

4 Experimental Setup

4.1 Datasets

We use the largest datatset from the sets used by Wiegand et al. (2019), the dataset from the Kaggle *Toxic Comment Classification Challenge*[1]. This dataset is an extension of the dataset by Wulczyn et al. (2017). The dataset contains 312 737 posts from Wikipedia Talkpages. It was created using random boosted sampling; the authors boosted the number of abusive posts by sampling posts from "users who where blocked for violating Wikipedia's policy on personal attack" (Wulczyn et al., 2017). We consider all posts abusive which are marked as either "toxic" or "severely toxic", following Wiegand et al. (2019). We will refer to this dataset as the *original Kaggle* set.

Additonally, we use the dataset from the Kaggle competition *Jigsaw Unintended Bias in Toxicity Classification*[2] with posts from the platform Civil Comments. The dataset contains 1 804 874 posts. Following Jigsaw's documentation, we consider every post with a target value of ≥ 0.5 abusive. We chose this dataset mainly because of its size since it gives enough posts for the sampling process, but also because the data are from a different domain than the first data set. We will refer to this dataset as the *large Kaggle* set.

4.1.1 Data Preprocessing and Features

For both datasets, we only use the posts and the abusive rating. We used the Scikit-learn (Pedregosa et al., 2011) tokenizer to tokenize the posts and then removed punctuation.

We use 5-fold cross-validation on all datasets, and we use word 1-3-grams as features.

4.2 Lexicons

Following Wiegand et al. (2019), we use a lexicon-based approach to determine whether a post is explicitly or implicitly abusive. As lexicons, we consider the base and extended lexicon by Wiegand et al. (2018). The base lexicon was created from negative polar expressions and annotated for abusive terms via crowdsourcing. This lexicon was used in a classifier to create the extended lexicon.

However, a manual inspection showed that many of the words in the base lexicon were not offensive. For this reason, we created a manually-vetted version of this lexicon[3]. Three native speakers were asked to rate each word in the base lexicon as either non-abusive, mildly abusive, or definitely abusive. For our manually-vetted lexicon, we consider all words abusive that 2 or three of our annotators have considered mildly or highly abusive. The base lexicon contains 551 abusive entries, the extended lexicon has 2 989 entries, and our manually-vetted lexicon 151 abusive words.

The native speakers disagreed with the original classification of 269 words from the base lexicon. Examples of words deemed inoffensive include "aloof", "chonky", and "gossip". There were only 6 words that were highly abusive, according to all three judges. Among them are n*gger, f*g, and c*nt.

4.3 Generating Sampling Variants

Our experiments utilize three types of sampling: boosted random sampling, biased topic sampling, and biased topic sampling with a narrowly defined topic (see below). For each sampling type, we sampled three subsets of 20 000 posts per dataset.

Random Boosted Sampling Since the original Kaggle dataset is based on random boosted sampling, we can use basic random sampling from the dataset to obtain our boosted random samples. For the large Kaggle set, it is unclear how these posts were collected, but it is more likely to be a variant of random boosted sampling than biased topic sampling, thus we used the same strategy as for the original Kaggle set.

Biased Topic Sampling Since the original Kaggle dataset is extracted from Wikipedia talkpages, the topics covered in the dataset are different from the topics in previous datasets using biased, topic-based sampling (Kumar et al., 2018; Waseem and Hovy, 2016; Warner and Hirschberg, 2012). Consequently, we had to create our own list of topic words. We created a list of (non-abusive) topic words covering a wide range of topics found in

---

[1]https://www.kaggle.com/c/
jigsaw-toxic-comment-classification-challenge
[2]https://www.kaggle.com/c/
jigsaw-unintended-bias-in-toxicity-
classification

[3]The manually-vetted lexicon is available at https://github.com/danterazo/ abusive-language-detection/blob/master/ data/lexicon.manual.csv

Set	Category	% in set	Precision	Recall	F1
set 1	not abusive	90.51	95.39	99.05	97.19
	abusive	9.49	85.73	54.50	66.56
set 2	not abusive	90.62	95.35	99.02	97.16
	abusive	9.38	85.00	53.44	65.62
set 3	not abusive	90.50	95.17	99.03	97.06
	abusive	9.50	84.92	52.13	64.60

Table 1: Results of repeating the random subset sampling process from the original Kaggle dataset.

Set	Category	% in set	Precision	Recall	F1
set 1	not abusive	91.89	93.55	98.96	96.18
	abusive	8.11	65.83	22.69	33.75
set 2	not abusive	91.83	93.41	98.86	96.06
	abusive	8.17	62.75	21.54	32.07
set 3	not abusive	91.94	93.66	99.14	96.33
	abusive	8.06	70.58	23.51	35.27

Table 2: Results of repeating the random subset sampling process from the large Kaggle dataset.

the Kaggle datasets, and which are known to incite abuse. The topics include, but are not limited to, politics, religion, and social justice initiatives, example words are "immigration", "muslim", and "feminism"[4].

Narrow Topic We chose the name "Trump" as our topic for the biased topic sampling with a narrow basis, assuming that the discussions around the last presidential elections will have incited abusive comments (the large Kaggle dataset covers posts from 2015 through 2017).

4.4 Classifier

We deviated from Wiegand et al. (2019) and used Support Vector Machines as our classifier. We used the SVC implementation of Scikit-learn (Pedregosa et al., 2011).

Scikit-learn's GridSearchCV was used to optimize our model parameters in an initial experiment. We then used the following optimal parameters for all consecutive experiments: regularization parameter: 1000, gamma: 0.001, and the radial basis function (RBF) kernel.

4.5 Evaluation

We report accuracy, macro-precision, macro-recall, and macro-F1 scores. For all classification experiments, we report averages over 3 samples and

5-fold cross-validation on each sample. For all statistics, we report averages over the 5 folds of the first sample.

5 Results

5.1 Repeated Subset Sampling

Here we investigate the consistency of datasets sampled from the two Kaggle datasets. We create 3 randomly sampled datasets of 20 000 posts, and then perform 5-fold CV on each set. Note that this type of sampling is different from the sampling investigated in the next sections; here the goal is to reduce the size of the dataset to a uniform, small size, and we need to determine how much variation we should expect from this random subset sampling.

The results for the original Kaggle set are shown in Table 1 and for the large Kaggle set in Table 2. They show that all three samples have a very similar distribution of classes. Both datasets also show a similar performance of the classifier on the majority class. For the minority class, in contrast, there are differences in the range of 2% absolute: The original dataset shows a decrease in the F-score from 66.56 in set 1 to 65.62 in set 2 and 64.60 in set 3. For the large Kaggle set, set 3 shows a noticeably higher performance (35.27) than set 1 and 2 result, which are similar in F-scores (33.75 and 32.07).

Given these results, we decided to use repeated subset sampling for all the remaining experiments,

<hr>

[4]The list of words is available at `https://github.com/danterazo/abusive-language-detection/blob/master/data/wordbank.py`.

Category	Boosted random sampling				Biased topic sampling			
	% in set	Precision	Recall	F1	% in set	Precision	Recall	F1
Not Abusive	90.54	95.31	99.03	97.13	93.85	96.14	99.23	97.66
Abusive	9.46	85.21	53.32	65.59	6.15	76.91	39.23	51.95
Accuracy		90.26				86.53		

Table 3: Comparing boosted random sampling and biased topic sampling on the original Kaggle dataset.

Category	Boosted random sampling				Biased topic sampling			
	% in set	Precision	Recall	F1	% in set	Precision	Recall	F1
Not Abusive	91.89	93.54	98.99	96.19	90.72	92.23	99.17	95.57
Abusive	8.11	66.38	22.58	33.70	9.28	69.12	18.23	28.85
Accuracy		92.79				91.67		

Table 4: Comparing boosted random sampling and biased topic sampling on the large Kaggle dataset.

thus all classification results below are based on an average over 3 subsets.

5.2 Comparing Random Boosted Sampling and Biased Topic Sampling

This question reproduces the comparison of the two sampling strategies by Wiegand et al. (2019), boosted random sampling and biased sampling (see section 4.3).

The results of this set of experiments for the original Kaggle set are shown in Table 3. A first look at the proportion of abusive posts in the datasets shows that the boosted random sampling results in 9.46% abusive posts while the biased topic sample reaches a lower percentage of 6.15%. This is directly reflected in accuracy, which is lower for the biased topic sample by about the same margin. However, a look at the large Kaggle set in Table 4 shows that the lower rate of abusive posts is not due to the biased topic sampling: In the large Kaggle set, the biased topic sample shows a higher rate of abusive posts than the boosted random set (9.28% vs. 8.11%).

It is also obvious that in both Kaggle sets, the abusive class in the biased topic sample is considerably harder to detect than in the boosted random sample: In the original Kaggle set, the biased topic sample reaches an F-score of 51.95 vs. 65.59 for the boosted random sample. For the large Kaggle set, the biased topic sample reaches 28.85 vs. 33.70. This trend is independent of the distribution of abusive and non-abusive posts, and it mirrors the findings of Wiegand et al. (2019) that the biased topic sampled datasets reach lower F-scores.

However, the differences that we have found are mostly distinct from those found by Wiegand et al.

(2019), shown in Table 5. While Wiegand et al. (2019) found that biased topic sampling tends to lead to higher proportions of abusive posts, our samples show that the difference is minimal, thus pointing to the hypothesis that the data source has more influence on the proportion of abusive language than the sampling strategy. They also found that boosted random sampling leads to higher F-scores (with the exception of the Waseem set, whose high F-score they trace back to the topic and author biases in this dataset). The same trend can be found in our samples, but to a much smaller degree: In our samples, the difference is about 1%, the most extreme difference in the datasets by Wiegand et al. (2019) is around 18%, when comparing the Kaggle and Kumar datasets (see Table 5, copied from their paper). This again points to the data source as the main determinant of classifier performance.

5.3 Comparing Wide and Narrow Topic Definitions for Biased Topic Sampling

Given the high performance we obtained on the biased topic sampling on the large Kaggle set, we decided to investigate this point more deeply. We are interested in how the definition of the topic, and more specifically the scope of the topic affects the distribution of abusive and non-abusive posts as well as the performance on this dataset. The first set of experiments for biased topic sampling uses a widely defined set of topics, including politics, religion, and social justice initiatives. Consequently, we created narrow topic samples by focusing on posts that mention the name "Trump". Note that this experiment is only possible on the large Kaggle set since the original Kaggle set is too diverse in topics and too limited in size to support the sam-

dataset	source	sampling	# posts	% abusive	F1	% explicit
Kaggle	Wikipedia	random	312 737	9.6	88.2	76.9
Founta	Twitter	random	59 357	14.1	87.3	75.9
Razavi	diverse	random	1 525	31.9	83.3	64.7
Warner	diverse	biased	3 438	14.3	71.8	51.3
Waseem	Twitter	biased	16 165	35.3	80.5	44.4
Kumar	Facebook	biased	15 000	58.1	70.4	32.7

Table 5: Dataset characteristics, from (Wiegand et al., 2019, p. 604).

Category	% in set	Wide topic sampling			% in set	Narrow topic sampling		
		Precision	Recall	F1		Precision	Recall	F1
Not Abusive	90.72	92.23	99.17	95.57	86.38	89.50	98.21	93.65
Abusive	9.28	69.12	18.23	28.85	13.62	70.41	26.91	38.93
Accuracy		91.67				88.50		

Table 6: Comparing topic sampling with wide or narrow topic scope on the large Kaggle set.

pling of a narrow topic.

The results for this experiment are shown in Table 6. We repeat the results for biased topic sampling using the wider range of topics from Table 4 for ease of comparison. Not unexpectedly, given the definition of the narrow topic, our sets using narrow topic sampling have a higher proportion of abusive posts compared to the wider topic sampling (13.62% vs. 9.28%). This means that the proportion of abusive posts is closer to the trend that Wiegand et al. (2019) observed, but well below two of the three datasets using biased topic sampling (Waseem with 35.3% and Kumar with 58.1%).

In terms of classifier performance, narrow topic sampling yields higher precision (70.41% vs. 69.12%) and recall (26.91% vs. 18.23%) for abusive posts. There are two possible explanations: Either the higher percentage of abusive posts in training boost performance on this class, or the abusive posts in this set is more consistent in that those posts lean towards explicit abuse. Since the F-score on the non-abusive class is lower for the narrow topic samples (93.65 vs. 95.57%), it is less likely that this sample is more homogeneous. We will investigate the latter aspect below.

The results for the narrow topic are closer to the trend reported by Wiegand et al. (2019) that biased topic sampling reaches lower F-scores. This shows that the definition of the topics included for sampling also have a considerable effect on results.

5.4 Explicit and Implicit Abuse

Wiegand et al. (2019) have also looked at the pro-

portion of explicit vs. implicit abuse on the abusive portion of the datasets, reported in the final column in Table 5. Explicit abuse means that the abusive post contains abusive words; the abuse in implicitly abusive posts is conveyed, for example, "via negation, sarcasm, or negative stereotypes" (Wiegand et al., 2019). They determine explicit abuse using their automatically created lexicon (Wiegand et al., 2018)[5]. We use the two versions of the lexicon by Wiegand et al. (2018) and ours discussed in section 4.2.

In Table 7, we show the proportions of abusive posts in the first sample per sampling condition, based on all 3 lexicons and the original Kaggle set. The first column corresponds to the proportion of explicit abuse in the abusive posts only. The second column shows the proportion in non-abusive posts, and the third column shows the proportion of abuse in *all* posts of the sample. We added the second and third column after a first look at the proportion of abusive posts when using the Wiegand extended lexicon: In all three sampling conditions, the proportion of explicit abuse based on this lexicon is 90.78% or higher. This hints at a significant amount of non-abusive words being included in the lexicon; i.e., over-generation. We test this by looking at the proportion of abusive words in the non-abusive posts and in all data of a sample. If there is a significant proportion beyond the proportion of abusive posts, we have an objective corroboration of our assumption, independent of human judgment. In this setting, using the Wiegand extended lexicon,

---

[5]More specifically, they use the extended version (p.c. M. Wiegand).

Lexicon	Abusive		Non-abusive		All	
	Random	Wide Topic	Random	Wide Topic	Random	Wide Topic
Wiegand extended	90.78	95.16	76.86	90.83	78.18	91.09
Wiegand base	79.83	84.09	41.32	59.83	44.98	61.30
manual	64.03	65.22	14.76	25.32	19.43	27.75

Table 7: Proportion of explicit abuse in different samples of the original Kaggle dataset.

Lexicon	Abusive			Non-abusive			All		
	Rand.	WT	NT	Rand.	WT	NT	Rand.	WT	NT
Wiegand extended	91.55	93.84	95.07	78.59	88.95	87.37	79.64	89.34	88.30
Wiegand base	68.25	74.65	76.28	44.01	56.48	56.77	45.98	58.15	59.42
manual	31.69	39.15	39.39	15.36	20.82	19.94	16.68	22.50	22.58

Table 8: Proportion of explicit abuse in different samples of the large Kaggle dataset (WT = wide topic, NT = narrow topic).

the proportion of explicit abuse is 78.18% in all posts and 76.86% in non-abusive posts, thus corroborating our assumption.

Overall, we see that the three versions of the lexicon have a significant influence on the proportions of abuse: If we use the Wiegand base lexicon, the proportion of explicit abuse in the whole sample ranges between 44.98% and 61.30%, which is still high given that the proportion of abusive posts in these samples are 9.50% for boosted random sampling and 6.10% for biased topic sampling. For the manually pruned lexicon, the proportions range between 14.76% and 27.75%. This shows the importance of having a high-quality lexicon rather than a large scale list.

When we focus on the manual lexicon and the two sampling methods, we see that the proportion of explicit abuse in both types of samples is very similar, 64.03% for the random sample and 65.22% for the biased topic sample. Thus, the proportion of explicit abuse cannot be the reason for the performance differences we have seen across sampling types for the abusive class.

Table 8 shows the proportions for the large Kaggle set. While we see similar trends with regard to the choice of lexicon, we also see a considerable difference between boosted random sampling and the two biased topic sampling strategies: Based on the manual lexicon, random sampling results in 31.69% explicitly abusive posts while the biased topic sampling strategies reach 39.15% and 39.39%. This may be an explanation of the difference in F-scores on the abusive class in Table 4, but it does not explain the difference in F-scores of around 10 points between the two biased topic

sampling methods in Table 6.

When comparing the proportions of explicit abuse across the two Kaggle sets, we see different trends, with more similarities across sampling strategies in the original Kaggle set, and major differences in the large Kaggle set. This indicates that the proportion of explicit and implicit abuse can be more dependent on the text sources than on the different sampling strategies.

5.5 Out-of-Vocabulary Rates

We calculated out-of-vocabulary percentages for both datasets on three conditions: all data, abusive posts only, and non-abusive posts only. These percentages are shown in Table 9. In a way, the OOV rates give us an indication of the topic diversity in given sample. It is to be expected that the original Kaggle set has a higher proportion of OOV words than the large Kaggle set since Wikipedia talkpages cover a wider range of topics than the comments in the large Kaggle set. However, it is interesting to see that this is also true for the biased topic sampling using the wide definition of topics. Here, one would expect the difference between the datasets to be smaller since we choose posts using the same list of topics. However, it is possible that the larger size of the large Kaggle set simply provides more variety to choose from.

It is surprising that the narrow topic has a higher proportion of OOV than the wide topic. In general, abusive posts have the highest OOV rate, independent of sampling strategies. These trends indicate that abusive language seems to be more creative in word choice, as are posts concerning Trump.

In terms of predictive power with regard to clas-

Sampling	original Kaggle			large Kaggle		
	all	non-abusive	abusive	all	non-abusive	abusive
Random	4.24	4.18	12.24	2.66	2.77	9.26
Wide Topic	3.17	3.19	9.65	1.88	2.02	5.27
Narrow Topic				2.17	2.27	7.36

Table 9: Out-of-vocabulary statistics for the two Kaggle datasets.

sifier performance, the OOV rate is also not useful. For example, the narrow topic sampling in the large Kaggle set results in a higher F-score by 10% absolute in comparison to the wide topic samples. However, in terms of OOV rate, the more difficult dataset has a lower OOV rate. Thus, the best predictor of classifier performance is the proportion of abusive posts in a sample. But the differences across datasets are generally larger than the differences across sampling conditions, again stressing that the textual sources of the datasets have more influence on classifier performance than sampling strategies.

6 Conclusion and Future Work

We have investigated the interaction between different sampling strategies with classification results for abusive language detection datasets. We have reproduced the two sampling strategies distinguished by Wiegand et al. (2019), boosted random sampling and biased topic sampling, but we applied them to the same dataset, in order to eliminate the differences resulting from the textual sources. We have then extended our experiments to a larger dataset to see how much influence the underlying textual source has on the result. We generally found similar trends to Wiegand et al. (2019), but much less pronounced, which indicates that the textual source has more influence on the results than the sampling strategy. Another important variable is the definition of topic: If we narrow the topic to one word, the proportion of abusive posts increases (but is still well below two of the three dataset using biased topic sampling, Waseem and Kumar), and the F-score decreases (but is still higher than all of the F-scores reported by Wiegand et al. (2019)[6]). All of our findings emphasize the importance of testing across different datasets. We have also seen the importance of having a high quality lexicon in order to determine the difference between explicit and implicit abuse.

For the future, we plan to have a closer look at

---
[6] Note than Wiegand et al. (2019) used a different classifier.

the datasets since it is still unclear why some of the datasets are more difficult to classify with high accuracy than others, which cannot be explained by class skewing, sampling technique, or proportion of explicit and implicit abuse. Additionally, we will experiment with settings in which training and test data have different biases, i.e., if we sampled using different sampling strategies. We will also extend our efforts to create high quality lexicons of explicit abuse. Our ultimate goal is to improve classification performance for implicit abuse.

References

Pinkesh Badjatiya, Manish Gupta, and Vasudeva Varma. 2019. Stereotypical bias removal for hate speech detection task using knowledge-based generalizations. In *WWW '19: The World Wide Web Conference*, pages 49–59, San Francisco, CA.

Thomas Davidson, Debasmita Bhattacharya, and Ingmar Weber. 2019. Racial bias in hate speech and abusive language detection datasets. In *Proceedings of the Third Workshop on Abusive Language Online*, pages 25–35, Florence, Italy.

He He, Sheng Zha, and Haohan Wang. 2019. Unlearn dataset bias in natural language inference by fitting the residual. In *Proceedings of the 2nd Workshop on Deep Learning Approaches for Low-Resource NLP (DeepLo 2019)*, pages 132–142, Hong Kong, China.

Ritesh Kumar, Atul Kr. Ojha, Shervin Malmasi, and Marcos Zampieri. 2018. Benchmarking aggression identification in social media. In *Proceedings of the First Workshop on Trolling, Aggression and Cyberbullying (TRAC)*, pages 1–11, Santa Fe, NM.

Ji Ho Park, Jamin Shin, and Pascale Fung. 2018. Reducing gender bias in abusive language detection. In *Proceedings of the Conference on Empirical Methods in Natural Language Processing (EMNLP)*, pages 2799–2804, Brussels, Belgium.

Fabian Pedregosa, Gaël Varoquaux, Alexandre Gramfort, Vincent Michel, Bertrand Thirion, Olivier Grisel, Mathieu Blondel, Peter Prettenhofer, Ron Weiss, Vincent Dubourg, et al. 2011. Scikit-learn: Machine learning in Python. *Journal of Machine Learning Research*, 12:2825–2830.

Juliet van Rosendaal, Tommaso Caselli, and Malvina Nissim. 2020. Lower bias, higher density abusive language datasets: A recipe. In *Proceedings of the LREC Workshop on Resources and Techniques for User and Author Profiling in Abusive Language*, pages 14–19, Marseille, France.

Maarten Sap, Dallas Card, Saadia Gabriel, Yejin Choi, and Noah A. Smith. 2019. The risk of racial bias in hate speech detection. In *Proceedings of the 57th Annual Meeting of the Association for Computational Linguistics*, pages 1668–1678, Florence, Italy.

William Warner and Julia Hirschberg. 2012. Detecting hate speech on the World Wide Web. In *Proceedings of the Second Workshop on Language in Social Media*, pages 19–26, Montréal, Canada.

Zeerak Waseem and Dirk Hovy. 2016. Hateful symbols or hateful people? Predictive features for hate speech detection on twitter. In *Proceedings of the NAACL Student Research Workshop*, pages 88–93, San Diego, CA.

Michael Wiegand, Josef Ruppenhofer, and Thomas Kleinbauer. 2019. Detection of abusive language: The problem of biased datasets. In *Proceedings of the 2019 Conference of the North American Chapter of the Association for Computational Linguistics: Human Language Technologies*, pages 602–608, Minneapolis, MN.

Michael Wiegand, Josef Ruppenhofer, Anna Schmidt, and Clayton Greenberg. 2018. Inducing a lexicon of abusive words – a feature-based approach. In *Proceedings of the 2018 Conference of the North American Chapter of the Association for Computational Linguistics: Human Language Technologies*, pages 1046–1056, New Orleans, LA.

Ellery Wulczyn, Nithum Thain, and Lucas Dixon. 2017. Ex Machina: Personal attacks seen at scale. In *Proceedings of the International World Wide Web Conference (WWW)*, pages 1391–1399, Perth, Australia.

Attending the Emotions to Detect Online Abusive Language

Niloofar Safi Samghabadi, Afsheen Hatami, Mahsa Shafaei
Sudipta Kar and Thamar Solorio
Department of Computer Science, University of Houston
{nsafisamghabadi, amhatami, mshafaei, skar3, tsolorio}@uh.edu

Abstract

In recent years, abusive behavior has become a serious issue in online social networks. In this paper, we present a new corpus for the task of abusive language detection that is collected from a semi-anonymous online platform, and unlike the majority of other available resources, is not created based on a specific list of bad words. We also develop computational models to incorporate emotions into textual cues to improve aggression identification. We evaluate our proposed methods on a set of corpora related to the task and show promising results with respect to abusive language detection.

1 Introduction

Nowadays, abusive behavior has become a rising problem in online communities (Jones et al., 2013; Ybarra and Mitchell, 2004). Such adverse behavior can have serious effects on the physical, mental, and social health of online users, among whom teenagers and young adults are the most vulnerable group.[1] To combat this problem at scale, automated Natural Language Processing (NLP) systems can help identify potentially abusive language.

In recent years, there have been several efforts to automate the detection of offensive language across social media platforms. Lexical features have been proven to work quite well for this task (Dinakar et al., 2012; Davidson et al., 2017). However, such features introduce some bias into the systems by heavily relying on profane words, whereas reports show that most profanities are used in a neutral way in today's teen talks (Samghabadi et al., 2017; Vidgen et al., 2019). The following examples signify the need for linguistically more sophisticated techniques beyond profanity dependent models to detect abusive language:

Neutral: *Damn you are such a BEAUTIFUL F*CKING MOMMY!*
Offensive: *u should use ur hands to choke urself.*

In fact, most of the resources available for abusive language detection have been created based on either a list of bad words or seed words related to abusive topics. In this paper, we aim at tackling this limitation by proposing a new method for sampling the data without focusing on a specific bad word list. We are interested to collect this new dataset from a social media website that is specifically popular among youth, since they are the most vulnerable group of users when it comes to online abuse.We scrape our data from Curious Cat,[2] a semi-anonymous question-answering website, that has increased in popularity among teenagers. This platform provides a way to interact anonymously, which opens the door for digital abuse. On this website, users can choose not to reveal any personal information on their account, as well as post comments/questions on other users' timelines anonymously. Additionally, on average, the posts are too short in length. These properties limit both the content of a post, as well as the information about the sender of that post.

To overcome the aforementioned challenges within the data, we propose a new methodology to integrate emotional information into textual cues from the input text to decide whether it is offensive or not. Our main contributions in this paper are as follows:

- We introduce a new corpus for the task of abusive language detection, which is not created based on a specific list of profane words.

- We develop approaches for incorporating emotions into textual information to improve abusive language detection, and create unified

---

[1] http://enough.org/stats_cyberbullying

[2] https://curiouscat.me

Proceedings of the Fourth Workshop on Online Abuse and Harms, pages 79–88
Online, November 20, 2020. ©2020 Association for Computational Linguistics
https://doi.org/10.18653/v1/P17

deep neural models that show promising results across several relevant corpora from various domains.

- We introduce Gated Emotion-Aware Attention (GEA) that dynamically learns the contribution of emotion and textual information to weigh the words inside a sequence. We show that this new attention mechanism significantly outperforms the regular attention, which only utilizes textual hidden representations to learn the word weights when the input text is short and noisy.

2 Related Work

Abusive language identification and hate speech detection have been addressed by many research papers (Mishra et al., 2019c; Schmidt and Wiegand, 2017). Most of the related works have employed feature engineering approaches, and use a combination of different types of lexical, syntactic, semantic, sentiment and lexicon-based features along with classic machine learning algorithms such as Support Vector Machines (SVM), and Logistic Regression (Samghabadi et al., 2018; Davidson et al., 2017; Nobata et al., 2016; Gitari et al., 2015; Van Hee et al., 2015).

Due to the popularity of deep neural networks, multiple studies have recently been conducted in order to explore the performance of these models on the task of aggression identification. Most of these studies are focused on hate speech detection within Twitter. Gambäck and Sikdar (2017) use a Convolutional Neural Network (CNN) based model, and investigate different textual and embedding features as the input to the model where word2vec produces the best results. Badjatiya et al. (2017) conduct an extensive evaluation on multiple traditional and deep learning approaches, and report the best results using an ensemble of LSTM and Gradient Boosted Decision Trees. There are also a few works that try to incorporate user information into the model, using approaches such as Graph Neural Networks (Mishra et al., 2019a,b; Ribeiro et al., 2018) to learn the structure of online communities along with the linguistic behaviors of the users within them. The main limitation of these approaches is that they are not applicable to the social media platforms that offer anonymity options to the users such as Curious Cat and ask.fm.

Several research papers have proven that emotion lexicons are helpful features for the tasks of

abusive language and hate-speech detection (Koufakou and Scott, 2020; Wiegand et al., 2018; Martins et al., 2018; Corazza et al., 2018; Alorainy et al., 2018; Gao and Huang, 2017). There is also one study that shows jointly modeling of emotion classification and abuse detection, through a multi-task approach, can improve the performance of the latter task (Rajamanickam et al., 2020).

Our methodology has two key differences in contrast to other existing methods: (1) Instead of using an ensemble approach, we create unified deep neural architectures that show very promising results across multiple domains, and (2) We do not use any user-level information in our model. Therefore, the model can be applied to various online platforms, even those that offer anonymity.

3 Dataset

We collected the data from Curious Cat, which is a semi-anonymous, question-answer social media platform. Curious Cat is very popular among the youth and has more than 15 million registered users. On this website, users can choose not to reveal any personal information on their account, as well as post comments/questions on other users' timelines anonymously. The anonymity option available on Curious Cat opens the door for digital abuse. Due to these properties, there are two significant limitations with respect to Curious Cat data: (1) The post content is usually too short making abuse detection harder, and (2) There is very limited information, if any, about the sender of a post.

3.1 Data Collection and Annotation

We crawled around 500K English question-answer pairs from 2K randomly chosen users of Curious Cat. To avoid having bias through some specific swear words in the data, we did not use a particular list of bad words to find potentially offensive messages. Instead, we exploited the state-of-the-art classification method for abusive language detection on ask.fm (Samghabadi et al., 2017)[3] because of two reasons: (1) The format of the data in Curious Cat and ask.fm is very similar,[4] and (2) This method utilizes lexical features that make it capable of learning new words and phrases related to the offensive class. This model combines lexical, domain-specific, and emotion-related features and

---

[3]We use the code available in `https://github.com/NiloofarSafi/Detecting-Nastiness`

[4]`https://ask.fm`

uses an SVM classifier to detect nastiness. We train that classifier on the full ask.fm dataset and apply it to Curious Cat to automatically label all rows of data. While ask.fm and Curious Cat have the same format, we noticed key differences between them, which may substantially affect the quality of automatic labeling. For instance, with Curious Cat, we observe numerous sexual posts that are full of profanities, yet not offensive to the user, e.g, a user may encourage others to post sexual comments to him/her, like the following example:

Question: *I wanna s*ck your d*ck so hard and taste your c*m.*
Answer: *Enter my DMs beautiful.*

Therefore, we randomly selected 2,482 question-answer pairs, where 60% were chosen from the negative/offensive labeled data, and 40% selected from the positive/neutral labeled data (we only considered the label of the questions). Four in-lab annotators[5] annotated the data. Each row was tagged by three different annotators, and the final label assigned to each instance by majority voting. Based on the annotations, the Fleiss's kappa (Fleiss, 1971) score is 0.5 that shows a moderate agreement among the annotators. Figure 1 shows the rate of "complete agreement" among all annotators for positive and negative questions and answers. By complete agreement, we mean the case where all the annotators assigned the same class to an instance (in Curious Cat data, an instance could be a question or an answer). Based on the figure, the complete agreement on the negative/offensive class is much less than the positive/neutral one. This observation demonstrates the fact that the perceived level of aggression is very subjective, so our final agreement score is reasonable Sap et al. (2019). It is also interesting that for negative instances, the annotation results show more complete agreements on top of the questions compared to answers. This indicates that it was more difficult for the annotators to decide whether a reply to a comment is offensive.

3.2 Data Statistics

Table 1 shows the final distribution of the proposed Curious Cat corpus. Statistics show that 95% of negative comments were posted on users' timelines anonymously. Looking at the labeled data, we also found that about 100 instances of abusive posts do not include any profanities, and 1327 pos-

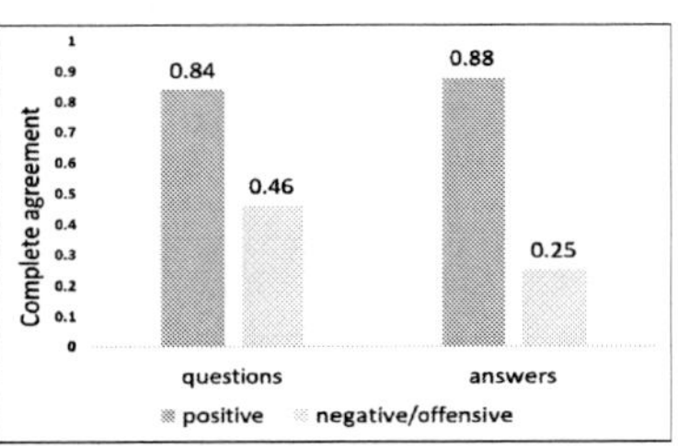

Figure 1: Complete agreement for questions and answers across negative/offensive and positive labeled data.

itive/neutral posts have at least one profane word. It shows that the proposed sampling method could capture the implicit forms of abusive language as well as explicit ones. This technique also samples the posts that include bad words, but are not attacking other users.

Class	Question	Answer	Total
Offensive	609	171	780
Neutral	1873	2311	4184
Total	2482	2482	4964

Table 1: Curious Cat data distribution.

3.3 Other Abusive Language Datasets

We also experimented with the following available corpora to better qualify the performance of the proposed models: (1) ask.fm dataset (Samghabadi et al., 2017), (2) Kaggle insult dataset,[6] and (3) Wikipedia personal attacks dataset (Wulczyn et al., 2017). Table 2 compares all resources that we use in this paper. Our Curious Cat data can be accessed through our website.[7]

Data	Size	%Negativity	Avg length
Curious Cat	4964	15.71%	15.30
ask.fm	11194	18.08%	13.92
Kaggle	6597	26.42%	38.35
Wikipedia	~115K	11.70%	81.29

Table 2: Data comparison. The last column shows the average length of the posts with respect to the number of words.

4 Methodology

Emojis help online users to better express their feelings within the text. With this notion, we hypothesize that emojis are effective tools to provide additional context for online comments, resulting in bet-

---

[5] Including one graduate and three undergraduate students

[6] https://www.kaggle.com/c/
detecting-insults-in-social-commentary
[7] https://ritual.uh.edu/
curious-cat-corpus/

ter offensive language recognition. For capturing emotions from the text, we use DeepMoji (Felbo et al., 2017) pre-trained on Twitter data. As for the output, this model creates a representation for 64 frequently used online emojis that shows how relevant each emoji is to a given text. Figure 2 illustrates the top 5 emojis that DeepMoji assigned to one neutral and one offensive instances in our Curious Cat data. Both of these comments are very short and include the bad word "die". We can see that DeepMoji correctly recognized the tone of the language in both examples. The colors also show the attention weights assigned by DeepMoji model. The darker colors indicate higher attention weights. Interestingly, the word "die" is attended the most in the offensive instance.

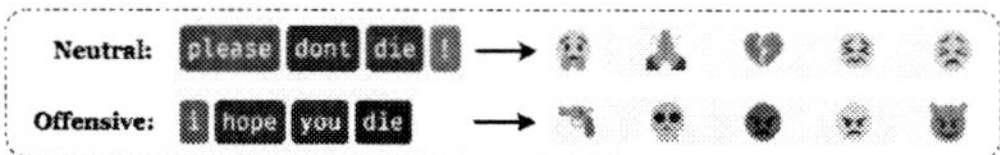

Figure 2: Top 5 emojis that the DeepMoji model assigned to one neutral and one offensive instances from our Curious Cat data. The words are colored based on the attention weights given by the DeepMoji model. Darker colors show higher attention weights.

In this paper, we examine two different approaches to create the model that combines Deep-Moji and textual representations to detect whether a given input text is offensive or not. The motivation behind this idea is to exploit emotional representation to better distinguish the use of profanities in an offensive way from a neutral way. Both models include the two following main modules:

1. **Bidirectional Long Short-Term Memory (BiLSTM):** This module has an embedding layer that generates the corresponding embedding matrix for the given input text. Then, we pass the embedding vectors to a Bidirectional LSTM (BiLSTM) layer to extract the contextual information from the sequences of words.

2. **DeepMoji:** This module feeds the input to the DeepMoji model and pass the last hidden representation through a non-linear layer to project it into the same space as the output from the BiLSTM module.

For combining the output of the above mentioned modules, we try two following approaches:

Concatenation: One popular way to incorporate information into deep neural models is concatenation. In this approach, we pass the output of BiLSTM to an attention layer, same as Bahdanau et al. (2015), to aggregate the output hidden states of BiLSTM into a single vector. Within this layer, we calculate the weighted sum of $r = \sum_i \alpha_i h_i$, where $h_i = [\overrightarrow{h_i}; \overleftarrow{h_i}]$ is the concatenation of the forward and backward hidden states of BiLSTM. α_i stands for the relative importance of words which is measured as follows:

$$\alpha_i = softmax(v^T tanh(W_h h_i + b_h)) \qquad (1)$$

where W_h is the weight matrix, and b_h and v are the parameters of the model. We refer to this attention model as the Regular Attention (RA) in the rest of paper. We concatenate the outputs of the RA and DeepMoji module. The resulting vector is then fed into a hidden dense layer with 100 neurons. To improve generalization of the model, we use batch normalization and dropout with a rate of 0.5 after the hidden layer. Finally, we use a two neuron output layer along with softmax activation to predict whether the input text is offensive or not.

Gated Emotion-Aware Attention (GEA): In this approach, instead of directly concatenating the text and DeepMoji representations, we hypothesize that it is not enough to only focus on the word representations in the attention model because of two reasons: (1) Many bad words may also be used in a neutral way to make jokes and provide compliments among friends, and (2) Some texts do not contain any profanities, but are still offensive to the receiver. Both reasons may confuse the model for final prediction. Therefore, we design the GEA mechanism to consider not only the word representations, but also the emotions behind the text to better determine the most relevant words in a post. We use the idea of Gated Multimodal Unit (Ovalle et al., 2017) to create GEA. The overall architecture of this model is shown in Figure 3.

Let us assume that h_i and e_i are the output representations of BiLSTM and DeepMoji modules, respectively. For each of them, we have a gate neuron (represented by σ nodes in Figure 3) that controls the contribution of each of these features to calculate the attention weights. We calculate the α_i as follows:

$$h_i' = tanh(W_h.h_i) \qquad (2)$$

$$e_i' = tanh(W_e.e_i) \qquad (3)$$

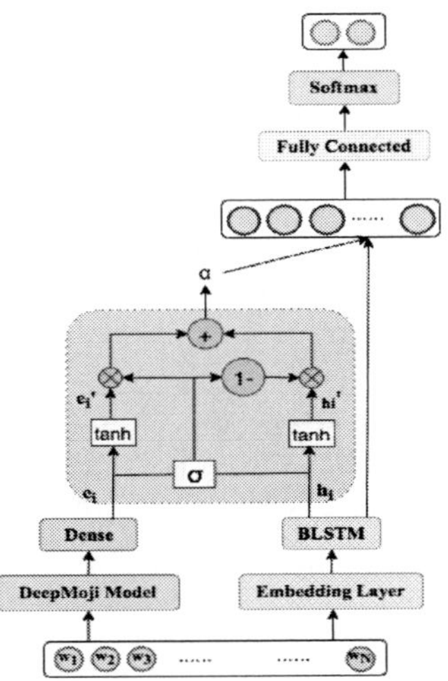

Figure 3: Overall architecture of the Gated Emotion-Aware Attention (GEA) model.

$$z_i = \sigma(W_z.[h_i', e_i']) \tag{4}$$

$$hid_i = z_i * h_i' + (1 - z_i) * e_i' \tag{5}$$

$$\alpha_i = softmax(v^T hid_i) \tag{6}$$

where $\{W_h, W_e, W_z\}$ are weight matrices, and v is the parameters of the model. W_e is shared across the words and adds emotion effects to the attention weights. The output of the attention layer is the weighted sum r calculated as follows:

$$r = \sum_i \alpha_i h_i \tag{7}$$

Finally, we pass the output of the attention mechanism to a fully connected layer with the same settings as the Concatenation model, and generate a two-dimensional output.

5 Experiments and Results

We stratified split Curious Cat data into train and test sets with a 70:30 training to test ratio, and use 20% of the train data as the validation set. For the other corpora, we use the same train, validation, and test folds as used by the original papers. As for preprocessing, we truncate the posts to 200 tokens, and right-pad the shorter sequences with zeros. We use Binary Cross Entropy to compute the loss between predicted and actual labels. To smooth the imbalance problem in the datasets, we add information about class weights to the loss function. The network weights were updated using Adam optimizer (Kingma and Ba, 2015) with a learning rate of $1e^{-5}$. We trained the model over

200 epochs, and reported the test results based on the best macro F1 obtained from the validation set.

5.1 Baselines and SOTA Approaches

We compared our proposed model against the state-of-the-art and several strong baselines listed bellow:

DeepMoji Baseline: We directly passed the output of the DeepMoji module to the dense and output layers. The motivation behind this baseline was to estimate the power of the DeepMoji model to detect abusive language on its own.

BiLSTM + RA: In this baseline, we do the classification, only using the textual information. This model uses the RA on top of BiLSTM module and directly passes the output representation to the fully connected and output layers. The motivation behind this model is to compare the performance of RA with GEA.

BERT Baseline: We directly passed the hidden representation of the BERT last layer for [CLS] token to the dense and output layer. With this model, we aim at testing the power of BERT as a feature extractor for the task of abusive language detection.

Sam'17 (Samghabadi et al., 2017): This is the state-of-the-art for the ask.fm corpus and applies an SVM classifier on top of a combination of various features.

Kaggle Winner: It shows the results of the winner of Kaggle competition on detecting insults in social commentary. This model includes an ensemble of several machine learning classifier with word n-grams and character n-grams lexical features.[8]

Bodapati'19 (Bodapati et al., 2019): This work reported the state-of-the-art results on the Wikipedia dataset. The authors added a single dense layer on top of BERT to fine-tune it for the task of abusive language detection. We implemented this model ourselves since the code was not released.

5.2 Classification Results

For the evaluation, we use the F1 score for the negative/offensive class, since this is the class of

---

[8]The code for this model is available through the competition discussion page: `https://www.kaggle.com/c/detecting-insults-in-social-commentary/leaderboard`

interest. We also report the weighted F1 score, which calculates the average performance over both classes. This is to ensure that the model does not sacrifice the positive/neutral class to increase the performance of the negative class.

The nature of the data could be different across various domains. For example, in Curious Cat and ask.fm data, informal language is used more often than Kaggle and Wikipedia. Therefore, the type of embeddings we use in our experiments could be an important factor for the final performance. We plan to use BERT language model in our experiments as the embeddings; however, we prefer not to fine-tune BERT weights because of the computational cost. Therefore, we run our BiLSTM + RA baseline with the two following embedding models to see which one works best across all corpora:

1. 200-dimensional *Glove*[9] embeddings trained on Twitter

2. $BERT_{base}$ (uncased) contextualized embeddings trained on the BookCorpus and English Wikipedia corpus (Devlin et al., 2019).[10]

Based on the results shown in Table 3, it seems that BERT performs better than Glove embeddings across all datasets, despite the fact that we do not fine-tune its weights. Therefore, we use BERT as the embeddings in the rest of the experiments.

	Glove		BERT	
	F1	W F1	F1	W F1
Curious Cat	60.16	87.1	**65.29**	**88.2**
ask.fm	51.69	83.9	**52.44**	**84.0**
Kaggle	69.73	85.1	**75.12**	**87.0**
Wikipedia	75.60	95.3	**79.21**	**95.9**

Table 3: Comparison between Glove and BERT embeddings using BiLSTM + RA baseline. We do not fine-tune BERT in our experiments and only use it as a feature extractor.

Table 4 compares the performance of GEA and RA attention mechanisms. For Curious Cat and ask.fm corpora, BiLSTM + GEA model performs significantly[11] better than BiLSTM + RA, which demonstrates the effectiveness of our proposed attention to detect offensive language in short and noisy texts. BiLSTM + RA shows slightly better performance on Kaggle, as well as significant improvement on Wikipedia datasets in comparison

<hr>

[9] https://nlp.stanford.edu/projects/glove

[10] We only use BERT as a feature extractor.

[11] All the significant testing are done using Mcnemar test.

with BiLSTM + GEA. This observation could be explained by the following reason: the length of documents are longer in Kaggle and Wikipedia compared to Curious Cat and ask.fm. Therefore, the DeepMoji module which is trained on short tweets has probably some difficulties to generate the emotion representation for Kaggle and Wikipedia data.

	BiLSTM + RA		BiLSTM + GEA	
	F1	W F1	F1	W F1
Curious Cat	65.29	88.2	**72.22***	**90.9***
ask.fm	52.44	84.0	**60.70***	**85.2***
Kaggle	**75.12**	**87.0**	74.98	86.7
Wikipedia	**79.21***	**95.9***	77.15	95.5

Table 4: Comparison between RA and GEA attention models. The starred results show significant improvement compared to the opposite model.

Table 5 shows the classification results, including the performance of our proposed models, Baselines, and state-of-the-art approaches across all four different corpora. For the Curious Cat data, DeepMoji Baseline shows very promising results. This model performs significantly better than fine-tuned BERT (Bodapati'19), which shows the power of DeepMoji representations. Combining the text and emotion information through either BiLSTM + RA + DeepMoji, or BiLSTM + GEA models produces results that are slightly better than DeepMoji Baseline.

For the ask.fm corpus, BiLSTM + RA + DeepMoji and BiLSTM + GEA + DeepMoji indicate almost similar performance. The former performs slightly better on the negative/offensive class (showing a higher F1), while the latter works better on the positive/neutral class (having a higher weighted F1, as well as a very promising F1). The reported results for both models are significantly better than the state-of-the-art results on ask.fm (Sam'17), DeepMoji baseline, and fine-tuned BERT (Bodapati'19) that prove the effectiveness of our proposed approaches to integrate emotion information into the textual representation.

For Kaggle, Bodapati'19 reports best results. However, the performance of that model compared to our best model, BERT Baseline + DeepMoji, is not significantly better under the Mcnemar test. Although none of our main models (BiLSTM + EA + DeepMoji and BiLSTM + GEA) is the winner for Kaggle, still, the best performing model across our proposed approaches and baselines (i.e., BERT Baseline + DeepMoji) has DeepMoji as part of its

Model		Curious Cat		ask.fm		Kaggle		Wikipedia	
		F1	W F1	F1	W F1	F1	W F1	F1	W F1
DeepMoji Baseline		71.90	91.0	59.21	85.1	73.45	86.0	72.20	94.5
BERT Baseline	–	40.86	81.6	37.29	80.1	64.72	81.4	50.84	89.6
	+ DeepMoji	70.17	89.9	60.79	85.6	76.50	87.6	73.24	94.9
BiLSTM + RA	–	65.29	88.2	52.44	84.0	75.12	87.0	79.21	**95.9**
	+ DeepMoji	72.05	**91.1**	**62.40**	85.7	76.06	87.7	78.35	95.7
BiLSTM + GEA	–	**72.22**	90.9	60.70	85.2	74.98	86.7	77.15	95.5
	+ DeepMoji	71.09	90.1	62.12	**86.0**	75.47	87.4	77.86	95.7
Sam'17		65.54	88.3	58.47	84.1	72.85	86.0	74.48	94.7
Kaggle Winner		65.86	90.0	51.49	84.4	72.03	86.5	74.45	95.2
Bodapati'19		68.19	89.9	56.38	85.0	**76.86**	**88.5**	**80.13**	**95.9**

Table 5: Classification results in terms of F1-score for the negative/offensive class and weighted F1. +DeepMoji refers to the experiments in which we directly concatenated DeepMoji vectors with the last hidden representation generated by the model.

architectures. This model significantly outperforms the Kaggle Winner results as well.

For Wikipedia, Bodapati et al. (2019) report the weighted F1 of 95.7 as the state-of-the-art results. However, when we re-implement their model, we achieve a slightly better weighted F1 of 95.9 as what we report in Table 5. Although we achieve the same weighted F1 of 95.9 with BiLSTM + RA model, we can see that the F1 for the offensive class is around 1% worse than Bodapati'19, indicating that our model probably works better for the neutral class. For this corpus, it seems that integrating the emotion information into the model decreases the performance, which is inline with what we observe in Table 4. A possible reason for this is that the Wikipedia corpus, in nature, is very similar to the data used for pre-training BERT, and is very different from the Twitter data used for pre-training DeepMoji. Therefore, in this case, the text representation generated by BERT is more powerful than the DeepMoji representation. Then, combining these two representations does not improve the results.

Overall, we can conclude that:

1. For short and noisy text data like Curious Cat and ask.fm, integrating the emotion information (by DeepMoji representation) into the textual representation produces the best results in comparison with all other baselines. It demonstrates the advantages of using DeepMoji representation to extract contextual information from online content. The reason is that DeepMoji considers fine-grained emoji categories, which capture different levels of emotional feelings (e.g., �😠, ☠, and 😡 show different levels of anger). Such information helps the model to determine the tone of language more precisely. In Section 5.3, we provide a more detailed analysis of the DeepMoji model.

2. For Kaggle and Wikipedia data that are longer and more structured, fine-tuned BERT (Bodapati'19) is the winner. However, the results reported by this model are not significantly better than our best performing approaches (i.e., BERT Baseline + DeepMoji for Kaggle, and BiLSTM + RA for Wikipedia). It should be noted that unlike Bodapati'19, we do not fine-tune BERT (fine-tuning BERT is computationally expensive, especially on large corpora like Wikipedia), which is a good achievement.

3. There are major differences between the performances of different models across the various datasets that we use. This observation shows that it is very challenging to build a model that works well in different domains. It also confirms the need to collect more data from a variety of social media platforms.

5.3 Why Does DeepMoji Work?

To show why emoji representations are helpful to detect the abusive language in social media, we plot the emoji distribution over the neutral and offensive classes for the Curious Cat training data (Figure 4). For creating this plot, we use the average DeepMoji vector extracted for each instance. This vector shows the relevance of each emoji to a specific comment. We create the overall emoji vector per class by averaging the emoji vectors extracted for all of the instances of the same class. Finally, we select 19 out of the 64 emojis used in the DeepMoji project to create the final plot. As it is shown in Figure 4, there are different patterns visible for the neutral and offensive classes. This

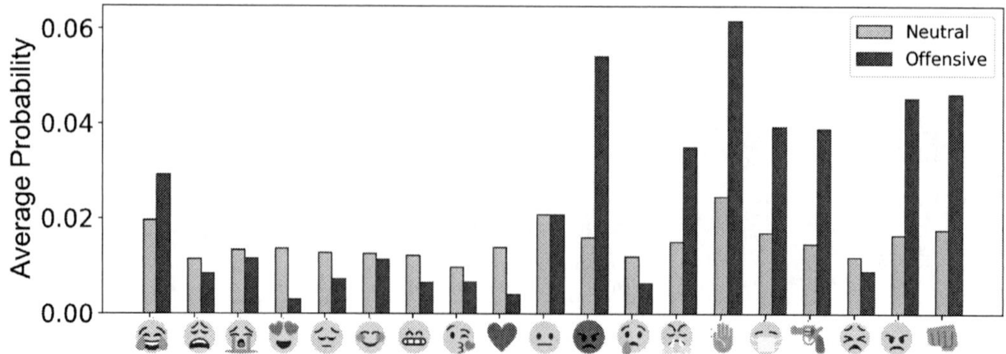

Figure 4: Emoji distribution over Curious Cat data.

observation validates our hypothesis on why it is useful to incorporate emoji information into the model.

Based on Figure 4, angry emojis (😡, 😤, 😠) are highly correlated with the offensive class, inversely happy and love faces (😄, 😍, ♥) appeared more frequently in the neutral class. For the happy and love faces, 😊 and 😘, the differences between offensive and neutral classes are much less. We believe that this represents the scenarios where a defender (a user who defends the victim of online attacks) tries to support an attacked user by complimenting him/her, while expressing their hatred towards the attackers. Sad faces (😓, 😭, 😔, 😢, 😖) are more frequent in neutral instances than offensive ones. It possibly shows the cases where a user expresses his/her unhappiness in response to an attack. Interestingly, the laughing face, 😆, shows a higher probability for the negative class. This can be linked to the scenario where someone attempts to bully a user by mocking him/her. Additionally, the plot shows exactly the same probabilities for the poker face (😐) over the offensive and neutral classes. So, we can conclude that this emoji does not convey any additional information related to offensive language. Other emojis (✊, ☝, 👊, and 🔫) that indicate the violent and threatening behavior towards the receiver also seem to appear in the offensive class frequently.

6 Conclusion and Future Work

In this paper, we create a new resource for the task of abusive language detection that does not focus on specific list of bad words. We also propose two different approaches for incorporating emotion information into textual representation by pre-

senting end-to-end deep neural models that show very promising results across three existing corpora, and our new corpus for abusive language detection. Based on the results, adding emotion information to the model can improve the performance, especially for short and noisy textual data. As for the future work, due to the fact that perceived level of aggression is very subjective to the user, we plan to jointly model the question and answer within a pair for the Curious Cat and ask.fm data. We believe that the reply that the user provides in response to a received question/comment is a strong indicator whether it was offensive or neutral towards the user. Another possible path in order to move the research forward, is to expand this task to the detection of cyberbullying incidents which has also become a growing concern in online communities.

References

Wafa Alorainy, Pete Burnap, Han Liu, Amir Javed, and Matthew L Williams. 2018. Suspended accounts: A source of tweets with disgust and anger emotions for augmenting hate speech data sample. In *2018 International Conference on Machine Learning and Cybernetics (ICMLC)*, volume 2, pages 581–586. IEEE.

Pinkesh Badjatiya, Shashank Gupta, Manish Gupta, and Vasudeva Varma. 2017. Deep learning for hate speech detection in tweets. In *Proceedings of the 26th International Conference on World Wide Web Companion*, pages 759–760. International World Wide Web Conferences Steering Committee.

Dzmitry Bahdanau, Kyunghyun Cho, and Yoshua Bengio. 2015. Neural machine translation by jointly learning to align and translate. In *3rd International Conference on Learning Representations, ICLR 2015*.

Sravan Bodapati, Spandana Gella, Kasturi Bhattacharjee, and Yaser Al-Onaizan. 2019. Neural word decomposition models for abusive language detection. In *Proceedings of the Third Workshop on Abusive Language Online*, pages 135–145, Florence, Italy. Association for Computational Linguistics.

Michele Corazza, Stefano Menini, Pinar Arslan, Rachele Sprugnoli, Elena Cabrio, Sara Tonelli, Serena Villata, and Fondazione Bruno Kessler. 2018. Comparing different supervised approaches to hate speech detection. *EVALITA Evaluation of NLP and Speech Tools for Italian*, 12:230.

Thomas Davidson, Dana Warmsley, Michael W. Macy, and Ingmar Weber. 2017. Automated hate speech detection and the problem of offensive language. In *Proceedings of the Eleventh International Conference on Web and Social Media, ICWSM 2017, Montréal, Québec, Canada, May 15-18, 2017*, pages 512–515. AAAI Press.

Jacob Devlin, Ming-Wei Chang, Kenton Lee, and Kristina Toutanova. 2019. Bert: Pre-training of deep bidirectional transformers for language understanding. In *Proceedings of the 2019 Conference of the North American Chapter of the Association for Computational Linguistics: Human Language Technologies, Volume 1 (Long and Short Papers)*, pages 4171–4186.

Karthik Dinakar, Birago Jones, Catherine Havasi, Henry Lieberman, and Rosalind Picard. 2012. Common sense reasoning for detection, prevention, and mitigation of cyberbullying. *ACM Transactions on Interactive Intelligent Systems (TiiS)*, 2(3):18.

Bjarke Felbo, Alan Mislove, Anders Søgaard, Iyad Rahwan, and Sune Lehmann. 2017. Using millions of emoji occurrences to learn any-domain representations for detecting sentiment, emotion and sarcasm. In *Proceedings of the 2017 Conference on Empirical Methods in Natural Language Processing, EMNLP 2017, Copenhagen, Denmark, September 9-11, 2017*, pages 1615–1625. Association for Computational Linguistics.

Joseph L Fleiss. 1971. Measuring nominal scale agreement among many raters. *Psychological bulletin*, 76(5):378.

Björn Gambäck and Utpal Kumar Sikdar. 2017. Using convolutional neural networks to classify hate-speech. In *Proceedings of the first workshop on abusive language online*, pages 85–90.

Lei Gao and Ruihong Huang. 2017. Detecting online hate speech using context aware models. In *Proceedings of the International Conference Recent Advances in Natural Language Processing, RANLP 2017*, pages 260–266.

Njagi Dennis Gitari, Zhang Zuping, Hanyurwimfura Damien, and Jun Long. 2015. A lexicon-based approach for hate speech detection. *International Journal of Multimedia and Ubiquitous Engineering*, 10(4):215–230.

Lisa M Jones, Kimberly J Mitchell, and David Finkelhor. 2013. Online harassment in context: Trends from three youth internet safety surveys (2000, 2005, 2010). *Psychology of violence*, 3(1):53.

Diederik P. Kingma and Jimmy Ba. 2015. Adam: A method for stochastic optimization. In *3rd International Conference on Learning Representations, ICLR 2015, San Diego, CA, USA, May 7-9, 2015, Conference Track Proceedings*.

Anna Koufakou and Jason Scott. 2020. Lexicon-enhancement of embedding-based approaches towards the detection of abusive language. In *Proceedings of the Second Workshop on Trolling, Aggression and Cyberbullying*, pages 150–157.

Ricardo Martins, Marco Gomes, José João Almeida, Paulo Novais, and Pedro Henriques. 2018. Hate speech classification in social media using emotional analysis. In *2018 7th Brazilian Conference on Intelligent Systems (BRACIS)*, pages 61–66. IEEE.

Pushkar Mishra, Marco Del Tredici, Helen Yannakoudakis, and Ekaterina Shutova. 2019a. Abusive language detection with graph convolutional networks. In *Proceedings of the 2019 Conference of the North American Chapter of the Association for Computational Linguistics: Human Language Technologies, NAACL-HLT 2019, Minneapolis, MN, USA, June 2-7, 2019, Volume 1 (Long and Short Papers)*, pages 2145–2150. Association for Computational Linguistics.

Pushkar Mishra, Marco Del Tredici, Helen Yannakoudakis, and Ekaterina Shutova. 2019b. Author profiling for hate speech detection. *CoRR*, abs/1902.06734.

Pushkar Mishra, Helen Yannakoudakis, and Ekaterina Shutova. 2019c. Tackling online abuse: A survey of automated abuse detection methods. *CoRR*, abs/1908.06024.

Chikashi Nobata, Joel Tetreault, Achint Thomas, Yashar Mehdad, and Yi Chang. 2016. Abusive language detection in online user content. In *Proceedings of the 25th International Conference on World Wide Web*, WWW '16, pages 145–153, Republic and Canton of Geneva, Switzerland. International World Wide Web Conferences Steering Committee.

John Edison Arevalo Ovalle, Thamar Solorio, Manuel Montes-y-Gómez, and Fabio A. González. 2017. Gated multimodal units for information fusion. In *5th International Conference on Learning Representations, ICLR 2017, Toulon, France, April 24-26, 2017, Workshop Track Proceedings*. OpenReview.net.

Santhosh Rajamanickam, Pushkar Mishra, Helen Yannakoudakis, and Ekaterina Shutova. 2020. Joint modelling of emotion and abusive language detection. In *Proceedings of the 58th Annual Meeting of the Association for Computational Linguistics*, pages 4270–4279, Online. Association for Computational Linguistics.

Manoel Horta Ribeiro, Pedro H Calais, Yuri A Santos, Virgílio AF Almeida, and Wagner Meira Jr. 2018. Characterizing and detecting hateful users on twitter. In *Twelfth International AAAI Conference on Web and Social Media*.

Niloofar Safi Samghabadi, Suraj Maharjan, Alan Sprague, Raquel Diaz-Sprague, and Thamar Solorio. 2017. Detecting nastiness in social media. In *Proceedings of the First Workshop on Abusive Language Online*, pages 63–72.

Niloofar Safi Samghabadi, Deepthi Mave, Sudipta Kar, and Thamar Solorio. 2018. Ritual-uh at TRAC 2018 shared task: Aggression identification. In *Proceedings of the First Workshop on Trolling, Aggression and Cyberbullying, TRAC@COLING 2018, Santa Fe, New Mexico, USA, August 25, 2018*, pages 12–18. Association for Computational Linguistics.

Maarten Sap, Dallas Card, Saadia Gabriel, Yejin Choi, and Noah A Smith. 2019. The risk of racial bias in hate speech detection. In *Proceedings of the 57th Annual Meeting of the Association for Computational Linguistics*, pages 1668–1678.

Anna Schmidt and Michael Wiegand. 2017. A survey on hate speech detection using natural language processing. In *Proceedings of the Fifth International Workshop on Natural Language Processing for Social Media*, pages 1–10.

Cynthia Van Hee, Els Lefever, Ben Verhoeven, Julie Mennes, Bart Desmet, Guy De Pauw, Walter Daelemans, and Véronique Hoste. 2015. Detection and fine-grained classification of cyberbullying events. In *International Conference Recent Advances in Natural Language Processing (RANLP)*, pages 672–680.

Bertie Vidgen, Alex Harris, Dong Nguyen, Rebekah Tromble, Scott Hale, and Helen Margetts. 2019. Challenges and frontiers in abusive content detection. In *Proceedings of the Third Workshop on Abusive Language Online*, pages 80–93, Florence, Italy. Association for Computational Linguistics.

Michael Wiegand, Josef Ruppenhofer, Anna Schmidt, and Clayton Greenberg. 2018. Inducing a lexicon of abusive words – a feature-based approach. In *Proceedings of the 2018 Conference of the North American Chapter of the Association for Computational Linguistics: Human Language Technologies, Volume 1 (Long Papers)*, pages 1046–1056, New Orleans, Louisiana. Association for Computational Linguistics.

Ellery Wulczyn, Nithum Thain, and Lucas Dixon. 2017. Ex machina: Personal attacks seen at scale. In *Proceedings of the 26th International Conference on World Wide Web*, pages 1391–1399. International World Wide Web Conferences Steering Committee.

Michele L Ybarra and Kimberly J Mitchell. 2004. Youth engaging in online harassment: Associations with caregiver–child relationships, internet use, and personal characteristics. *Journal of adolescence*, 27(3):319–336.

Enhancing the Identification of Cyberbullying through Participant Roles

Gathika Ratnayaka[1], Thushari Atapattu[2], Mahen Herath[1], Georgia Zhang[2] and **Katrina Falkner[2]**
[1]Department of Computer Science & Engineering, University of Moratuwa, Katubedda, Sri Lanka
[2]School of Computer Science, The University of Adelaide, Adelaide, Australia
email: thushari.atapattu@adelaide.edu.au

Abstract

Cyberbullying is a prevalent social problem that inflicts detrimental consequences to the health and safety of victims such as psychological distress, anti-social behaviour, and suicide. The automation of cyberbullying detection is a recent but widely researched problem, with current research having a strong focus on a binary classification of bullying versus non-bullying. This paper proposes a novel approach to enhancing cyberbullying detection through role modeling. We utilise a dataset from ASKfm to perform multi-class classification to detect participant roles (e.g. victim, harasser). Our preliminary results demonstrate promising performance including 0.83 and 0.76 of F1-score for cyberbullying and role classification respectively, outperforming baselines.

1 Introduction

The surge of Internet and social media has led to the unprecedented social crisis of cyberbullying, particularly among adolescents. It can lead to various damaging consequences on the health and safety of victims, such as feelings of isolation, depression, and suicide. Cyberbullying is the *repetitive use of aggressive language among peers, with the intention to harm others through digital media* (Rosa et al., 2019). Despite the illegality of harassing others, most social media platforms are susceptible to cyberbullying due to the openness and anonymisation of platforms. Research conducted by Patchin and Hinduja (2019) indicates that cyberbullying victimisation rates have approximately doubled between the years 2007 and 2019. Adolescents, minorities (e.g. refugees, LGBTQI) and women are among common targets of cyberbullying. The sheer amount of cyberbullying-related incidents vastly exceeds the capacity of manual detection and demands the need to develop technology to effectively and automatically detect this.

You're a fucking moron. [harasser]

Why do you talk shit about me? Leave me alone. [victim]

Stop making fun of people, I think she's a good person. [bystander-defender]

LOL, you're right, he is a nobody. [bystander-assistant]

Figure 1: An excerpt from a cyberbullying episode (Van Hee et al., 2015)

The development of automated models to detect cyberbullying is a widely researched problem in recent years, with current research focusing on classifying posts as bullying or non-bullying (Rosa et al., 2019; Al-garadi et al., 2016; Salawu et al., 2020). One of the fundamental gaps in current research is that *all texts from all users are treated equally* without differentiating who has authored bullying and who has been targeted. These models provide a temporary solution by filtering offensive contents. Bullies often find novel ways to bypass technology such as incorporating implicit and subtle forms of language (e.g. sarcasm) and pseudo profiles. Identifying the roles of authors and targets introduces a novel approach to enable more information-rich models and to foster precise detection. A small number of recent studies focus on cyberbullying-related *'participant roles'* (e.g. bully, victim, bystander) (see Figure 1) (Van Hee et al., 2018; Xu et al., 2012; Jacobs et al., 2020).

Motivated by this idea, our work focuses on two tasks, 1) detecting cyberbullying as a binary classification problem, and 2) detecting participant roles as a multi-class classification problem. We build upon previous role identification research and the AMiCA dataset proposed by Van Hee et al. (2018).

Proceedings of the Fourth Workshop on Online Abuse and Harms, pages 89–94
Online, November 20, 2020. ©2020 Association for Computational Linguistics
https://doi.org/10.18653/v1/P17

2   Related Works

In addition to modeling bullying and non-bullying content as a binary classification task (Rosa et al., 2019; Al-garadi et al., 2016; Salawu et al., 2020), several research studies focus on participant role identification (Salawu et al., 2020; Van Hee et al., 2018; Xu et al., 2012) within the cyberbullying context. Xu et al. (2012) defined 8 roles - *bully, victim, bystander, assistant, defender, reporter, accuser* and *reinforcer*, based on the theoretical framework of Salmivalli (2010). The majority of previous studies addressing role identification incorporate user- (e.g., age, gender, location) and social network-based features (e.g., number of followers, network centrality). Although these features have demonstrated a tendency to increase classification performance (Huang et al., 2014; Singh et al., 2016), relying on user and network features is logistically challenging in real-world application due to the creation of pseudo profiles and ethical restrictions imposed by platforms. Alternatively, lexical and semantic features (e.g., subjectivity lexicons, character n-grams, topic models, profanity word lists, and named entities) of participants' posts are considered in few research studies (Van Hee et al., 2018; Xu et al., 2012).

Our research aims to automatically identify cyberbullying and roles are based on supervised learning mechanisms that utilizes pretrained language models and advanced contextual embedding techniques. Therefore, such mechanisms will mitigate the need for rule-based approaches and will also minimize the requirement for creating task-specific feature extraction mechanisms.

3   Model Description

This study focuses on two tasks 1) detecting cyberbullying as a binary classification problem, and 2) detecting cyberbullying-related participant roles as a multi-class classification problem.

3.1   Cyberbullying classification

Instead of building new models, we extend an ensemble model originally designed by the authors (Herath et al., 2020) for SemEval-2020 Task on offensive language identification (Zampieri et al., 2020), to classify posts in the current dataset. The reused ensemble model (Herath et al., 2020) was built using three single classifiers, each based on DistilBERT (Sanh et al., 2019), a lighter, faster version of BERT (Devlin et al., 2018). Each of the single classifiers A, B, and C was trained on a Twitter dataset containing Tweets annotated as offensive ('OFF') or non-offensive('NOT') posts. Models A and B were trained on imbalanced sets of Twitter data where the majority class instance was OFF and NOT respectively. Model C was trained using a balanced subset of Tweets which were assigned opposing class labels by the models A and B.

Each classifier was trained using a learning rate of 5e-5 and a batch size of 32 for 2 epochs. A voting scheme was then used to combine the single models and build an ensemble model. If the biased classifiers A and B agreed upon a label for a given data instance, we assigned it that particular label. If the predictions from the biased classifiers were different, we assigned the data instance the prediction from the model C. This ensemble model achieved 0.906 of F1 score on the evaluation dataset of OffensEval challenge (Zampieri et al., 2020).

3.2   Role classification

According to a theoretical framework developed by Salmivalli (2010) and the annotation guide by Van Hee et al. (2015), 'bystander assistant' also engages in bullying while helping or encouraging the 'harasser'. Similarly, 'bystander defender' helps the 'victims' to defend themselves from the harassment. Therefore, we consider 'bystander assistant' as a role which contributes to bullying. Accordingly, we categorise the posts of harassers and bystander assistants in AMiCA dataset into a category called 'bullying' and victim and bystander defender's posts into a category called 'defending'. Then, we divide the posts in each category into the roles as shown in Figure 3. The final ensemble model contains 3 sub models as follows,

1. **Outer Model**: Classifies a post as Bullying or Defending

2. **Bullying Model**: Classifies a post as 'Harasser' or 'Bystander assistant'

3. **Defending Model**: Classifies a post as 'Victim' or 'Bystander defender'

Each of these models have the same model architecture, that consists of a pre-trained BERT embedding layer, hidden neural layer and a softmax output layer (Figure 2). In order to extract BERT embeddings, 'bert-based uncased' model (Devlin et al., 2018) used. As discussed in section 5, each

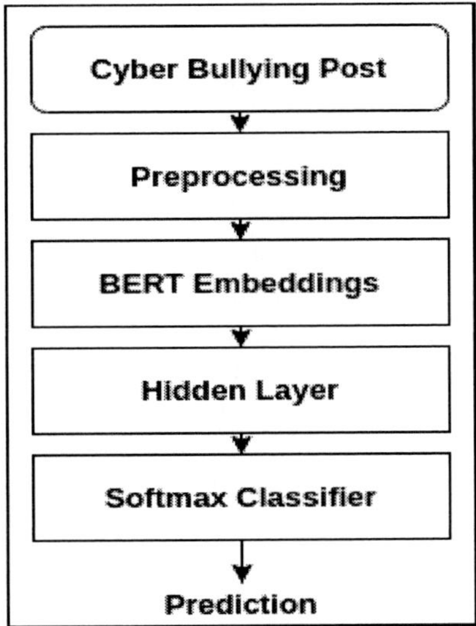

Figure 2: Model architecture

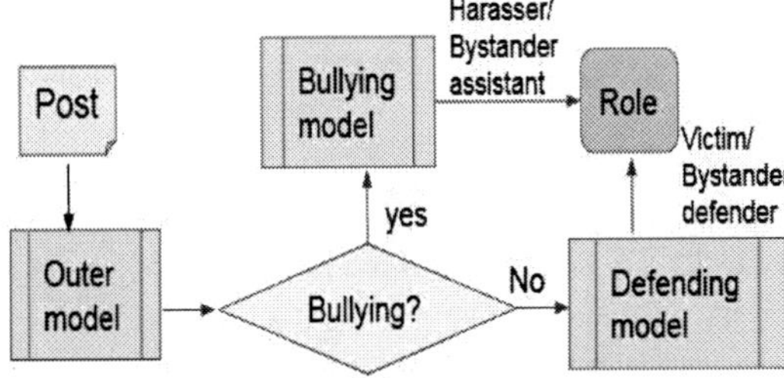

Figure 3: Overview of the Ensemble model

model was experimented with different sampling strategies and cost functions to obtain optimal performance.

4 Methods

Our research is guided by two tasks, which focus on evaluating the performance of models that could classify whether a given post is,

1. cyberbullying-related or not, and

2. if cyberbullying-related, predicting the role of the user who authored that post.

4.1 Dataset

AMiCA dataset contains data collected from the social networking site ASKfm[1] by Van Hee et al. (2018) in April and October, 2013. ASKfm is very popular among adolescents and has increasingly been used for cyberbullying (Kao et al., 2019). We

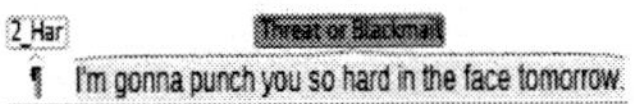

- Harmfulness score = 2, the message contains serious indications of cyberbullying.
- Author's role = harasser

Figure 4: An example of BRAT annotation (Van Hee et al., 2015)

used the English dataset, where posts are annotated and presented in chronological order within their original conversation (see Figure 1). AMiCA dataset is annotated by linguists using BRAT[2], a web-based tool for text annotation, and considers the following four roles.

- **Harasser**: person who initiates the harassment

- **Victim**: person who is harassed

- **Bystander defender**: person who helps the victim and discourages the harasser from continuing his actions

- **Bystander assistant**: person who does not initiate, but takes part in the actions of the harasser.

Figure 4 shows the annotation mechanism where '2_Har' refers that the author's role is 'harasser' while the harmfulness score is 2.

At post-level, the harmfulness of a post is scaled from 0 (no harm) to 2 (severely harmful). We merge harmfulness scores 1 and 2 together (e.g. 1_victim, 2_victim as 'victim') to increase training examples for each cyberbullying role. The cyberbullying class contained 5,380 instances (Harasser - 3,576, Victim - 1,356, Bystander assistant - 24, Bystander defender - 424). AMiCA dataset also provides annotations of cyberbullying-related textual categories such as threat, insult, curse. This study does not focus on those annotations during our model development.

Van Hee et al. (2018) have used 10% of the data as the hold-out test set. However, their hold-out is not publicly available. Therefore, in this study, we perform 10-fold cross validation while having 10% of the dataset as the test set in each fold. In order to maintain a similar data distribution ratio among the classes and to make sure that test set of

---

[1]https://ask.fm/

[2]https://brat.nlplab.org/

one fold is mutually exclusive with the test sets of other folds, we use the 'StratifiedKFold' method in the Scikit-Learner.

4.2 Data preprocessing and balancing

In order to minimise the noise of ASKfm posts, we performed some pre-processing steps such as replacing slang words and abbreviations [3] and decoding emoticons[4] in addition to standard data preprocessing steps (e.g. removal of punctuations) while fine-tuning BERT (Devlin et al., 2018).

Before feeding the posts into the models, we performed more preprocessing steps such as converting to lower case, tokenisation using the bert-tokenizer, and special token additions (adding [CLS] and [SEP] tokens to appropriate positions to perform BERT based sequence classification).

5 Results and Discussion

Evaluation metric. To evaluate our models and compare the performance with baselines, we use metrics similar to Van Hee et al. (2018): 1) **F1-score:** The harmonic mean of precision and recall and 2) **Error rate:** 1- recall of the class.

Baseline. We use the best system of Van Hee et al. (2018) as our baseline to compare our models. This baseline used feature combinations such as subjectivity lexicons, character n-grams, term lists, and topic models.

5.1 Evaluation of cyberbullying classification

As discussed in section 3.1, our cyberbullying classification experiments extended an ensemble model (refer as 'OffensEval ensemble' hereafter) based on DistilBERT developed by authors for SemEval 2020 challenge (Herath et al., 2020). To test the performance of OffensEval ensemble on ASKfm dataset, we constructed three test datasets. Each test dataset consisted of 10,872 non-bullying posts randomly sampled from the non-cyberbullying class and all the 5,380 posts belonging to the cyberbullying class. The class distribution in test datasets was selected such that it would be compatible with Van Hee et al. (2018). The averaged performance using three test sets is presented in Table 1 along with the baselines.

According to the results, our OffensEval ensemble model outperforms the best system of Van Hee

[3]https://floatcode.wordpress.com/2015/11/28/internet-slang-dataset/

[4]https://github.com/carpedm20/emoji

Model	F1	P	R
OffensEval ensemble	**0.83**	**0.84**	**0.82**
Van Hee et al. (2018)	0.64	0.74	0.56

Table 1: Hold-out scores of cyberbullying classification

et al. (2018) by a margin of 0.2 (F1 score). Since present results were obtained by evaluating a pre-built model for a separate task, in our future works, we expect to improve our performance through fine-tuning our previous model on AMiCA dataset. Further, the presence of obscene slang words in non-cyberbullying posts could have led to some of the false positives. A sample of examples in this category is provided in section 5.2. The presence of very short posts with 'chat-related slang words (e.g., *Fgt, No to the woah hoe)*' the model has not seen during the training could have led to some of the false negatives.

5.2 Evaluation of role classification

Table 2 demonstrates the 10-fold cross-validation results of our role classification models. As discussed in section 3.2, we created the BERT-based 'outer model' to classify posts into two classes - bullying and defending. At the initial experiments, we obtained low recall for 'defending' class mainly due to the class imbalance in the dataset. To overcome this drawback, we have carried out experiments with different techniques such as weighted random sampling and weighted cross-entropy loss (as cost function). Based on the results of our experiments, weighted random sampling was used when training the outer model as it has shown considerable improvement in performance. Weighted random sampling is an sampling technique that attempts to maintain an approximately equal distribution of data instances among classes in a batch while training.

Our BERT-based 'defending model' demonstrated promising performance including 0.93 of weighted F1 score and 0.96 (victim class) and 0.86 (bystander defender class) of F1 score (Table 2). Our BERT-based 'bullying model' was not successful in classifying bystander assistants. We have experimented several strategies to improve the performance of bystander assistant detection such as choosing different training samples, limiting the number of instances taken from 'Harasser' class (100, 500) when training the 'Bullying' model, using weighted random sampling to under sample the harasser class while oversampling the bystander assistant class in order to keep the distribution among two classes at a ratio near to 1:1. However, these strategies failed to enable the 'Bullying' model or the overall ensemble model to detect bystander assistant class properly. Based on these experiments, we assume that the issue of the bystander assistant being classified as a harasser may not be due to class imbalance, however, based on the fact that examples in both classes have the overlapping language (see sample posts of 'bystander assistant' below).

"[..] wanna kill him? let's do it together"

*"[..] she's a massive sl*t! I agree with you [..] I'm on your side"*

While training each of the three models (Outer, Bullying, Defending), batch size of 8 was used with a maximum sequence length of 256 characters. Cross entropy loss was used as the cost function and stochastic gradient descent with a learning rate of 2×10^{-5} was used as the optimizer.

As shown in the Table 2, our BERT-based 'ensemble model' has achieved 'good' performance (weighted F1-score is 0.76) except in the classes - victim and bystander assistant. According to the confusion matrix of ensemble model, most misclassified instances are related to victims being classified as harassers. An error analysis of misclassified posts revealed that bullying language widely overlaps with victims when victims use swear words to respond the harasser. These posts increase the difficulty for models to detect victims and require efforts in future research to develop effective models that can handle aggressive victims. A sample of posts where victims have aggressively responded to harassers is shown below.

*"[..] whoever is saying that sh*t that its me needs to cut your sh*t out you need to shut the f*** up [..]"*

"and you're living proof that abortion should be legal"

The comparison of our role classification model with the baselines is restricted since Van Hee et al. (2018) do not report cross-validation results[5], However, if the 'error rates' are compared using our 10-fold cross-validation results with their hold-out results, our model outperforms the baseline by 0.26 and 0.11 of 'error rate' in harasser and victim classes respectively. Both the models were not able to detect bystander assistant successfully (i.e. error

---

[5] https://doi.org/10.1371/journal.pone.0203794.t009

Model	WF	Class	P	R	F1
Outer	0.78	Bully	0.84	0.83	0.83
		Defend	0.66	0.67	0.67
Bullying	0.99	Harasser	0.99	1.00	1.00
		B.assist	0.20	0.05	0.08
Defending	0.93	Victim	0.95	0.96	0.95
		B.defend	0.86	0.84	0.85
Ensemble	0.76	Harasser	0.84	0.82	0.83
		Victim	0.59	0.61	0.60
		B.assist	0.00	0.00	0.00
		B.defend	0.68	0.73	0.70

Table 2: 10-fold cross-validation scores of our models; WF: Weight F1

rate is 1). The baseline outperforms us by 0.01 (error rate) in the bystander defender class. Van Hee et al. (2018) reported that error rates often being lowest for the profanity baseline, confirming that it performs well in terms of recall, however, precision is also an important metric to be considered. In our future work, we intend to further improving recall of each role class while stabilizing good precision.

6 Conclusions

This paper proposes an approach to classify cyberbullying and associated roles (e.g., harasser, victim) as a novel contribution to enhance automated cyberbullying detection. Cyberbullying is a growing social problem that inflicts detrimental impacts on online users. The identification of roles is a valuable contribution to future research as it can prompt closer monitoring of bullies and implicitly help victims through potential prevention. Currently, our approaches to identifying cyberbullying related roles focus only on individual posts on a forum. In our future work, we aim to expand this further by considering an entire discussion and the discourse relationships between the posts within the considered discussion. This will enable us to get a better understanding of the roles played by different users in a discussion. Moreover, we intend to integrate cyberbullying and role classification as a single model and optimise performance further to provide an effective solution to the cyberbullying problem.

Acknowledgments

Authors would like to acknowledge the researchers on the AMiCA project for sharing the dataset.

References

Mohammed Ali Al-garadi, Kasturi Dewi Varathan, and Sri Devi Ravana. 2016. Cybercrime detection in online communications: The experimental case of cyberbullying detection in the twitter network. *Computers in Human Behavior*, 63:433 – 443.

Jacob Devlin, Ming-Wei Chang, Kenton Lee, and Kristina Toutanova. 2018. Bert: Pre-training of deep bidirectional transformers for language understanding.

Mahen Herath, Thushari Atapattu, Hoang Dung, Christoph Treude, and Katrina Falkner. 2020. AdelaideCyC at SemEval-2020 Task 12: Ensemble of Classifiers for Offensive Language Detection in Social Media. In *Proceedings of SemEval*.

Qianjia Huang, Vivek Kumar Singh, and Pradeep Kumar Atrey. 2014. Cyber bullying detection using social and textual analysis. In *Proceedings of the 3rd International Workshop on Socially-Aware Multimedia*, page 3–6. Association for Computing Machinery.

Gilles Jacobs, Cynthia Van Hee, and Véronique Hoste. 2020. Automatic classification of participant roles in cyberbullying: Can we detect victims, bullies, and bystanders in social media text? *Natural Language Engineering*. In-print.

Hsien-Te Kao, Shen Yan, Di Huang, Nathan Bartley, Homa Hosseinmardi, and Emilio Ferrara. 2019. Understanding cyberbullying on instagram and ask.fm via social role detection. In *Companion Proceedings of The 2019 World Wide Web Conference*, page 183–188. Association for Computing Machinery.

J. Patchin and S. Hinduja. 2019. Lifetime cyberbullying victimization rates.

H. Rosa, N. Pereira, R. Ribeiro, P. C. Ferreira, J. P. Carvalho, S. Oliveira, L. Coheur, P. Paulino, A. M. Veiga Simão, and I. Trancoso. 2019. Automatic cyberbullying detection: A systematic review. *Computers in Human Behavior*, 93:333 – 345.

S. Salawu, Y. He, and J. Lumsden. 2020. Approaches to automated detection of cyberbullying: A survey. *IEEE Transactions on Affective Computing*, 11(01):3–24.

Christina Salmivalli. 2010. Bullying and the peer group: A review. *Aggression and Violent Behavior*, 15(2):112 – 120. Special Issue on Group Processes and Aggression.

Victor Sanh, Lysandre Debut, Julien Chaumond, and Thomas Wolf. 2019. Distilbert, a distilled version of bert: smaller, faster, cheaper and lighter.

Vivek K. Singh, Qianjia Huang, and Pradeep K. Atrey. 2016. Cyberbullying detection using probabilistic socio-textual information fusion. In *Proceedings of the 2016 IEEE/ACM International Conference on Advances in Social Networks Analysis and Mining*, page 884–887.

Cynthia Van Hee, Gilles Jacobs, Chris Emmery, Bart Desmet, Els Lefever, Ben Verhoeven, Guy De Pauw, Walter Daelemans, and Véronique Hoste. 2018. Automatic detection of cyberbullying in social media text. *PLOS ONE*, 13(10):1–22.

Cynthia Van Hee, Ben Verhoeven, Els Lefever, Guy De Pauw, Walter Daelemans, and Véronique Hoste. 2015. Guidelines for the Fine-Grained Analysis of Cyberbullying, version 1.0. LT3,. Technical report, Language and Translation Technology Team Ghent University.

Jun-Ming Xu, Kwang-Sung Jun, Xiaojin Zhu, and Amy Bellmore. 2012. Learning from bullying traces in social media. In *Proceedings of the 2012 Conference of the North American Chapter of the Association for Computational Linguistics: Human Language Technologies*, page 656–666. Association for Computational Linguistics.

Marcos Zampieri, Preslav Nakov, Sara Rosenthal, Pepa Atanasova, Georgi Karadzhov, Hamdy Mubarak, Leon Derczynski, Zeses Pitenis, and Çağrı Çöltekin. 2020. SemEval-2020 Task 12: Multilingual Offensive Language Identification in Social Media (OffensEval 2020). In *Proceedings of SemEval*.

Developing a New Classifier for Automated Identification of Incivility in Social Media

Sam Davidson*, Qiusi Sun[†], Magdalena Wojcieszak[†‡]
*Dept. of Linguistics, [†] Dept. of Communication
University of California, Davis
[‡]University of Amsterdam
{ssdavidson, qssun, mwojcieszak}@ucdavis.edu

Abstract

Incivility is not only prevalent on online social media platforms, but also has concrete effects on individual users, online groups, the platforms themselves, and the society at large. Given the prevalence and effects of online incivility, and the challenges involved in human-based incivility detection, it is urgent to develop validated and versatile automatic approaches to identifying uncivil posts and comments. This project advances both a neural, BERT-based classifier as well as a logistic regression classifier to identify uncivil comments. The classifier is trained on a dataset of Reddit posts, which are annotated for incivility, and further expanded using a combination of labeled data from Reddit and Twitter. Our best performing model achieves an F_1 of 0.802 on our Reddit test set. The final model is not only applicable across social media platforms and their distinct data structures, but also computationally versatile, and - as such - ready to be used on vast volumes of online data. All trained models and annotated data are made available to the research community.

1 Introduction

Given the growing polarization in the United States, the increasing popularity of partisan media, and the widespread use of social media for information and discussion (see Iyengar et al. (2019) for a review), many scholars and observers worry about the accelerated use and spread of incivility in the online environment. Incivility, defined as "features of discussion that convey disrespectful tone toward the discussion forum, its participants, or its topics" (Coe et al., 2014) is a common aspect of many online communities, especially anonymous forums (Reader, 2012) such as Reddit. Estimates suggest that more than 84% of Americans have experienced incivility online, and among those who have ever experienced it, the number of average weekly encounters with incivility was as high as 10.6 times (KRC Research, 2018). In addition to lowering the standards of public discourse, incivility has concrete effects on users, online discussions, and social media platforms. The use of and exposure to incivility generates negative emotions, such as anger, anxiety, or mental distress, and is related to aggression (Gervais, 2015) and hostile communication (Groshek and Cutino, 2016). Incivility also turns users away from online discussions altogether (Anderson et al., 2014; Bauman et al., 2013; Moor et al., 2010; Ransbotham et al., 2016). Given these reasons for the public and industry to be concerned with online incivility, many companies seek to automatically detect incivility in order to understand its scope, identify the online communities in which incivility is particularly prevalent, and - ultimately - address the problem.

This project offers a step in this direction. We present machine learning models for detecting incivility in social media, models that are not only computationally efficient but also applicable across platforms. We propose both a BERT-based neural classifier as well as a logistic regression based classifier trained on manually annotated and artificially labeled data. Our results suggest that the proposed models perform well across distinct data/communication structures of different platforms, and, as such, can be easily applied to detect incivility.

2 Previous Work

There is considerable conceptual and operational ambiguity in the literature on incivility and related concepts under the umbrella of offensive or intolerant speech (see (Rossini, 2020) for a review). Some studies use incivility interchangeably with hate speech, which refers to speech that aims to discriminate against a certain identity group, or

Proceedings of the Fourth Workshop on Online Abuse and Harms, pages 95–101
Online, November 20, 2020. ©2020 Association for Computational Linguistics
https://doi.org/10.18653/v1/P17

aggressive or toxic language, which includes personal attacks (Rösner and Krämer, 2016). However, incivility is a broader concept, which focuses on content that goes against acceptable social norms in terms of vulgarity, name-calling, or offensive language (Papacharissi, 2004), whereas hate speech or aggressive language captures more specifically discourse that offends, derogates, or silences others and may promote harm (Rossini, 2020). Increasingly, incivility is conceptually and operationally distinguished from such intolerant discourse, and evidence suggests that the effects of these two forms of expressions also differ (Rossini, 2020). Definitions of incivility vary, ranging from "a norm-defying behavior" (Gervais, 2015), "an explicit attack" (Anderson and Huntington, 2017), to the violation of interpersonal politeness norms (Mutz, 2015; Mutz and Reeves, 2005), yet most include a lack of respect toward discussion participants or arguments (Santana, 2014), and a impolite tone of discourse (Papacharissi, 2004). The often used definition, which we adopt for the purpose of our machine learning model, sees incivility as features of discussion that convey disrespectful tone toward the discussion participants or its topics, including name-calling, mean-spirited or disparaging words directed at a person or group of people, an idea, plan, policy, or behavior, vulgarity, using profanity or language that would not be considered proper in professional discourse, and pejorative remarks about the way in which a person communicates (Coe et al., 2014). As such, our approach encompasses both the less societally detrimental foul language or harsh tone as well as the more intolerant discourse.

From a technical perspective, previous research using machine learning models to detect incivility and other offensive or intolerant language online has focused primarily on the use of logistic regression (Theocharis et al., 2020; Daxenberger et al., 2018; Maity et al., 2018), support vector machines (Joksimovic et al., 2019; Maity et al., 2018), and various neural classification models (Sadeque et al., 2019). BERT (Devlin et al., 2019) and related transfomer language models have been used in related tasks, such as identifying abusive language on Twitter (Nikolov and Radivchev, 2019; Risch et al., 2019), including many entrants in the OffensEval task at SemEval-2020 (Zampieri et al., 2020). To our knowledge, this paper is the first to utilize a fine-tuned BERT model to identify incivility on social media platforms, and one of few projects that train the classifier on data from more than one platform. Also, past work on identifying incivility over time has mostly analyzed Twitter data during certain political events, such as the 2016 presidential election in the US (Siegel et al., 2018), and/or looked at political incivility in specific contexts (e.g., among politicians, e.g., (Theocharis et al., 2020). These rather narrow, single-platform foci limit the applicability of the developed classifications, a limitation we address in this project.

In addition to these contributions of our work, our primary contribution may lie in our data augmentation method. Specifically, we extend recent approaches to automatically label additional training data to improve the performance of a logistic regression classifier. Previous work in detection of offensive language has used back-translation (Ibrahim et al., 2020) and data transformation techniques (Rizos et al., 2019) to augment limited training data. While some work (Theocharis et al., 2020) utilizes the Google Perspectives API to label additional training data, which introduces noise to the operationalization of incivility, we take advantage of our well-performing BERT classification model to generate artificial training data for a logistic regression classifier. The resulting classifier can be efficiently run on CPU and is far less computationally expensive than our comparably performing BERT model. This extension makes our classifier easily applicable to vast amounts of data and readily implemented on social media platforms or the comments sections of websites of news media organizations.

3 Dataset

We present a corpus of Reddit data annotated for incivility at the post level, and further annotated for political/non-political content at the subreddit level. We chose to use Reddit as the source of our dataset because Reddit is the sixth most popular website in the US and the third most visited social media platform following YouTube and Facebook (Alexa.com, 2019). There are more than 430 million active users worldwide on Reddit (Perez, 2019). Also, the anonymous nature of Reddit makes it popular for sharing information and engaging in long and complex discussions, making it ideal for observing online discourse. Furthermore, the public nature of Reddit allowed us to gather a large number of posts from across various user communities, known as subreddits. Each subreddit has a general topic, behavioral norms, and community standards, allowing for a creation of a diverse dataset, which further increases the applicability of the resulting machine learning model.

To tackle the detection problem, we identified the most popular subreddits from 2006 to 2019 that contained 95% of the total comments by (1) the number of comments in the subreddit each year, and (2) the number of followers that commented in the subreddit each year, which resulted in 9355 subreddits across the years. We then collected 5000 comments from these subreddits using stratified random sampling technique, such that the random sampling from each year is based on each year's proportion in the total number of comments. These 5000 posts were the manually labeled.

3.1 Dataset Annotation

Instead of adapting annotation schema that focused on profanity and swear words or phrases (i.e., the more narrow definition of incivility) (Zampieri et al., 2019; Mohan et al., 2017; Almerekhi et al., 2020), we developed a coding manual to classify comments according to four dimensions present in offensive speech more broadly. We account for whether a comment contains: (1) name-calling, mean-spirited or disparaging words directed at a person or a group of people; (2) aspersion, mean-spirited or disparaging words directed at an idea, plan, policy or behavior; (3) pejorative or disparaging remark about the way in which a person communicates, and (4) vulgarity, profanity or language that would not be considered proper. Our operational approach accounted for the content aspect (e.g., vulgarity or profanity, such as "you're a dumbass for simplifying the issue and trying to jump right into the helm of the 'y'r all hypocrites' bandwagon") and the different targets of incivility or foul content included in the intolerant discourse (e.g., "... the interests of left-handed black female dwarves"), to create a comprehensive and inclusive annotated dataset for model building. Annotators were asked to apply a binary label to indicate whether or not the comment contains incivility. The annotators were three undergraduate students in social sciences at UC Davis, two native English speakers and one with English as the second language. Two annotators are heavy Reddit users and one is a user of other social media. The annotators were trained on the definitions and proce-

dures, and each of them completed five pilot coding exercises. Each annotator first independently coded a random set of 50 comments with Fleiss's kappa of 0.618. They then compared results, discussed and resolved discrepancies, and clarified confusions. These steps were repeated multiple times with increasingly large comment sets until an acceptable agreement level was reached. In total, all three annotators completed 1000 comments together during training, with Fleiss's kappa of 0.663. The major discrepancies pertain to potentially sarcastic comments (e.g., "Great, now we're paying for CBC to promote cuckoldry"), which some coders saw as uncivil and others as innocent sarcasm. After an acceptable coding precision was established among the three annotators, the remaining 4000 comments were randomly divided into three sets and each annotator independently coded an assigned set. The final result of this process is a set of 5000 comments labeled for incivility. Additionally, our dataset includes coding at the subreddit level to identify subreddits that were political, non-political, or mixed (i.e., contained some political and some non-political content). This allows us to analyze the prevalence of incivility across different kinds of online discussions and across the political spectrum.

4 Classifier Training

To demonstrate the efficacy of our collected dataset, we use supervised machine learning to automatically identify uncivil Reddit posts. However, annotating a dataset large enough to train a state-of-the-art neural classifier from scratch is a costly and time-consuming undertaking. We experimented with several neural binary classifiers, with our best-performing models built on top of transformer-based language models, namely BERT (Devlin et al., 2019) and its relative, DistilBERT (Sanh et al., 2019). Past work has demonstrated that fine-tuning large, pre-trained language models, such as BERT and DistilBERT, is an effective method for creating a high-quality neural classifier with limited supervised training data. As described in Sun et al. (2019), we conduct additional pretraining of the BERT-base and DistilBERT-base models on a large collection of Reddit posts as in-domain data. Once pretrained, we fine-tune our models for classification on our annotated dataset of Reddit comments, which trained annotators classified with binary labels for incivility.

Finally, in an effort to extend past work by creating a more flexible, platform agnostic classifier, we train a logistic regression classifier for incivility prediction in social media by combining the data presented in Theocharis et al. (2020) with our annotated and artificially labeled datasets.

Our Reddit dataset (including annotation disagreements), test predictions, scripts and models are available on the project GitHub repository [1].

5 Experiments and Results

Our BERT and DistilBERT models begin with the respective base pretrained language models, as implemented in HuggingFace's Transformer's package. We then further pretrain these models on dataset of 3 million Reddit posts, for 100,000 training steps (as suggested by Sun et al. (2019)) using the masked word prediction task (Devlin et al., 2019). We then utilize these pretrained models in a classification setup, utilizing a softmax layer to predict binary class probability based on the [CLS] token in BERT's final hidden layer. For classification fine-tuning, all inputs to the models are limited to 256 tokens in length, with a training batch size of 16. We use the AdamW optimizer (Gugger and Howard, 2018) with default learning rate and epsilon values. We fine-tune our model for classification for four epochs on our dataset of 5,000 Reddit posts which are coded for incivility, with 10% of the data set aside for training validation, and 1000 annotated posts set aside for model testing. Classification results using BERT and DistilBERT are shown in Table 1.

Model	Precision	Recall	F_1
BERT	0.814	0.76	0.786
DistilBERT	0.936	0.702	0.802

Table 1: Results - Models trained on Reddit data

One major goal of this project is to classify multiple years of Reddit data for further analysis of incivility across political and non-political subreddits. Despite the acceptable performance of our BERT classification models, the models were too computationally expensive to classify the approximately 800 million posts per year we collected from Reddit. To address this constraint, we also train a logistic regression classification model to be able to classify large amounts of Reddit data without the use of expensive neural classifiers. However, given the small size of our annotated training set, we must generate additional training data to train an effective logistic regression model. In order to improve system performance, we first use our fine-tuned DistilBERT model to classify a large collection of Reddit posts. We then uptrain a logistic regression model on this synthetic data, along with our annotated data. As detailed in Section 5, the resulting model achieves an F_1 score which is competitive with our BERT and DistilBERT models, while also being able to classify data more quickly and at lower computational cost, making our model widely applicable.

All logistic regression models are trained using TFIDF of stemmed unigrams as features. Given the relative imbalance of labels in our training data, in which positive examples of incivility represent only 10.3% of annotated posts, we use ADASYN (He et al., 2008) to generate additional synthetic data for oversampling. We train a second model on synthetic data consisting of 5 million Reddit posts which are labeled for incivility using our trained DistilBERT model. Results are shown in Table 2

To test the overlap of concepts such as hate speech and offensive language with incivility, we applied the classifier provided by Davidson et al. (2017) to the test portion of our Reddit dataset. To conduct our test, we combined the classes "offensive language" and "hate speech" predicted by the Davidson et al. (2017) classifier into a single class. On our Reddit data, this classifier achieves an F1 of 0.242, indicating limited overlap between the these domains. This test demonstrates that the definitional, conceptual, and operational differences between incivility and related domains of offensive speech are indeed represented in our labeled data.

In order to further test the efficacy of our implementation, we train a logistic regression model as outlined above using Twitter data collected and annotated by Theocharis et al. (2020). Finally, to create our platform agnostic model, we train a logistic regression model by combining our annotated and synthetic Reddit data with the annotated and synthetic data from Theocharis et al. (2020), which we test on the Theocharis et al. (2020) Twitter test set, as shown in Table 3.

6 Analysis and Discussion

Our encouraging results in classifying incivility in Reddit posts demonstrate the efficacy of our dataset

---

[1] https://github.com/ssdavidson/reddit_incivility

Training Data	Precision	Recall	F_1
Annotated Reddit	1	0.173	0.295
Synthetic Reddit	0.835	0.731	0.779
Reddit + Twitter	0.828	0.74	0.782

Table 2: Results - Logistic Regression Models on Reddit Test Data

Training Data	Precision	Recall	F_1
Synthetic Reddit	0.872	0.158	0.267
Reddit + Twitter	0.711	0.474	0.569

Table 3: Results - Logistic Regression Models on Twitter Data

for classifier training. We have applied our trained classifier to 95% of Reddit comments from the year 2017, finding that 9.21% of non-political comments are uncivil, compared to 14.75% of political comments; initial results that indicate relative prevalence of incivility in online *political* discourse.

Due to the scale of the data to be ultimately classified, we were concerned as much with computational efficiency as with prediction accuracy when building our incivility classifier. When we use our trained BERT model to generate a large quantity of synthetically labeled training data, the performance of our log regression model is comparable to that of the our fine-tuned BERT models.

Concern with computational efficiency also informed our choice of features in our logistic regression model. While alternate features could be used, such as Doc2Vec or Word2Vec embeddings, we chose to use TFIDF due to the simplicity of calculating these features. Additionally, the choice of TFIDF was informed by the work of Theocharis et al. (2020), who demonstrate the utility of TFIDF for the task for incivility classification. Finally, the fact that our TFIDF-based logistic regression model performs similarly well to the BERT model is evidence of the effectiveness of the choice of TFIDF features. That said, the use of alternate features may improve model performance, and we leave this to future work.

The similarity between the predictions made by our BERT model and our logistic regression model indicates that the logistic regression model retains much of the predictive power of the BERT model. In fact, across 996 test comments, the two models disagreed on only 27 comments, for a rate of 2.7%. From reviewing the disagreements we can identify several classes of comment on which the two models often disagree. The first, and most obvious, is very long comments. BERT is designed to truncate long input text (our implementation truncates inputs longer than 256 tokenized word pieces). Thus, our BERT model may mislabel longer comments in which the incivility occurs later in the comment. Another source of disagreement comes from the fact that our TFIDF-based classifier tends to be more sensitive to individual lexical items, which is to be expected as BERT is known to condense far more semantic information than do count-based vectorization techniques such as TFIDF (Jawahar et al., 2019). For example, our regression model mislabels the comment "This is dope! Does anyone know where I can purchase one for myself?" as an uncivil comment, presumably due to the presence of the word "dope", while our BERT model labels the comment correctly. In future work, we plan to conduct a more rigorous analysis of labelling disagreements between the two models to better understand the role of lexicon and compositional semantics in the incivility classification task.

Finally, we demonstrate the flexibility of our model training strategy by creating a combined incivility prediction model using our automatically labeled Reddit data with the synthetic data provided by Theocharis et al. (2020). The resulting model has shown promise as a platform agnostic incivility classifier model for social media.

7 Conclusion and Future Work

In this paper, we present a new dataset of Reddit posts annotated at the comment level for incivility, as well as at the subreddit level for political content. Further, we demonstrate the efficacy of this dataset to train machine learning models for incivility detection, both alone and in combination with previously available datasets, to create a platform agnostic classifier for incivility on social media.

Using our trained classifier, our future goal is to provide a systematic overview of trends in incivility on social media, across time and variety of discussion topics. The project aims to capture the fluctuations in the prevalence of incivility in political and non-political online spaces, politically homogeneous and heterogeneous discussions, liberal and conservative ones, and also among different non-political topics. The anticipated study will add our understanding of the development of online incivility and shed light on incivility interventions.

References

Alexa.com. 2019. Alexa - Top Sites in United States - Alexa.

Hind Almerekhi, Supervised by Bernard J Jansen, and co-supervised by Haewoon Kwak. 2020. Investigating Toxicity Across Multiple Reddit Communities, Users, and Moderators. In *Companion Proceedings of the Web Conference 2020*, pages 294–298.

Ashley A Anderson, Dominique Brossard, Dietram A Scheufele, Michael A Xenos, and Peter Ladwig. 2014. The "nasty effect:" Online incivility and risk perceptions of emerging technologies. *Journal of Computer-Mediated Communication*, 19(3):373–387.

Ashley A Anderson and Heidi E Huntington. 2017. Social media, science, and attack discourse: How Twitter discussions of climate change use sarcasm and incivility. *Science Communication*, 39(5):598–620.

Sheri Bauman, Russell B Toomey, and Jenny L Walker. 2013. Associations among bullying, cyberbullying, and suicide in high school students. *Journal of adolescence*, 36(2):341–350.

Kevin Coe, Kate Kenski, and Stephen A Rains. 2014. Online and uncivil? patterns and determinants of incivility in newspaper website comments. *Journal of Communication*, 64(4):658–679.

Thomas Davidson, Dana Warmsley, Michael Macy, and Ingmar Weber. 2017. Automated Hate Speech Detection and the Problem of Offensive Language. In *Proceedings of the 11th International AAAI Conference on Web and Social Media*, ICWSM '17, pages 512–515.

Johannes Daxenberger, Marc Ziegele, Iryna Gurevych, and Oliver Quiring. 2018. Automatically Detecting Incivility in Online Discussions of News Media. In *2018 IEEE 14th International Conference on e-Science (e-Science)*, pages 318–319. IEEE.

Jacob Devlin, Ming-Wei Chang, Kenton Lee, and Kristina Toutanova. 2019. BERT: Pre-training of Deep Bidirectional Transformers for Language Understanding. In *Proceedings of the 2019 Conference of the North American Chapter of the Association for Computational Linguistics: Human Language Technologies, Volume 1 (Long and Short Papers)*, pages 4171–4186.

Bryan T Gervais. 2015. Incivility online: Affective and behavioral reactions to uncivil political posts in a web-based experiment. *Journal of Information Technology & Politics*, 12(2):167–185.

Jacob Groshek and Chelsea Cutino. 2016. Meaner on mobile: Incivility and impoliteness in communicating contentious politics on sociotechnical networks. *Social Media+ Society*, 2(4):2056305116677137.

Sylvain Gugger and Jeremy Howard. 2018. AdamW and Super-convergence is now the fastest way to train neural nets. `https://www.fast.ai/2018/07/02/adam-weight-decay/`.

Haibo He, Yang Bai, Edwardo A Garcia, and Shutao Li. 2008. ADASYN: Adaptive synthetic sampling approach for imbalanced learning. In *2008 IEEE international joint conference on neural networks (IEEE world congress on computational intelligence)*, pages 1322–1328. IEEE.

Mai Ibrahim, Marwan Torki, and Nagwa El-Makky. 2020. Alexu-backtranslation-tl at semeval-2020 task [12]: Improving offensive language detection using data augmentation and transfer learning. In *Proceedings of the International Workshop on Semantic Evaluation (SemEval)*.

Shanto Iyengar, Yphtach Lelkes, Matthew Levendusky, Neil Malhotra, and Sean J Westwood. 2019. The origins and consequences of affective polarization in the United States. *Annual Review of Political Science*, 22:129–146.

Ganesh Jawahar, Benoît Sagot, and Djamé Seddah. 2019. What Does BERT Learn about the Structure of Language? In *Proceedings of the 57th Annual Meeting of the Association for Computational Linguistics*, pages 3651–3657.

Srecko Joksimovic, Ryan S Baker, Jaclyn Ocumpaugh, Juan Miguel L Andres, Ivan Tot, Elle Yuan Wang, and Shane Dawson. 2019. Automated Identification of Verbally Abusive Behaviors in Online Discussions. In *Proceedings of the Third Workshop on Abusive Language Online*, pages 36–45.

Powell Tate KRC Research, Weber Shandwick. 2018. Civility in America 2018: Civility at work and in our public squares. `https://www.webershandwick.com/wp-content/uploads/2018/06/Civility-in-America-VII-FINAL.pdf`.

Suman Kalyan Maity, Aishik Chakraborty, Pawan Goyal, and Animesh Mukherjee. 2018. Opinion conflicts: An effective route to detect incivility in Twitter. *Proceedings of the ACM on Human-Computer Interaction*, 2(CSCW):1–27.

Shruthi Mohan, Apala Guha, Michael Harris, Fred Popowich, Ashley Schuster, and Chris Priebe. 2017. The impact of toxic language on the health of Reddit communities. In *Canadian Conference on Artificial Intelligence*, pages 51–56. Springer.

Peter J Moor, Ard Heuvelman, and Ria Verleur. 2010. Flaming on YouTube. *Computers in human behavior*, 26(6):1536–1546.

Diana C Mutz. 2015. Incentivizing the manuscript-review system using REX. *PS, Political Science & Politics*, 48(S1):73.

Diana C Mutz and Byron Reeves. 2005. The new videomalaise: Effects of televised incivility on political trust. *American Political Science Review*, pages 1–15.

Alex Nikolov and Victor Radivchev. 2019. Nikolov-Radivchev at SemEval-2019 Task 6: Offensive tweet classification with BERT and ensembles. In *Proceedings of the 13th International Workshop on Semantic Evaluation*, pages 691–695.

Zizi Papacharissi. 2004. Democracy online: Civility, politeness, and the democratic potential of online political discussion groups. *New media & society*, 6(2):259–283.

Sarah Perez. 2019. Reddit's monthly active user base grew 30% to reach 430M in 2019.

Sam Ransbotham, Robert G Fichman, Ram Gopal, and Alok Gupta. 2016. Special section introduction—ubiquitous IT and digital vulnerabilities. *Information Systems Research*, 27(4):834–847.

Bill Reader. 2012. Free press vs. free speech? The rhetoric of "civility" in regard to anonymous online comments. *Journalism & mass communication quarterly*, 89(3):495–513.

Julian Risch, Anke Stoll, Marc Ziegele, and Ralf Krestel. 2019. hpiDEDIS at GermEval 2019: Offensive Language Identification using a German BERT model. In *KONVENS*.

Georgios Rizos, Konstantin Hemker, and Björn Schuller. 2019. Augment to prevent: short-text data augmentation in deep learning for hate-speech classification. In *Proceedings of the 28th ACM International Conference on Information and Knowledge Management*, pages 991–1000.

Leonie Rösner and Nicole C Krämer. 2016. Verbal venting in the social web: Effects of anonymity and group norms on aggressive language use in online comments. *Social Media+ Society*, 2(3):2056305116664220.

Patrícia Rossini. 2020. Beyond Incivility: Understanding Patterns of Uncivil and Intolerant Discourse in Online Political Talk. *Communication Research*, page 0093650220921314.

Farig Sadeque, Stephen Rains, Yotam Shmargad, Kate Kenski, Kevin Coe, and Steven Bethard. 2019. Incivility Detection in Online Comments. In *Proceedings of the Eighth Joint Conference on Lexical and Computational Semantics (*SEM 2019)*, pages 283–291.

Victor Sanh, Lysandre Debut, Julien Chaumond, and Thomas Wolf. 2019. DistilBERT, a distilled version of BERT: smaller, faster, cheaper and lighter. *arXiv preprint arXiv:1910.01108*.

Arthur D Santana. 2014. Virtuous or vitriolic: The effect of anonymity on civility in online newspaper reader comment boards. *Journalism practice*, 8(1):18–33.

Alexandra A Siegel, Evgenii Nikitin, Pablo Barberá, Joanna Sterling, Bethany Pullen, Richard Bonneau, Jonathan Nagler, and Joshua A Tucker. 2018. Measuring the prevalence of online hate speech, with an application to the 2016 US election. https://smappnyu.wpcomstaging.com/wp-content/uploads/2018/11/Hate_Speech_2016_US_Election_Text.pdf.

Chi Sun, Xipeng Qiu, Yige Xu, and Xuanjing Huang. 2019. How to fine-tune BERT for text classification? In *China National Conference on Chinese Computational Linguistics*, pages 194–206. Springer.

Yannis Theocharis, Pablo Barberá, Zoltán Fazekas, and Sebastian Adrian Popa. 2020. The Dynamics of Political Incivility on Twitter. *Sage Open*, 10(2):2158244020919447.

Marcos Zampieri, Shervin Malmasi, Preslav Nakov, Sara Rosenthal, Noura Farra, and Ritesh Kumar. 2019. Predicting the Type and Target of Offensive Posts in Social Media. In *Proceedings of the 2019 Conference of the North American Chapter of the Association for Computational Linguistics: Human Language Technologies, Volume 1 (Long and Short Papers)*, pages 1415–1420.

Marcos Zampieri, Preslav Nakov, Sara Rosenthal, Pepa Atanasova, Georgi Karadzhov, Hamdy Mubarak, Leon Derczynski, Zeses Pitenis, and Çağrı Çöltekin. 2020. Semeval-2020 task 12: Multilingual offensive language identification in social media (offenseval 2020). *arXiv preprint arXiv:2006.07235*.

Countering hate on social media: Large-scale classification of hate and counter speech

Joshua Garland[*]
Santa Fe Institute
Santa Fe, NM 87501 USA
joshua@santafe.edu

Keyan Ghazi-Zahedi[*]
Max Planck Institute for Mathematics in the Sciences
Inselstrasse 22, 04103
Leipzig, Germany

Jean-Gabriel Young
Center for the Study of Complex Systems
University of Michigan
Ann Arbor, MI 48109, USA

Laurent Hébert-Dufresne
Vermont Complex Systems Center
University of Vermont,
Burlington, VT 05405 USA

Mirta Galesic
Santa Fe Institute
Santa Fe, NM 87501 USA

Abstract

Hateful rhetoric is plaguing online discourse, fostering extreme societal movements and possibly giving rise to real-world violence. A potential solution to this growing global problem is citizen-generated counter speech where citizens actively engage with hate speech to restore civil non-polarized discourse. However, its actual effectiveness in curbing the spread of hatred is unknown and hard to quantify. One major obstacle to researching this question is a lack of large labeled data sets for training automated classifiers to identify counter speech. Here we use a unique situation in Germany where self-labeling groups engaged in organized online hate and counter speech. We use an ensemble learning algorithm which pairs a variety of paragraph embeddings with regularized logistic regression functions to classify both hate and counter speech in a corpus of millions of relevant tweets from these two groups. Our pipeline achieves macro F1 scores on out of sample balanced test sets ranging from 0.76 to 0.97—accuracy in line and even exceeding the state of the art. We then use the classifier to discover hate and counter speech in more than 135,000 fully-resolved Twitter conversations occurring from 2013 to 2018 and study their frequency and interaction. Altogether, our results highlight the potential of automated methods to evaluate the impact of coordinated counter speech in stabilizing conversations on social media.

1 Introduction

Hate speech is a growing problem in many countries [Bakalis, 2015, Hawdon et al., 2017], it can have serious psychological consequences [Oksanen et al., 2018], and is related to, and perhaps even contributing to, real-world violence [Müller and Schwarz, 2019]. While censorship can help curb hate speech [Álvarez-Benjumea and Winter, 2018], it can also impinge on civil liberties and might merely disperse rather than reduce hate [Chandrasekharan et al., 2017]. A promising alternative approach to reduce toxic discourse without recourse to censorship is so-called *counter speech*, which broadly refers to citizens' response to hateful speech in order to stop it, reduce its consequences, and discourage it [Benesch et al., 2016, Rieger et al., 2018].

It is unknown, however, whether counter speech is actually effective due to the lack of systematic large-scale studies on its impact [Gaffney et al., 2019, Gagliardone et al., 2015]. A major reason has been the difficulty of designing automated algorithms for discovering counter speech in large online corpora, stemming mostly from the lack of labeled training sets including both hate and counter speech. Past studies that provided insightful analyses of the effectiveness of counter speech mostly used hand-coded examples and were thus limited to small samples of discourse [Mathew et al., 2018, 2019, Wright et al., 2017, Ziegele et al., 2018, Ziems et al., 2020].

We perform the first large-scale classification

---

[*]Denotes equal contribution.

Proceedings of the Fourth Workshop on Online Abuse and Harms, pages 102–112
Online, November 20, 2020. ©2020 Association for Computational Linguistics
https://doi.org/10.18653/v1/P17

study of hate and counter speech, using a unique situation in Germany, where self-labeling hate and counter speech groups engaged in discussions around current societal topics such as immigration and elections. One is "Reconquista Germanica" (RG), a highly-organized hate group which aimed to disrupt political discussions and promote the right-wing populist, nationalist party Alternative für Deutschland (AfD). At their peak time, RG had between 1,500 and 3,000 active members. The counter group "Reconquista Internet" (RI) formed in late April 2018 with the aim of countering RG's hateful messaging through counter speech and to re-balance the public discourse. Within the first week, approximately 45,000 users joined the discord server where RI was being organized. At their peak, RI had an estimated 62,000 registered and verified members, of which over 4,000 were active on their discord server for the first few months. However, RI quickly lost a significant amount of active members, splintering into independent though cooperating smaller groups. We collected millions of tweets from members of these two groups and built labeled training set orders of magnitude larger than past studies of counter speech. By building an ensemble learning system with this large corpus we trained highly accurate classifiers which matched human judgment. We also used this system to study more than 135,000 conversations on German Twitter to understand the interactions between counter and hate groups online—an important first step in studying the impacts of counter speech on a large scale.

2 Background and Past Research

2.1 Hate and counter speech

There are many definitions of online hate speech and its meaning is developing over time. According to more narrow definitions, it refers to insults, discrimination, or intimidation of individuals or groups on the Internet, on the grounds of their supposed race, ethnic origin, gender, religion, or political beliefs [Blaya, 2019, Weber, 2009]. However, the term can also be extended to speech that aims to spread fearful, negative, and harmful stereotypes, call for exclusion or segregation, incite hatred, and encourage violence against a particular group [Gagliardone et al., 2015, you, 2019, twi, 2019, fac, 2019], be it using words, symbols, images, or other media.

Counter speech entails a citizen-generated response to online hate in order to stop and prevent the spread of hate speech, and if possible discourage it by changing perpetrators' attitudes and prevailing social norms. Counter speech intervention programs focus on empowering Internet users to speak up against online hate [Gagliardone et al., 2015]. For instance, programs such as *seriously* [ser, 2019] and the *Social Media Helpline* [smh, 2019] help users to recognize different kinds of online hate and prepare appropriate responses. Counter speech is seen as a feasible way of countering online hate, with a potential to increase civility and deliberation quality of online discussions [Ziegele et al., 2018, Habermas, 2015].

2.2 Classification of Hate and Counter Speech

There has been a lot of work on developing classifiers to detect hate speech online (e.g., [Brassard-Gourdeau and Khoury, 2018, Basile et al., 2019, Burnap et al., 2015, Burnap and Williams, 2016, Ribeiro et al., 2018, Zhang and Luo, 2019, Bosco et al., 2018, de Gibert et al., 2018, Kshirsagar et al., 2018, MacAvaney et al., 2019, Malmasi and Zampieri, 2018, Pitsilis et al., 2018, Al-Hassan and Al-Dossari, 2019, Vidgen and Yasseri, 2020, Zimmerman et al., 2018]). Many different learning algorithms have been used to perform this classification, ranging from support vector machines and random forests to convolutional and recurrent neural networks [Zhang and Luo, 2019, Burnap and Williams, 2016, Bosco et al., 2018, de Gibert et al., 2018, Kshirsagar et al., 2018, Malmasi and Zampieri, 2018, Pitsilis et al., 2018, Al-Hassan and Al-Dossari, 2019, Vidgen and Yasseri, 2020, Zimmerman et al., 2018]. These algorithms use a variety of feature extraction methods, for example, frequency scores of different n-grams, word and document embeddings [Le and Mikolov, 2014, Pennington et al., 2014], sentiment scores [Brassard-Gourdeau and Khoury, 2018, Burnap et al., 2015], part-of-speech scores such as the frequency of adjectives versus nouns used to describe target groups, 'othering' language (e.g., 'we' vs. 'them' [Burnap and Williams, 2016]), and meta-information about the text authors (e.g., keywords from user bios, usage patterns, their connections based on replies, retweets, and following patterns [Ribeiro et al., 2018]). Zhang and Luo [2019] compare several state-of-the art methods for automatic detection of hate speech, including

SVM and different implementations of convolutional neural networks (CNN) using word embeddings, on seven different Twitter data sets. The best performing methodology, based on a combination of CNN and gated recurrent networks (GRU), yields macro F1 scores ranging from 0.64 to 0.83. Other promising approaches include an ensemble of different CNNs with different weight initializations proposed by Zimmerman et al. [Zimmerman et al., 2018], BERT [Devlin et al., 2019], and a multi-view stacked SVM approach proposed by McAvaney et al. [MacAvaney et al., 2019]. The best results reported for these approaches are achieved by MacAvaney et al. [2019] using the `hatebase.org` database (a set of 24,802 tweets provided by Davidson et al. [2017], receiving F1 scores of 0.91 with a neural ensemble and 0.89 using BERT.

Compared to the number of studies investigating automatic detection of online hate, there have been far fewer studies that aim to automatically detect counter speech. One reason for this is the difficulty and subjectivity of automated identification of counter speech [Kennedy et al., 2017]. As a result, most past studies use hand-coded examples for this task. For instance, Mathew et al. [2019] analyzed more than 9,000 hand-coded counter speech and neutral comments posted in response to hateful YouTube videos. They found that for discriminating counter speech vs. non-counter speech, the combination of tf-idf vectors as features and logistic regression as the classifier performed best, achieving an F1 score of 0.73. In another study, Mathew et al. [2018] analyzed 1,290 pairs of Twitter messages containing hand-coded hate and counter speech. In this data set, a boosting algorithm based mostly on tf-idf values and lexical properties of tweets performed best, achieving F1 score of 0.77. Wright et al. [2017] provide a qualitative analysis of individual examples of counter speech. Ziegele et al. [2018] employed 52 undergraduate students to hand-code 9,763 Facebook messages. A study concurrent to ours [Ziems et al., 2020] investigated hate and counter speech in the context of racist sentiment surrounding COVID-19. They hand-coded 2,319 tweets, of which they labeled 678 as hateful, 359 as counter speech, and 961 as neutral. They were able to achieve F1 scores on unbalanced sets of 0.49 for counter and 0.68 for hate.

While extremely useful as a first step in analyzing counter speech, these studies are intrinsically limited because manual coding of counter speech is costly and hard to scale to the size needed to train sophisticated classifiers.

3 Data and Methods

3.1 Data Collection Strategy

We built our corpus of hate speech by collecting the timelines of 2,120 publicly known members of RG using the Twitter API. We used the list of hate accounts known as the "Böhmermann Liste," which was promoted as a list of accounts that spread hateful rhetoric, promote alt-right propaganda, or engage in directly hateful speech. As a secondary check of the list, we further verified these accounts by ensuring that the names and/or bios of these accounts contained known RG badges and no known badges of RI (see Table S1 in the Supplementary Materials for a list of these features). Finally, we had an expert hand-verify a large random sample of these accounts to ensure they were indeed actively taking part in hate speech. This resulted in more than 4.6 million tweets which with high likelihood contained some hateful rhetoric. While we cannot guarantee that every single one of these tweets was hate speech, given the purpose of these accounts, we can be reasonably confident in labeling the tweets sent from these accounts as hate speech.

Building our corpus of counter speech was a bit more challenging. We began our search with a hand-curated list of 103 accounts comprised of the core RI Twitter team, each of which were highly focused to their primary objective of engaging in various forms of counter speech. We collected the timelines of each of these known members of RI using the Twitter API. While we were highly confident in this sample of tweets being counter speech, it did not provide enough examples to build balanced training sets. Therefore, to expand our counter speech corpus we also collected the follower-followee network of these 103 core RI members using the Twitter API. This resulted in a list of 70,537 potential counter accounts.

We narrowed down this list of potential counter accounts by only including users that appeared in at least 5 of the follower-followee networks of core RI members. We then further required that each user self-identify as an RI member by using language features typical of RI members in their bios (see Table S1 in the Supplementary Materials for a list of these features) and also eliminated all users from this subset who used any RG features in their bios, to remove troll accounts that used both classes of features in their bios. Finally, we also enrolled an expert to check many of these accounts to ensure they were actively taking part in counter speech. This process resulted in a total of 1,472 profiles which we labeled as counter accounts.

To build our corpus of counter speech we collected the timelines of each of these additional accounts as well as the timelines of the core RI Twitter team. This resulted in a total of 4,323,881 tweets which had a high probability of containing counter speech. For training, we labeled all of these tweets as counter speech. It is likely that not all of these tweets in fact contained counter speech, especially those written by users that were identified through our network search. However, one can think of our data gathering process as trading-off some accuracy for a significant increase in scale. To check that accuracy was not strongly impacted, we verified that our classification of counter speech aligned with human judgment after classification (see Section 3.2) and added a post-hoc criterion to eliminate tweets that are not confidently labeled as counter speech (or hate speech) by the trained classifier.

In addition to these labeled tweets, we collected 204,544 fully-resolved conversations (reply trees) that grew in response to tweets of prominent accounts engaged in political speech on German Twitter from 2013 to 2018. These included accounts of large news organizations (e.g., faznet, tagesschau, tagesthemen, derspiegel and spiegelonline, diezeit, and zdfheute), well-known journalists and bloggers (e.g., annewilltalk, dunjahayali, janboehm, jkasek, maischberger, nicolediekmann), and politicians (e.g. cem_oezdemir, c_lindner, goeringeckardt, heikomaas, olafscholz, renatekuenast), all of which were known to be targets of hate speech. Indeed, the majority of these conversations involve instances of both hate and counter speech. We focused on 137,725 trees which originated from 11 accounts that contributed trees in at least 69 of 72 possible months throughout the examined period: derspiegel, goeringeckardt, jkasek, olafscholz, regsprecher, zdfheute, c_lindner, faznet, janboehm, nicolediekmann, and tagesschau. The tweets in these trees were used to study the dynamics of hate and counter speech over time and were not used to train or evaluate the accuracy of the classifiers. Figure 1 shows a few example trees

labeled using the pipeline described in Section 3.2.

3.2 Classification Pipeline

As is common in the literature [Schmidt and Wiegand, 2017] we split our classification pipeline into two stages: extraction of features from text, and classification based on those features. Before tweets were used in this pipeline they went through a minor preprocessing stage. All of the text was made lower case, and hashtags, usernames e.g., @username, punctuation and "RT:" were all stripped out of the tweet's text. Finally, depending on the model being trained, we removed stop words using one of two lists ("heavy" and "light"), or we did not remove any stop words. The "heavy" stop word list eliminated 231 German words based on nltk's German stop word list. The "light" stop word list was based on the heavy list without all words which have been shown to be relevant identifiers in an "us vs. them" discourse [Burnap and Williams, 2016], e.g., wir, uns, sie (we, us, them). This list eliminated 48 words (see Supplementary Materials).

To extract features from each processed timeline tweet, we constructed paragraph embeddings, also known as doc2vec models [Le and Mikolov, 2014], using the standard gensim implementation [Řehůřek and Sojka, 2010]. We will refer to a generic doc2vec model as $\mathcal{M}_{d2v}$. We performed a parameter sweep following standard practice and the guidelines of [Lau and Baldwin, 2016]. This sweep includes the analysis of several doc2vec parameters e.g, maximum distance between current and predicted words, "distributed-memory" vs "distributed bag of words" frameworks, and five different document label types, as well as three levels of stop word removal.

The five different document label types used to train $\mathcal{M}_{d2v}$ were as follows. 1) Each tweet was treated as a single document and labeled with a *unique* label, *viz.*, the unique tweet-id assigned by Twitter. 2) All tweets by a single *author* used the same document label, *viz.*, the user-id assigned by Twitter. This effectively made every tweet by a particular user a single document. These are the more traditional choices for document labeling. We also used three other labels which incorporate the classification stage into the feature development: 3) Each tweet was assigned a *group* label, with all tweets from RG accounts labeled "hate" and all

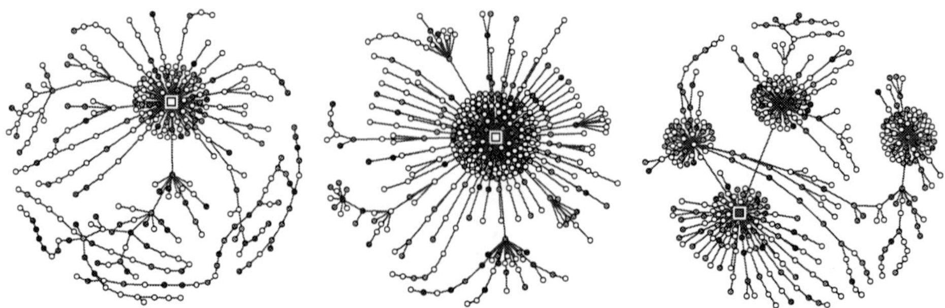

Figure 1: Examples of Twitter conversations (reply trees) with labeled hate (red), counter (blue), and neutral speech (white). The root node is shown as a large square. We used a confidence threshold of $\gamma = 0.75$ and a panel of 25 experts to classify these tweets, as described later in Section 3.2.

tweets from RI labeled "counter". This treats all RG tweets as one document and all RI tweets as another document, incorporating the the label we care about into the feature development stage. However, it conflates all the tweets into two documents. To avoid this we also trained $\mathcal{M}_{d2v}$ using multi-label setups. In particular, we trained models where we 4) labeled each tweet using both the author's identifier as well as the group identifier and separate models which 5) labeled each tweet with a unique identifier as well as the group identifier.

Every $\mathcal{M}_{d2v}$ was trained on five different but partially overlapping training sets (approximately 27% overlap). Each training set included 500,000 randomly selected tweets originating from RG accounts and another 500,000 coming from RI accounts. This produced a balanced training set with 50% hate speech and 50% counter speech. This is important in interpreting our classification results correctly, and avoiding accuracy inflation due to unbalanced sets, an apparent frequent problem with much of the current literature where hate speech is highly under sampled [Zhang and Luo, 2019, MacAvaney et al., 2019]. We refer to these training sets as $\mathcal{T}_{in,i}$, to denote the ith in-sample training set.

Let $\{\mathcal{M}_{d2v}, \mathcal{T}_{in,i}\}$ be a trained doc2vec model and the corresponding training set it was trained on. For each tweet $t_j \in \mathcal{T}_{in,i}$ we use $\mathcal{M}_{d2v}$ to infer a corresponding feature vector $x_j \in \mathbb{R}^{300}$, as $x_j = \mathcal{M}_{d2v}(t_j)$. With each tweet mapped to a feature vector we constructed a decision boundary between tweets from RG members and tweets from RI members using regularized logistic regression. In other words, we wrote the likelihood that tweet

j is labeled as coming from an RG/RI account as:

$$h_\theta(x_j) = g(\theta^T x_j), \qquad g(z) = \frac{1}{1 + e^{-z}}. \quad (1)$$

where $\theta \in \mathbb{R}^{300}$ is the vector of feature weights. Given a set of labels $\mathcal{L} = \{H, C\}$ for all tweets, we then learned the vector θ that best separates the data by minimizing the loss $-\sum_j \log h_\theta(x_j)$ under an ℓ_2 regularization constraint $\frac{1}{\lambda}||\theta||_2$, where λ is a fixed regularization parameter. We finally solved for θ using the the LBFGS algorithm as implemented in scikit-learn [Pedregosa et al., 2011].

To evaluate the accuracy of the resulting hypothesis function h_θ we evaluated its predictive accuracy on an out of sample test set denoted $\mathcal{T}_{out,i}$. Each out of sample test set $\mathcal{T}_{out,i}$ consisted of 50,000 tweets from both groups, chosen at random while ensuring that $\mathcal{T}_{out,i} \cap \mathcal{T}_{in,i} = \emptyset$. For each, $\mathcal{M}_{d2v}, h_\theta, \mathcal{T}_{out,i}$ combination we determined the probability of each class label $l \in \mathcal{L}$ for each $t \in \mathcal{T}_{out,i}$. In particular, for each tweet $t \in \mathcal{T}_{out,i}$ and each label $l \in \{H, C\}$ we computed $h_\theta(\mathcal{M}_{d2v}(t)) = p(l|\mathcal{M}_{d2v}(t); \theta)$, where $p(l|\mathcal{M}_{d2v}(t); \theta)$ denotes the probability that a tweet t has label l when classified with the feature vector calculated with model $\mathcal{M}_{d2v}$. The accuracy of this prediction was then assessed against the known labels.

In addition to logistic regressions, we also used word bias and n-gram based classifiers like those used in [Jaki and De Smedt, 2019], as well as xgboost [Chen and Guestrin, 2016] with a variety of parameters. However, in both cases the accuracy was worse (only slightly so for xgboost) than the logistic regression experiments reported in Section 4, so we omit these details for brevity.

Instead of looking for the single optimal

$(\mathcal{M}_{d2v}, h_\theta)$ parameterization we used an ensemble learning approach to classification by constructing a "panel of experts." The panel is comprised of N experts which are defined to be the combination of a feature extraction method $\mathcal{M}_{d2v}$ as well as a classification or hypothesis function h_θ. An ensemble learning approach combines multiple hypothesis functions to form a more robust hypothesis jointly which can lead to greater generalizability and increased out-of-sample accuracy.

In this ensemble classification method, each expert is given a tweet in a balanced out-of-sample test set $\mathcal{T}_{out,i}$ and asked to assign to it a probability that it belongs to each class $l \in \mathcal{L}$. For each tweet $t \in \mathcal{T}_{out,i}$ we computed a hate and counter score, S_h and S_c respectively, in the following way:

$$S_h(t) = \frac{1}{N} \sum_{i=1}^{N} \mathcal{E}_i(t; H), \qquad (2)$$

where $\mathcal{E}_i(t; l)$ is the probability that expert i assigns to label $l \in \{H, C\}$ for tweet t. Note that $S_c(t) = 1 - S_h(t)$. Note that $\mathcal{T}_{out,i} \cap \mathcal{T}_{in,j}$ need not be empty when $i \neq j$. As such, if a tweet appeared in the training set of an expert, we withheld its vote to avoid leaking training data.

For final classification we then defined a "confidence threshold" $\gamma \in [1/2, 1]$, and used a confidence voting system with thresholding to assign labels to tweets. If $S_h(t) > \gamma$ then t is labeled H, and if $S_c(t) > \gamma$ then t is labeled C. If $S_c(t)$ and $S_h(t)$ are both less than the given threshold the tweet is marked as neutral speech and the panel effectively abstains from voting. This results in some tweets which the panel of experts is not confident labeling as hate or counter speech—a crucial feature of the classifier. Indeed, the primary goal of our classifier is to identify hate and counter speech in online political discourse. Since not all online political discourse is hate or counter speech, the classifier must be able to flag neutral speech, too. The confidence threshold allows us to identify neutral speech by contrasting it with counter and hate speech.

An alternative solution would be to build a ternary classifier that can distinguish between hate, counter and neutral speech. A big challenge would then be to obtain a corpus of neutral speech relevant to political discourse, yet free of hate or counter speech. One could use tweets from politicians or news outlets to build a neutral corpus but then one would have to be careful to have a balanced representation across the political spectrum so that the neutral class is not biased toward the speech patterns of a particular party or news outlet. As we were confident in our hate and counter speech labeling and not confident in labeling an unbiased neutral corpus we chose to use our ranked classification method instead. However, this is certainly a potentially fruitful area for future research.

3.3 Crowdsourcing

To test whether the automated classifier corresponded to human judgment, we conducted a crowdsourcing study in which human judges evaluated some of the same tweets evaluated by the classifier. Since our corpus mostly contained German tweets, judges were recruited among members of Mechanical Turk who indicated that they can speak German. To qualify, they had to complete a relatively difficult German test item taken from a Goethe Institut's test for B1 German level, which asked them to interpret comments of three individuals about violence in video games. They also evaluated a test sample of a few dozen tweets from across the score spectrum. We also checked their answers to ensure a basic level of conscientiousness. Of the initial 55 candidate raters, 28 raters both solved the German test correctly and gave ratings to the test sample of tweets which indicated that they paid attention to their content. These 28 raters were asked to evaluate 5000 randomly selected tweets evenly spread across the whole range of scores $S_h(t)$. Raters ranked tweets on a scale of 1 to 5, from "very likely counter speech" to "very likely hate speech," with 3 corresponding to neutral content. Each tweet was evaluated by at least 2 different raters. Standard inter-rater reliability measures are not possible because most tweets were evaluated by a different pair of raters. However, median difference in ratings of each tweet was 0, and absolute mean was 0.57. In other words, different raters evaluated the tweets well within one point on our 5-point scale, suggesting reasonable correspondence of evaluations by different raters.

4   Results

Classification Results All combinations of feature extraction models $\mathcal{M}_{d2v}$ and classification functions h_θ produced a total of $N = 289$ possible experts. We found that the top 10 highest performing parameter sets across all five balanced training sets were the same for all $\mathcal{M}_{d2v}$. In particular, a maximum distance between the current and predicted word within a sentence of 5, ignoring all words that occurred less than 10 times, and an initial learning rate of 0.025 with a minimum learning rate of 0.00025, resulted in the highest accuracy. Each of these top performing experts were trained for 20 epochs, with a distributed bag-of-words framework. The optimal preprocessing parameters were also the same across the top 10. Each of these used light stop word removal. The optimal document labeling was also the same across these 10 experts, namely the author-group labeling. Recall that this labeling scheme tagged each tweet with the authors' unique identifier as well as the known group identification (RG vs RI). While the top models had the same training parameters aside from λ, the models were trained across 5 different training sets, which led to experts that could differ significantly.

These top 10 experts had individual F1 scores of 0.755 ± 0.0012 on their individual test sets, when forced to make a classification (confidence $\gamma = 1/2$). Taking into account that each $\mathcal{T}_{out,i}$ was balanced, containing 50,000 hate tweets and 50,000 counter tweets, these F1 scores do not suffer from accuracy inflation that would occur with an unbalanced test set [Zhang and Luo, 2019, MacAvaney et al., 2019]. This result compares well to previous studies that used smaller unbalanced data sets and achieved F1 scores ranging from 0.49 to 0.77 [Mathew et al., 2019, 2018, Ziems et al., 2020].

As mentioned in Section 3, we did not only use experts in isolation, but also in an ensemble learning approach where the experts could vote on the class label for each tweet in a given test set. Due to variations in the training sets and parameters, each expert had a slightly different view of the language, suggesting that combining their knowledge might be beneficial. Using the top 10 experts as a panel, instead of individually as just discussed, we obtained an improved average F1 score across all 5 out-of-sample test sets of 0.7616 ± 0.00083. Increasing the size of the panel to include the top 25 experts resulted in an average F1 score across the 5 test sets of 0.7618 ± 0.0007, see Table 1. We used this large panel for all of our subsequent results.

We also obtained improved results when we varied confidence threshold γ and allowed the experts to withhold their vote on contentious tweets. Increasing the confidence threshold naturally decreased the number of tweets classified as hate or counter speech. As expected, we found that this led to an increased overall precision, recall, and F1 score, since the labeled tweets were those for which the panel was more certain (see Table 1).

The scores for $\gamma > 1/2$ should be viewed with cautious optimism. The thresholding procedure causes many examples—correctly and incorrectly labeled—to be ignored from these calculations, which obviously may bias these scores in unpredictable ways. Even so, these scores provide a rough approximation of how accurate we can expect the classifier to be when applied to the reply tree dataset at a given confidence threshold. As discussed earlier, while this makes these scores challenging to interpret, the threshold is necessary to avoid mislabeling neutral speech in these conversations.

Comparison to Human Judgment Our crowdsourcing results, shown in Figure 2, suggest that our automated classifier aligns well with human judgment. Overall correlation between classifier scores and human judgments was $r = 0.94$. The correlation was somewhat lower for tweets classified as counter speech ($r = 0.75$) than for those classified as hate ($r = 0.96$). This could indicate that to humans counter speech looks more like 'neutral' discourse than hate speech does, or this could be a reflection of the slightly weaker counter speech labeling scheme described in Section 3.1 and suggest that counter speech is more challenging for the classifier to identify, or a combination of both. As expected, classifier scores around 0.5 received intermediate hate scores from human judges as well. The labels assigned by human judges were not used during the classification training or annotation process and were only used as a sanity check on the alignment of the classifier with human judgment.

Tree Coloring and Analysis We next used our classifier to label 137,725 fully-resolved conversations (reply trees) related to current societal and political issues on German Twitter between 2013 and 2018. Due to limited space, here we focus our analysis on two primary questions. For the interested reader, please see [Garland et al., 2020] for a much deeper analysis of this rich dataset.

First, how do hate and counter speech develop over time? To study this, we calculated the proportion of hate and counter speech of all speech occurring in each month (using $\gamma = 0.75$), as well as the average hate and counter score for all tweets

Results for Top Classifier Overall					Results for Panel of Experts				
γ	Precis.	Recall	F1	Labeled	γ	Precis.	Recall	F1	Labeled
0.50	0.757	0.757	0.757	100.0%	0.50	0.763	0.762	0.762	100.0%
0.65	0.837	0.837	0.837	70.29%	0.65	0.854	0.854	0.854	66.44%
0.75	0.883	0.882	0.882	53.99%	0.75	0.897	0.897	0.897	49.43%
0.85	0.924	0.924	0.924	37.93%	0.85	0.939	0.939	0.939	33.45%
0.95	0.970	0.970	0.970	18.49%	0.95	0.977	0.977	0.977	15.38%

Table 1: Classification scores for the top classifier (left) and a panel of experts using the top 25 experts (right). γ is the confidence threshold, and "Labeled" is the percentage of examples in the test set that are labeled as either hate or counter at a confidence level of γ. The top row represents traditional accuracy measures, which compare favorably to previous studies that used smaller unbalanced data sets and achieved F1 scores ranging from 0.49 to 0.77. The remaining rows are more nuanced and need to be viewed with cautious optimism, see text for a discussion of these issues.

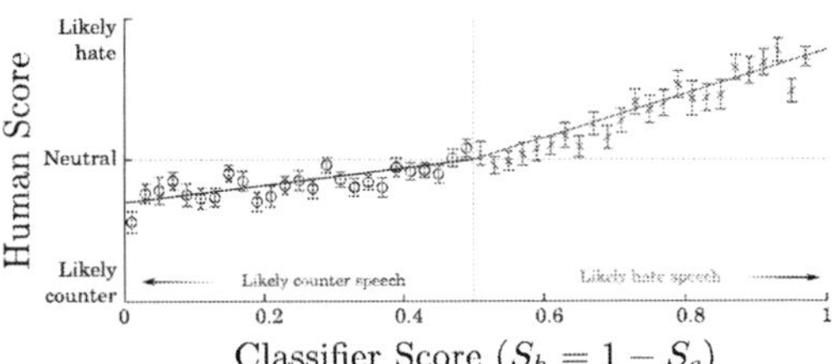

Figure 2: Human judgment of hate and counter speech corresponds to automated classification (panel of 25 experts). Average human judgments of tweets classified as counter speech by our method are shown in blue (left-half), and judgments for tweets classified as hate are shown in red (right-half). Individual human judgments are averaged across bins of width 0.02 of classifier scores for the original tweet. Error bars represent ± one standard error.

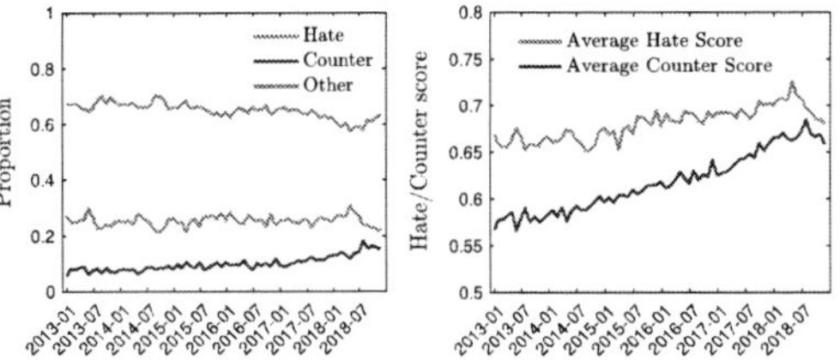

Figure 3: Proportion of hate, counter, and other speech in reply trees from 2013-2018, using a $\gamma = 0.75$ threshold (left panel), and average hate and counter score of tweets exceeding the $\gamma = 1/2$ threshold (right panel). After the establishment of RI in April 2018, the proportion of counter speech increases, and the ongoing increase in polarization is slowed down as indicated by a decrease in average hate and counter scores.

exceeding $\gamma = 1/2$. As Figure 3 shows, the proportion of hate speech was rather stable throughout the examined period, slightly increasing towards the end (red line in the left panel). However, its average score was consistently increasing over time (red line in the right panel). The proportion of counter speech was increasing somewhat throughout this period (blue line in the left panel), but its score increased quite strongly towards more extreme speech (blue line in the right panel). A notable change occurred in May 2018, when RI became active: the proportion of counter and other speech increased, and the proportion as well as extremity of hate speech decreased in the following months. This result suggests that organized counter speech might have helped in balancing polarized and hateful discourse, although causality is difficult to establish given the complex web of online and offline events and process in the broader society throughout that time.

Second, we conducted an initial analysis of how hate and counter speech interact in reply trees. We asked, how do tweets identified as hate or counter speech change the expected frequency of future hate and counter speech in a reply tree? For this analysis, we used reply trees that have at least 10 tweets identified as hate and at least 10 identified as counter speech, using a 70% threshold on scores assigned by a panel of the top 25 experts. We measured the overall frequency of assigned labels in every individual tree, and tracked how this frequency increases or decreases in time as more tweets identified as hate or counter are posted. We compared 6-month periods before and after the establishment of RI. Results are shown in Figure 4. Before RI was founded (Figure 4a), a low amount of hate tweets

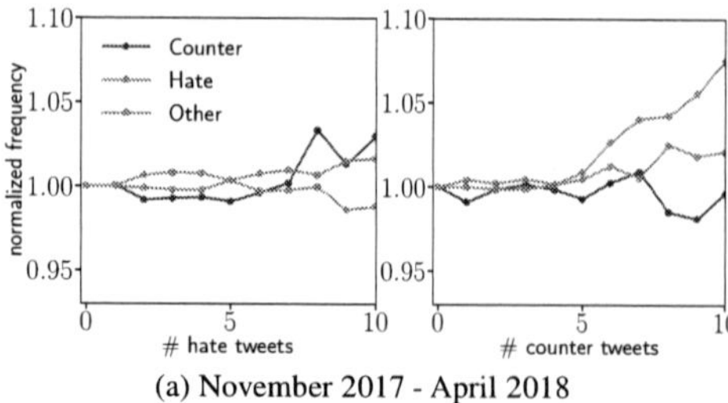

(a) November 2017 - April 2018

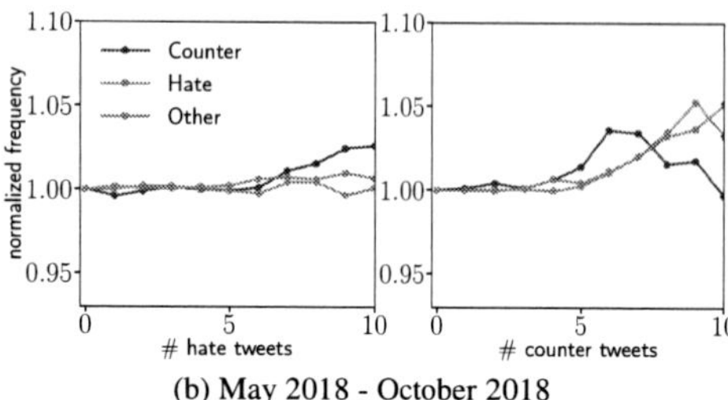

(b) May 2018 - October 2018

Figure 4: Frequency of hate, counter, and other tweets following a hate (counter) tweet, normalized by the overall frequency of these types of tweets in a tree. Panel (a) shows the 6-months period before the establishment of RI, and panel (b) shows the 6-months period after RI was formed. By comparing the right panels of both (a) and (b), tweets from organized counter speech tend to attract more counter and other speech and attract less hate speech than tweets from non-organized counter speech.

(first panel) somewhat attracted additional hate and suppressed counter speech. However, once many hate tweets were posted, counter speech increased and hate decreased. Similarly, counter tweets (second panel) did not have much effect on hate at first but once there were many counter tweets in a tree they attracted much more hate speech. Importantly, counter speech attracted less hate and stimulated additional counter speech more effectively after RI was formed in April 2018 (Figure 4b). In all time periods, we also found that counter speech tweets were more likely than hate speech to stimulate neutral or unclassified speech; suggesting that counter speech contributed to depolarizing individual discussions.

Taken together, these results suggest that organized counter speech was associated with a more balanced discourse, reflected in an increased proportion of counter speech in discussions and reduced extremity of hate (Figure 3) and counter speech having a strong influence in attracting more counter and neutral speech while not attracting more hate (Figure 4).

5 Conclusion

Online hate speech is a problem shared by every social media platform, and yet there are still no clear solutions to this growing problem. A potential solution aimed at returning online discourse to civility is citizen-generated counter speech. Until now, studying counter speech and its effectiveness has been limited to small-scale hand-labeled studies. In this paper, we leveraged a unique situation in Germany to perform the first large-scale automated classification of counter speech. Our methods provided F1 scores on a balanced set of 100,000 out-of-sample tweets ranging from 0.76 to 0.97 depending on the confidence threshold being used. Beyond accuracy measures, we used crowdsourcing to verify that the conclusions reached by our classifier were in-line with human judgment.

We were able to use this classification algorithm to identify hate and counter speech in over 135,000 fully resolved Twitter conversations from 2013-2018. Our results suggest that counter speech might have contributed to depolarization of discussions and that organized counter speech by RI might have stimulated further counter speech and attracted less hateful responses. While causality cannot be established due to the many other ongoing societal processes at the time, our results suggest that organized counter speech may be a powerful solution to combating the spread of hate online. We hope that the framework developed in this paper will be a starting point to understand the dynamics between hate and counter speech and help develop actionable strategies.

Acknowledgments

The authors would like to thank Will Tracy and Santa Fe Institute's Applied Complexity team for support and resources throughout this project. J.G. was partially supported by an Omidyar and an Applied Complexity Fellowship at the Santa Fe Institute. J.-G.Y. was supported by a James S. McDonnell Foundation Postdoctoral Fellowship Award. J.-G.Y and L.H.-D. were supported by Google Open Source under the Open-Source Complex Ecosystems And Networks (OCEAN) project. M.G. was partially supported by NSF-DRMS 1757211. Any opinions, findings, and conclusions or recommendations expressed in this material are those of the authors and do not necessarily reflect the views of any of the funders.

References

Chara Bakalis. *Cyberhate: An issue of continued concern for the council of Europe's anti-racism commission.* Council of Europe, 2015.

James Hawdon, Atte Oksanen, and Pekka Räsänen. Exposure to online hate in four nations: A cross-national consideration. *Deviant Behav.*, 38(3):254–266, 2017.

Atte Oksanen, Markus Kaakinen, Jaana Minkkinen, Pekka Räsänen, Bernard Enjolras, and Kari Steen-Johnsen. Perceived societal fear and cyberhate after the November 2015 paris terrorist attacks. *Terror. Political Violence*, pages 1–20, 2018.

Karsten Müller and Carlo Schwarz. Fanning the flames of hate: Social media and hate crime. *SSRN:3082972*, 2019.

Amalia Álvarez-Benjumea and Fabian Winter. Normative change and culture of hate: An experiment in online environments. *Eur. Sociol. Rev.*, 34(3):223–237, 2018.

Eshwar Chandrasekharan, Umashanthi Pavalanathan, Anirudh Srinivasan, Adam Glynn, Jacob Eisenstein, and Eric Gilbert. You can't stay here: The efficacy of Reddit's 2015 ban examined through hate speech. In *Proceedings of the ACM on Human-Computer Interaction*, volume 1, pages 1–22, 2017.

S Benesch, D Ruths, KP Dillon, H M Saleem, and L Wright. Considerations for successful counterspeech, 2016. URL https://https://dangerousspeech.org/considerations-for-successful-counterspeech/.

Diana Rieger, Josephine B Schmitt, and Lena Frischlich. Hate and counter-voices in the internet: Introduction to the special issue. *SCM Stud. Commun. Media*, 7(4):459–472, 2018.

Hannah Gaffney, David P Farrington, Dorothy L Espelage, and Maria M Ttofi. Are cyberbullying intervention and prevention programs effective? A systematic and meta-analytical review. *Aggress. Violent Behav.*, 45:134–153, 2019.

Iginio Gagliardone, Danit Gal, Thiago Alves, and Gabriela Martinez. *Countering online hate speech.* Unesco Publishing, 2015.

Binny Mathew, Navish Kumar, Pawan Goyal, and Animesh Mukherjee. Analyzing the hate and counter speech accounts on Twitter. *arXiv:1812.02712*, 2018.

Binny Mathew, Punyajoy Saha, Hardik Tharad, Subham Rajgaria, Prajwal Singhania, Suman Kalyan Maity, Pawan Goyal, and Animesh Mukherjee. Thou shalt not hate: Countering online hate speech. In *Proceedings of the International AAAI Conference on Web and Social Media*, volume 13, pages 369–380, 2019.

Lucas Wright, Derek Ruths, Kelly P Dillon, Haji Mohammad Saleem, and Susan Benesch. Vectors for counterspeech on Twitter. In *Proceedings of the first workshop on abusive language online*, pages 57–62, 2017.

Marc Ziegele, Pablo Jost, Marike Bormann, and Dominique Heinbach. Journalistic counter-voices in comment sections: Patterns, determinants, and potential consequences of interactive moderation of uncivil user comments. *SCM Stud. Commun. Media*, 7(4):525–554, 2018.

Caleb Ziems, Bing He, Sandeep Soni, and Srijan Kumar. Racism is a virus: Anti-asian hate and counterhate in social media during the COVID-19 crisis. *arXiv:2005.12423*, 2020.

Catherine Blaya. Cyberhate: A review and content analysis of intervention strategies. *Aggress. Violent Behav.*, 45:163–172, 2019.

Anne Weber. *Manual on hate speech.* Council Of Europe, 2009.

Youtube: Hate speech policy, 2019. URL https://support.google.com/youtube/answer/2801939.

Twitter: Hateful conduct policy, 2019. URL https://help.twitter.com/en/rules-and-policies/hateful-conduct-policy.

Facebook: Hate speech, 2019. URL https://www.facebook.com/communitystandards/hate_speech.

Seriously, 2019. URL http://www.seriously.ong.

Social Media Helpline, 2019. URL https://socialmediahelpline.com/counterspeech-dos-and-donts-for-students/.

Jürgen Habermas. *Between facts and norms: Contributions to a discourse theory of law and democracy.* John Wiley & Sons, 2015.

Éloi Brassard-Gourdeau and Richard Khoury. Impact of sentiment detection to recognize toxic and subversive online comments. *arXiv:1812.01704*, 2018.

Valerio Basile, Cristina Bosco, Elisabetta Fersini, Nozza Debora, Viviana Patti, Francisco Manuel Rangel Pardo, Paolo Rosso, Manuela Sanguinetti, et al. Semeval-2019 task 5: Multilingual detection of hate speech against immigrants and women in twitter. In *13th International Workshop on Semantic Evaluation*, pages 54–63. Association for Computational Linguistics, 2019.

Pete Burnap, Omer F Rana, Nick Avis, Matthew Williams, William Housley, Adam Edwards, Jeffrey Morgan, and Luke Sloan. Detecting tension in online communities with computational Twitter analysis. *Technol. Forecast. Soc. Change*, 95:96–108, 2015.

Pete Burnap and Matthew L Williams. Us and them: identifying cyber hate on Twitter across multiple protected characteristics. *EPJ Data science*, 5(1):11, 2016.

Manoel Horta Ribeiro, Pedro H Calais, Yuri A Santos, Virgílio AF Almeida, and Wagner Meira Jr. Characterizing and detecting hateful users on Twitter. In *Twelfth international AAAI conference on web and social media*, 2018.

Ziqi Zhang and Lei Luo. Hate speech detection: A solved problem? the challenging case of long tail on Twitter. *Semantic Web*, 10(5):925–945, 2019.

Cristina Bosco, Dell'Orletta Felice, Fabio Poletto, Manuela Sanguinetti, and Tesconi Maurizio. Overview of the evalita EVALITA hate speech detection task. In *EVALITA 2018-Sixth Evaluation Campaign of Natural Language Processing and Speech Tools for Italian*, volume 2263. CEUR, 2018.

Ona de Gibert, Naiara Perez, Aitor García-Pablos, and Montse Cuadros. Hate speech dataset from a white supremacy forum. In *Proceedings of the 2nd Workshop on Abusive Language Online (ALW2)*, pages 11–20. Association for Computational Linguistics, 2018.

Rohan Kshirsagar, Tyus Cukuvac, Kathleen McKeown, and Susan McGregor. Predictive embeddings for hate speech detection on Twitter. In *Proceedings of the 2nd Workshop on Abusive Language Online (ALW2)*, pages 26–32. Association for Computational Linguistics, 2018.

Sean MacAvaney, Hao-Ren Yao, Eugene Yang, Katina Russell, Nazli Goharian, and Ophir Frieder. Hate speech detection: Challenges and solutions. *PLOS ONE*, 14(8), 2019.

Shervin Malmasi and Marcos Zampieri. Challenges in discriminating profanity from hate speech. *J. Exp. Theor. Artif. Intell.*, 30(2):187–202, 2018.

Georgios K Pitsilis, Heri Ramampiaro, and Helge Langseth. Effective hate-speech detection in Twitter data using recurrent neural networks. *Appl. Intell.*, 48(12):4730–4742, 2018.

Areej Al-Hassan and Hmood Al-Dossari. Detection of hate speech in social networks: a survey on multilingual corpus. In *6th International Conference on Computer Science and Information Technology*, 2019.

Bertie Vidgen and Taha Yasseri. Detecting weak and strong islamophobic hate speech on social media. *J. Inf. Technol. Politics*, 17(1):66–78, 2020.

Steven Zimmerman, Udo Kruschwitz, and Chris Fox. Improving hate speech detection with deep learning ensembles. In *Proceedings of the Eleventh International Conference on Language Resources and Evaluation (LREC 2018)*, 2018.

Quoc Le and Tomas Mikolov. Distributed representations of sentences and documents. In *International conference on machine learning*, pages 1188–1196, 2014.

Jeffrey Pennington, Richard Socher, and Christopher D Manning. Glove: Global vectors for word representation. In *Proceedings of the 2014 conference on empirical methods in natural language processing*, pages 1532–1543, 2014.

Jacob Devlin, Ming-Wei Chang, Kenton Lee, and Kristina Toutanova. BERT: Pre-training of deep bidirectional transformers for language understanding. In *Proceedings of NAACL-HLT 2019*, pages 4171—4186, 2019.

Thomas Davidson, Dana Warmsley, Michael Macy, and Ingmar Weber. Automated hate speech detection and the problem of offensive language. In *Eleventh international AAAI conference on Web and social media*, 2017.

George Kennedy, Andrew McCollough, Edward Dixon, Alexei Bastidas, John Ryan, Chris Loo, and Saurav Sahay. Technology solutions to combat online harassment. In *Proceedings of the first workshop on abusive language online*, pages 73–77, 2017.

Anna Schmidt and Michael Wiegand. A survey on hate speech detection using natural language processing. In *Proceedings of the Fifth International Workshop on Natural Language Processing for Social Media*, pages 1–10, 2017.

Radim Řehůřek and Petr Sojka. Software framework for topic modelling with large corpora. In *Proceedings of the LREC 2010 Workshop on New Challenges for NLP Frameworks*, pages 45–50, Valletta, Malta, 2010. ELRA.

Jey Han Lau and Timothy Baldwin. An empirical evaluation of doc2vec with practical insights into document embedding generation. In *Proceedings of the 1st Workshop on Representation Learning for NLP*, pages 78–86. Association for Computational Linguistics, 2016.

F. Pedregosa, G. Varoquaux, A. Gramfort, V. Michel, B. Thirion, O. Grisel, M. Blondel, P. Prettenhofer, R. Weiss, V. Dubourg, J. Vanderplas, A. Passos, D. Cournapeau, M. Brucher, M. Perrot, and E. Duchesnay. Scikit-learn: Machine learning in Python. *J. Mach. Learn. Res.*, 12: 2825–2830, 2011.

Sylvia Jaki and Tom De Smedt. Right-wing German hate speech on Twitter: Analysis and automatic detection. *arXiv:1910.07518*, 2019.

Tianqi Chen and Carlos Guestrin. xgboost: A scalable tree boosting system. In *Proceedings of the 22nd ACM SIGKDD international conference on knowledge discovery and data mining*, pages 785–794, 2016.

Joshua Garland, Keyan Ghazi-Zahedi, Jean-Gabriel Young, Laurent Hébert-Dufresne, and Mirta Galesic. Impact and dynamics of hate and counter speech online. *arXiv preprint arXiv:2009.08392*, 2020.

Moderating Our (Dis)Content: Renewing the Regulatory Approach

Claire Pershan

October 2020

Proceedings of the Fourth Workshop on Online Abuse and Harms, page 113
Online, November 20, 2020. ©2020 Association for Computational Linguistics
https://doi.org/10.18653/v1/P17

Six Attributes of Unhealthy Conversations

Ilan Price
University of Oxford
ilan.price@maths.ox.ac.uk

Jordan Gifford-Moore
jordan.gifford-moore@flinders.edu.au

Jory Fleming
University of South Carolina
fleminj6@mailbox.sc.edu

Saul Musker
saul@presidency.gov.za

Maayan Roichman
University of Oxford
maayan.roichman@anthro.ox.ac.uk

Guillaume Sylvain
gs1867@nyu.edu

Nithum Thain
Google Brain
nthain@google.com

Lucas Dixon
Google Research
ldixon@google.com

Jeffrey Sorensen
Jigsaw
sorenj@google.com

Abstract

We present a new dataset of approximately 44000 comments labeled by crowdworkers. Each comment is labelled as either 'healthy' or 'unhealthy', in addition to binary labels for the presence of six potentially 'unhealthy' sub-attributes: (1) hostile; (2) antagonistic, insulting, provocative or trolling; (3) dismissive; (4) condescending or patronising; (5) sarcastic; and/or (6) an unfair generalisation. Each label also has an associated confidence score. We argue that there is a need for datasets which enable research based on a broad notion of 'unhealthy online conversation'. We build this typology to encompass a substantial proportion of the individual comments which contribute to unhealthy online conversation. For some of these attributes, this is the first publicly available dataset of this scale. We explore the quality of the dataset, present some summary statistics and initial models to illustrate the utility of this data, and highlight limitations and directions for further research.

1 Introduction

Analysis of online user discussion continues to be a critical area of interdisciplinary research. Increasing rates of internet access and the development of a diverse range of online forums has allowed for conversation between individuals across the globe on an extraordinary range of topics. However, this has been accompanied by a surge in abuse and other negative behaviours online, the impacts of which have been well-documented in academic research. It has been found that targeted negative comments and harassment online can seriously impact individual well-being (Weingartner and Stahel, 2019; Bauman, 2013), force users to leave a community or reduce online participation (Wulczyn et al., 2017; Blackburn and Kwak, 2014), and potentially lead to offline hate-crimes (Mulki et al., 2019; Hassan et al., 2018). While these forms of comments may be explicit or overtly harmful, they are also often difficult to detect or ambiguous. Where there are insufficient moderation resources to scale with a forum's user-base, this can lead to unchecked negative discourse, or cause website administrators to restrict user comment functions. This means that research which aims to enable automated moderation, provide a review triage service for human moderation teams, or design systems to nudge users towards healthier conversation, has significant potential for contributing to both the availability and quality of online discourse.

A persistent challenge for researchers and site administrators in this area is the need to: (a) establish a typology of comments which are undesirable in online discussions; (b) apply this typology in a consistent and reliable manner; and (c) account for adversarial user behaviour in response to moderation. This is complicated by the fact that there is no single objective set of categories for speech which ought to be excluded in all contexts, with

Proceedings of the Fourth Workshop on Online Abuse and Harms, pages 114–124
Online, November 20, 2020. ©2020 Association for Computational Linguistics
https://doi.org/10.18653/v1/P17

perceptions of undesirable speech differing across individuals, cultures, geographies, and online communities (Vidgen et al., 2019).

Prior research on toxic comments online has found that classifiers trained on crowdsourced data can be effective at detecting the most overt forms of toxic comments. However, there remain difficulties in detecting subtler forms of toxicity which may be implicit, require idiosyncratic knowledge, familiarity with the conversation context, or familiarity with particular cultural tropes (Kohli et al., 2018; van Aken et al., 2018; Parekh and Patel, 2017). One of the key ingredients to progress on this front will be high quality, large, annotated datasets addressing these more subtle harmful attributes, from which machine learning models will be able to learn. Unfortunately, for most subtler toxic attributes there are few available datasets (or none, particularly in many languages other than English), which is a bottleneck preventing further research (Fortuna et al., 2019).

We aim to contribute to research in this area through the release of the Unhealthy Comment Corpus (UCC) of approximately 44,000 comments and corresponding crowdsourced labels and confidence scores. The labelling typology for the dataset identifies for each comment a higher-level classification of whether that comment 'has a place in a healthy online conversation', accompanied for each comment by binary labels for whether it is: (1) hostile, (2) antagonistic, insulting, provocative or trolling (together, 'antagonistic'), (3) dismissive, (4) condescending or patronising (together, 'condescending'), (5) sarcastic, and/or (6) an unfair generalisation. For each label there is also an associated confidence score (between 0.5 and 1). The UCC is open source and available on Github.[1]

The UCC contributes further high quality data on attributes like sarcasm, hostility, and condescension, adding to existing datasets on these and related attributes (Wang and Potts, 2019; Davidson et al., 2017; Wulczyn et al., 2017; Chen et al., 2017), and provides (to the best of our knowledge) the first dataset of this scale with labels for dismissiveness, unfair generalisations, antagonistic behavior, and overall assessments of whether those comments fall within 'healthy' conversation. We also make use of and illustrate the benefits of annotator trustworthiness scores when crowdsourcing labels on subjective data of this sort.

This paper is structured as follows. Section 2 outlines the motivation and background to the UCC attribute typology. Section 3 details the data collection and quality control processes. In Section 4 we present some summary statistics, benefits, and limitations of the data, and in Section 5 we present a baseline classification model for this dataset, and evaluate its performance. Section 6 highlights potential sources of bias in this dataset, and the need to be cognisant of these when conducting further research in this area (Dixon et al., 2018).

2 From 'toxic' comments to 'unhealthy' conversation

In this paper, we broadly characterise a healthy online public conversation as one where posts and comments are made in good faith, are not overly hostile or destructive, and generally invite engagement. Such a conversation may include robust engagement and debate, and is generally (though not always) focused on substance and ideas. Importantly, though, healthy contributions to online conversations are not necessarily friendly, grammatically correct, well constructed, intellectual, substantive, or even free of any vulgarity.

Some harmful contributions to conversations are obviously derogatory, threatening, violent, or insulting (Anderson et al., 2018), and these are the sorts of comments which have been the primary focus of research in algorithmic moderation assistance and related areas. However, many of those comments which deter people from engagement or create downward spirals in interactions can be more subtle (Zhang et al., 2018). This is especially the case with conversations *online*, many of which (i) take place in a 'public' forum that is visible to thousands of others, and (ii) involve strangers who have never met and know little about one another (Santana, 2014). These two features of online conversations can sometimes enhance commenters' sensitivity to subtler forms of toxicity like sarcasm, condescension, or dismissiveness, amplifying their negative impact on conversations despite the fact that these attributes may be less (or not at all) harmful in other specific contexts.

Identifying subtle indicators of problematic online comments is a difficult task. There are at least three reasons for this. First, they are less extreme and therefore less likely to use clearly identifiable explicit or inflammatory language. Second, a substantive point might be made in an inflammatory

---

[1] github.com/conversationai/unhealthy-conversations

way, or a remark may be perceived differently depending on the context, norms, and expectations of the reader. Third, there is an even greater risk of identifying 'false positives' and 'false negatives', since many of the expressions used in subtle forms of toxicity can also be deployed for positive contributions. For example, sarcasm is often used in derisive or bullying ways, but it can also be used for humour or to express a substantive, inoffensive point (Vidgen et al., 2019).

The challenge is to identify the subtle characteristics of harmful comments online despite their ambiguity, without falsely identifying healthy comments. We differentiate between two categories. The first, which is the most well studied to date, are those whose explicit intention is to insult, threaten, or abuse. The second category, are comments which engage with others, share an opinion, or contribute to the conversation, but are written in a way which is likely to antagonise, hurt, or deter others. We found these comments to be at least as prevalent in the sample data (Table 1). Our typology of unhealthy attributes aims to include this second category of comments, and determine whether annotators believe they belong in a healthy online conversation.

Our hypothesis was that together these 6 attributes account for the majority of 'unhealthy' comments online, but that there will still be some comments that are 'unhealthy' but do not display any sub-attribute, and also some which are 'healthy' despite representing one or more sub-attributes (see Figure 1). In general, whether the presence of these attributes indicates healthy or unhealthy conversation will also depend significantly on the nature of the forum and users. Nonetheless, the combination of an abstract 'health' rating with the other 6 attributes provides a useful dataset for investigating nuanced comments, and could be used to help develop a broader range of models that are customised for specific production environments.

3 Source data and annotation

The dataset comprises randomly chosen comments from the Globe and Mail news site (sampled from the SFU Opinion and Comment Corpus dataset) (Kolhatkar et al., 2019), of 250 characters or less. Comment scores were crowdsourced using Figure Eight (now Appen). The annotation job consisted of 588 crowdworkers (annotators) providing

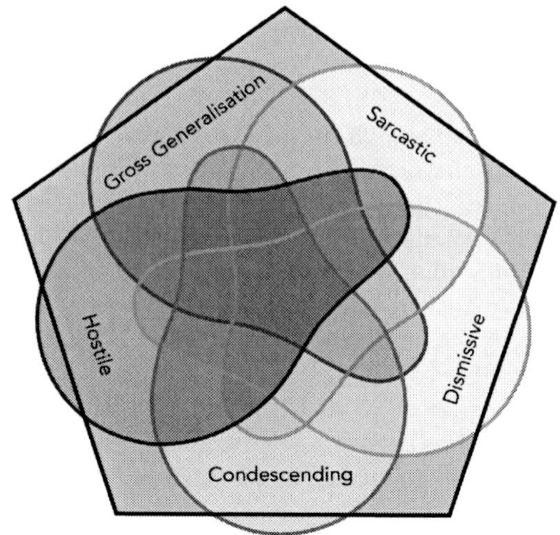

Figure 1: A visualisation of the proposed typology of unhealthy online comments. The grey pentagon represents unhealthy comments. Note that in this figure, 'hostile' and 'antagonistic' are represented jointly as 'hostile'.

244468 judgements on 44355 comments.[2] Each annotator was asked to identify for each comment whether it was healthy and if any of the attributes were present, in the form of a standard questionnaire (see Appendix A). Annotators were not given any wider context or additional information about where a comment was posted or how it was engaged with by other users.

To both accommodate and attempt to resolve meaningful disagreement, we applied a dynamic judgement method which requests additional annotations for those comments on which there was insufficient consensus (either yes or no with a confidence of less than 75%). All comments were annotated at least three times, and more annotators were added, up to a limit of five annotators per comment until sufficient consensus was reached.

Annotation Job Refinement. The inherent subtlety, subjectivity, and frequent ambiguity of the attributes covered in this dataset make crowdsourcing quality attribute labels an unavoidably difficult process.

Typically the goal in an annotation task would simply be to maximise agreement between the multiple annotators of each comment. However, when the annotation task is inherently subjective and

---

[2]According to statistics provided by Appen, the average time spent on those annotations which were included in the final dataset was between 12 and 13 seconds per comment.

meaningful difference of opinion is itself valuable data, the goal becomes instead to maximise common understanding of the task across annotators. This entails tailoring the phrasing of the questions put to annotators, so as to create as common an understanding as possible of what each question is really asking. This way, disagreement between annotators reflected in the dataset will represent different reasonable readings of the same comment which are themselves important to capture. In research on irony and sarcasm, for example, Filatova noted the difficulty even among expert researchers in formally defining these terms (Filatova, 2012). For the other attributes included in this dataset which are as (if not more) ambiguous and subtle than sarcasm, we expect this to hold true as well.

The exact wording of each question on the questionnaire went through multiple iterations, tested by smaller scale experiments to evaluate effectiveness. The quality of the resulting data was evaluated manually by our team, calculating the proportion of perceived mistaken annotations and their 'severity': to what extent a judgement was 'obviously wrong', as opposed to an understandable alternative reading of a comment.

We found that providing annotators with precise and more comprehensive definitions of each attribute was not more likely to produce inter-annotator agreement or better quality data. Neither, however, were best results produced by asking simple, 'yes or no' questions such as 'Is this comment dismissive?' for all attributes. The best results were achieved by relying primarily on annotators implicit understandings of and intuitions about the attributes, aided by brief inline explanations. We added explanations to avoid mistakes for those attributes which are more ambiguous, and for which our smaller tests had indicated required further guidance. These can be seen in the questionnaire included as Appendix A.

To ensure that disagreement reflects reasonable difference of opinion, rather than inattention or misunderstanding of the task, it is necessary to apply a method of quality control. The attempt to create a labeled dataset is premised on the assumption of some 'ground truth'; that it is possible for comments to have labels and confidence scores accurately representing the presence of one or more attributes to some extent. However, the extent to which a comment displays one or more attribute is subjective, and the scores would be unhelpful

if they did not capture what a wider and more diverse audience than our team of authors would understand the comments to mean. Our process of quality control therefore aimed to reduce the number of 'bad' annotators, those who either do not understand or appropriately engage with the task, while still allowing for differences of opinion.

Our primary quality control mechanism was to collate a set of 'test comments', for which we had manually established the correct answers. Annotators encountered one test comment per batch of seven comments they reviewed, without knowing which of the seven was the test comment, and their running accuracy on these test comments was defined as their 'trustworthiness score'. The task required that annotators maintain a trustworthiness score of more than 78%. If an annotator dropped below this level, they were removed from the annotator pool for this task, and all of their prior annotations were discarded[3]. The removed 'bad' annotator judgements were replaced by newly collected trusted judgements as necessary.

We restricted our test comments to what were (in our view) clear and definitive examples of the attributes, such that one would fail on the test comments only if one has an incorrect understanding of what is meant by a particular attribute. In the course of our preliminary small-scale refining iterations of the questionnaire, analysis of responses revealed some recurring misunderstandings or mistakes. For example, a common error was to label all non-sarcastic humour as sarcasm, or to conflate polite disagreement with dismissiveness. As a result, we identified and included specific test comments, drawn from real examples, aimed at reducing these common errors.

We included very few test comments for the higher level question on whether a comment belongs in a healthy conversation. Any test questions on this topic were very extreme examples, such as highly abusive explicit comments, to ensure that annotators were not randomly answering that question. We had two reasons for minimising the use of test comments for this question. Firstly, since this was in our view the most open-ended question, it is difficult to establish tests on the basis of which to exclude annotators. Secondly, allowing greater

---

[3]This was a threshold selected through initial test jobs, to balance budget and quality considerations. A higher threshold yields more trustworthy annotations, but consequently discards more existing data when annotators drop below that threshold.

annotator discretion on this question provides insight on whether there is a correlation between the six attributes and being labelled as unhealthy.[4]

4 The UCC dataset

The dataset comprises a total of 44355 comments labelled 'yes' or 'no' for each attribute, along with a confidence score for each label. The labels and corresponding confidence scores for each attribute are based on an aggregation of the answers given by different annotators, weighted by their respective 'trustworthiness' scores. As an example to demonstrate this process, consider a comment annotated by 5 annotators with trustworthiness scores 0.78, 0.85, 0.9, 1.0, and 0.95, who judge a comment for a particular attribute with judgements 'yes', 'yes', 'yes', 'no', 'yes' respectively. Let T be the sum of their trustworthiness scores, and T_y, T_n the sum of the trustworthiness scores of those who answered 'yes' and 'no' respectively. The label is then determined by which of T_y or T_n is larger, in this case it is T_y, and the confidence score is T_y/T, in this case 0.78.

The proportion of comments that contain each attribute is shown in Table 1 and the confidence distributions are shown in Figure 2.

Attribute	Proportion
Antagonistic/Insulting/Trolling	4.7 %
Condescending/Patronising	5.5%
Dismissive	3.1%
(Unfair) Generalisation	2%
Hostile	2.5%
Sarcastic	4.3%
Unhealthy	7.5%

Table 1: Percentage of positive labels for each attribute.

As the comments were sampled from the SFU Opinion and Comment Corpus dataset, the prevalence for each attribute is inevitably low. Despite the label imbalance, the dataset represents an important contribution to identification of this wider variety of subtle attributes, with thousands of positive examples for each. Our manual analysis during initial iterations of the annotation job indicated that

---

[4]There remains a clear methodological issue with using this data for comparing the set of comments classed as 'unhealthy' with those classed as one or more of the other attributes: having been asked all questions as part of the same questionnaire, annotators may have been primed to associate the attributes with 'unhealthiness', even if they would not have done so otherwise.

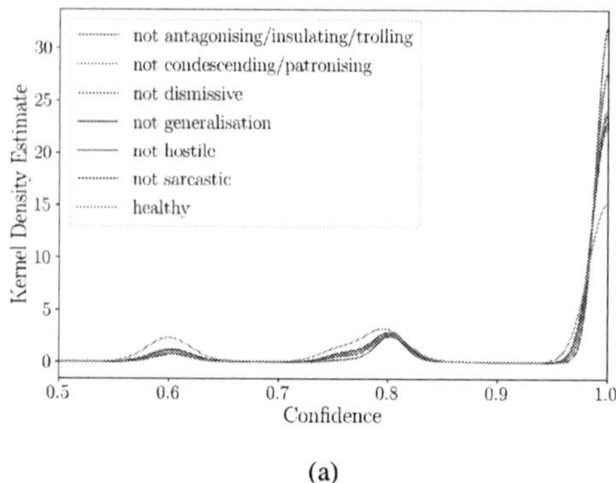

(a)

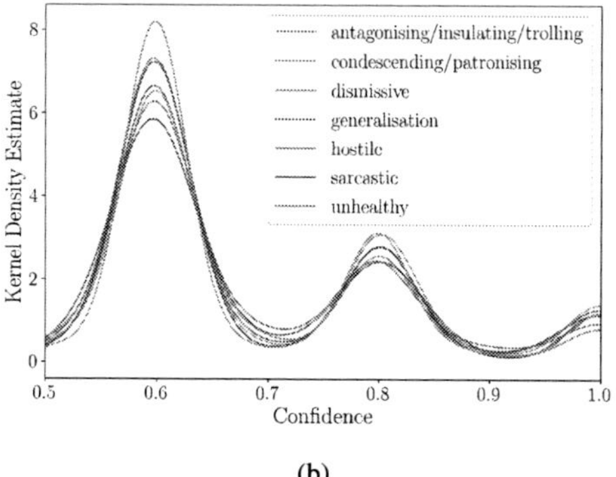

(b)

Figure 2: Density estimation (Rosenblatt et al., 1956) of confidence scores for each attribute. Figure 2a shows confidence scores for those comments labelled as 'no' for each unhealthy attribute, while Figure 2b represents those of comments labelled 'yes'.

these final proportions are roughly representative of the prevalence of these attributes in similar live contexts, such as North American online newspaper comment sections. There are specific attributes, notably sarcasm, for which it can be possible to collate a corpus of self-labelled data, for example by scraping tweets with '#sarcastic' from Twitter, or comments followed by '/s' on Reddit (Khodak et al., 2018). In these specific circumstances, the avoidance of the need to crowdsource and pay for annotations can permit much larger and more balanced datasets. However, for all other attributes we consider, and in fora like the comment sections of news sites, relying on self-labelled data is not possible. For these attributes, crowdsourcing is the only feasible way to obtain high quality data, and as such we would expect proportions reflecting those observed in similar contexts.

Inspection of random subsets of the new UCC

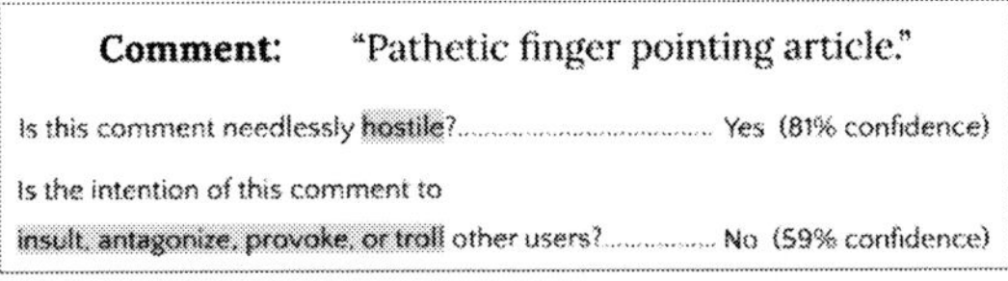

(a) A distinction between a hostile comment and one which intends to insult, antagonize, provoke or troll other users.

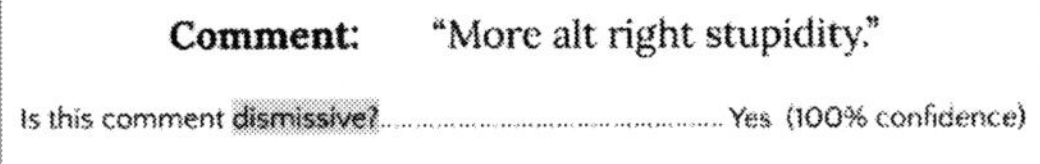

(b) Subtle condescension

(c) Implicit yet clear dismissiveness.

Figure 3: Examples of subtleties correctly picked up by annotators, with confidence scores shown in brackets alongside the resultant label.

dataset reveals that the data is generally of a high quality, and captures important nuances, accurately identifying these subtle attributes, both when they overlap (as is common), and also when they do not (see Figure 3 for examples).

Figure 4 shows the correlations between attributes, calculated based on the pool of comments which are labelled as one or more of the six unhealthy attributes. The figure highlights two important facts. First, the relatively low correlation between most attributes indicates that the dataset succeeds in differentiating between these different types of subtle unhealthy attributes. As expected, there is significant correlation between antagonistic and hostile comments. There is some correlation between the often more subtle attributes like dismissiveness/condescension and antagonism, while these are less correlated with hostility. We also include correlations with the 'toxicity' scores produced by Jigsaw's Perspective API (perspectiveapi.com), which again confirms that our attributes, in particular those other than antagonistic and hostile, capture something distinct from overt toxicity. A notable feature of Figure 4 is the slightly negative correlations between sarcasm and other attributes, indicating that annotators generally did not associate sarcasm with other unhealthy attributes. Secondly, 'unhealthy' correlates significantly with

antagonism and hostility, but very little with the other attributes, indicating a fairly broad general notion of healthy conversation on the part of the annotators, which mostly includes dismissive, condescending, sarcastic and generalising comments.

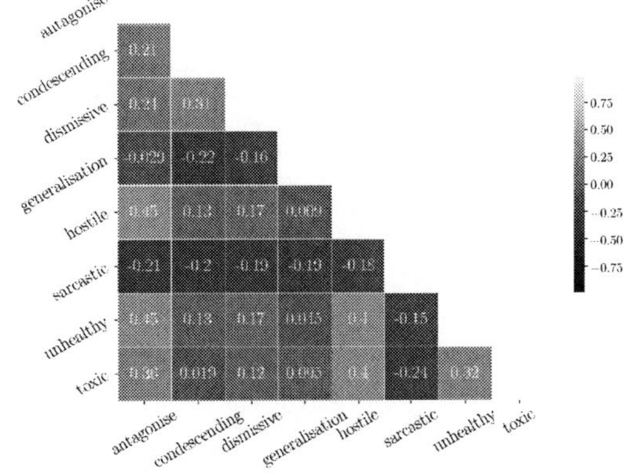

Figure 4: Inter-attribute correlations, including with 'toxicity' as scored by Perspective API.

Despite its generally high quality, the nature of the task and the annotation method entails some level of noise in the dataset. This noise is particularly difficult to quantify given the need to distinguish between different but reasonable interpretations of a comment, and simply incorrect annotations caused by a lack of understanding or care on the part of an annotator (for example, one comment reading "You are an ignorant *sshole" was judged not to be needlessly hostile, an obvious error).

This highlights the difficulties of using traditional reliability metrics like Krippendorff's α for crowdsourced annotations on subjective tasks (D'Arcey et al., 2019). Krippendorff's α is a number between 0 and 1 intended to indicate the extent to which annotators agree compared with what would have happened if they guessed randomly. The base assumption then is that all disagreement between annotators decreases reliability, which is not necessarily the case for subjective attributes (Salminen et al., 2018b; Swanson et al., 2014).

Despite the above caveat, we conduct analysis using Krippendorff's α (K-α) for two reasons. Firstly, to allow for comparison with other literature in the field, we report the K-α for judgements on each attribute in Table 2. They range from 0.31 - 0.39, which is comparable with other datasets labelling 'similar' phenomenon, such as sarcasm (0.24-0.38) (Swanson et al., 2014; Justo et al., 2018; D'Arcey et al., 2019), and hate speech with sub-attributes from Figure Eight annotators (0.21) (Lazaridou et al., 2020). The one exception is the set of judgements on whether a comment has a place in a healthy conversation, with a lower K-α of 0.26. Given that this is a more open-ended question, this is not necessarily surprising.

Attribute	K-α
Antagonistic/Insulting/Trolling	0.39
Condescending/Patronising	0.36
Dismissive	0.31
Generalisation	0.35
Hostile	0.36
Sarcastic	0.34
Unhealthy	0.26

Table 2: Krippendorff's alpha by attribute.

Secondly, to the extent that K-α is an important reliability metric for this form of data, it supports our use of 'trustworthiness' scores when aggregating judgements on a given comment to decide labels and confidence scores. Specifically, as shown in Figure 5, we see that as we increase the trustworthiness threshold for annotators whose judgements are included, the resulting K-α steadily increase. This provides some indication that our trustworthiness scores do capture the reliability of our annotators, and thus that their judgements ought to be weighted more highly in the final confidence in a comment's labels.

Also included in the UCC dataset are the individual annotations for each comment by all 'trusted' annotators. Users of the data may therefore apply any alternative trustworthiness threshold, or use a preferred aggregation method to derive labels.

5   Models and results

Use of a pre-trained BERT model (Devlin et al., 2019) and fine-tuning on this dataset produces classifiers with modest performance (Figure 6), compared to the state of the art for sequence classification. The best performing attributes, 'hostile' and 'antagonistic' are also those most similar to the types of attributes typically annotated in comment classification work. The other attributes seem to cluster together, with the 'sarcastic' label particularly noteworthy for its low performance.

To give context to the model performance, we follow (Wulczyn et al., 2017) and compare our performance with human workers. For each comment,

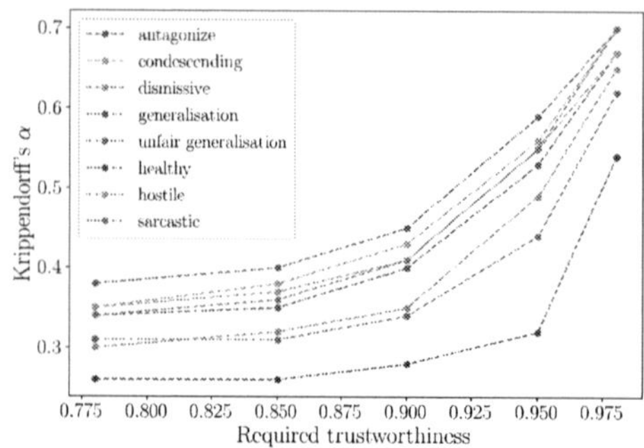

Figure 5: Krippendorff's α for various threshold levels of annotator trustworthiness.

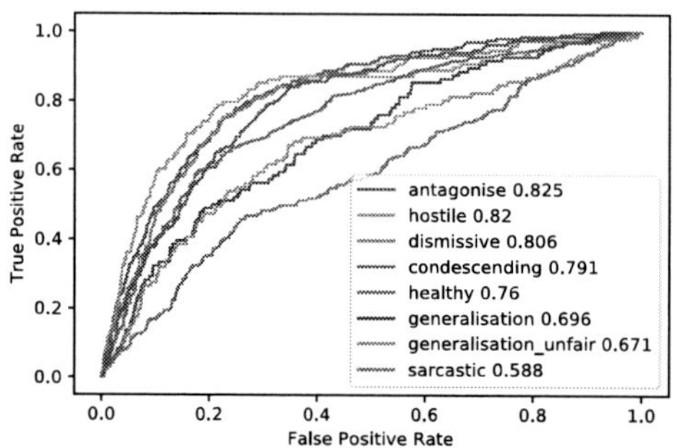

Figure 6: Receiver operating characteristic curves and AUC for class each attribute.

we hold out one annotator to act as our 'human model' and use the aggregated score of the other annotators as the ground truth to compute the ROC AUC. To stabilize our results, this procedure is repeated five times and the average reported. We use the same test sets to compute the ROC AUC of the trained BERT model and average those scores as well. As we can see, for all attributes other than 'sarcastic' the BERT model outperforms a randomly selected human annotator, indicating that it has sufficiently captured the semantic and syntactic structures for these attributes. For 'sarcastic', the gap between the BERT model and human annotators indicates a rich area for studying whether model performance can be improved.

6   Potential Unintended Biases

One further challenge which comes with annotating more subtle unhealthy attributes is the potential to encode unintended societal biases and value judgements in models trained on this data. For example,

Attribute	Human AUC	BERT AUC
Antagonistic	0.71	0.82
Condescending	0.72	0.78
Dismissive	0.68	0.82
Generalisation	0.73	0.74
Hostile	0.76	0.84
Sarcastic	0.72	0.64
Unhealthy	0.62	0.69

Table 3: Comparing Human and BERT performance

sarcasm is often communicated by stating something which the author presumes to be so obviously untrue that it will be read as sarcastic. These presumptions reflect the author's biases - or in the cases of comment annotation, labelling comments as sarcastic reflects the annotators beliefs of what is obviously untrue.

With the comment corpus being in English, and given the subtlety of the attributes, higher quality annotations were likely to be achieved by annotators with first-language proficiency in English. The best proxy for this available on the Figure Eight platform was to restrict the country of origin of our annotators to a limited subset of countries with a large English-speaking population (as either an official language or primary second language), in particular: the United States, the United Kingdom, South Africa, Sweden, New Zealand, Norway, Netherlands, Denmark, Canada, and Australia. Although our early iterations of this annotation job indicated a significant reduction in annotators failing test comments once this was enforced, this introduces a clear cultural and geographic bias. For example, the comment 'Iran and Turkey are the BEST places to be a woman!', was scored as sarcastic with 72% confidence by the annotators. Finding this comment sarcastic relies on an assumption by the annotators (of which the pool excludes residents of Iran and Turkey) that Iran and Turkey are clearly not the best places to be women. Our annotators were not selected as broadly representative across language, geography, culture, or other attributes and this assumption is not universal. While important research has begun to explore the composition of the global crowd workforce, it remains difficult to select for annotators representative of specific characteristics on crowd work platforms (Posch et al., 2018). In the current version of the Appen platform, unless annotators are asked standalone questions on demographics, the only available de-

tails are the annotators' country and/or city (and even then, only for some annotators). Research and modelling based on this dataset, and similar datasets, requires the exercise of great care in mitigating biases produced by the underlying data collection. This potential selection bias is likely to be evident across the broader healthy/unhealthy categorisation along with each of the attributes. Prior research has found substantial disagreement on subtle attributes of speech both among individuals and across geographies (Salminen et al., 2018a).

Finally, the source of the comments and their manner of presentation could introduce bias into the dataset. The source data is solely from a Canadian online newspaper comment section and comments were presented in isolation to annotators, without the surrounding context of the news article and other comments. Annotators were also provided with the standard questionnaire (Appendix A), which includes high level descriptions of the attributes that may not generalise across cultures. There is a substantial body of research demonstrating the potential impact of introducing biased datasets, and Vidgen *et al.* (Vidgen et al., 2019) note that public datasets in this area are prone to systematic bias and mislabelling, with interannotator agreement typically low for complex multi-class tasks of this kind. These challenges are to be expected in a relatively new field which aims to improve on human baseline moderation for highly subjective characteristics of online discussion. At this early stage of research, we must be mindful of addressing these biases and cognisant that the manner in which this data is collected can have critical impacts on users in a production environment. It is important to note at this stage of the field in general, and with our understanding of this dataset in particular, that the UCC dataset is not designed to train models which are immediately available for automated moderation without human intervention in a live online setting. As the field develops further, initial use-cases may include less interventionist 'nudges' or reminders of how a comment could be perceived by a reader to assist participants in discussions online.

7   Conclusions and Further work

We introduced a new corpus of labelled comments and a typology for some of the more subtle aspects of unhealthy online conversation. Our typology provides 6 sub-attributes of typically unhealthy contributions, and confidence scores for the labels. We described the process and challenges in creating such a dataset, and provided statistics to convey the scale of data. In particular, we note that although there is a substantial body of research on more extreme forms of negative contributions, such as toxicity, the subtler forms of unhealthy comments in our typology are often similarly prevalent online. Our analysis also shows that the sub-attributes are largely independent from overt toxicity, and mostly correlated with unhealthy contributions.

We also provide results from a modern baseline ML model (fine tuning BERT) and note that performance exceeds that of a crowd-worker. This suggests that further work could also be done to collect a larger corpus of annotations to improve the capacity to measure models in this domain. While this dataset provides a new contribution in gathering the 6 attributes under the umbrella of an 'unhealthy' conversation, there also remains an open question as to how exhaustive this typology of unhealthy contributions is. Future research and annotation work could further refine the typology, amend the standard questionnaire, or apply it to forums which differ in cultural and geographic context.

Further work also includes exploring the unintended biases in the model and data. This dataset is well-placed to further explore early signs of conversations going awry (Zhang et al., 2018), while models based on the data could be explored to provide assistance to moderating online conversations.

References

Betty van Aken, Julian Risch, Ralf Krestel, and Alexander Löser. 2018. Challenges for toxic comment classification: An in-depth error analysis. In *Proceedings of the 2nd Workshop on Abusive Language Online (ALW2)*, pages 33–42.

Ashley A Anderson, Sara K Yeo, Dominique Brossard, Dietram A Scheufele, and Michael A Xenos. 2018. Toxic talk: How online incivility can undermine perceptions of media. *International Journal of Public Opinion Research*, 30(1):156–168.

Sheri Bauman. 2013. Cyberbullying: What does research tell us? *Theory into practice*, 52(4):249–256.

Jeremy Blackburn and Haewoon Kwak. 2014. Stfu noob! predicting crowdsourced decisions on toxic behavior in online games. In *Proceedings of the 23rd international conference on World wide web*, pages 877–888.

Hao Chen, Susan Mckeever, and Sarah Jane Delany. 2017. Presenting a labelled dataset for real-time detection of abusive user posts. In *Proceedings of the International Conference on Web Intelligence*, pages 884–890.

J Trevor D'Arcey, Shereen Oraby, and Jean E Fox Tree. 2019. Wait signals predict sarcasm in online debates. *Dialogue & Discourse*, 10(2):56–78.

Thomas Davidson, Dana Warmsley, Michael Macy, and Ingmar Weber. 2017. Automated hate speech detection and the problem of offensive language. In *Proceedings of the Eleventh International AAAI Conference on Web and Social Media*.

J. Devlin, Ming-Wei Chang, Kenton Lee, and Kristina Toutanova. 2019. Bert: Pre-training of deep bidirectional transformers for language understanding. In *NAACL-HLT*.

Lucas Dixon, John Li, Jeffrey Sorensen, Nithum Thain, and Lucy Vasserman. 2018. Measuring and mitigating unintended bias in text classification. In *Proceedings of the 2018 AAAI/ACM Conference on AI, Ethics, and Society*, pages 67–73.

Elena Filatova. 2012. Irony and sarcasm: Corpus generation and analysis using crowdsourcing. In *Proceedings of the Eighth International Conference on Language Resources and Evaluation (LREC 2012)*, pages 392–398.

Paula Fortuna, Joao Rocha da Silva, Leo Wanner, Sérgio Nunes, et al. 2019. A hierarchically-labeled portuguese hate speech dataset. In *Proceedings of the Third Workshop on Abusive Language Online*, pages 94–104.

Ghayda Hassan, Sébastien Brouillette-Alarie, Séraphin Alava, Divina Frau-Meigs, Lysiane Lavoie, Arber Fetiu, Wynnpaul Varela, Evgueni Borokhovski, Vivek Venkatesh, Cécile Rousseau, et al. 2018. Exposure to extremist online content could lead to violent radicalization: A systematic review of empirical evidence. *International journal of developmental science*, 12(1-2):71–88.

Raquel Justo, José M Alcaide, M Inés Torres, and Marilyn Walker. 2018. Detection of sarcasm and nastiness: new resources for spanish language. *Cognitive Computation*, 10(6):1135–1151.

Mikhail Khodak, Nikunj Saunshi, and Kiran Vodrahalli. 2018. A large self-annotated corpus for sarcasm. In *Proceedings of the Eleventh International Conference on Language Resources and Evaluation (LREC 2018)*.

Manav Kohli, Emily Kuehler, and John Palowitch. 2018. Paying attention to toxic comments online. *Web: https://stanford.io/2YfKMvE*.

Varada Kolhatkar, Hanhan Wu, Luca Cavasso, Emilie Francis, Kavan Shukla, and Maite Taboada. 2019. The sfu opinion and comments corpus: A corpus for the analysis of online news comments. *Corpus Pragmatics*, pages 1–36.

Konstantina Lazaridou, Alexander Löser, Maria Mestre, and Felix Naumann. 2020. Discovering biased news articles leveraging multiple human annotations. In *Proceedings of the 12th Conference on Language Resources and Evaluation*, pages 1268–1277.

Hala Mulki, Hatem Haddad, Chedi Bechikh Ali, and Halima Alshabani. 2019. L-hsab: a levantine twitter dataset for hate speech and abusive language. In *Proceedings of the Third Workshop on Abusive Language Online*, pages 111–118.

Pooja Parekh and Hetal Patel. 2017. Toxic comment tools: A case study. *International Journal of Advanced Research in Computer Science*, 8(5).

Lisa Posch, Arnim Bleier, Fabian Flöck, and Markus Strohmaier. 2018. Characterizing the global crowd workforce: A cross-country comparison of crowdworker demographics.

Murray Rosenblatt et al. 1956. Remarks on some nonparametric estimates of a density function. *The Annals of Mathematical Statistics*, 27(3):832–837.

Joni Salminen, Fabio Veronesi, Hind Almerekhi, Soon-Gvo Jung, and Bernard J Jansen. 2018a. Online hate interpretation varies by country, but more by individual: A statistical analysis using crowdsourced ratings. In *2018 Fifth International Conference on Social Networks Analysis, Management and Security (SNAMS)*, pages 88–94. IEEE.

Joni O. Salminen, Hind A. Al-Merekhi, Partha Dey, , and Bernard James Jansen. 2018b. Inter-rater agreement for social computing studies. In *Proceedings of the 5th International Conference on Social Networks Analysis, Management and Security*, pages 80–87.

Arthur D Santana. 2014. Virtuous or vitriolic: The effect of anonymity on civility in online newspaper reader comment boards. *Journalism practice*, 8(1):18–33.

Reid Swanson, Stephanie Lukin, Luke Eisenberg, Thomas Corcoran, and Marilyn Walker. 2014. Getting reliable annotations for sarcasm in online dialogues. In *Proceedings of the Ninth International Conference on Language Resources and Evaluation (LREC'14)*, pages 4250–4257.

Bertie Vidgen, Alex Harris, Dong Nguyen, Rebekah Tromble, Scott Hale, and Helen Margetts. 2019. Challenges and frontiers in abusive content detection. In *Proceedings of the Third Workshop on Abusive Language Online*, pages 80–93, Florence, Italy. Association for Computational Linguistics.

Zijian Wang and Christopher Potts. 2019. Talkdown: A corpus for condescension detection in context. In *Proceedings of the 2019 Conference on Empirical Methods in Natural Language Processing and the 9th International Joint Conference on Natural Language Processing (EMNLP-IJCNLP)*, pages 3702–3710.

Sebastian Weingartner and Lea Stahel. 2019. Online aggression from a sociological perspective: An integrative view on determinants and possible countermeasures. In *Proceedings of the Third Workshop on Abusive Language Online*, pages 181–187.

Ellery Wulczyn, Nithum Thain, and Lucas Dixon. 2017. Ex machina: Personal attacks seen at scale. In *Proceedings of the 26th International Conference on World Wide Web*, pages 1391–1399.

Justine Zhang, Jonathan P Chang, Cristian Danescu-Niculescu-Mizil, Lucas Dixon, Yiqing Hua, Nithum Tahin, and Dario Taraborelli. 2018. Conversations gone awry: Detecting early signs of conversational failure. In *Proceedings of the 56th Annual Meeting of the Association for Computational Linguistics.*, volume 1.

A Annotator Questionnaire

Overview

In this job, you will be asked to read a comment and to express an overall opinion about whether you think it has a place in a healthy conversation online.

You will also be asked to identify whether it displays a range of characteristics that may lead to unhealthy conversations. These characteristics include: sarcasm, gross generalisations, hostility, aggression, dismissiveness, condescension and patronization.

All of the comments you will see are real comments posted by users in online conversations. Most of them will have been posted in response to one or more comments made by others (which you are not given). However, the questions are designed in such a way that you should be able to answer them without seeing these other comments.

The data collected here will be used to help build tools which promote healthier conversations online.

Note:

- Please bear in mind that the questions do not ask whether you agree or disagree with the substance of each comment. Do your best to ignore your own opinion on the substantive idea or claim made in the comment when answering the questions.

- Please be sure to read the full text of the comment before answering the questions. Sometimes the part of a comment which displays one or more of the attributes you will be asked about, appears close to the end of the comment.

---

1. Healthy Online Conversations:

   What are the characteristics of a healthy conversation?

   - Posts and comments are made in good faith
   - Posts and comments are not overly hostile, and are not destructive
   - The comments in the conversation generally invite engagement
   - The conversation may include robust engagement and debate
   - The conversation is generally focused on substance and ideas

   A healthy conversation does not necessarily require all posts and comments to be:

   - friendly
   - grammatically correct
   - well constructed or well structured
   - sanitized and free of any vulgarity
   - intellectual or substantive

   With this in mind please answer the following question: Do you think this comment has a place in a healthy online conversation?

2. A comment is sarcastic if it uses irony in order to mock or convey contempt, or if its intended meaning is different from what is literally said. Sarcasm can be used playfully, or harshly. Note: Not all humour (or nastiness) is sarcastic.

   Is this comment sarcastic?

3. Does this comment make a generalisation about a specific group of people?

4. If yes, would a member of that group feel that the generalisation is unfair?

5. Is this comment needlessly hostile?

6. Is the intention of this comment to insult, antagonize, provoke, or troll other users?

7. A comment with a condescending or patronising tone will generally assume an attitude of superiority, and imply that the other commenter(s) is ignorant, child-like, naive, or unintelligent. Such comments will usually imply that the other commenter shouldn't be taken seriously.

   Is this comment condescending and/or patronising?

8. A comment is dismissive if it rejects or ridicules another comment without good reason, or tries to push another commenter and their ideas out of the conversations. Note: A comment which expresses *disagreement* is not necessarily dismissive.

   Is this comment dismissive?

A Unified Typology of Harmful Content

Michele Banko, Brendon MacKeen and Laurie Ray
Sentropy Technologies
380 Portage Avenue
Palo Alto, CA 94306
{mbanko,brendon,laurie}@sentropy.io

Abstract

The ability to recognize harmful content within online communities has come into focus for researchers, engineers and policy makers seeking to protect users from abuse. While the number of datasets aiming to capture forms of abuse has grown in recent years, the community has not standardized around how various harmful behaviors are defined, creating challenges for reliable moderation, modeling and evaluation. As a step towards attaining shared understanding of how online abuse may be modeled, we synthesize the most common types of abuse described by industry, policy, community and health experts into a *unified typology of harmful content*, with detailed criteria and exceptions for each type of abuse.

1 Introduction

Content moderation, the practice of monitoring and reviewing user-generated content to ensure compliance with legal requirements, community guidelines, and user agreements, is important for creating safe and equitable online spaces. While traditional content moderation systems rely heavily on human reviewers who use a set of proprietary guidelines to determine if content is in violation of policy, the use of algorithmic approaches has become a part of moderation workflows in recent years. While not a full replacement for human content moderators, the use of AI promises to reduce trauma and cost incurred by purely human-centric workflows.

As a result, the ability to recognize abusive content using data-driven approaches has attracted attention from researchers in the computational and social sciences. To study, model and measure systems designed to recognize online abuse, researchers typically create labelled datasets using crowdsourcing platforms or in-house annotators. While the number of research datasets continues to grow (Vidgen and Derczynski, 2020), the research

community has not reached a consensus on how common abuse types are defined. Despite the use of best practices that leverage multiple annotators, definitional ambiguity can lead to the creation of datasets of questionable consistency (Ross et al., 2017; Waseem, 2016; Wulczyn et al., 2017). Furthermore, without thorough domain understanding, research datasets built to capture abusive content may be prone to unintended bias (Wiegand et al., 2019). Together, these shortcomings create challenges for reliable modeling and study of abuse as it occurs in the real world.

Harmful content has also drawn attention from internet companies, such as those in the social media, online gaming, and dating industries, who seek to protect their users from abuse. These companies typically employ a Trust and Safety organization to define and enforce violations of content policies, and to develop tools aimed at identifying instances of abuse on their platforms. Several online platforms which have seen large volumes of harmful content on their platforms, have created content policies that can be useful in specifying definitions of various abuse classes. In the absence of a standard upon which content policies can be based, community standards within digital platforms are largely shaped by users who report abuse they have experienced firsthand. Additionally, some aspects of content policies are informed by requirements handed down from local law enforcement agencies wishing to prosecute users engaging in illegal activity online.

Recently, the demand for internet companies to more aggressively reduce the spread of cyberbullying, radicalization, deception, exploitation, and other forms of dangerous content has been increasingly called for by governmental and civil society organizations. The proposed Online Harms Bill in the UK and amendments to Section 230 in the United States call for stricter accountability, trans-

Proceedings of the Fourth Workshop on Online Abuse and Harms, pages 125–137
Online, November 20, 2020. ©2020 Association for Computational Linguistics
https://doi.org/10.18653/v1/P17

parency, and regulations to be imposed on companies hosting user-generated content. Civil society organizations have yielded numerous proposals for better describing types of harmful content online so that internet companies may better understand the nature and impact of such content.

In this paper, we enumerate, consolidate and define the most common types of abuse described in content policies for several major online platforms and white papers from civil society organizations. We look for commonalities in both *what* types of abuse have been identified and *how* they are defined. Our goal is to provide a unified typology of harmful content, with clear criteria and exceptions for each type of abuse. While hate speech and harassment have attracted attention from the natural language processing community in recent years, upon close study, we find that the domain of harmful content is broader than many may have realized. We hope this typology will benefit content moderation systems by:

- Defining abuse types that are readily usable by content moderators, both human and algorithmic

- Encouraging the construction of accurate, complete and unbiased datasets used for model training and evaluation

- Creating awareness of types of abuse that have received limited attention in the research community thus far

2 Background and Related Work

2.1 Abuse Typologies

Several efforts to categorize online abuse began by closely studying specific types of harm. With a focus on cyberbullying, Van Hee et al. (2015) published a scheme for annotation, which considers the presence, severity, role of the author (harasser, victim or bystander) and a number of fine-grained categories, such as insults and threats. Waseem et al. (2017) discussed the lack of consensus around how hate speech is defined, noting that messages labeled as hate speech in some datasets are only considered to be offensive in others. They devised a two-fold typology that considers whether hate is directed at a specific target (as opposed to taking the form of a general statement), and the degree of explicitness. Anzovino et al. (2018) studied misogynistic social media posts, and modeled seven types

of abuse, most of which extend beyond abuse directed at women. Similar to these works, we break apart class definitions into fine-grained categories when possible in an attempt to disambiguate potentially underspecified requirements. We build upon this body of work by considering a larger set of abuse types, as opposed to just cyberbullying or hate speech.

More broadly, Vidgen et al. (2019) noted the difficulties in categorizing abusive content, and proposed a three dimensional scheme for defining abuse classes. They suggest to consider (1) the type of the abuse target (e.g. individual, identity, entity or concept), (2) the recipient of the abuse (e.g. a specific individual, women, capitalism), and (3) the manner in which the abuse is articulated (e.g. as an insult, aggression, stereotype, untruth). We consider target type and manner in our categorization and take the suggested scheme one step further by instantiating a large set of what the authors refer to as subtasks. In some cases, where there is no clear or uniform target (e.g. misinformation) we found it helpful to organize types based on topic or possible outcome that can be easily reasoned about by those impacted by moderation systems.

2.2 Hate Speech

The natural language processing community has largely focused on detection of hate speech and cyberbullying (Schmidt and Wiegand, 2017). As a result, a number of research datasets have been produced (Vidgen and Derczynski, 2020), yet none have used the same definition, or have annotated only partial phenomena (e.g. annotating racist and sexist speech, but not hate speech directed at all groups who require protection).

While building a hate speech corpus from Twitter data, Ross et al. (2017) investigated how the reliability of the annotations is affected by the provision of accompanying definitions. They compared annotations in which the annotators were provided Twitter's definition of hate speech versus no definition. While annotators shown the definition were more likely to ban the tweet, the authors found that even when presented with Twitter's definition, inter-annotator agreement, measured using Krippendorf's alpha, was at best 0.3, depending on the question asked.[1] Ross et al. concluded that more detailed coding schemes are needed to be

---

[1] Krippendorff (2004) suggests that for annotations to be considered reliable, a minimum score of 0.80 is desirable, with 0.667 being the lowest conceivable limit

able to distinguish hate speech from other content.

Other works which report the difficulty of achieving high levels of interannotator agreement when compiling hate speech datasets include Davidson et al. (2017), who found that 5% of tweets were coded as hate speech by the majority of annotators with only 1.3% being annotated unanimously as containing hate speech. The creators of the 2018 Kaggle Toxic Comment Classification Challenge (Wulczyn et al., 2017) report that while the challenge dataset was built using ten annotators per label, agreement was weak (Krippendorff alpha of 0.45).

Demonstrating the importance of having well-defined annotation guidelines, Waseem and Hovy (2016) articulated an eleven-point definition of gendered and racial attacks. The use of detailed criteria yielded a high level of agreement. The authors measured inter-annotator agreement, defined using Cohen's kappa, to be 0.84.

2.3 Other Forms of Harmful Content

In recent years, machine learning has been used to recognize forms of self-harm such as pro-eating disorder content in social media posts (Chancellor et al., 2016; Wang et al., 2017) and suicidal ideation (Burnan et al., 2015; Cao et al., 2019).

Snyder et al. (2017) developed an automated framework for detecting dox files, i.e. files which reveal personally identifiable data without consent, and measuring the frequency, content, targets, and effects of doxing on popular dox-posting sites.

Detection of sexually explicit content includes efforts to recognize instances of child sexual abuse (Lee et al., 2020) and human trafficking (Dubrawski et al., 2015; Tong et al., 2017).

Another endeavor related to online harm that has gained attention within the research community is the detection of misinformation, which is surveyed by Su et al. (2020).

3 Methodology

To develop a unified typology of harmful content, we employed a grounded theory approach, in which we synthesized inputs from several sources:

- Community guidelines and content policy made public by large online platforms, specifically Discord,[2] Facebook,[3] Pinterest,[4] Reddit,[5] Twitter,[6] and YouTube[7]

- The International Covenant on Civil and Political Rights,[8] an international human rights treaty developed by the United Nations

- Proposals from members of civil society organizations such as the Women's Media Center; Internet and Jurisdiction Policy Network (2019) and Benesch (2020)

- Recommendations from experts and health organizations who study psychological and physical impact of abuse, including the American Association of Suicidology and the Conflict Tactics Scale

3.1 Principles

While qualitatively analyzing the data mentioned above, we used the following principles to guide the creation of the typology:

Avoid the use of subjective adjectives as core definitions. As prior research has shown, annotation tasks that make use of underspecified or subjective phrases such as "hateful," "toxic" or "would make you leave a conversation," without further explanation are likely to be interpreted differently depending on the annotator. Enumerate problematic content types using precise objective criteria when possible.

Prefer fine-grained classes over those spanning multiple behaviors. Behavior that is casually described as "toxic" or "bullying" may contain a mix of identity-based hate speech, general insults, threats and inappropriate sexual language. Narrowly defined classes simplify annotation requirements and provide a level of explainability that is missing from underspecified labels.

Consider the type of the subject of abuse. To keep definitions well-scoped, we consider the subject of the attack, and avoid mixing subject types within a single definition when possible. For instance, instead of having a generic class aimed at recognizing sexually explicit content, we advocate for annotating sexually charged content directed at an individual separately from content advertising for adult sexual services. However, we find that

---

there are some instances in which a broad form
of harm can not be uniformly defined by the type
of the target, and employ a topical approach that
may be more understandable to moderators and
users of social platforms. An example of this is
Misinformation.

Consider potential downstream actions. If a
type of behavior is universally associated with an
outcome, avoid definitions that mix behaviors that
do not share the outcome. For instance, child sexual abuse content is not tolerated under any circumstances in most countries and must be reported to
law enforcement, whereas insults that make use
of sexual terms are unlikely to have legal ramifica-
tions. A platform may have strict policies against attacks on protected groups but permit mild forms of
non-identity based insults. Distinguishing between
the two simplifies the ability to enforce policy and
therefore, improves the usefulness of a moderation
system.

Despite our preference for fine-grained classes,
they are not defined to be mutually exclusive. Additionally, hierarchical arrangement of types is not
always possible. As a result, there are cases where
multiple types may apply to a single input. For
example, *Time to shoot this n******, where the last
word represents a racial slur, should be classified as
both *Identity Attack* and *Threat of Violence*. *Time
to shoot up this school* is a violent threat without
an identity-based attack. *N***** aren't welcome
here* is a non-violent *Identity Attack*.

3.2 Severity

All forms of abuse are problematic and require
some means to identify and address them in order to mitigate their impact on users. While the
strength of statements involving abuse may be interpreted differently depending on the recipient and
context, some forms of online harm present immediate or lasting danger to individuals or stand in
violation of the law. For each type of abuse we
present, we establish qualifications for what may
be considered *severe abuse*. The ability to detect
severe abuse is critical for content moderation systems seeking to identity extreme or time-sensitive
violations quickly.

The concept of "severe toxicity" is annotated
in the Kaggle Toxic Comment Classification Challenge (2018), where it is defined it as "rude, disrespectful, or unreasonable comments that are very
likely to make people leave a discussion." Mov-

ing away from the use of subjective adjectives, we
consider the following attributes when determining
severity:

- Use of language expressing direct intent (severe) vs. use of language that is passive or
  merely wishful (not severe)

- Time-sensitive or immediate threats of harm
  are considered to be severe

- Consequences of, or degree of harm associated with, the abuse, i.e. actions resulting in
  death or long-lasting physical or psychological trauma shall be treated as severe

- Vulnerability of the target, e.g. attacks directed at members of groups that have been
  historically marginalized, dehumanized or ob-
  jectified are considered to be severe

- Violations of personal privacy and consent are
  treated as severe

- Violations of applicable laws, including internationally recognized policies are handled as
  severe

4 Abuse Class Definitions

Using the data and guidelines described in Section
3, we arrived at the typology depicted in Figure 1.
In the remainder of this section, we describe each
type in detail. Within each section, we present the
types in lexicographic order.

4.1 Hate and Harassment

Hate and Harassment describes abuse directed at a
specific individual or group of people (e.g. identity)
meant to torment, demean, undermine, frighten or
humiliate the target. Abuse directed at institutions
or abstract concepts is not included in this set of
definitions. In the remainder of this section, we
present criteria for defining common forms of hate
and harassment: *Doxing, Identity Attack, Identity
Misrepresentation, Insult, Sexual Aggression*, and
Threat of Violence.

4.1.1 Doxing

Doxing is a form of severe abuse in which a malicious party tries to harm an individual by releasing personally identifiable information about the
target to the general public. During a doxing attack, sensitive information is typically distributed
on web sites that permit anonymous posting and

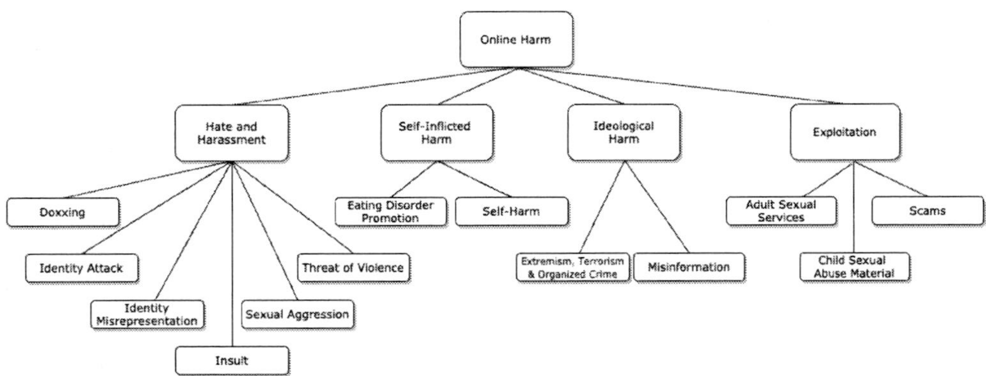

Figure 1: A Typology of Harmful Content

do not proactively remove harassing content, such as onion sites, torrents, IRC, and anonymous text sharing websites such as pastebin.com, 4chan and 8chan. Doxing can lead to another form of harm known as SWATing, in which someone calls law enforcement with false reports of violence at an address in order to cause harm at the target's residence (e.g. a SWAT team kicking in their door).

Personal data that should not be shared without the consent of others includes:

- Physical or virtual locations such as home, work and IP addresses, or GPS locations

- Contact information such as private email address and phone numbers

- Identification numbers such as Social Security, passport, government or school ids

- Digital identities such as social network accounts, chat identities, and passwords

- Personal financial information such as bank account or credit card information

- Criminal and medical histories

Mentions of data already in the public domain such as one's place of education or employment, email addresses that have been voluntarily shared (such as on a personal homepage) are not considered instances of doxing, nor are cases where people willingly share their own private information.

4.1.2 Identity Attack

Identity Attack is a form of online abuse where malicious actors severely attack individuals or groups of people based on their membership in a protected or vulnerable group. During an *Identity Attack*, a bad actor will use language reflecting the intent to dehumanize, persecute or promote violence based on the identity of the subject. The use of slurs and/or derogatory epithets may be present but is not a requirement.

While there is neither agreement in what constitutes hate speech across academic datasets, nor is there any industry or legal standard of this definition, constructions of *Identity Attack* definitions typically attempt to: 1) protect vulnerable groups, 2) protect specific characteristics or attributes of individuals, 3) prohibit hate speech but fail to offer a definition. For platforms that fall into either of the first two categories the policies described protect users from attacks and violence on the basis of identity-based attributes including age, disability, ethnicity, gender identity, military status, nationality, race, religion, and sexual orientation. Some platforms offer additional protections for vulnerable groups such as immigration status, socio-economic class or the presence of a medical condition.

Jigsaw (Kaggle, 2018) defines *Identity Attack* as: "Negative or hateful comments targeting someone because of their identity." Underspecified definitions such as this are difficult to use in practice due to the open-endedness of how "negative" or "hateful" may be interpreted by annotators or community moderators. As mentioned in our survey of related work, we promote the use of more fine-grained classes, focusing here on severe attacks (e.g. those with dehumanizing and/or violent intent) and defining a separate class for more mild phenomena such as spread of negative stereotypes or misinformation related to vulnerable groups. Another distinction we suggest is to ensure the subject of the attack refers to a human or group thereof, as

129

opposed to institutions or organizations. For example, an attack on people who practice a religion (e.g. Jews, Muslims) falls under the class, but attacks on religion itself (e.g. Judiasm, Islam) itself do not. As a result, statements such as *You deserve to be euthanized, you dirty ***** and *****s deserve to be euthanized"*[9] would be treated as *Identity Attack*, whereas ***** is a religion that should cease to exist* would not. In some cases, it is possible that use of organizations are replacements for the individuals belonging to them, but for the first version of the typology we propose to maintain this distinction.

Here we summarize types of content that warrant a classification of *Identity Attack*, all of which are considered severe forms of abuse:

- Explicit use of slurs and other derogatory epithets referencing an identity group

- Violent threats or calls for harm directed at an identity group

- Calls for exclusion, domination or suppression of rights, directed at an identity group

- Dehumanization of an identity group, including comparisons to animals, insects, diseases or filth, generalizations involving physical unattractiveness, low intelligence, mental instability and/or moral deficiencies

- Expressions of superiority of one group over a protected or vulnerable group

- Admissions of hate and intolerance towards members of an identity group

- Denial of another's identity, calls for conversion therapy, deadnaming

- Support for hate groups communicating intent described above

The following should be considered non-examples for the *Identity Attack* abuse class:

- Attacks on institutions or organizations (as opposed to the people belonging to them)

- Promotion of negative stereotypes, fear or misinformation related to an identity group (defined as *Identity Misrepresentation* in Section 4.1.3)

---

[9]As per the WOAH guidelines we use **** in place of any group identifier to avoid reproducing harm

- In-group usage of slurs and their variants, reclamation of hateful terms by the those who have been historically targeted

- Discussion of meta-linguistic nature or education related to slurs or hate speech

- Accounts of the speech behavior of parties external to the immediate conversational context

4.1.3 Identity Misrepresentation

Identity Misrepresentation is defined by statements or claims that are used to convey pejorative misrepresentations, stereotypes, and other insulting generalizations about protected or vulnerable populations. As with *Identity Attack*, protected groups are defined by attributes including age, disability, ethnicity, gender identity, military status, nationality, race, religion, and sexual orientation. Vulnerable groups such as those defined by immigration status, socio-economic class or the presence of a medical condition, may also be offered protection.

Statements belonging to this class fall below the severity of *Identity Attack*. They may be presented as fact but may lack supporting evidence or be opinions in disguise. Criteria outlined in the definition of *Identity Attack* belong uniquely to that class. For example, a stereotype suggesting that group of people is inferior (e.g. has low IQ) would fall under the definition of *Identity Attack*, whereas generalizations regarding food preferences (e.g. eats foods that are unappealing to others, without conveying explicit hatred towards the group), non-dehumanizing assumptions about physical appearance (e.g. wearing a style of facial hair implies support for extremism) or stereotypes about spending habits (e.g. frugality) should be treated as *Identity Misrepresentation*.

A summary of qualifying criteria for the *Identity Misrepresentation* class is as follows:

- Dissemination of negative stereotypes and generalizations about a protected or vulnerable group, apart from those that involve explicit dehumanization or claims of inferiority

- Statements about protected or vulnerable groups presented as declarative truth without supporting evidence

- Microaggressions, subtle expressions of bias towards a protected or vulnerable group

- Intent to spread fear of protected or vulnerable groups, without calls for violence

Positive criteria defined for *Identity Attack* and *Insult* should be considered non-examples of *Identity Misrepresentation*.

4.1.4 Insult

Two datasets shared by Kaggle (2012, 2018) have provided guidelines used to determine whether or not content can be considered insulting. The latter defines *Insult* as: "insulting, inflammatory, or negative comment towards a person or a group of people." The earlier task provides more detail, whereupon insults are constrained to be person-to-person speech acts in which the target is assumed to be active in the conversation. This definition allows for the presence of profanity, racial slurs and other offensive terms. Using these specifications, it is not obvious how to distinguish between an *Insult* and an *Identity Attack* (which is also defined in the 2018 challenge). We propose an important distinction in that statements that make use of identity-based slurs and epithets are to be elevated to the level of *Identity Attack*.

With the assumption that the subject of an *Insult* is a participant in the conversation, an *Insult* is defined as:

- General name-calling, directed profanity and other insulting language or imagery not referencing membership in a protected group or otherwise meeting the criteria for *Identity Attack*

- Content mocking someone for their personality, opinions, character or emotional state

- Body shaming, attacks on physical appearance, or shaming related to sexual or romantic history

- Mocking someone due to their status as a survivor of assault or abuse

- Encouraging others to insult an individual

- Images manipulated with the intent to insult the subject

The following should be considered non-examples of insults:

- Insults strictly based on the target's membership in a group with protected status, including use of slurs

- Insults aimed at non-participant subjects, such as celebrities and other high-profile individuals

- Self-referential insults and self-deprecation

- Insults directed at inanimate objects

- Harassment education or awareness

With regard to the scale of severity, *Insults* are not elevated to the level of severe abuse, as they do not explicitly threaten physical safety, contain identity-based attacks, compromise personal privacy or involve criminal behavior.

4.1.5 Sexual Aggression

Various forms of sexual content are present online, such as pornography, nudity, and offers for adult services. Here we focus on a type of person-to-person abuse, *Sexual Aggression*. This type of content includes unwanted sexual advances, undesirable sexualization, non-consensual sharing of sexual content, and other forms of unsolicited sexual conversations. *Sexual Aggression* is defined as:

- Threats or descriptions of sexual activity, fantasy or non-consensual sex acts directed at an individual

- Unsolicited graphic descriptions of a person (including oneself) that are sexual in nature

- Unwanted sexualization, sexual advances or comments intended to sexually degrade an individual

- Solicitations or offers of non-commercial sexual interactions

- Unwanted requests for nude or sexually graphic images or videos

- Sharing of content depicting any person in a state of nudity or engaged in sexual activity created or shared without their permission, including fakes (e.g. revenge porn)

- Sharing of content revealing intimate parts of a person's body, even if clothed or in public, created or posted without their permission (e.g., "creepshots" or "upskirt" images)

- Sextortion, threat of exposing a person's intimate images, conversations or other intimate information

Sexual Aggression does not refer to:

- Pornography created with consent of all participants

- Solicitation or offers of commercial sex transactions

- Definitions of sexual terms

- Sexual health and wellness discussions

- Non-graphic use of words associated with sex

- Insults that make use of sexual terms

- Flirting, compliments, or come-ons that are not sexually graphic or degrading

Using our criteria for severe abuse, the following subset of content meeting the definition of *Sexual Aggression* is to be considered severe:

- Threats of non-consensual sexual activity

- Sharing of sexual content without consent from an involved party

- Demand for sexual activity

- Graphic and/or violent descriptions of sex

4.1.6 Threat of Violence

Many online platforms do not permit users to state a desire to kill or inflict physical harm towards others. Statements which celebrate, encourage or condone violent acts are also prohibited, as they may incite others to commit violent acts. *Threat of Violence* refers to content that contains at least one of the following:

- Desire to physically harm a person or group of people, including violent sexual acts

- Call for the death, serious injury or illness of a person or group of people

- Encouragement of another individual to commit self-harm or suicide

- Incitement to commit acts of violence

- Glorification of violence or violent events

Non-examples of this class include:

- Anecdotal or personal accounts of violence without glorification (e.g. survivor stories, criminal rehabilitation accounts)

- Historical descriptions or research studies of violence

- Hyperbolic or metaphorical violence

Taxonomies of violence (Straus et al., 1996) treat physical threats as more severe than verbal or psychological threats. While threats made via online communication are technically verbal, severe threats are those in which there is credible belief that the aggressor could or would carry out a threat physically. Severe forms of violent threats intend to do at least one of the following:

- Create the fear or belief that the violent act will occur in real life

- Threaten acts that result in serious consequences, such as a long-term injury or illness or fatality

- Convey the abuser's desire to carry out the threat personally

Mild forms of physically violent threats have at least one of the following features:

- The abuser's intent is to insult or dismiss the target, with little to no harmful consequences (e.g. "I could easily take you down")

- Threaten acts that result in minor or no lasting harm to a person's health or well-being, (e.g. "I'll slap you if you don't stop")

- Passive threats stated as wishes or hopes for an unfortunate event or illness to occur

4.2 Self-Inflicted Harm

Self-Inflicted Harm describes forms of harmful behavior, both physical and psychological, directed at one's self. The detection of content belonging to this class is intended to flag such behaviors in order to provide help to those in distress and prevent the spread of dangerous behavior within online communities. In the remainder of this section, we discuss definitions for two common forms of self-inflicted harm: *Eating Disorder Promotion* and *Self-Harm*.

4.2.1 Eating Disorder Promotion

Eating disorders (EDs) are mental disorders characterized by abnormal eating habits and attitudes towards food. Many online platforms explicitly prohibit pro-ED content in order to prevent the spread of unhealthy behavior. While the DSM-V offers clinical definitions of such disorders, here we summarize types of dangerous content related to the way eating disorders may be discussed online:

- Promotion of eating disorders as legitimate lifestyle choices (e.g. pro-ana, pro-mia content)

- Glorification of slim or emaciated bodies (e.g. thinspiration)

- Content featuring high-fat food or overweight people intended to induce disgust (e.g. reverse thinspiration)

- Sharing instructions for unhealthy weight loss methods

The following should be considered non-examples of *Eating Disorder Promotion*:

- Research, advocacy, and education related to eating disorders

- Discussion of recovery mechanisms and resources to prevent eating disorders

- Anecdotes of individuals who have suffered from eating disorders in a manner that does not glorify the disorder

Pro-ED content potentially creates long-lasting impact to one's health and therefore is considered to be severe.

4.2.2 Self-Harm

Self-Harm is a behavior in which a person purposefully physically hurts themself using methods such as cutting with a sharp object, burning, biting, and pulling out hair. Practitioners of such behavior do so in order to cope with emotional distress. While according to the DSM-V, people who exhibit self-harming behaviors do not intend to cause long-term, serious harm or fatality, suicide is an additional, albeit extremely different, form of self-harm, which we include in our definition.

Self-Harm includes the following content:

- Discussion of current or recent acts of deliberately harming one's own body.

- Suicidal ideation, discussing details of a suicide plan, or stating that one intends to commit suicide

- Requests for instructions on how to conduct or hide self-harm or suicide

- Describing emotions or symptoms of mental illness explicitly related to self-harm, or traumatic experiences and triggers

- Promotion of or assistance with self-harming behaviors

Self-Harm content does not refer to:

- Anecdotes of personal recovery, treatment

- Sharing coping methods for addressing thoughts of self-harm or suicide

- Support for individuals who are considering or are actively harming themselves

- Recollection of self-harming behaviors or suicidal attempts that occurred at least 12 months in the past that does not promote self-harm or suicide

- Research or education related to prevention of self-harm or suicide

- Discussion of depression or other mental illnesses, symptoms, or depressed thoughts and feelings that are not explicitly tied to self-harm or suicide

Identifying severe expressions of *Self-Harm* primarily rests on determining the individual's intent. An individual who is cutting or punching walls is doing so in order to help them cope with emotional pain. Suicidal individuals are not attempting to cope but rather responding to unbearable physical or emotional pain by ending their lives.

Severe forms of *Self-Harm* include:

- Suicidal ideation and planning

- Threatening to take action to kill, cut or otherwise hurt oneself

- Asking for or providing instructions or how to commit suicide or self-harm

- Positive reflections on death and dying or the perceived benefits of the individual's death

Less severe forms of *Self-Harm* include:

- Advice on hiding evidence of non-suicidal self-harm

- Showing off self-harm scars or positive reflections on self-harm behaviors

- Admitting to active or recent acts of non-suicidal self-harm

- Discussing events or objects that have recently "triggered" an individual to harm one's self

- Discussing reductions in recent non-suicidal self-harming behaviors without clear evidence of cessation

4.3 Ideological Harm

Ideological Harm describes the spread of beliefs that may lead to real world harm to society at large over time. Content belonging to this class may include statements without an explicit human target at the time of creation, for example, statements that openly question health or government policies that may lead to public crises, or expressions of praise for ideologies associated with crime, violence or exclusion. In this section, we present definitions of two common forms of ideological harm: *Extremism, Terrorism and Organized Crime* and *Misinformation*.

4.3.1 Extremism, Terrorism and Organized Crime

While to date there is no internationally agreed upon definition of terrorism, the UN General Assembly defines it as "criminal acts intended or calculated to provoke a state of terror in the public, a group of persons or particular persons for political purposes are in any circumstance unjustifiable, whatever the considerations of a political, philosophical, ideological, racial, ethnic, religious or any other nature that may be invoked to justify them." Various national governments and international organizations maintain lists of organizations they officially recognize as terrorist.

While terrorist groups are predominantly associated with violent behaviors, extremism refers to both violent and peaceful forms of expression. Organized crime groups, which frequently engage in violent criminal behavior, are not typically driven by political or ideological goals, but instead operate for economic gain.

Harmful content related to with *Extremism, Terrorism and Organized Crime* includes:

- Recruiting for a terrorist organization, extremist group or organized crime group

- Praise and promotion of organized crime, terrorist or extremist groups, or acts committed by such groups

- Assisting a terrorist organization, extremist group or organized crime group

- Content that includes symbols known to represent a terrorist organization, extremist group or organized crime group

At its core, every goal or belief of this class fits the criteria of severely abusive content. Either through exclusion, segregation, eradication or criminal activity, severe harm is intended.

White Supremacist Extremism One notable subtype of this type that we draw attention to is *White Supremacist Extremism* (*WSE*). The United States Congress recently identified white supremacist extremism as the most significant domestic terrorism threat facing the United States.[10]

WSE describes content seeking to revive and implement various ideologies of white supremacy. Content policies developed to address white supremacist ideologies are often established as part of a broader "hate speech" definition. While certain *WSE* statements attacking individuals based on religion, race or immigration status indeed overlap with our definition of *Identity Attack*, the motivation to elevate *WSE* to its own type of abuse is driven by a few factors. *WSE* content is often marked by various ideologies and linguistic patterns not expressed in direct person-to-person abuse. Attributes of the abuser are often in focus (e.g. whiteness and national identity), as opposed to characteristics of the abused. Additional features of *WSE* language include the use of dog whistle phrases and emoji, nostalgic references to "better times" in history, and the promotion of conspiracies and pseudo-science related to race, religion and sexuality.

WSE content can be generalized as belonging to one or more of the following ideologies:

- Neo-Nazism: idolization of Adolph Hitler, praise of Nazi policies or beliefs, use of Nazi symbols or slogans

- White racial supremacy: belief in white racial superiority, promotion of eugenics, incitement or allusions to a race war, concerns about "white genocide," cynicism towards interracial relationships and miscegenation

---

[10]https://www.congress.gov/116/bills/s894/BILLS-116s894is.xml

- White cultural supremacy: promotion of a white ethnostate, xenophobic attitudes, nostalgia for times of segregation

- Holocaust denial, propagation of Jewish conspiracy theories

- Recruitment or requests for financial support for WSE ideology, incitement of extreme physical fitness as a readiness measure for race-driven conflict

4.3.2 Misinformation

Simply stated, *Misinformation* is false or misleading information. It may be spread by users who are unaware of its credibility and lack a deliberate intent to harm. Disinformation, a subset of misinformation, refers to the knowing spread of misinformation. The intent behind disinformation is malicious, such as to damage the credibility of a person or organization, or to gain political or financial advantage.

Types of *Misinformation* include fake news, false rumors, conspiracy theories, hoaxes, and opinion spam. Increasingly more forms of misinformation are disallowed on many online platforms, including:

- Medically unproven health claims that create risk to public health and safety, including the promotion of false cures, incorrect information about public health or emergencies

- False or misleading content about members of protected or vulnerable groups

- False or misleading content that compromises the integrity of an election, or civic participation in an election

- Conspiracy theories

- Denial of a well-documented event

- Opinion spam, fabricated product reviews

- Removal of factual information with intent to erode trust or inflict harm, such as the omission of date, time or context

- Manipulation of visual or audio content with the intent to deceive

The spread of misinformation poses risks to society, erodes trust, hurts decision-making abilities, and may even lead to harmful global health or political events. *Misinformation* that may result in physical harm, civil unrest or health crises should be considered severe.

4.4 Exploitation

In order to provide safe online spaces, content created by users seeking to benefit by causing harm to others financially, sexually or physically is not permitted within digital communities. Forms of *Exploitation* include *Adult Sexual Services*, *Child Sexual Abuse Material* and *Scams*.

4.4.1 Adult Sexual Services

Certain forms of sexual solicitation and commerce cross over into illegal behavior that exploit often vulnerable participants, and are thus treated as a type of severe abuse. *Adult Sexual Services* includes:

- Promotion or solicitation of illegal sexual services such as prostitution, escort services, paid sexual fetish/domination services and sensual massages

- Organization of human trafficking

- Recruitment for live sex performances, sex chat

4.4.2 Child Sexual Abuse Material

Child Sexual Abuse Material (*CSAM*), sometimes referred to as "child pornography," is defined as content involving sexual abuse and exploitation of anyone under the age of eighteen. Materials included in the definition of *CSAM* have expanded beyond sexual images involving minors to include exploitative text content as well. *CSAM* is a severe form of abuse that includes:

- Images and videos which depict minors in a pornographic, sexually suggestive, or sexually violent manner, including illustrated or digitally altered pornography that depicts minors (e.g. lolicon, shotacon, or cub)

- Sharing adult pornography or CSAM with a minor

- Grooming of minors (the development of relationships of trust with the intent to sexually exploit)

- Sexual remarks directed at minors

- Arranging real-world sexual encounters or direct solicitation of sexual material from a minor

- Providing advice for or advocacy of child sexual abuse

4.4.3 Scams

Online scams are attempts to trick a person into providing funds or sensitive information using deceptive or invasive techniques. The perpetrator of a scam may attempt to build insincere relationships over the course of a conversation or misrepresent themselves as someone with skill or authority. Types of *Scams* that are commonly prohibited from digital communities include:

- Attempts to trick users into sending money or sharing personal information (e.g. phishing)

- Promise of funds in return for a smaller initial payment via wire transfer, gift cards, or prepaid debit card (e.g. money-flipping)

- Offers promising cash or gifts, such as lottery scams

- Romantic and military impersonation

- Promises of debt relief or credit repair

- Recruitment into pyramid schemes

5 Conclusions and Future Work

Upon careful synthesis of content policies, human rights treaties and recommendations from experts in physical and psychological harm, we have presented a typology of harmful content along with a set of best practices for developing precise definitions of types. In the future, we plan to report on the impact of how the proposed definitions impact the quality of datasets and models built using them, and to share public datasets based on this typology that may be used by the research community. We have published the typology at `https://gitlab.com/sentropy-technologies/typology-of-online-harm` and encourage those who study online abuse to contribute.

Acknowledgments

We wish to thank Cindy Wang, Taylor Rhyne, Bertie Vidgen and the WOAH reviewers for providing detailed feedback on this work.

References

Internet and Jurisdiction Policy Network. 2019. Content and jurisdiction program: Operational approaches, norms, criteria, mechanisms.

Maria Anzovino, Elisabetta Fersini, and Paolo Rosso. 2018. *Automatic Identification and Classification of Misogynistic Language on Twitter*, pages 57–64.

Susan Benesch. 2020. Proposals for Improved Regulation of Harmful Online Content.

Pete Burnan, Walter Colombo, and Jonathan Scourfield. 2015. Machine classification and analysis of suicide-related communication on twitter. In *Proceedings of the 26th ACM Conference on Hypertext & Social Media*, HT '15, page 75–84, New York, NY, USA. Association for Computing Machinery.

Lei Cao, Huijun Zhang, Ling Feng, Zihan Wei, Xin Wang, Ningyun Li, and Xiaohao He. 2019. Latent suicide risk detection on microblog via suicide-oriented word embeddings and layered attention. In *Proceedings of the 2019 Conference on Empirical Methods in Natural Language Processing and the 9th International Joint Conference on Natural Language Processing (EMNLP-IJCNLP)*, pages 1718–1728, Hong Kong, China. Association for Computational Linguistics.

Stevie Chancellor, Zhiyuan (Jerry) Lin, and Munmun De Choudhury. 2016. "this post will just get taken down": Characterizing removed pro-eating disorder social media content. In *Proceedings of the 2016 CHI Conference on Human Factors in Computing Systems*, CHI '16, page 1157–1162, New York, NY, USA. Association for Computing Machinery.

Thomas Davidson, Dana Warmsley, Michael Macy, and Ingmar Weber. 2017. Automated hate speech detection and the problem of offensive language. In *Proceedings of the Eleventh International AAAI Conference on Web and Social Media*.

Artur Dubrawski, Kyle Miller, Matthew Barnes, Benedikt Boecking, and Emily Kennedy. 2015. Leveraging publicly available data to discern patterns of human trafficking activity. In *Journal of Human Trafficking*.

Kaggle. 2012. Detecting insults in social commentary.

Kaggle. 2018. Toxic comment classification challenge.

Klaus Krippendorff. 2004. *Content analysis: An introduction to its methodology*. Sage.

Hee-Eun Lee, Tatiana Ermakova, Vasilis Ververis, and Benjamin Fabian. 2020. Detecting child sexual abuse material: A comprehensive survey". *Forensic Science International: Digital Investigation*, 34:301022.

Björn Ross, Michael Rist, Guillermo Carbonell, Benjamin Cabrera, Nils Kurowsky, and Michael Wojatzki. 2017. Measuring the reliability of hate speech annotations: The case of the european refugee crisis. In *Proceedings of the Workshop on Natural Language Processing for ComputerMediated Communication*.

Anna Schmidt and Michael Wiegand. 2017. A survey on hate speech detection using natural language processing. In *Proceedings of the Fifth International workshop on natural language processing for social media*, pages 1–10.

Peter Snyder, Periwinkle Doerfler, Chris Kanich, and Damon McCoy. 2017. Fifteen minutes of unwanted fame: Detecting and characterizing doxing. In *Proceedings of the 2017 Internet Measurement Conference*, page 432–444, New York, NY, USA. Association for Computing Machinery.

Murray A. Straus, Sherry L. Hamby, Sue Boney-McCoy, and David B. Sugarman. 1996. The revised conflict tactics scales (cts2): Development and preliminary psychometric data. *Journal of Family Issues*, 17(3):283–316.

Qi Su, Mingyu Wan, Xiaoqian Liu, and Chu-Ren Huang. 2020. Motivations, methods and metrics of misinformation detection: An nlp perspective. *Natural Language Processing Research*, 1:1–13.

Edmund Tong, Amir Zadeh, Cara Jones, and Louis-Philippe Morency. 2017. Combating human trafficking with deep multimodal models. *CoRR*, abs/1705.02735.

Cynthia Van Hee, Els Lefever, Ben Verhoeven, Julie Mennes, Bart Desmet, Guy De Pauw, Walter Daelemans, and Véronique Hoste. 2015. Detection and fine-grained classification of cyberbullying events. In *International Conference Recent Advances in Natural Language Processing (RANLP)*, pages 672–680.

Bertie Vidgen and Leon Derczynski. 2020. Directions in abusive language training data: Garbage in, garbage out. *ArXiv*, abs/2004.01670.

Bertie Vidgen, Alex Harris, Dong Nguyen, Rebekah Tromble, Scott Hale, and Helen Margetts. 2019. Challenges and frontiers in abusive content detection. Association for Computational Linguistics.

Tao Wang, Markus Brede, Antonella Ianni, and Emmanouil Mentzakis. 2017. Detecting and characterizing eating-disorder communities on social media. In *Proceedings of the Tenth ACM International conference on web search and data mining*.

Zeerak Waseem. 2016. Are you a racist or am i seeing things? annotator influence on hate speech detection on twitter. In *Proceedings of the First Workshop on NLP and Computational Social Science*, pages 138–142.

Zeerak Waseem, Thomas Davidson, Dana Warmsley, and Ingmar Weber. 2017. Understanding abuse: A typology of abusive language detection subtasks. In *Proceedings of the First Workshop on Abusive Language Online*, pages 78–84. Association for Computational Linguistics.

Zeerak Waseem and Dirk Hovy. 2016. Hateful symbols or hateful people? predictive features for hate speech detection on twitter. In *Proceedings of the NAACL Student Research Workshop*, pages 88–93. Association for Computational Linguistics.

Michael Wiegand, Josef Ruppenhofer, and Thomas Kleinbauer. 2019. Detection of Abusive Language: the Problem of Biased Datasets. In *Proceedings of the 2019 Conference of the North American Chapter of the Association for Computational Linguistics: Human Language Technologies, Volume 1 (Long and Short Papers)*, pages 602–608, Minneapolis, Minnesota. Association for Computational Linguistics.

Women's Media Center. Online abuse 101.

Ellery Wulczyn, Nithum Thain, and Lucas Dixon. 2017. Ex machina: Personal attacks seen at scale. In *Proceedings of the 26th International Conference on World Wide Web*, WWW '17, page 1391–1399, Republic and Canton of Geneva, CHE. International World Wide Web Conferences Steering Committee.

Towards a Comprehensive Taxonomy and Large-Scale Annotated Corpus for Online Slur Usage

Jana Kurrek [†]
McGill University
School of Computer Science
jana.kurrek@mail.mcgill.ca

Haji Mohammad Saleem [†]
McGill University
School of Computer Science
haji.saleem@mail.mcgill.ca

Derek Ruths
McGill University
School of Computer Science
derek.ruths@mcgill.ca

Abstract

Abusive language classifiers have been shown to exhibit bias against women and racial minorities. Since these models are trained on data that is collected using keywords, they tend to exhibit a high sensitivity towards pejoratives. As a result, comments written by victims of abuse are frequently labelled as hateful, even if they discuss or reclaim slurs. Any attempt to address bias in keyword-based corpora requires a better understanding of pejorative language, as well as an equitable representation of targeted users in data collection. We make two main contributions to this end. First, we provide an annotation guide that outlines 4 main categories of online slur usage, which we further divide into a total of 12 sub-categories. Second, we present a publicly available corpus based on our taxonomy, with 39.8k human annotated comments extracted from Reddit. This corpus was annotated by a diverse cohort of coders, with Shannon equitability indices of 0.90, 0.92, and 0.87 across sexuality, ethnicity, and gender. Taken together, our taxonomy and corpus allow researchers to evaluate classifiers on a wider range of speech containing slurs.

1 Introduction

Detecting abusive language is important for two substantive reasons. First is the mitigation of harm to individuals. Exposure to hate speech can result in a wide range of psychological effects, including degradation of mental health, depression, reduced self-esteem, and greater stress expression (Saha et al., 2019; Tynes et al., 2008; Boeckmann and Liew, 2002). Second is the broader impact of unregulated speech on the participation gap in social media (Jenkins, 2009; Notley, 2009). Overexposure to hateful language results in user desensitization (Soral et al., 2018) and radicalization (Norman and

---

†These authors made equal contributions.

Mikhael, 2017), both of which have been shown to worsen racial relations (Sène, 2019). Moreover, hateful echo-chambers promote a "spiral of silence" that discourages counter-speech in conversations online (Duncan et al., 2020).

Access to large-scale training data is the first step towards robust automated systems for abusive language detection. While industry researchers can access moderator logs and user reports, proprietary data is not the standard for academics. Instead, pejorative keywords are commonly used as filters in the data collection process. These include, but are not limited to, slurs and other curated lists of profane language (Waseem and Hovy, 2016; Waseem, 2016; Khodak et al., 2018; Rezvan et al., 2018), terms borrowed from Hatebase, a multilingual repository for hate speech (Silva et al., 2016; Davidson et al., 2017; Founta et al., 2018; ElSherief et al., 2018), offensive hashtags (Chatzakou et al., 2017; Golbeck et al., 2017), and manually selected threads or subreddits (Gao and Huang, 2017; Hammer et al., 2019; Qian et al., 2019). Although the drawbacks of keyword-based approaches are known to researchers, there are currently no clear alternatives to this technique (Waseem and Hovy, 2016; Davidson et al., 2017; ElSherief et al., 2018).

There has been a recent focus on how technical choices involving data curation can introduce systemic bias in the resultant corpus. For instance, Wiegand et al. (2019) discover that terms like *football*, *announcer*, and *sport* have the strongest correlation to abusive posts in Waseem and Hovy (2016). Furthermore, Davidson et al. (2019), Xia et al. (2020) and Sap et al. (2019) reveal how classifiers trained on data with systemic racial bias have a higher tendency to label text written in African-American English as abusive. Cited examples include: "Wussup, nigga!", and "I saw his ass yesterday". Left unaddressed, bias has a real impact on users. Automated recruiting tools

Proceedings of the Fourth Workshop on Online Abuse and Harms, pages 138–149
Online, November 20, 2020. ©2020 Association for Computational Linguistics
https://doi.org/10.18653/v1/P17

used by Amazon.com were shown to discriminate against women (Cook, 2018). Similarly, Microsoft released a public chatbot that learned to share racist content on Twitter (Vincent, 2016). A common solution is to debias language representations (Bolukbasi et al., 2016). However, these methods conceal but do not remove systemic bias in the overall data (Gonen and Goldberg, 2019).

A way of beginning to address the issue of racial and gender bias is therefore to understand the implications of forced sampling. Our paper focuses specifically on data that is collected using derogatory keywords and we make two main contributions to this end. First, we provide an annotation guide that outlines 4 main categories of online slur usage, which we further divide into a total of 12 subcategories. Second, we present a publicly available corpus based on our taxonomy, with 39.8k human annotated comments extracted from Reddit. We also propose an approach to data collection and annotation that prioritizes inclusivity both by design and application:

Inclusivity by Design: Data selection and annotation achieves weighted group representation. We sample from a variety of subreddits in order to capture non-derogatory slur usage. We then hire a diverse set of coders under strict ethical standards as a means of engaging the perspectives of various target communities. We encourage opinion diversity by pairing annotators into teams based on maximum demographic differences.

Inclusivity by Application: Our coding guidelines are extensible to language that targets multiple protected groups. We collect data using the slurs: *faggot*, a pejorative term used primarily to refer to gay men, *nigger*, an ethnic slur typically directed at black people, especially African Americans, and *tranny*, a derogatory slur for a transgender person. This is only time we mention the actual slurs. From hereon, We refer to each term as the f-slur, n-slur, and t-slur, respectively. We specifically choose these slurs because they enable us to study discrimination across sexuality, ethnicity, and gender.

Our work does not directly eliminate bias in existing datasets. Rather, it aids in truly understanding the different ways in which slurs can be used online so that models can be trained and assessed more effectively.

2   Related Work

2.1   Existing Hate Speech Corpora

The earliest and most notable corpus for hate speech research is Waseem and Hovy (2016). It contains 16k comments from Twitter, annotated according to the offense criteria of McIntosh (1988). Waseem (2016) is an extension of this corpus by 6,909 comments and it considers amateur as well as expert annotations. The authors make use of offensive hashtags for data collection, but it was not until Nobata et al. (2016) that slurring language was formally introduced as a sub-problem of hate speech. This paper uses a variety of linguistic features, such as modal words, insulting and hate blacklist words, and politeness words, in order to separate the three notions of hate, derogation, and profanity based on their relative degrees of harm to the target. These guidelines inspired the Fox News user comments corpus of Gao and Huang (2017). Both works emphasize the capacity for hateful language to exist in implicit and explicit forms and collect the explicit form using derogatory keywords. Silva et al. (2016) is a target-based analysis of the explicit form. They leverage the syntactic structure "I <intensity><user intent><hate target>", where each hate target is one of 1,078 terms selected from Hatebase, in order to identify ten top targets of hate within Twitter and Whisper content. Next, Davidson et al. (2017) investigate intentional group-based humiliation and derogation. They reinforce the role of slurs as archetypal representations of hate by acknowledging that "tweets with the highest predicted probabilities of being hate speech tend to contain multiple racial or homophobic slurs." More recently, de Gibert Bonet et al. (2018) sample from a white supremacist sub-forum and, in doing so, encourage community-based filtering. The emerging theme from these research efforts is the consensus that we require an alternative to random sampling for reliably capturing hateful content. What that alternative is remains unclear but keywords are currently the dominant choice.

Other researchers have expanded on this definition and shown that it is applicable to more nuanced categories of online misbehaviour, such as abuse, threats, personal attacks, and cyberbullying. For instance, Khodak et al. (2018) is a self-annotated corpus for sarcasm on Reddit. Sprugnoli et al. (2018) focuses on cyberbullying within WhatsApp conversations. Rezvan et al. (2018) points out sexual,

Authors	Size	Platform	Annotation	Agreement
KEYWORD BASED DATA COLLECTION				
Qian et al. (2019)	34k	Gab	Hate Speech (Binary)	Unknown
Qian et al. (2019)	22k	Reddit	Hate Speech (Binary)	Unknown
Waseem and Hovy (2016)	16k	Twitter	Racism, Sexism	$\kappa = 0.84$
Waseem (2016)	7k	Twitter	Racism, Sexism	$\kappa = 0.34$ (Majority Vote) $\kappa = 0.70$ (Full Agreement)
Golbeck et al. (2017)	35k	Twitter	Hate Speech, Threats, Harassment, Offense	$\kappa = 0.84$
Chatzakou et al. (2017)	9k	Twitter	Aggressors, Bullies, Spammers	Inter-rater agreement = 0.54
Davidson et al. (2019)	25k	Twitter	Hate Speech, Offense	Inter-rater agreement = 0.92
Rezvan et al. (2018)	25k	Twitter	Harassment	$\kappa = 0.70$; 0.84; 1.0; 0.80; 0.69 for respective categories
Founta et al. (2018)	80k	Twitter	Hate Speech, Spam, Abuse	Unknown
ElSherief et al. (2018)	2k	Twitter	Hate Speech	$\alpha = 0.622$
Jha and Mamidi (2017)	1k	Twitter	Sexism	$F\kappa = 0.74$
Silva et al. (2016)	539.5m	Twitter Whisper	Hate Speech	Not applicable
Fersini et al. (2018)	3k	Twitter	Sexism	Unknown
Basile et al. (2019)	19.6k	Twitter	Hate Speech, Target, Aggressiveness	F8 confidence = 0.83 0.70, 0.73
Zampieri et al. (2019)	14.1k	Twitter	Offense, Target	$F\kappa = 0.83*$ *on 21 tweets
MANUAL SELECTION				
Gao and Huang (2017)	1.5k	Fox News	Hate Speech	$\kappa = 0.98$
Hammer et al. (2019)	30k	Youtube	Threats	Unknown
PROPRIETARY DATA				
Sprugnoli et al. (2018)	15k	WhatsApp	Cyberbullying	SDC = 0.80 - 0.88
Nobata et al. (2016)	1.2m	Yahoo	Hate Speech	$F\kappa = 0.40$; 0.21 for AMT $F\kappa = 0.84$; 0.46 for Trained (Binary; Fine-grained)
RANDOM DATA SELECTION				
de Gibert Bonet et al. (2018)	10k	Stormfront	Hate Speech (Binary)	$\kappa = 0.61$; $F\kappa = 0.61$ (Batch1) $\kappa = 0.63$; $F\kappa = 0.63$ (Batch2)
Napoles et al. (2017)	10k	Yahoo	Positive Conversations	$\alpha = 0.79$ (Group) $\alpha = 0.71$ (Trained)
OTHER METHODS				
Wulczyn et al. (2017)	100k	Wikipedia	Harassment, Attacks	$\alpha = 0.45$
Kennedy et al. (2017)	20k	Twitter, Reddit, The Guardian,	Harassment (Binary)	Inter-rater agreement = 0.88

Table 1: An overview of the main corpora on abusive language and similar behaviours. $F\kappa$ is Fleiss' Kappa, κ is Cohen's Kappa, SDC is the Sørensen–Dice coefficient, and inter-rater agreement refers to raw disagreement.

appearance-related, intellectual, and political harassment on Twitter. Hammer et al. (2019) is a corpus for detection of violent threats on YouTube. Holgate et al. (2018), Cachola et al. (2018), and Pamungkas et al. (2020) examine vulgarity and swearing. A number of corpora on mixed behaviours have also been produced. Golbeck et al. (2017) is a study on harassment and offense on Twitter. Chatzakou et al. (2017) labels Twitter users, not comments, as aggressors, bullies, or spammers. Founta et al. (2018) considers spam in conjunction with abuse, bullying, and aggression on Twitter. Napoles et al. (2017) works on the converse of the problem. This paper uses Yahoo! News data to advance a corpus on constructive conversations.

We have collected a list of the major English-language corpora and summarized their sizes, platforms of focus, annotation schemes, and agreement scores in Table 1. With that said, the study of online misbehavior has been extend beyond the traditional focus on English. It now includes resources in Italian, Indonesian, Hindi-English, Tunisian, etc. (Sanguinetti et al., 2018; Ibrohim and Budi, 2018; Kumar et al., 2018; Bohra et al., 2018; Haddad et al., 2019; Mulki et al., 2019; Chung et al., 2019).

2.2 Slurs

To model the contents of slur-based data, it is crucial that we first examine the properties of slurs themselves. Slurs are pejoratives that derogate based on in-group membership, that is, they categorize targets based on institutionally defined

f-slur	n-slur	t-slur
SUPPORTIVE COMMUNITIES		
askgaybros	BlackPeopleTwitter	transgendercirclejerk
gaybros	Blackfellas	traaaaaaannnnnnnnnns
lgbt	blackladies	asktransgender
ainbow	beholdthemasterrace	ainbow
LGBTeens	AgainstHateSubreddits	transgender
ANTAGONISTIC COMMUNITIES		
4chan	CoonTown	TumblrInAction
ImGoingToHellForThis	uncensorednews	MGTOW
The_Donald	WhiteRights	Braincels
CringeAnarchy	GreatApes	metacanada
TheRedPill	european	GenderCritical
GENERAL DISCUSSION COMMUNITIES		
funny	todayilearned	rupaulsdragrace
pics	videos	cars
politics	changemyview	Drama
AskReddit	worldnews	AdviceAnimals
atheism	movies	unpopularopinion

Table 2: This table presents the major supportive, antagonistic, and general discussion subreddits that were used in data collection. Their range of views towards the targets of each slur facilitates equitable representation.

archetypes (Croom, 2015). Studies on slurs are built on the recognition by Kaplan (1999) that meaning in natural language comes from convention and from context: a sentence is *expressively correct* if it is true by interpretation; a sentence is *descriptively correct* if it is literally true.

Hom (2008) advocates in favor of the expressive view of slurs. He identifies nine adequacy conditions that characterize and explain racial epithets: A slur exhibits (1) derogatory force. The force of any slur is (2) variable across epithets and (3) fundamentally offensive, independently of the intents and beliefs of the speaker. While slurs are capable of being (7) reclaimed or (8) used towards a non-derogatory, non-appropriative end, they are generally (4) taboo unless (6) their force changes over time. This is because slurs are (5) meaningful insofar as they contribute to the truth-conditions of the sentence in which they arise. Hom's account of slurs is (9) generalizable across pejoratives.

Hom implies that there are three main categories of slur usage, which are derogatory, non-derogatory non-appropriative, and appropriative. His adequacy conditions are central to our research. The three categories are the basis of our annotation scheme and they enable us to make assessments of abuse with ambiguous user intent.

3 Inclusive Design Process

Random sampling of slur-based data allows for proportional representation because the share of each usage in the corpus is reflective of its probability of occurrence online. However, this approach is not equitable. Less common usages, such as reclamation, discussion, and counter-speech, are not captured. Consequently, language models can overfit on pejoratives and further codify institutional biases (Caliskan et al., 2017; Garg et al., 2018). A top-down approach to debiasing is simply insufficient. We advocate in favor of affirmative action during data collection and make an effort to represent a wider range of slur usages through community targeting. We also tailor our study to include individuals that belong to targeted communities, both as authors and annotators.

3.1 Data Collection

We use the Pushshift Reddit corpus (Baumgartner et al., 2020) and filter for the three slurs (f-slur, n-slur, t-slur) and their plurals. The data ranged from October 2007 to September 2019 at the time of filtering. We extracted a total of 2.6 million comments. We applied the following filtering process:

Author Level: We remove comments written by users with no history in order to leave open the possibility of a future analysis with user meta-data. We remove comments written by users that were identified as bots. We limit the number of comments written by the same author.

Comment Level: Reddit comments vary in length, with an upper limit of 40,000 characters. For ease of annotation, we remove comments from the top and bottom quartiles by length. We limit our corpus to English-language comments and use the

Slur Usages	Example Text
DEROGATORY	
Attribution	he's an ugly [f-slur] with greasy hair.
Community Focus	lol don't be a [f-slur]
Stand Alone	[t-slur]
Sexualization	I love the taste of a nice hot [t-slur] load
Self-Deprecation	as mizkif i can agree i look like a [f-slur]
APPROPRIATIVE	
Reclamation	get in [t-slur] Formation everyone, it's time to march against the tyranny of heteronormatives trying to appropriate OUR WORDS
NON-DEROGATORY, NON-APPROPRIATIVE	
Counter Speech	[t-slur] is a slur please don't use it.
Direct Quotations	actual quote: de [n-slur] woman is de mule uh de world so fur as ah can see.
Discussion	You could call someone a [f-slur] in the 70s and 80s with absolutely no recourse.
Recollection	I never got so much shit until I graduated high school. :— I get called a [f-slur] by some random clitdick almost every day I have class.
Sarcasm	Yeah because apparently [f-slur] all of a sudden isn't a slur used against homosexuals.
HOMONYMS	
	transmissions are beautiful pieces of engineering, why not have a [t-slur] tattoo?
	[f-slur] Hill, 969th tallest peak in Massachusetts... why even count at that point?
	Damn talk about being able to skate anything. Rips [t-slur] then throws in kickflip back lips on rails.

Table 3: Our taxonomy of slur usage, with 4 main categories broken down into 12 subcategories. Examples are provided for each subcategory and further detail can be found in the Appendix.

Compact Language Detector v3[1] to detect them.

Community Level: Communities that antagonise or support a group talk about similar topics but with opposing valence (Saleem et al., 2016). To capture such polarity, we compile a list of subreddits based on their disdain for, neutrality towards, or support of the f-slur, n-slur, and t-slur (see Table 2). We do this by building on an existing list of toxic Reddit communities (Caffier, 2017). We consider the name, rules, extent of moderation, description text, and polarity of comments containing slurs (overall score) of each subreddit in our assessment of whether or not to include them. We then extract the top comments in terms of polarity.

Our post-filter corpus has 40,000 comments, sourced from 2704 individual subreddits and 37,133 unique authors. The median and maximum number of comments per author is 1 and 5.

3.2 Taxonomy Design

Our coding guide is based on the three major categories of slur usage identified in Hom (2008). By open coding data collected using slurs, we identify a fourth major category as well as twelve subcategories. The complete taxonomy, along with examples for each subcategory, is provided in Table 3. In general, comments containing more than one slur were labelled according to the most derogatory usage. The four main categories are explained below:

[1]https://github.com/google/cld3

Derogatory Usage (DER): Any usage that is understood to convey contempt towards a targeted individual or group.

Appropriative Usage (APR): Meaningful usage by the targeted group for an alternate, non-derogatory purpose. Text belonging to this label loses its derogatory force.

Non-Derogatory, Non-Appropriative Usage (NDG): Meaningful usage by targeted or non-targeted groups for an alternate non-derogatory, non-appropriative purpose. Text belonging to this label retains its derogatory force.

Homonyms (HOM): A slur with one or more non-derogatory alternative meanings.

3.3 Annotator Selection

Following approval by the university Research Ethics Board (REB), we shared messages on social media and university mailing lists as well as physical posters across faculties in order to look for participants. The application consisted of eight short answer questions, in which candidates were asked to disclose their name, email, field and year of study, age, sexuality, ethnicity, and gender. We specifically collected the demographic information in free-form text. The free-form allows participants to choose best demographic identifiers for themselves. The demographic information is confidential and used solely for selecting annotators and creating their teams.

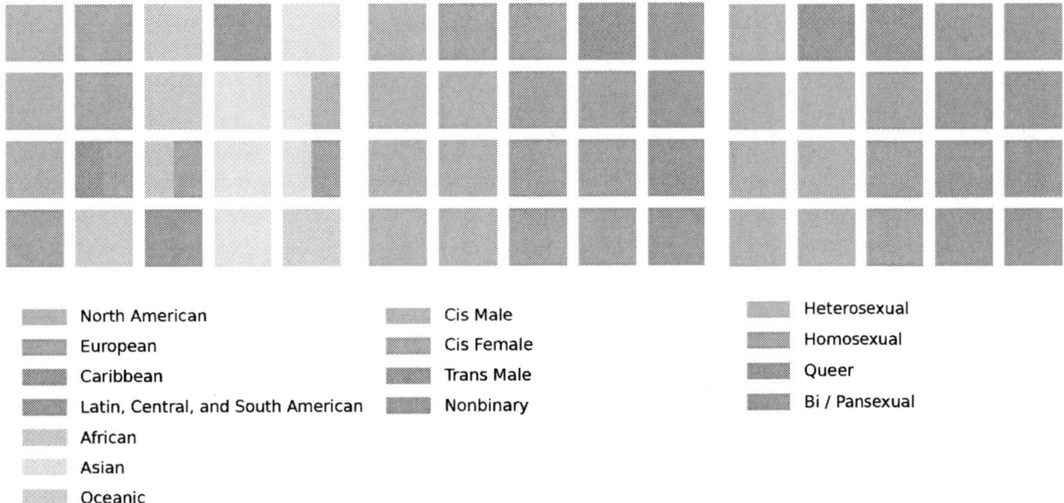

Figure 1: The diverse demographic details of our annotator cohort, aggregated on ethnicity, gender and sexuality.

All demographics were collapsed into categories (see Figure 1) primarily based on the classification structure approved as a departmental standard by Statistics Canada (2017). Of the four hundred and twelve applications received, 20 participants, ranging between 19 and 65 years of age (M = 26.7, SD = 10.8), were chosen using iterative proportional fitting. Overall, our annotator cohort has a Shannon equitability index of 0.90, 0.92, and 0.87 across sexuality, ethnicity, and gender. We did not have the REB clearance to perform any further analysis on the relationship between annotator demographics and annotations. We leave this as an area for future work.

3.4 Training and Annotation

A 4-session on-campus training program was developed for annotators to attend over 2 days. On Day 1, we presented the annotation scheme obtained through open coding. Annotators were then guided through two group annotation exercises of 20 and 40 comments respectively. On Day 2, annotators were randomly divided into 4 teams. Each team completed 2 rounds of 200 training annotations. After each round, they discussed their annotations and the reasons behind their labels. The discussion was aimed at fostering a common understanding of the annotation process.

The final annotations were divided into 4 tasks of 10,000 comments each. The 20 annotators were grouped into 10 teams of 2. The team creation process maximized the demographic distance between members across sexuality, ethnicity, and gender. It was treated as an assignment problem and solved using the Kuhn-Munkres algorithm. Each team annotated 1000 comments per task and annotators were grouped into new pairs for each subsequent task. Comments with no disagreement were added to the final corpus. Comments with disagreement were resolved by the authors. The final annotations were performed remotely on the open source text annotation tool Doccano (Nakayama et al., 2018).

4   Labeled Corpus

40,000 Reddit comments were annotated, of which 189 were removed as noise. The remaining 39,811 were closely split across slurs: 13,290, 13,267 and 13,267 for f-slur, n-slur and t-slur respectively. In total, 20,531 comments were labelled derogatory, 16,729 non-derogatory, 1,998 homonym, and 553 appropriative. We anticipated a large portion of derogatory comments in our corpus because our data is slur-based. However, only 52% of comments were labelled as such. We attribute this to our community-targeted data collection process and efforts to sample from supportive subreddits.

4.1   Label Distribution Across Slurs

In Figure 2, we present the label distribution across slurs. We observe that roughly 59% of comments collected using the f-slur and t-slur were labelled as derogatory. In comparison, about 37.9% of comments containing the n-slur were similarly labelled. The majority of found homonyms include the t-

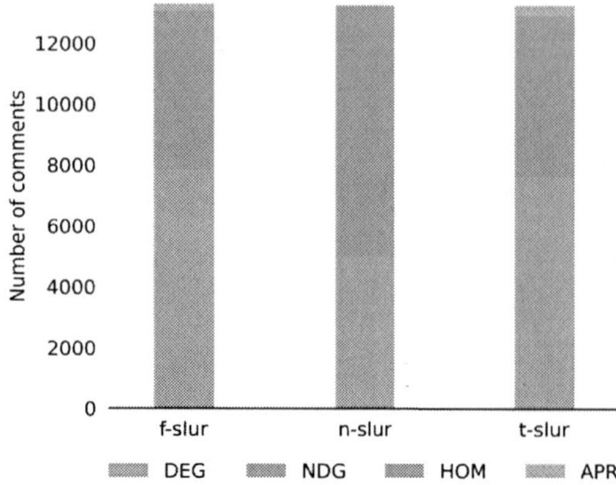

Figure 2: The label distribution across slurs.

slur, which accounts for 95.9% of the label. This is largely because the term is used in automotive communities to mean vehicle transmission (see Figure 3) and in skateboarding communities to describe skating transition. The remaining homonyms include the f-slur, with the meaning "bundle" or in reference to a form of British meatball. The n-slur has the smallest share of homonyms (0.02%) and appropriative (0.16%) comments.

4.2 Label Distribution Across Subreddits

In Figure 3, we present the label distribution across the 50 most common subreddits in our corpus. The graph is sorted by the proportion of derogatory comments in each subreddit. Consequently, it can be seen as a scale of derogatory behavior. On the far right are communities that we had previously identified as antagonistic. Many of their comments were labelled as derogatory and examples include MGTOW, CoonTown, 4chan and, The_Donald. In the middle we find general discussion subreddits such as videos, todayilearned, and politics. They generally have an even split of derogatory and non-derogatory labels. On the far left we observe mostly supportive subreddits, with small portions of derogatory comments. Automotive subreddits like cars have a large number of homonyms. Meanwhile, subreddits such as traaaaaaannnnnnnnnnns, askgaybros, and rupaulsdragrace contain significant portion of appropriative speech. These findings align with our initial hypothesis about supportive, antagonistic, and general discussion communities.

	Agreement (%)	Cohen's κ
overall	78.6	0.60
f-slur	79.7	0.58
n-slur	75.4	0.51
t-slur	80.5	0.65

Table 4: Raw and inter-rater agreement. We achieve moderate to substantial agreement with Cohen's κ.

4.3 Agreement Analysis

Both annotators agreed on the same label for 31,034 of the comments in our corpus. The remaining 8,777 comments were resolved by the authors. Overall we achieve a raw agreement score of 78.6%, corresponding to a Cohen's κ of 0.60. Our scores indicate substantial agreement and are in line with what has been observed in the literature (see Table 1). We obtain similar agreement across the three slurs, which are presented in Table 4.

APR had the highest amount of disagreement, with 67.99% comments requiring resolution, followed by NDG (35.36%), and HOM (31.58%). DEG was the lowest at 9.034%. During the resolution process, we identified three probable causes for disagreement:

Label Overlap Discussions of derogation or reclamation created ambiguity and were falsely labelled as DER or APR, rather than NDG. A similar issue arose in comments acknowledging slurs as homonyms. For instance: *"When i was telling my skate friends about me being trans i asked them if they knew why it was so ironic that i love skating [t-slur] so much."*.

Satire Our annotators found many derogatory comments in transgendercirclejerk (see Figure 3), which is a subreddit that self-identifies as a "parody for trans people, mocking all transgender-related topics". However, the sarcastic or satirical nature of these comments was not always evident: *"We don't need gun control we need [T-SLUR] CONTROL! [t-slurs] are not in the Constitution or Bible, like guns are! If we don't outlaw t-slurs, only [t-slurs] will have outlaws!"*. We leave this area for future work.

Lack of Context In an independent assessment of label reliability, we re-annotated 100 DEG comments from transgendercirclejerk with complete access to user and thread history. 44 of our labels did not match those submitted by annotators. For instance, the following comment came from a transgender poster: *"LA LA LA CAN'T*

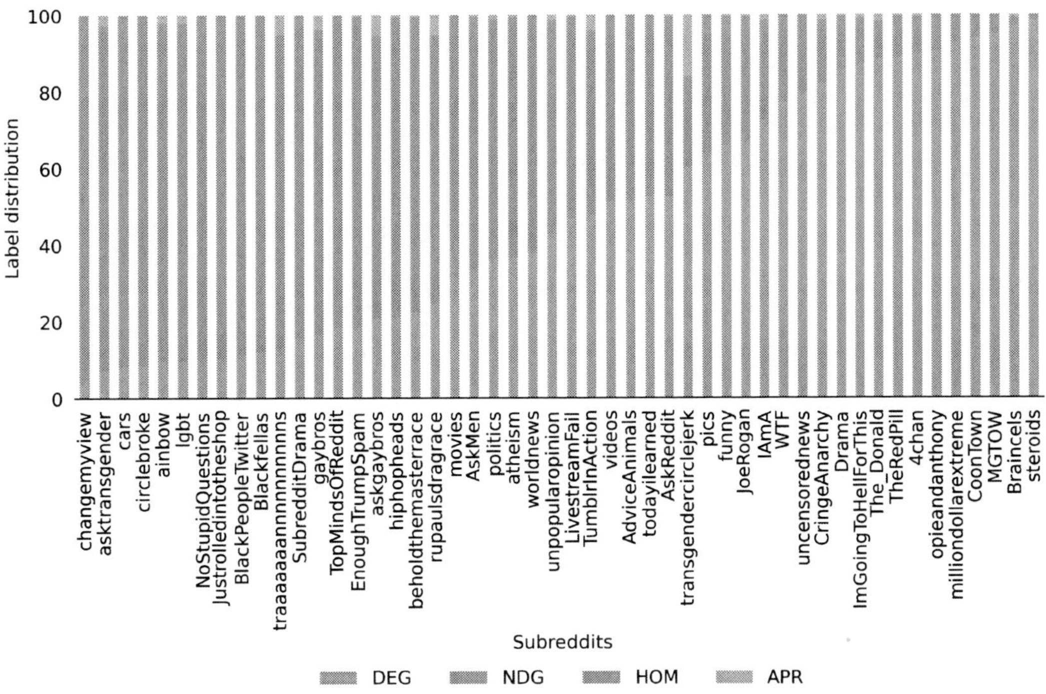

Figure 3: The normalized label distribution across the 50 most common subreddits in our corpus, sorted by their portion of derogatory comments.

HEAR YOU I'M STUCK IN [T-SLUR] REALITY" but was mislabelled. This testifies the difficulty of annotating appropriative language without context. Other instances that requires context are reference to lyrics and dialogues from pop culture.For example "Dead [n-slur] Storage" from the movie Pulp Fiction.

4.4 Benchmarking the Perspective API

We use a state-of-the-art model for derogatory content detection to assess whether current classifiers are subject to overfitting on pejoratives. We choose the Perspective API by Conversation AI, which "identifies whether a comment could be perceived as toxic to a discussion". We obtain the toxicity scores for 100 random comments for each of the DEG, NDG, HOM, and APR labels. The results are summarized in Figure 4. As expected, the overall score distribution is high for DEG. However, it is equally high for NDG and APR comments. This perfectly illustrates the issue of potentially biased models failing to identify non-derogatory content.

Further analysis of toxicity scores across comments underlines the challenges faced by existing models. First, instances of slur reclamation re-

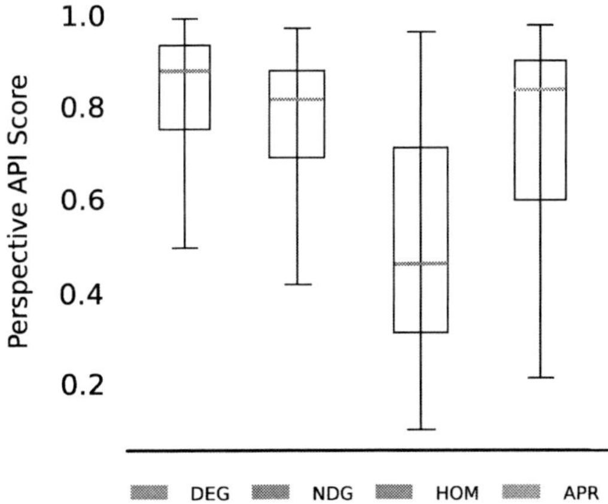

Figure 4: Benchmarking the Perspective API. Scores indicate a comment's degree of toxicity.

ceived high toxicity scores. For example: *"Psh my [t-slur] agony sits atop that steed with militant fervour. The world shall hear me roar, I AM A [T-SLUR] FREAK!!!! /uj Not even kidding, I'm 100% out as a [t-slur] freak. World can suck my shenis"* and *"When I've got a guy I'm crushing on I will sometimes say 'He makes me feel like a silly [f-slur] all over again'"* have toxicity scores above 0.93. Reclamation is an attempt at empowerment and community cohesion. The mislabelling of such examples further censors communities already targeted by hate. Second, recollections of past harassment received high toxicity scores. For example: *"A homeless dude called me a spic [f-slur] once while I was with my ex"* is rated as high as 0.889. This belittles victims' experiences with abuse, rather than protecting them from it. Finally, counter speech received high toxicity scores. For example: *"Ummmm, yeah no, [t-slur] is a slur and youre ignorant as hell"* is rated 0.953. This undermines community-level efforts at removing derogatory language. Overall, these three outcomes are counterproductive to the detection process since empowering and vulnerable conversations of targeted communities may be flagged down.

5 Conclusion

We present a comprehensive taxonomy and large-scale annotated corpus for online slur usage. Our findings are an attempt at integrating a qualitative understanding of slurs into their usage in natural language. We believe that they provide a significant contribution to the hate speech research community, not only as resources for training machine and deep learning models, but also as a means of achieving a nuanced understanding of the phenomenon of slurs. We encourage researchers to replicate and expand our efforts by studying language that targets other marginalized communities. With that said, our corpus is a challenging benchmark that will help expose over-fitting on pejoratives and our taxonomy introduces a systematic approach for dealing with derogatory keywords and epithets. Our corpus can be accessed by emailing the authors.

References

Valerio Basile, Cristina Bosco, Elisabetta Fersini, Debora Nozza, Viviana Patti, Francisco Manuel Rangel Pardo, Paolo Rosso, and Manuela Sanguinetti. 2019. SemEval-2019 task 5: Multilingual detection of hate speech against immigrants and women in Twitter. In *Proceedings of the 13th International Workshop on Semantic Evaluation*, pages 54–63, Minneapolis, Minnesota, USA. Association for Computational Linguistics.

Jason Baumgartner, Savvas Zannettou, Brian Keegan, Megan Squire, and Jeremy Blackburn. 2020. The pushshift reddit dataset. *Proceedings of the International AAAI Conference on Web and Social Media*, 14(1):830–839.

Robert J Boeckmann and Jeffrey Liew. 2002. Hate speech: Asian american students' justice judgments and psychological responses. *Journal of Social Issues*, 58(2):363–381.

Aditya Bohra, Deepanshu Vijay, Vinay Singh, Syed Sarfaraz Akhtar, and Manish Shrivastava. 2018. A dataset of hindi-english code-mixed social media text for hate speech detection. In *Proceedings of the second workshop on computational modeling of people's opinions, personality, and emotions in social media*, pages 36–41.

Tolga Bolukbasi, Kai-Wei Chang, James Y Zou, Venkatesh Saligrama, and Adam T Kalai. 2016. Man is to computer programmer as woman is to homemaker? debiasing word embeddings. In *Advances in neural information processing systems*, pages 4349–4357.

Isabel Cachola, Eric Holgate, Daniel Preoţiuc-Pietro, and Junyi Jessy Li. 2018. Expressively vulgar: The socio-dynamics of vulgarity and its effects on sentiment analysis in social media. In *Proceedings of the 27th International Conference on Computational Linguistics*, pages 2927–2938, Santa Fe, New Mexico, USA. Association for Computational Linguistics.

Justin Caffier. 2017. Here are reddit's whiniest, most low-key toxic subreddits. *Vice.com*.

Aylin Caliskan, Joanna J. Bryson, and Arvind Narayanan. 2017. Semantics derived automatically from language corpora contain human-like biases. *Science*, 356(6334):183–186.

Elisabeth Camp. 2012. Sarcasm, pretense, and the semantics/pragmatics distinction. *Noûs*, 46(4):587–634.

Despoina Chatzakou, Nicolas Kourtellis, Jeremy Blackburn, Emiliano De Cristofaro, Gianluca Stringhini, and Athena Vakali. 2017. Mean birds: Detecting aggression and bullying on twitter. In *Proceedings of the 2017 ACM on web science conference*, pages 13–22.

Yi-Ling Chung, Elizaveta Kuzmenko, Serra Tekiroglu, and Marco Guerini. 2019. Conan - counter narratives through nichesourcing: a multilingual dataset of responses to fight online hate speech. In *Proceedings of the 57th Annual Meeting of the Association for Computational Linguistics*, pages 2819–2829.

James Cook. 2018. Amazon scraps 'sexist ai' recruiting tool that showed bias against women. *The Telegraph*.

Adam M Croom. 2015. The semantics of slurs: A refutation of coreferentialism. *Ampersand*, 2:30–38.

Thomas Davidson, Debasmita Bhattacharya, and Ingmar Weber. 2019. Racial bias in hate speech and abusive language detection datasets. In *Proceedings of the Third Workshop on Abusive Language Online*, pages 25–35. Association for Computational Linguistics.

Thomas Davidson, Dana Warmsley, Michael Macy, and Ingmar Weber. 2017. Automated hate speech detection and the problem of offensive language. In *Eleventh international aaai conference on web and social media*.

Megan Duncan, Ayellet Pelled, David Wise, Shreenita Ghosh, Yuanliang Shan, Mengdian Zheng, and Doug McLeod. 2020. Staying silent and speaking out in online comment sections: The influence of spiral of silence and corrective action in reaction to news. *Computers in Human Behavior*, 102:192–205.

Mai ElSherief, Vivek Kulkarni, Dana Nguyen, William Yang Wang, and Elizabeth Belding. 2018. Hate lingo: A target-based linguistic analysis of hate speech in social media. In *Twelfth International AAAI Conference on Web and Social Media*.

Elisabetta Fersini, Paolo Rosso, and Maria Anzovino. 2018. Overview of the task on automatic misogyny identification at ibereval 2018. In *IberEval@ SEPLN*, pages 214–228.

Antigoni Maria Founta, Constantinos Djouvas, Despoina Chatzakou, Ilias Leontiadis, Jeremy Blackburn, Gianluca Stringhini, Athena Vakali, Michael Sirivianos, and Nicolas Kourtellis. 2018. Large scale crowdsourcing and characterization of twitter abusive behavior. In *Twelfth International AAAI Conference on Web and Social Media*.

Lei Gao and Ruihong Huang. 2017. Detecting online hate speech using context aware models. In *Proceedings of the International Conference Recent Advances in Natural Language Processing, RANLP 2017*, pages 260–266, Varna, Bulgaria. INCOMA Ltd.

Nikhil Garg, Londa Schiebinger, Dan Jurafsky, and James Zou. 2018. Word embeddings quantify 100 years of gender and ethnic stereotypes. *Proceedings of the National Academy of Sciences*, 115(16):E3635–E3644.

Ona de Gibert Bonet, Naiara Perez Miguel, Aitor García-Pablos, and Montse Cuadros. 2018. Hate speech dataset from a white supremacy forum. In *Proceedings of the 2nd Workshop on Abusive Language Online (ALW2)*, pages 11–20. Association for Computational Linguistics.

Jennifer Golbeck, Zahra Ashktorab, Rashad O Banjo, Alexandra Berlinger, Siddharth Bhagwan, Cody Buntain, Paul Cheakalos, Alicia A Geller, Rajesh Kumar Gnanasekaran, Raja Rajan Gunasekaran, et al. 2017. A large labeled corpus for online harassment research. In *Proceedings of the 2017 ACM on web science conference*, pages 229–233.

Hila Gonen and Yoav Goldberg. 2019. Lipstick on a pig: Debiasing methods cover up systematic gender biases in word embeddings but do not remove them. In *Proceedings of the 2019 Conference of the North American Chapter of the Association for Computational Linguistics: Human Language Technologies, Volume 1 (Long and Short Papers)*, pages 609–614.

Philip B Gove. 1964. Noun often attributive" and" adjective. *American Speech*, 39(3):163–175.

Hatem Haddad, Hala Mulki, and Asma Oueslati. 2019. T-hsab: A tunisian hate speech and abusive dataset. In *International Conference on Arabic Language Processing*, pages 251–263. Springer.

Hugo L Hammer, Michael A Riegler, Lilja Øvrelid, and Erik Velldal. 2019. Threat: A large annotated corpus for detection of violent threats. In *2019 International Conference on Content-Based Multimedia Indexing (CBMI)*, pages 1–5. IEEE.

Eric Holgate, Isabel Cachola, Daniel Preoţiuc-Pietro, and Junyi Jessy Li. 2018. Why swear? analyzing and inferring the intentions of vulgar expressions. In *Proceedings of the 2018 Conference on Empirical Methods in Natural Language Processing*, pages 4405–4414, Brussels, Belgium. Association for Computational Linguistics.

Christopher Hom. 2008. The semantics of racial epithets. *The Journal of Philosophy*, 105(8):416–440.

Muhammad Okky Ibrohim and Indra Budi. 2018. A dataset and preliminaries study for abusive language detection in indonesian social media. *Procedia Computer Science*, 135:222–229.

Henry Jenkins. 2009. *Confronting the challenges of participatory culture: Media education for the 21st century*. Mit Press.

Akshita Jha and Radhika Mamidi. 2017. When does a compliment become sexist? analysis and classification of ambivalent sexism using twitter data. In *Proceedings of the second workshop on NLP and computational social science*, pages 7–16.

David Kaplan. 1999. The meaning of ouch and oops. explorations in the theory of meaning as use. University of California.

George Kennedy, Andrew McCollough, Edward Dixon, Alexei Bastidas, John Ryan, Chris Loo, and Saurav Sahay. 2017. Technology solutions to combat online harassment. In *Proceedings of the first workshop on abusive language online*, pages 73–77.

Mikhail Khodak, Nikunj Saunshi, and Kiran Vodrahalli. 2018. A large self-annotated corpus for sarcasm. In *Proceedings of the Linguistic Resource and Evaluation Conference (LREC)*.

Ritesh Kumar, Aishwarya Reganti, Akshit Bhatia, and Tushar Maheshwari. 2018. Aggression-annotated corpus of hindi-english code-mixed data. In *Proceedings of the Eleventh International Conference on Language Resources and Evaluation (LREC 2018)*. European Language Resources Association (ELRA).

Peggy McIntosh. 1988. White privilege: Unpacking the invisible knapsack.

Hala Mulki, Hatem Haddad, Chedi Bechikh Ali, and Halima Alshabani. 2019. L-hsab: A levantine twitter dataset for hate speech and abusive language. In *Proceedings of the Third Workshop on Abusive Language Online*, pages 111–118.

Hiroki Nakayama, Takahiro Kubo, Junya Kamura, Yasufumi Taniguchi, and Xu Liang. 2018. doccano: Text annotation tool for human. Software available from https://github.com/doccano/doccano.

Courtney Napoles, Aasish Pappu, and Joel Tetreault. 2017. Automatically identifying good conversations online (yes, they do exist!). In *Eleventh International AAAI Conference on Web and Social Media*.

Chikashi Nobata, Joel Tetreault, Achint Thomas, Yashar Mehdad, and Yi Chang. 2016. Abusive language detection in online user content. In *Proceedings of the 25th international conference on world wide web*, pages 145–153.

Julie Norman and Drew Mikhael. 2017. Youth radicalization is on the rise. here's what we know about why. *The Washington Post*.

Tanya Notley. 2009. Young people, online networks, and social inclusion. *Journal of Computer-Mediated Communication*, 14(4):1208–1227.

Endang Wahyu Pamungkas, Valerio Basile, and Viviana Patti. 2020. Do you really want to hurt me? predicting abusive swearing in social media. In *Proceedings of the 12th Language Resources and Evaluation Conference*, pages 6237–6246, Marseille, France. European Language Resources Association.

Jing Qian, Anna Bethke, Yinyin Liu, Elizabeth Belding, and William Wang. 2019. A benchmark dataset for learning to intervene in online hate speech. In *Proceedings of the 2019 Conference on Empirical Methods in Natural Language Processing and the 9th International Joint Conference on Natural Language Processing (EMNLP-IJCNLP)*, pages 4757–4766. Association for Computational Linguistics.

Mohammadreza Rezvan, Saeedeh Shekarpour, Lakshika Balasuriya, Krishnaprasad Thirunarayan, Valerie L Shalin, and Amit Sheth. 2018. A quality type-aware annotated corpus and lexicon for harassment research. In *Proceedings of the 10th ACM Conference on Web Science*, pages 33–36.

Koustuv Saha, Eshwar Chandrasekharan, and Munmun De Choudhury. 2019. Prevalence and psychological effects of hateful speech in online college communities. In *Proceedings of the 10th ACM Conference on Web Science*, pages 255–264.

Haji Mohammad Saleem, Kelly P Dillon, Susan Benesch, and Derek Ruths. 2016. A web of hate: Tackling hateful speech in online social spaces.

Manuela Sanguinetti, Fabio Poletto, Cristina Bosco, Viviana Patti, and Marco Stranisci. 2018. An italian twitter corpus of hate speech against immigrants. In *Proceedings of the Eleventh International Conference on Language Resources and Evaluation (LREC 2018)*.

Maarten Sap, Dallas Card, Saadia Gabriel, Yejin Choi, and Noah A Smith. 2019. The risk of racial bias in hate speech detection. In *Proceedings of the 57th Annual Meeting of the Association for Computational Linguistics*, pages 1668–1678.

Yaye Nabo Sène. 2019. Hate speech exacerbating societal, racial tensions with 'deadly consequences around the world', say un experts. *UN News*.

Leandro Silva, Mainack Mondal, Denzil Correa, Fabrício Benevenuto, and Ingmar Weber. 2016. Analyzing the targets of hate in online social media. In *Tenth International AAAI Conference on Web and Social Media*.

Wiktor Soral, Michał Bilewicz, and Mikołaj Winiewski. 2018. Exposure to hate speech increases prejudice through desensitization. *Aggressive behavior*, 44(2):136–146.

Rachele Sprugnoli, Stefano Menini, Sara Tonelli, Filippo Oncini, and Enrico Piras. 2018. Creating a whatsapp dataset to study pre-teen cyberbullying. In *Proceedings of the 2nd Workshop on Abusive Language Online (ALW2)*, pages 51–59.

Robert Truswell. 2004. *Attributive adjectives and the nominals they modify*. Ph.D. thesis, Citeseer.

Brendesha M Tynes, Michael T Giang, David R Williams, and Geneene N Thompson. 2008. Online racial discrimination and psychological adjustment among adolescents. *Journal of adolescent health*, 43(6):565–569.

James Vincent. 2016. Twitter taught microsoft's ai chatbot to be a racist asshole in less than a day. *The Verge*, 24.

Zeerak Waseem. 2016. Are you a racist or am i seeing things? annotator influence on hate speech detection on twitter. In *Proceedings of the first workshop on NLP and computational social science*, pages 138–142.

Zeerak Waseem and Dirk Hovy. 2016. Hateful symbols or hateful people? predictive features for hate speech detection on twitter. In *Proceedings of the NAACL student research workshop*, pages 88–93.

Michael Wiegand, Josef Ruppenhofer, and Thomas Kleinbauer. 2019. Detection of abusive language: the problem of biased datasets. In *Proceedings of the 2019 Conference of the North American Chapter of the Association for Computational Linguistics: Human Language Technologies, Volume 1 (Long and Short Papers)*, pages 602–608.

Deirdre Wilson. 2006. The pragmatics of verbal irony: Echo or pretence? *Lingua*, 116(10):1722–1743.

Ellery Wulczyn, Nithum Thain, and Lucas Dixon. 2017. Ex machina: Personal attacks seen at scale. In *Proceedings of the 26th International Conference on World Wide Web*, pages 1391–1399.

Mengzhou Xia, Anjalie Field, and Yulia Tsvetkov. 2020. Demoting racial bias in hate speech detection. In *Proceedings of the Eighth International Workshop on Natural Language Processing for Social Media*, pages 7–14, Online. Association for Computational Linguistics.

Marcos Zampieri, Shervin Malmasi, Preslav Nakov, Sara Rosenthal, Noura Farra, and Ritesh Kumar. 2019. Predicting the type and target of offensive posts in social media. In *Proceedings of the 2019 Conference of the North American Chapter of the Association for Computational Linguistics: Human Language Technologies, Volume 1 (Long and Short Papers)*, pages 1415–1420, Minneapolis, Minnesota. Association for Computational Linguistics.

In Data We Trust: A Critical Analysis of Hate Speech Detection Datasets

Kosisochukwu Judith Madukwe, Xiaoying Gao, Bing Xue
School of Engineering and Computer Science
Victoria University of Wellington
PO Box 600 ,Wellington 6012, New Zealand
`{kosisochukwu.madukwe,xiaoying.gao,bing.xue}@ecs.vuw.ac.nz`

Abstract

Recently, a few studies have discussed the limitations of datasets collected for the task of detecting hate speech from different viewpoints. We intend to contribute to the conversation by providing a consolidated overview of these issues pertaining to the data that debilitate research in this area. Specifically, we discuss how the varying pre-processing steps and the format for making data publicly available result in highly varying datasets that make an objective comparison between studies difficult and unfair. There is currently no study (to the best of our knowledge) focused on comparing the attributes of existing datasets for hate speech detection, outlining their limitations and recommending approaches for future research. This work intends to fill that gap and become the one-stop shop for information regarding hate speech datasets.

1 Introduction

It is imperative to detect hateful speech on social media platforms and other online spaces because its real life implications are usually dire. The research community working towards achieving this goal spans from the Social Sciences to Computer Science. Under the field of Computer Science, Natural Language Processing (NLP) and Machine Learning (ML) techniques have been applied to this task of detecting hate speech by mostly framing it as a text classification task. Here, text is classified into different categories based on its innate content or features. Text classification is a supervised ML task; which means it requires a considerable amount of labelled data. Each data instance needs a label or a class/category that it belongs to. Although the majority of the studies in this research area use labelled data as they conduct a classification task, there are some that do not (Gao et al., 2017; Xiang et al., 2012).

In this study, we concentrate on datasets for hate speech detection in the English language while briefly highlighting other languages and similar concepts such as cyberbullying and abuse detection. The same issue discussed here are also true in other languages, thus all suggested solutions would persist.

The overall aim of this work is to provide insight into the existing datasets and a consolidated analysis into their strengths and weaknesses and most importantly suggest methods to forward research in this area. To achieve this, we ask several questions:

- What makes a dataset benchmark?

- How do we handle class imbalanced dataset? In its unbalanced form or not?

- What typology should we follow for hate speech research? What should or shouldn't it include?

- What is the best ethical format for collating and sharing such a sensitive dataset so as to avoid data degradation?

Although this work will be critiquing a few studies, it is not meant to be negative in any form.

2 Motivations

The importance of hate speech detection research cannot be overemphasised. Now, more than ever, with the current inflammatory political climate and discourse all around the world and minorities in various locations demanding for equality and equity, we cannot allow additional bias to be introduced into their lives through artificial intelligence. The problem of hate speech detection is one yet to be solved even to an acceptable level. It would be counter-productive if all the research efforts are not focused and channeled towards a better tomorrow

Proceedings of the Fourth Workshop on Online Abuse and Harms, pages 150–161
Online, November 20, 2020. ©2020 Association for Computational Linguistics
https://doi.org/10.18653/v1/P17

by building on top one another. So we were motivated to go back to a root of the problem: the data. One of the foundations of this research work (that we can easily make changes on) is the data set. We can only build solid structures on solid foundations. Furthermore, research efforts would be futile if the proposed state-of-the-art for this task fail to perform well on a realistic dataset.

3 Summary of Existing Datasets

In this section, we highlight the currently existing datasets used in literature for the task of detecting hate speech. In the broad area of abusive language detection, there exists several other datasets collected and annotated for cyberbullying, toxicity, aggression and so on (we would not discuss those in-depth as they are out of the scope of this work). As highlighted in (Fortuna and Nunes, 2018), the majority of the studies in this area of hate speech detection collected and annotated their own datasets, however, some were not made publicly available. The existing datasets are:

1. **BURNAP Dataset**: This dataset collected by (Burnap and Williams, 2016) comprises of cyber-hate targeted at four different protected characteristics (sexual orientation, race, disability and religion) in roughly equal amounts. Of the annotated sample, 10.15% of sexual orientation category, 3.73% of race category, 2.66% of disability category and 11.68% of religion category are considered offensive or antagonistic. The dataset was collected after different trigger events for each category.

2. **WASEEM Dataset**[1]: This dataset was published by (Waseem and Hovy, 2016). It contains 16k English tweets annotated into three classes (1972 are Racism, 3383 are Sexism and 11559 are Neither) and was made publicly available using TweetIDs. The authors annotated the data themselves, then used a third party to validate the annotations. They record an inter-annotator agreement of 0.84. This dataset is unbalanced and also biased toward specific users since all of the tweets labelled as racist where from 9 users only, while the other classes were from more than 600 users. This dataset was extended in (Waseem, 2016) by 4033 additional tweets, were they experimented with amateur and expert annotations

to investigate their influence based on an existing knowledge of the research area.

3. **DAVIDSON Dataset**[2]: This was published by (Davidson et al., 2017). The dataset contains 24,802 tweets in English (5.77% labelled as Hate speech, 77.43% as Offensive and 16.80% as Neither) and was published in raw text format. They report collecting this data from Twitter using a lexicon from HateBase[3] containing hateful words and phrases. They used a crowdsourcing platform (Figure-Eight[4] formerly CrowdFlower) for annotating the tweets into the 3 classes. The annotators were provided with the authors' definitions and specific instructions. They record an inter-rater agreement of 92% as provided by the crowdsourcing platform.

4. **FOUNTA Dataset**[5]: (Founta et al., 2018) published a dataset of 80k tweets, annotated for various abusive behaviors (abusive, hateful speech, spam, normal) and made publicly available using TweetIDs. They use a boosted random sampling technique through an iterative and incremental process to generate the final dataset in order to improve the number of derogatory samples. They use a larger number of annotators (20) through crowdsourcing. Their classes are None at 59%, Spam at 22.5%, Abusive at 11% and Hateful at 7.5%. Recently, as part of the ICWSM Data challenge, an updated version of this dataset, now containing 100k was made available in text format.

5. **WARNER Dataset**: The constituent data was collated by (Warner and Hirschberg, 2012) from Yahoo News Group and URLs from the American Jewish Society. It contains 9000 paragraphs, manually annotated into seven (7) categories (anti-semitic, anti-black, anti-Asian, anti-woman, anti-Muslim, anti-immigrant or other hate(anti-gay and anti-white)). It doesn't seem to be publicly available.

---

6. **DJURIC Dataset**: (Djuric et al., 2015) collected comments from the Yahoo Finance website. 56,280 comments were labeled as hateful while 895,456 labeled as clean from 209,776 users.

7. **NOBATA Dataset**: The authors in (Nobata et al., 2016) collected data from Yahoo Finance and News comment section. Their definition of abusive language conflates hate speech, profanity and derogatory language. It was labelled as clean or abusive by Yahoo employees. In the primary dataset, 7.0% of Finance and 16.4% News comment were labelled as abusive. In the temporal dataset, 3.4% of Finance and 10.7% News comment were labelled as abusive. The dataset was reported to be at `https://webscope.sandbox.yahoo.com/`, however it currently cannot be found. They reported an annotation agreement rate of 0.867 and Fleiss Kappa of 0.401.

8. **ZHANG Dataset**[6]: The authors in (Zhang et al., 2018) created a dataset using refugee and muslim specific words and hashtags from Twitter. The dataset contains 2,435 tweets with 414 labelled as hate and 2,021 labelled as non-hate. The dataset was initially publicly available but not anymore due to the data sharing policy of the authors' institution.

9. **QIAN Dataset**[7]: (Qian et al., 2019) collected data from Reddit and Gab including intervention responses written by humans. Their data preserves the conversational thread as a way to provide context. From Reddit, they collect 5,020 conversations which includes a total of 22,324 comments labelled as hate or non-hate. 76.6% of the conversations contain hate speech while only 23.5% of the comments are labelled as hateful. They were mined from known toxic subbreddit using hate keywords. Similarly, from Gab, they collected 11,825 conversations containing 33,776 posts. 94.5% of the conversations contained hate speech while about 43.2% of the comments are labelled as hateful. Each entry in the dataset is a conversation of several indexed comments. The index (in another column) is used to identify which comment is considered hateful, then a response intervention is provided. The entries with no hate speech do not have an intervention response. The number of responses do not correspond to the number of hateful comments in the conversation. Therefore, a conversation with 5 hateful comments can have just 3 responses to intervene.

10. **HATEVAL Dataset**[8]: This is a very small dataset for detecting hate speech against women and immigrants. It contains English and Spanish tweets labelled into hateful or not hateful.

In other languages, hate speech detection research have also progressed.

11. **ROSS Dataset**[9]: (Ross et al., 2017) collected and annotated 541 German tweets with key hashtags on the refugee crisis that could be offensive. The tweets were rated on their level of offensiveness on a 6 point Likert scale. They reported a Krippendorff's alpha from 0.18 to 0.29.

12. **BENIKOVA Dataset**[10]: (Benikova et al., 2018) contains 36 German tweets with 33% labelled as hatespeech and 67% as non-hatespeech.

13. **VIGNA Dataset**: (Vigna et al., 2017) labeled 17,567 Facebook comments from 99 posts as No hate, Weak hate and Strong hate. They recorded a Fleiss' kappa inter-annotator agreement metric of 0.19 with 5 annotators. It doesn't seem to be publicly available.

14. **EVALITA Dataset**[11]: EVALITA[12] published two datasets in Italian in 2018 and 2020 for a shared task in hate speech detection.

15. **TULKENS Dataset**: (Tulkens et al., 2016) crawled and collected data from comments on Dutch Facebook pages most likely to contain derogatory statements such as a Belgian anti-islamic organization and a right-wing organization. They recorded an inter-annotator

[6] `https://github.com/ziqizhang/data#hate`

[7] `https://github.com/jing-qian/A-Benchmark-Dataset-for-Learning-to-Intervene-in-Online-Hate-Speech`

[8] `https://competitions.codalab.org/competitions/19935#phases`

[9] `UCSM-DUE/IWG_hatespeech_public`

[10] `github.com/MeDarina/HateSpeechImplicit`

[11] `https://github.com/msang/haspeede`

[12] `"http://www.evalita.it/2020"`

agreement using the Cohen Kappa score of
0.60. The train set contains 5,424 comments
while the test set contains 607 comments labelled as non-racist and racist. The dataset is
not publicly available, however the dictionary
used can be accessed at `https://github.c
om/clips/hades`

Finally, since hate speech can occur in different modes such as text, images, audio and
video, there are some multimodal datasets to
address this issue:

16. **MMHS150K Dataset**[13]: (Gomez et al., 2019)
    made publicly available a multimodal (image
    and text) dataset collected from Twitter using
    Hatebase terms. It contains 150,000 tweets
    manually annotated into six classes of No at-
    tacks to any community, Racist, Sexist, Ho-
    mophobic, Religion based attacks or Attacks
    to other communities.

17. **HATEFUL MEMES Dataset**: Facebook AI
    (Kiela et al., 2020) collected a multimodal
    dataset for detecting and classification of hate
    speech containing images and text. It was an-
    notated using their specific definition of hate
    speech. It contains 10k memes with a 5% dev
    and 10% test set. The memes belong to the
    following classes: multimodal hate (benign
    confounders were found for both modalities),
    unimodal hate (one or both modalities were
    already hateful on their own), benign text con-
    founder, benign image confounder, random
    non-hateful. A benign confounder is defined
    as "*a minimum replacement image or replace-
    ment text that flips the label for a given mul-
    timodal meme from hateful to non-hateful.*"
    They record a Cohen's kappa score (inter an-
    notators reliability) of 67.2%. The dataset
    is available upon joining a currently ongoing
    competition[14].

4 The Need For A Benchmark Dataset

In the field of ML, benchmark datasets are datasets
used to evaluate or compare the performance of
ML methods on a particular task. It is used

---

[13] `https://gombru.github.io/2019/10/09/MMHS/`

[14] `https://www.drivendata.org/competitions/64/hateful-memes/page/205/`

Datasets	Availability	Classes/Labels	Size	Format
1	No	Sexual Orientation Race Disability Religion	-	-
2	Yes	Racism Sexism Neither	11.69% 20.00% 68.33% 16,914 tweets	TweetID
3	Yes	Hate Speech Offensive Neither	5.77% 77.43% 16.80% 24k tweets	Raw text
4	Yes	Abusive Hateful Spam Normal/None	11% 7.5% 22.5% 59% 80,000 tweets	TweetID
5	No	Anti-Semitic Anti-Black Anti-Asian Anti-Woman Anti-Muslim Anti-Immigrant Other hate	-	-
6	No	Hate Speech Clean	5.91% 94.08% 951,736 comments	- -
7	No	Abusive Clean	7 %of F + 16.4% of N 3.4 %of F + 10.7% of N	- -
9	Yes	Hate Speech Non-Hate Speech	23.5% 76.5% 22,324 Reddit comments	Raw text
9	Yes	Hate Speech Non-Hate Speech	43.2% 51.8% 33,776 Gab comments	Raw text
11	Yes	6 Point Likert Scale	- 541 tweets	-
12	Yes	Hate Speech Non-Hate Speech	33% 67% 33 tweets	-
13	No	No Hate Weak Hate Strong Hate	- 6,031 Facebook comments	-
15	No	Racist Non-Racist	- 17,567 Facebook comments	-

Table 1: Analysis of some of the existing hate speech
datasets

by researchers to test how their new ideas perform against existing ones (Caruana and Niculescu-
Mizil, 2006) and to objectively measure progress
on a particular problem. The dataset is usually the
only necessary consistent/constant aspect of a study.
Benchmark datasets have been shown in areas like
image processing to be of paramount importance
in enabling research progress and a fair/objective
comparison between studies and proposed methods.
Datasets like CIFAR10, CIFAR100 (Krizhevsky,
2009) and MNIST (LeCun and Cortes, 2010) for
image processing and computer vision were published and are maintained by a large research institution. The CIFAR10 and CIFAR100 have desig-
nated train and test sets, which makes comparison
between studies and proposed methods fair.

4.1 Dataset Accessibility and Availability

In Table 1, we show the state of availability and accessibility of some of the discussed datasets. Making datasets available on personal repositories is problematic because the user can take it down at anytime. For example, a hate speech dataset listed in (Fortuna and Nunes, 2018) on Annie Thorbun's personal github page[15] does not exist anymore. This problem can also occur when a website address changes. For example, in (Watanabe et al., 2018), one of the dataset used was listed to be at `www.crowdflower.com/data-for-everyone/` which now redirects to `https://appen.com/reso urces/datasets/`. However, the dataset cannot be found as at 19th June, 2020

Data degradation occurs when a dataset, published in an encrypted format, needs to be regenerated by the researcher on-demand, does not produce the same number/amount of data as on the publication date. This phenomenon occurs with hate speech data harvested from Twitter and published in form of tweetIDs which are identification number that linked to each individual tweet. In some cases, the author of the tweet deletes it, or the account owner deactivates the account, or it might be reported to Twitter as breaking one of their guidelines and Twitter takes it down. This has been reported in (Zhang and Luo, 2018; Arango et al., 2019). Also (Watanabe et al., 2018), noted that the WASEEM dataset had only 6,655 tweets left, out of the 6,909 initially published. (Osho et al., 2020) reported that for FOUNTA dataset they only found 69k out of 80k tweets. As compared to the distribution highlighted in Table 1, the new distribution over the classes were now 62% normal, 20% as abusive, 14% as spam and 4% as hateful. The hateful class was even more reduced. Both the FOUNTA and WASEEM data suffer from data degradation. As at June 2020, we found that the first batch of WASEEM data was completely degraded while the second batch has only 2,412 out of 6,090 tweets left. We also found that the FOUNTA data has 18,943 tweets out of the 80,000 left. The already minute class of interest bears the brunt of this phenomena.

For a persistent benchmark dataset to succeed, we need to make data available in a better format. The nature of the data and the fact that it provides a consolidated source of harmful information makes it very tricky. Therefore, we suggest a submission portal for the data, where each researcher can request for a copy of the data using a verifiable email address and then a copy of the benchmark dataset is sent to them. This might restrict access for those that might want to use this data for malicious purposes. This service can be provided by large institutional data repositories like Dataverse[16] or ICPSR[17].

4.2 Class Imbalance Issue

Unlike most text classification task such as sentiment analysis; hate speech detection suffers from a severe class imbalance issue, with the hate class being in most cases less than 12% for the multi-class datasets and less than half of the total dataset for the binary datasets (Table 1) .

Usually when the classes in a dataset are unbalanced, it is because one of the following reasons: Its either

- the data is rarely occurring (more specifically the class of interest is rare compared to the other class(es))

- or the data collection and labelling is difficult, time consuming and expensive;

- or the overlap between the classes is high.

For the hate speech detection task, it is all of the above. It becomes increasingly difficult to train ML algorithms on such small samples, which leads to subpar performance. The class imbalance problem is probably inevitable when collecting data, as there is an estimated maximum of 3% derogatory tweets on Twitter (Founta et al., 2018). Thus, the open question of whether to work with the dataset in its unbalanced form or to look into methods to make it balanced remains unanswered. It is desirable to develop a model that does a good job in identifying hateful instances even with the small sample size. Certainly, such a model will perform well in real life scenarios during deployment. Therefore a naturally occurring question is; *Are the methods for learning with a small data size more easily accessible and less computationally expensive than methods for reducing the class imbalance?* It is worthwhile to look into both and compare. Several studies (Davidson et al., 2017; Founta et al., 2019;

---

[15] `https://github.com/anniethorburn/Hat e-Speech-M`

[16] `https://dataverse.org/`
[17] `https://www.icpsr.umich.edu/web/page s/index.html`

Madukwe and Gao, 2019; Mozafari et al., 2020; Zhang et al., 2018) have used the datasets in its unbalanced form with the claim that since this is the naturally occurring state, it shouldn't be altered. However, we argue that this is not advantageous to existing supervised ML algorithms that depend on a large supply of data with balanced classes for optimum performance. Similarly, (Swamy et al., 2019) showed that models generalize better when trained on data containing a high amount of samples in the positive class which also unfortunately the minority class in most datasets.

Since the collection and annotation of data for this task is time-consuming, expensive, error-prone with low yield, we recommend more studies into the best way to augment existing data. This would assist in increasing the data size and inadvertently solving the class imbalance problem. A few studies have discussed and proposed solution for augmenting related datasets (Chung et al., 2019; Karatsalos and Panagiotakis, 2020; Sharifirad et al., 2018). However, employing data augmentation as a pre-processing step to cater to the class imbalance problem will lead to an unfair comparison amongst other proposed solutions as there are wide of augmentation techniques. Also, data augmentation methods such as oversampling the minority class not done right (Agrawal and Awekar, 2018), will introduce bias into the model (Arango et al., 2019). Another suggestion is to look into ML methods that are unaffected by the class size such as one-class and active learning. Rigorous investigations are required to answer the question of how to handle class imbalance in hate speech datasets.

4.3 Varying Definitions and How it Affects Annotation

It is known that there are varying definitions of hate speech, however there are some consistencies amongst them. (Fortuna and Nunes, 2018) have analysed some available definitions of hate speech and highlighted the major similarities amongst them. Specifically, hate speech:

- has a specific target.

- incites violence or hate.

- attacks or diminishes.

- can contain humor or sarcasm.

Varying definitions imply that, of course, it might be impossible to rid social media platforms

completely of hateful instances. Despite this fact, the agreed upon similarities is a good place to start. Currently, existing datasets are affected by these variations because the annotations are powered by the definitions. Thus, similar instances can fall under different annotation categories. (Ross et al., 2017) investigated the effects of the presence and absence of a definition during annotation on the annotation reliability of a hate speech dataset. They conclude that hate speech requires a stronger definition. Similarly, (Fortuna et al., 2020) empirically find that most of the publicly available datasets are incompatible due to different definitions assigned to similar concepts.

In order to measure the annotation reliability of the labels in a dataset, a numerical index known as the Inter-Rater/Inter-Coder/Inter-Annotator Agreement (Artstein and Poesio, 2008) is usually adopted. The studies that collected data, use it to measure the level of agreement among their annotators on the labels they chose for each text or sentence. Examples of this score are Fleiss (Fleiss, 1971) or Cohens (Cohen, 1960) Kappa. This score is affected by annotator bias and imbalance in the classes making it unreliable. In addition, different studies suggest different thresholds for acceptable annotation (Di Eugenio and Glass, 2004; Artstein and Poesio, 2008). As can be seen from the datasets highlighted in Section 3, the annotation reliability is relatively low. In (Awal et al., 2020), the authors propose a framework to analyse the annotation inconsistency in the WASEEM, DAVIDSON and FOUNTA dataset. They found major inconsistencies in the labels of all the three dataset most especially in FOUNTA dataset where duplicate tweets exists in great number and the exact same tweet can have opposing labels. ML models built on this data will find it difficult to learn anything useful. Additionally, using different names for the same concept can be misleading. (Waseem et al., 2017) examined the relationship between abusive language, hate speech, cyberbullying and trolling. A lax use of typology affects annotation. For example in (Wiegand et al., 2019) they conflated the racism and sexism class in WASEEM data into one class and changed the labels to Abuse and No Abuse.

4.4 Conflating Classes/Labels

Hate speech datasets sometimes have very similar labels and some studies merge some of them together into one class, often as a way to combat the level of class imbalance. However, this conflation could negatively affect research progress as distinction between them is very necessary. One example is the DAVIDSON data with the Offensive and Hate class or the WASEEM data with the Racist and Sexist class. Classes in the DAVIDSON data were conflated in (Zhang and Luo, 2018; Zhang et al., 2018) where they merged the Hate and Offensive class into one class while (Miok et al., 2019) conflated the Offensive and Neither class into a Non-hate class. (Watanabe et al., 2018; Wiegand et al., 2019) conflated classes in the WASEEM data and for the FOUNTA data, (Davidson and Bhattacharya, 2020) deleted the Spam class and conflated the Hate and Abusive Class into Abusive.

These last two sections (4.3 and 4.4) affect the typology used in this research. There aren't any enforced or strict demarcations, therefore the use of varying terms to mean one thing negatively affects research progress. An author searching for hate speech data or studies, might miss out on ones that used abusive language or toxic comment as an umbrella term encompassing several paradigms. We suggest that the terms be used strictly following the available definitions. Similar to suggestion in (Davidson et al., 2017), offensive language is not the same as hate speech and should not be merged. Also, abusive language and cyberbullying should not be merged with hate speech.

4.5 Varying Preprocessing Steps and Train-Test Splits

Social media data is often very noisy since it is a user-generated data. Different researchers have employed varying steps to clean the data in preparation for an ML algorithm. We show that these choice of steps can affect the data size, therefore obstructing an objective comparison between studies even more. Table 2 shows a few papers using three commonly used hate speech datasets and the preprocessing applied which leads to variations that negatively affect a fair comparison. Some of the existing studies select different train-test splits such as 70:30 or 80:20, some do a train-test-validation split of 70:15:15 or 60:20:20 or 80:10:10 while some do a 10-fold or 5-fold cross validation. This varying setting means that fair comparison amongst studies is not possible except if every researcher reruns all existing studies they wish to compare with. This is both impractical and costly.

Datasets	Paper	Stem or Lemmatize	Username	URLs	Lowercase	Hashtags	Remove Punctuation	Remove Stopwords	Train-Test Split	Final DataSize
WASEEM	(Badjatiya et al., 2017)	-	replaced	replaced	added <allcaps> after an all capitalized word	replaced # sign with <hashtag>	No. Repetition replaced with <repeat>	-	-	-
	(Founta et al., 2019)	both	counted	counted	No. counted all capital words	counted	-	Yes	-	16,059
	(Mozafari et al., 2020)	-	replaced with placeholder <user>	replaced with placeholder <url>	Yes	removed # sign only	Yes	No	-	-
DAVIDSON	(Davidson et al., 2017)	stem	counted	counted	Yes	counted	-	-	5-fold CV	24,802
	(Malmasi and Zampieri, 2017, 2018)	-	removed	removed	Yes	-	-	-	10-fold CV	14,509
	(Founta et al., 2019)	both	counted	counted	No. counted all capital words	counted	-	Yes	-	24,783
	(Madukwe and Gao, 2019)	lemmatize	removed	removed	Yes	removed	Yes	Yes. Custom stop words	75/25	-
	(Mozafari et al., 2020)	-	replaced with placeholder <user>	replaced with placeholder <url>	Yes	removed # sign only	Yes	No	-	-
	(Miok et al., 2019)	lemmatize	remove	remove	-	expanded into words	Yes	Yes	-	3000
FOUNTA	(Verma et al., 2020)	-	replaced	replaced	Yes	Dropped # sign only	No	Yes	80/10/10	-
	(Liu et al., 2020)	-	-	removed	-	removed	Yes	-	80% 20%	99603 from 100000
	(Davidson et al., 2017)	-	replaced	replaced	-	-	Yes	Yes	-	75,023 from 100000
	(Kim et al., 2020)	Stem	-	-	Yes	-	-	-	80 /20	-

Table 2: Varying Pre-processing Steps

4.6 What Makes a Dataset Benchmark

Here, we highlight factors that qualifies a dataset to be considered as benchmark.

- A publicly available dataset: The dataset should be considerably easy to access by potential researchers. This will increase the chances of these researchers to use the dataset to measure the performance of their proposed methods.

- Consistent Train-Test-Validation Split: Likewise, this will contribute to fairer comparison between studies.

- Accessible data format: The data should preferably be in a format that does not degrade or change in time. Therefore the exact same dataset is available to Researcher A now and Researcher Z later.

- Absence of bias: A benchmark data lacks (for the most part) bias. A benchmark dataset for hate speech detection needs to be devoid of racial (Davidson et al., 2019; Sap et al., 2019), gender (Park et al., 2018) or intersectional (Kim et al., 2020) biases. Bias introduced by the data collection process was discussed in (Wiegand et al., 2019). Likewise, (Waseem et al., 2018) noted that more than 2k tweets in the DAVIDSON dataset, written in African American Vernacular English were labeled as hateful or offensive simply because they used the n-word. A diverse group of annotators would have significantly reduced this bias. In (Arango et al., 2019), they showed that a bias in user distribution adversely affected the generalization ability of the proposed models. Therefore, it is important that benchmark dataset are not biased towards particular users and that information on the distribution of the users whose tweets make up the dataset are provided in an anonymized format. (Davidson and Bhattacharya, 2020) reported that in the FOUNTA dataset, there are several duplicated tweets which can introduce a strong bias in the model as some instances are contained in both the training and testing sets.

- A common evaluation method/metric: Different studies use different metrics which affect comparison without re-implementation which might not be feasible if the said method is expensive to re-implement. Also, some metric choices do not reflect the true performance of the proposed methods.

  (Olteanu et al., 2017) argues for evaluation metrics that are directly proportional to user perception of correctness, thus more human-centered.

- It should be preferably pre-processed to an extent. If this is not feasible, then the authors should endeavor to make their pre-processing code public so that other researchers can apply it to keep the resulting dataset consistent and uniform.

Datasets	Publicly Available	Consistent Split	Accessible data format	Common Evaluation Metric	Unbiased	Pre-processed
WASEEM	✓	✗	✗	✗	✗	✗
DAVIDSON	✓	✗	✓	✗	✗	✗
FOUNTA	✓	✗	✗	✗	✗	✗
QIAN	✓	✗	✓	✗	✗	✗
HATEVAL	✓	✗	✓	✗	✗	✗

Table 3: Benchmark criteria met by datasets

Table 3 highlights the existing publicly available datasets and the benchmark criteria they fulfil. From this summary, it is clear that there currently exits no benchmark hate speech detection dataset.

5 Discussions and Implications for future research

First, we want to encourage researchers to put in more efforts towards a less biased, benchmark dataset taking the prior discussed factors into consideration.

Second, we also implore social media platforms to make the access easier for researchers.

Collaboration with these platforms is also another way to ensure better data sharing. Twitter has been known to release datasets for research purposes[18] (Vidgen et al., 2019).

We suggest that all datasets are anonymized before release because some of the username left in the dataset have ended up in research publications; which is a glaring ethical breach. Although some studies have extracted user information as a feature, we argue that it constitutes some ethical concerns and should be avoided. For a more in-depth survey on the issues surrounding social data bias see (Olteanu et al., 2019).

---

[18]https://www.wired.com/story/twitters-disinformation-data-dumps-helpful/

Also, we purport that the specific terms be used to avoid confusions and conflations of ideas. Even better, a clear definition should be provided on what the researcher defines a term as, e.g. what is offensive, abusive, or hate speech for the researcher. Unnecessary conflations dampens the research efforts. Moreover, a clear demarcation should be made for for proposed methods to solve hate speech, abusive language and cyberbullying detection. Their characteristics differ and proposed solutions might not generalize.

Finally, making codes public is always in best interest of the research community and when that is not possible, the hyperparameter choices and other necessary settings should be reported to support replicability of research work.

6 Conclusion

This work assisted in understanding the limitations of existing hate speech data for future research and the way forward. The contributions of this work include:

- Recommendation on a better approach to make datasets publicly available in the future.

- Requirements for any future researcher/organization interested in collecting and labelling data
    - Persistently publicly available
    - Consistent train-test split
    - Less bias
    - Lack of data degradation
    - Common evaluation metric
    - Basic pre-processing

These suggestions can be easily applied to other NLP applications apart from hate speech detection that require real-world datasets. We acknowledge the fact that an unbiased dataset does not exist, however, there are steps to be taken to make them less biased. Finally, even though we might have highlighted limitations in datasets and approaches, it is not meant as a negative criticism of the authors or their work. We acknowledge that their individual and collective efforts have brought us so far in this research area.

Acknowledgements: The authors are grateful for the insightful comments from the reviewers that helped improve this work.

References

Sweta Agrawal and Amit Awekar. 2018. Deep learning for detecting cyberbullying across multiple social media platforms. In *Advances in Information Retrieval*, pages 141–153, Cham. Springer International Publishing.

Aymé Arango, Jorge Pérez, and Barbara Poblete. 2019. Hate speech detection is not as easy as you may think: A closer look at model validation. In *Proceedings of the 42nd International ACM SIGIR Conference on Research and Development in Information Retrieval*, SIGIR'19, page 45–54, NY, USA. ACM.

Ron Artstein and Massimo Poesio. 2008. Inter-coder agreement for computational linguistics. *Comput. Linguist.*, 34(4):555–596.

Md Rabiul Awal, Rui Cao, Roy Ka-Wei Lee, and Sandra Mitrović. 2020. On analyzing annotation consistency in online abusive behavior datasets. In *Proceedings of the 14th International AAAI Conference on Web and Social Media*.

Pinkesh Badjatiya, Shashank Gupta, Manish Gupta, and Vasudeva Varma. 2017. Deep Learning for Hate Speech Detection in Tweets. *Proceedings of the 26th International Conference on World Wide Web Companion - WWW '17 Companion*.

Darina Benikova, Michael Wojatzki, and Torsten Zesch. 2018. What does this imply? examining the impact of implicitness on the perception of hate speech. *Lecture Notes in Computer Science*, 10713 LNAI:171–179.

Pete Burnap and Matthew L. Williams. 2016. Us and them: identifying cyber hate on Twitter across multiple protected characteristics. *EPJ Data Science*, 5(1).

Rich Caruana and Alexandru Niculescu-Mizil. 2006. An empirical comparison of supervised learning algorithms. In *Proceedings of the 23rd International Conference on Machine Learning*, ICML '06, page 161–168, NY, USA. Association for Computing Machinery.

Yi-Ling Chung, Elizaveta Kuzmenko, Serra Sinem Tekiroglu, and Marco Guerini. 2019. CONAN - COunter NArratives through Nichesourcing: a Multilingual Dataset of Responses to Fight Online Hate Speech. pages 2819–2829.

Jacob Cohen. 1960. A coefficient of agreement for nominal scales. *Educational and Psychological Measurement*, 20(1):37–46.

Thomas Davidson and Debasmita Bhattacharya. 2020. Examining racial bias in an online abuse corpus with structural topic modeling. In *Proceedings of the 14th International AAAI Conference on Web and Social Media*.

Thomas Davidson, Debasmita Bhattacharya, and Ingmar Weber. 2019. Racial Bias in Hate Speech and Abusive Language Detection Datasets. In *Third Abusive Language Workshop, Annual Meeting for the Association for Computational Linguistics 2019*.

Thomas Davidson, Dana Warmsley, Michael Macy, and Ingmar Weber. 2017. Automated Hate Speech Detection and the Problem of Offensive Language. In *Proceedings of the 11th International AAAI Conference on Web and Social Media*, ICWSM '17, pages 512–515.

Barbara Di Eugenio and Michael Glass. 2004. The kappa statistic: A second look. *Comput. Linguist.*, 30(1):95–101.

Nemanja Djuric, Jing Zhou, Robin Morris, Mihajlo Grbovic, Vladan Radosavljevic, and Narayan Bhamidipati. 2015. Hate Speech Detection with Comment Embeddings. In *Proc. 24th Int. Conf. World Wide Web*, pages 29–30.

JL Fleiss. 1971. Measuring nominal scale agreement among many raters. *Psychological bulletin*, 76(5):378—382.

Paula Fortuna and Sérgio Nunes. 2018. A Survey on Automatic Detection of Hate Speech in Text. *ACM Computing Surveys*, 51(4):1–30.

Paula Fortuna, Juan Soler, and Leo Wanner. 2020. Toxic, hateful, offensive or abusive? what are we really classifying? an empirical analysis of hate speech datasets. In *Proceedings of the 12th Language Resources and Evaluation Conference*, pages 6786–6794, Marseille, France. European Language Resources Association.

Antigoni Maria Founta, Despoina Chatzakou, Nicolas Kourtellis, Jeremy Blackburn, Athena Vakali, and Ilias Leontiadis. 2019. A unified deep learning architecture for abuse detection. In *Proceedings of the 10th ACM Conference on Web Science*, WebSci '19, page 105–114, New York, NY, USA. Association for Computing Machinery.

Antigoni-Maria Founta, Constantinos Djouvas, Despoina Chatzakou, Ilias Leontiadis, Jeremy Blackburn, Gianluca Stringhini, Athena Vakali, Michael Sirivianos, and Nicolas Kourtellis. 2018. Large Scale Crowdsourcing and Characterization of Twitter Abusive Behavior. In *AAAI International Conference on Web and Social Media (ICWSM)*.

Lei Gao, Alexis Kuppersmith, and Ruihong Huang. 2017. Recognizing explicit and implicit hate speech using a weakly supervised two-path bootstrapping approach. In *Proceedings of the Eighth International Joint Conference on Natural Language Processing (Volume 1: Long Papers)*, pages 774–782, Taipei, Taiwan. Asian Federation of Natural Language Processing.

Raul Gomez, Jaume Gibert, Lluis Gomez, and Dimosthenis Karatzas. 2019. Exploring hate speech detection in multimodal publications. In *2020 IEEE Winter Conference on Applications of Computer Vision (WACV)*, pages 1459–1467.

Christos Karatsalos and Yannis Panagiotakis. 2020. Attention-based method for categorizing different types of online harassment language. *Communications in Computer and Information Science*, page 321–330.

Douwe Kiela, Hamed Firooz, Aravind Mohan, Vedanuj Goswami, Amanpreet Singh, Pratik Ringshia, and Davide Testuggine. 2020. The hateful memes challenge: Detecting hate speech in multimodal memes. In *ArXiv Preprint*.

Jae Yeon Kim, Carlos Ortiz, Sarah Nam, Sarah Santiago, and Vivek Datta. 2020. Intersectional bias in hate speech and abusive language datasets. In *ArXivPreprint*.

Alex Krizhevsky. 2009. Learning multiple layers of features from tiny images. Technical report.

Yann LeCun and Corinna Cortes. 2010. MNIST handwritten digit database.

Ruibo Liu, Guangxuan Xu, and Soroush Vosoughi. 2020. Enhanced offensive language detection through data augmentation. In *ICWSM'20 Safety Data Challenge*.

Kosisochukwu Judith Madukwe and Xiaoying Gao. 2019. The Thin Line Between Hate and Profanity. In *AI 2019: Advances in Artificial Intelligence*, pages 344–356, Cham. Springer International Publishing.

Shervin Malmasi and Marcos Zampieri. 2017. Detecting Hate Speech in Social Media. In *Proceedings of Recent Advances in Natural Language Processing (RANLP)*, pages 467–472, Varna, Bulgaria.

Shervin Malmasi and Marcos Zampieri. 2018. Challenges in discriminating profanity from hate speech. *Journal of Experimental and Theoretical Artificial Intelligence*, 30(2):187–202.

Kristian Miok, Dong Nguyen-Doan, Blaž Škrlj, Daniela Zaharie, and Marko Robnik-Šikonja. 2019. Prediction uncertainty estimation for hate speech classification. *Lecture Notes in Computer Science*, page 286–298.

Marzieh Mozafari, Reza Farahbakhsh, and Noël Crespi. 2020. A bert-based transfer learning approach for hate speech detection in online social media. In *Complex Networks and Their Applications VIII*, pages 928–940, Cham. Springer International Publishing.

Chikashi Nobata, Joel Tetreault, Achint Thomas, Yashar Mehdad, and Yi Chang. 2016. Abusive language detection in online user content. In *Proceedings of the 25th International Conference on World*

Wide Web, WWW '16, page 145–153, Republic and Canton of Geneva, CHE. International World Wide Web Conferences Steering Committee.

Alexandra Olteanu, Carlos Castillo, Fernando Diaz, and Emre Kıcıman. 2019. Social data: Biases, methodological pitfalls, and ethical boundaries. *Frontiers in Big Data*, 2:13.

Alexandra Olteanu, Kartik Talamadupula, and Kush R. Varshney. 2017. The limits of abstract evaluation metrics: The case of hate speech detection. In *Proceedings of the 2017 ACM on Web Science Conference*, WebSci '17, page 405–406, NY, USA. ACM.

Abiola Osho, Ethan Tucker, and George Amariucai. 2020. Implicit crowdsourcing for identifying abusive behavior in online social networks. In *ArXiv PrePrint*.

Ji Ho Park, Jamin Shin, and Pascale Fung. 2018. Reducing gender bias in abusive language detection. In *Proceedings of the 2018 Conference on Empirical Methods in Natural Language Processing*, pages 2799–2804, Bxl, Belgium. ACL.

Jing Qian, Anna Bethke, Yinyin Liu, Elizabeth Belding, and William Yang Wang. 2019. A benchmark dataset for learning to intervene in online hate speech. In *Proceedings of the 2019 Conference on Empirical Methods in Natural Language Processing and the 9th International Joint Conference on Natural Language Processing (EMNLP-IJCNLP)*, pages 4757–4766.

Björn Ross, Michael Rist, Guillermo Carbonell, Benjamin Cabrera, Nils Kurowsky, and Michael Wojatzki. 2017. Measuring the Reliability of Hate Speech Annotations: The Case of the European Refugee Crisis.

Maarten Sap, Dallas Card, Saadia Gabriel, Yejin Choi, and Noah A. Smith. 2019. The risk of racial bias in hate speech detection. In *Proceedings of the 57th Annual Meeting of the Association for Computational Linguistics*, pages 1668–1678, FLR, Italy. ACL.

Sima Sharifirad, Borna Jafarpour, and Stan Matwin. 2018. Boosting text classification performance on sexist tweets by text augmentation and text generation using a combination of knowledge graphs. In *Proceedings of the 2nd Workshop on Abusive Language Online (ALW2)*, pages 107–114, Brussels, Belgium. Association for Computational Linguistics.

Steve Durairaj Swamy, Anupam Jamatia, and Björn Gambäck. 2019. Studying generalisability across abusive language detection datasets. In *Proceedings of the 23rd Conference on Computational Natural Language Learning (CoNLL)*, pages 940–950, Hong Kong, China. Association for Computational Linguistics.

Stéphan Tulkens, Lisa Hilte, Elise Lodewyckx, Ben Verhoeven, and Walter Daelemans. 2016. A dictionary-based approach to racism detection in Dutch social media. In *Proceedings of the LREC 2016 Workshop on Text Analytics for Cybersecurity and Online Safety (TA-COS)*. European Language Resources Association (ELRA).

Gaurav Verma, Niyati Chhaya, and Vishwa Vinay. 2020. "to target or not to target": Identification and analysis of abusive text using ensemble of classifiers. In *ICWSM'20 Safety Data Challenge*.

Bertie Vidgen, Alex Harris, Dong Nguyen, Rebekah Tromble, Scott Hale, and Helen Margetts. 2019. Challenges and frontiers in abusive content detection. In *Proceedings of the Third Workshop on Abusive Language Online*, pages 80–93, FLR, Italy. ACL.

Fabio Del Vigna, Andrea Cimino, and Felice Dell Orletta. 2017. Hate me, hate me not: Hate speech detection on facebook. In *ITA-SEC 17*, Venice.

William Warner and Julia Hirschberg. 2012. Detecting Hate Speech on the World Wide Web. In *Proceedings of the 2012 Workshop on Language in Social Media*, pages 19–26.

Zeerak Waseem. 2016. Are you a racist or am I seeing things? annotator influence on hate speech detection on Twitter. In *Proceedings of the First Workshop on NLP and Computational Social Science*, pages 138–142, Austin, Texas. Association for Computational Linguistics.

Zeerak Waseem, Thomas Davidson, Dana Warmsley, and Ingmar Weber. 2017. Understanding abuse: A typology of abusive language detection subtasks. In *Proceedings of the First Workshop on Abusive Language Online*, pages 78–84, Vancouver, BC, Canada. Association for Computational Linguistics.

Zeerak Waseem and Dirk Hovy. 2016. Hateful symbols or hateful people? predictive features for hate speech detection on Twitter. In *Proceedings of the NAACL Student Research Workshop*, pages 88–93, San Diego, California. Association for Computational Linguistics.

Zeerak Waseem, James Thorne, and Joachim Bingel. 2018. Bridging the gaps: Multi task learning for domain transfer of hate speech detection. In *Golbeck J. (eds) Online Harassment. Human–Computer Interaction Series*, pages 29–55, Cham. Springer International Publishing.

Hajime Watanabe, Mondher Bouazizi, and Tomoaki Ohtsuki. 2018. Hate Speech on Twitter: A Pragmatic Approach to Collect Hateful and Offensive Expressions and Perform Hate Speech Detection. *IEEE Access*, 6:13825–13835.

Michael Wiegand, Josef Ruppenhofer, and Thomas Kleinbauer. 2019. Detection of Abusive Language: the Problem of Biased Datasets. *Proceedings of the*

2019 Conference of the North American Chapter of the Association for Computational Linguistics: Human Language Technologies, Volume 1, pages 602–608.

Guang Xiang, Bin Fan, Ling Wang, Jason Hong, and Carolyn Rose. 2012. Detecting offensive tweets via topical feature discovery over a large scale twitter corpus. In *Proceedings of the 21st ACM International Conference on Information and Knowledge Management*, CIKM '12, page 1980–1984, NY, USA. ACM.

Ziqi Zhang and Lei Luo. 2018. Hate speech detection: A solved problem? the challenging case of long tail on twitter. *Semantic Web*, page 925 – 945.

Ziqi Zhang, David Robinson, and Jonathan Tepper. 2018. Detecting hate speech on twitter using a convolution-gru based deep neural network. In *The Semantic Web: European Semantic Web Conference*, pages 745–760, Cham. Springer International Publishing.

Detecting East Asian Prejudice on Social Media

Bertie Vidgen
The Alan Turing Institute
bvidgen@turing.ac.uk

Austin Botelho
University of Oxford

David Broniatowski
The George Washington
University

Ella Guest
The Alan Turing Institute

Matthew Hall
The University of Surrey

Helen Margetts
The Alan Turing Institute

Rebekah Tromble
The George Washington
University

Zeerak Waseem
University of Sheffield

Scott A. Hale
University of Oxford
Meedan

Abstract

During COVID-19 concerns have heightened about the spread of aggressive and hateful language online, especially hostility directed against East Asia and East Asian people. We report on a new dataset and the creation of a machine learning classifier that categorizes social media posts from Twitter into four classes: Hostility against East Asia, Criticism of East Asia, Meta-discussions of East Asian prejudice, and Non-related. The classifier achieves a macro-F1 score of 0.83. We then conduct an in-depth ground-up error analysis and show that the model struggles with edge cases and ambiguous content. We provide the 20,000 tweet training dataset (annotated by experienced analysts), which also contains several secondary categories and additional flags. We also provide the 40,000 original annotations (before adjudication), the full codebook, annotations for COVID-19 relevance and East Asian relevance and stance for 1,000 hashtags, and the final model.

1 Introduction

The outbreak of COVID-19 has raised concerns about the spread of Sinophobia and other forms of East Asian prejudice across the world, with reports of online and offline abuse directed against East Asian people, including physical attacks (Flanagan, 2020; Wong, 2020; Liu, 2020; Walton, 2020; Solomon, 2020; Guy, 2020). The United Nations High Commissioner for Human Rights has drawn attention to these issues, calling on UN member states to fight the 'tsunami' of hate and xenophobia (Shields, 2020).

As digital technologies become even more important for maintaining social connections, it is crucial that online spaces remain safe, accessible and free from abuse (Cowls et al., 2020)—and that people's fears and distress are not exploited during the pandemic. Computational tools, including machine learning and natural language processing, offer powerful ways of creating scalable and robust systems for detecting and measuring prejudice. These, in turn, can assist with both online content moderation processes and further research into the dynamics, prevalence, causes, and impact of abuse.

We report on the creation of a new dataset and classifier to detect East Asian prejudice in social media data. The classifier distinguishes between four primary categories: Hostility against East Asia, Criticism of East Asia, Meta-discussions of East Asian prejudice, and Non-related. It achieves a macro-F1 score of 0.83. The 20,000 tweet training dataset used to create the classifier and the annotation codebook are also provided. The dataset contains annotations for several secondary categories, including threatening language, interpersonal abuse, and dehumanization, which can be used for further research. In addition, we provide the 40,000 original annotations given by our experienced annotators, which can be used for further investigation of annotating prejudice. We also annotated 1,000 hashtags in our dataset for East Asian relevance and stance, as well as other attributes. These are also provided for other researchers.[1]

To provide insight into what types of content causes the model to fail, we conduct a ground-up qualitative error analysis. We show that 17% of errors are due to annotation mistakes and 83% due to the machine learning model. Of these, 29% are clear errors (i.e. obvious mistakes) and 54% are edge cases (i.e. more complex and nuanced cases). In the machine learning edge cases, we show that the model struggles with lexically similar content (e.g. distinguishing Hostility against East Asia from Criticism of East Asia), as well as ambiguous content (i.e. where there is uncertainty among the annotators about the correct label).

---

[1] All research artefacts are available at: https://zenodo.org/record/3816667

Proceedings of the Fourth Workshop on Online Abuse and Harms, pages 162–172
Online, November 20, 2020. ©2020 Association for Computational Linguistics
https://doi.org/10.18653/v1/P17

Finally, we analyze the hashtags most closely associated with the primary categories in the training dataset, identifying several terms which could guide future work.

2 Background

East Asian prejudice, such as Sinophobia, can be understood as fear or hatred of East Asia and East Asian people (Billé, 2015). This prejudice has a long history in the West: in the 19th century the term "yellow peril" was used to refer to Chinese immigrants who were stereotyped as dirty and diseased and considered akin to a plague (Goossen et al., 2004). Often, the association of COVID-19 with China plays into these old stereotypes, as shown by derogatory references to 'bats' and 'monkeys' online (Zhang, 2020). In 2017 a study found that 21% of Asian Americans had received threats based on their Asian identities, and 10% had been victims of violence (Neel, 2017). Likewise, a 2009 report on the discrimination and experiences of East Asian people in the UK, described Sinophobia as a problem that was 'hidden from public view' (Adamson et al., 2009).

New research related to East Asian prejudice during COVID-19 has already provided insight into its nature, prevalence and dynamics with Schild et al. (2020) finding an increase in Sinophobic language on some social media platforms such as 4chan. Analysis by the company Moonshot CVE also suggests that the use of anti-Chinese hashtags has increased substantially (The New Statesman, 2020). They analysed more than 600 million tweets and found that 200,000 contained either Sinophobic hate speech or conspiracy theories, and identified a 300% increase in hashtags that supported or encouraged violence against China during a single week in March 2020. Similarly, Velásquez et al. (2020) show the existence of a Sinophobic 'hate multiverse', with hateful content following contagion patterns and clusters which are similar to the epidemiological diffusion of COVID-19 itself.

Ziems et al. (2020) argue that racism 'is a virus', and study a dataset of 30 million COVID-19 tweets using a classifier trained on 2,400 tweets. They identify 900,000 hateful tweets and 200,000 counter-hate, and find that 10% of users who share hate speech are bot accounts. Toney et al. (2020) used the Word Embedding Association Test in the context of COVID-19 to analyse anti-China sentiment on Twitter, finding substantial biases in how Asian people are viewed. East Asian prejudice has also been linked to the spread of COVID-19 health-related misinformation (Cinelli et al., 2020) and in March 2020 the polling company YouGov found that 1 in 5 Brits believed the conspiracy theory that the coronavirus was developed in a Chinese lab (Nolsoe, 2020).

Research into computational tools for detecting, categorizing, and measuring online hate has received substantial attention in recent years (Waseem et al., 2017). However, a systematic review of hate speech training datasets conducted by Vidgen and Derczynski (2020) shows that classifiers and training datasets for East Asian prejudice are not currently available. Somewhat similar datasets are available, pertaining to racism (Waseem and Hovy, 2016) Islamophobia (Chung et al., 2019) and 'hate' in general (Davidson et al., 2017; de Gibert et al., 2018) but they cannot easily be re-purposed for East Asian prejudice detection. The absence of an appropriate training dataset (and automated detection tools) means that researchers have to rely instead on less precise ways of measuring East Asian prejudice, such as using keyword searches for slurs and other pejorative terms. These methods create substantial errors (Davidson et al., 2017) as more covert prejudice is missed because the content does not contain the target keywords, and non-hateful content is misclassified simply because it does contain a keyword.

Developing new detection tools is a complex and lengthy process. The field of hate speech detection sits at the intersection of social science and computer science and is fraught with not only technical challenges but also deep-routed ethical and theoretical considerations (Vidgen et al., 2019). If machine learning tools are to be effective then they need to be developed with consideration of their social implications (Vidgen et al., 2019; Sap et al., 2019; Davidson et al., 2019; Garg et al., 2019).

3 Dataset Collection

To create our 20,000 tweet training dataset, we collected tweets from Twitter's Streaming API using 14 hashtags that relate to both East Asia and the novel coronavirus.[2] Some of these hashtags ex-

---

[2] We query for: #chinavirus, #wuhan, #wuhanvirus, #chinavirusoutbreak, #wuhancoronavirus, #wuhaninfluenza, #wuhansars, #chinacoronavirus, #wuhan2020, #chinaflu, #wuhanquarantine, #chinesepneumonia, #coronachina and #wohan.

press anti-East Asian sentiments (e.g. '#chinaflu') but others, such as '#wuhan' are more neutral, referring to the geographic origin of the virus. Data collection ran initially from 11 to 17 March 2020, returning 769,763 tweets, of which 96,283 were unique entries in English. To minimize biases that could emerge from collecting data over a relatively short period of time, we then collected tweets from 1 January to 10 March 2020 using the same keywords from a 10% random sample of Twitter (the 'Decahose'), provided by a third party. We identified a further 63,037 unique tweets in English, which we added to our dataset. The full dataset comprises 159,320 unique tweets.

To create a training dataset for annotation we sampled from the full dataset. To guide the sampling process, we extracted the 1,000 most used hashtags from the 159,320 tweets. Three annotators independently marked them for: (1) whether they are East Asian relevant and, if so, (2) what Asian entity is discussed (e.g., China, Xi Jinping, South Korea), (3) what the stance is towards the Asian entity (Very Negative, Negative, Neutral, Positive, or Very Positive) and also (4) whether they relate to COVID-19. 97 hashtags were marked as either Negative or Very Negative toward East Asia by at least one annotator. All annotations for hashtags are available in our data repository.

We then sampled 10,000 tweets at random from the full dataset and a further 10,000 tweets which used one of the 97 hashtags identified as Negative or Very Negative towards East Asia, thereby increasing the likelihood that prejudicial tweets would be identified and ensuring that our dataset is suitable for training a classifier (Schmidt and Wiegand, 2017; Vidgen et al., 2019). The training dataset comprises 20,000 tweets in total.

3.1 Data pre-processing for annotation

Initial qualitative inspection of the dataset showed that hashtags played a key role in how COVID-19 was discussed and how hostility against East Asia was expressed. Hashtags often appeared in the middle of tweets, especially when they related to East Asia and/or COVID-19. For example:

> its wellknown #covid19 originated from #china. Instead of #Doingtherightthing they're blaming others, typical. You cant trust these #YellowFever to sort anything out.

Without the hashtags it is difficult to discern whether this tweet expresses prejudice against East Asia. In this regard, it is important that they are seen by annotators to ensure high quality labels. However, in other cases, the inclusion of hashtags risked low quality labels. In a test round of annotation (not included in the dataset presented here) annotators over-relied on the prejudicial hashtags, marking up nearly all tweets which contained them as prejudiced against East Asia, even if they were otherwise neutral. This is problematic because we used hashtags to sample the training data so they are highly prevalent. If all of their uses were identified as prejudicial then any systems trained on the dataset would likely overfit to just a few keywords. This could severely constrain the system's generalizability, potentially leading to poor performance on new content.

To address this challenge, we performed a hashtag replacement on all tweets prior to presenting them to the annotators. For the 1,000 most used hashtags (annotated as part of the data sampling phase), we had one annotator identify appropriate *thematic replacement* hashtags. We used five thematic replacements:

- #EASTASIA: Relate only to an East Asian entity, e.g. #China or #Wuhan

- #VIRUS: Relate only to COVID-19, e.g. #coronavirus or #covid19.

- #EASTASIAVIRUS: Relate to both an East Asian entity and COVID-19, e.g. #wuhanflu.

- #OTHERCOUNTRYVIRUS: Relate to both a Country (which is not East Asian) and COVID-19, e.g. #coronacanada or #italycovid.

- #HASHTAG: Not directly relevant to COVID-19 or East Asia, e.g. #maga or #spain.

Annotators could still discern the meaning of tweets because they were presented with the hashtags' topics. However, they were not unduly biased by the substantive *outlook*, stance, and sentiment the hashtags express. All hashtags beyond our annotated list of 1,000 were replaced with a generic replacement, #HASHTAG. The 1,000 thematic hashtag replacements are available in our data repository. With this process, the quote above is transformed to:

its wellknown #HASHTAGVIRUS originated from #HASHTAGEASTASIA. Instead of #HASHTAG they're blaming others, typical. You cant trust these #HASHTAGEASTASIAVIRUS to sort anything out.

This process, although time consuming, strikes a balance between preserving the meaning of the tweet for annotation and minimizing the risk of overfitting. It means that the text the annotators are presented with is also the same text that is fed into our final models (i.e. both annotations and the model classifications are based on the replaced hashtags). In principle, it would be easy for anyone applying our final classification model to a new dataset to update the hashtag replacement list and then apply it to their data.

4 Dataset Annotation and Taxonomy

4.1 Annotators

Annotation was completed by a team of 26 annotators, all of whom had completed at least 4 weeks of training on a previous hate speech annotation project. The annotators were all aged between 18 and 35, spoke English fluently (50% were native speakers), were 75% female and were all educated to at least an undergraduate level. 25% were studying for higher degrees. Annotators came from the United Kingdom (60%), elsewhere in Europe (30%) and South America (10%). Information about their sexuality, religious and political affiliation is not available due to their sensitivity.

Two experts were used to adjudicate decisions on the primary categories. Both experts were final year PhD students working on extreme behaviour online. One was male; one was female. They were both aged between 25 and 35, and were native English speakers.

4.2 Themes

Tweets were first annotated for the presence of two themes: (1) East Asia and (2) COVID-19. If a tweet was not East Asian relevant then no further annotations were required and it was automatically assigned to the Non-related class. Annotators then used an additional flag for how they marked up the two themes, which we call 'hashtag dependence.' For this label, annotators were asked whether they had used the hashtags to identify the themes or the themes were apparent without the hashtags.

Our approach to annotating themes and the role of hashtags required substantial training for annotators (involving one-to-one on-boarding sessions). This detailed annotation process means that we can provide insight into not only what annotations were made but also *how*, which we anticipate will be of use to scholars working on online communications beyond online prejudice.

4.3 Primary categories

Each tweet was assigned to one of five mutually exclusive primary categories.

- **Hostility against an East Asian (EA) entity**: Express abuse or intense negativity against an East Asian entity, primarily by derogating/attacking them (e.g. "Those oriental devils don't care about human life" or "Chinks will bring about the downfall of western civilization"). It also includes: conspiracy theories, claiming East Asians are a threat, and expressing negative emotions about them.

- **Criticism of an East Asian entity**: Make a negative judgement/assessment of an East Asian entity, without being abusive. This includes commenting on perceived social, economic and political faults, including questioning their response to the pandemic and how they are governed.

  The Hostility/Criticism distinction is crucial for addressing a core issue in online hate speech research, namely ensuring that freedom of speech is protected (Ullmann and Tomalin, 2020). The Criticism category minimizes the chance that users who engage in what has been termed 'legitimate critique' (Imhoff and Recker, 2012) will have their comments erroneously labelled as hostile.

- **Counter speech**: Explicitly challenge or condemn abuse against an East Asian entity. It includes rejecting the premise of abuse (e.g., "it isn't right to blame China!"), describing content as hateful or prejudicial (e.g., "you shouldn't say that, it's derogatory") or expressing solidarity with target entities (e.g., "Stand with Chinatown against racists").

- **Discussion of East Asian prejudice** Tweets that discuss prejudice related to East Asians but do not engage in, or counter, that prejudice (e.g., "It's not racist to call it the Wuhan

Theme	Number of Entries	Percentage
COVID-19 relevant / Both said No	2,940	14.7%
COVID-19 relevant / Both said Yes	12,255	61.3%
COVID-19 relevant / Disagreement	4,805	24.0%
East Asian relevant / Both said No	6,593	33.0%
East Asian relevant / Both said Yes	9,790	49.0%
East Asian relevant / Disagreement	3,617	18.0%

Table 1: Prevalence of themes in the dataset.

Category	Number of Entries	Percentage
Hostility	3,898	19.5%
Criticism	1,433	7.2%
Counter speech	116	0.6%
Discussion of EAP	1,029	5.1%
Non-related	13,528	67.6%
TOTAL	**20,000**	**100%**

Table 2: Prevalence of primary categories in the dataset.

Measure	Mean	Min.	Max.
Percentage agreement	78%	67%	84%
Fleiss' Kappa			
All categories	0.54	0.36	0.66
Hostility	0.53	0.22	0.66
Criticism	0.27	0.14	0.41
Counter Speech	0.33	0.11	0.61
Discussion of EAP	0.46	0.14	0.65
Non-related	0.64	0.51	0.78

Table 3: Agreement scores for primary categories.

virus"). It includes content which discusses whether East Asian prejudice has increased during COVID-19, the supposed media focus on prejudice, and/or free speech.

- **Non-related** Do not fall into any of the other categories. Note that they could be abusive in other ways, such as expressing misogyny.

The primary categories were annotated with a two step process. First, each tweet was annotated independently by two trained annotators. Second, one of two expert adjudicators reviewed cases where annotators disagreed about the primary category. Experts could decide an entirely new primary category if needed. Expert adjudication was not used for the themes and secondary categories.

Agreement is reported for each pair of annotators in Table 3, with the average, minimum, and maximum. Overall, agreement levels are moderate, with better results for the two most important and prevalent categories (Hostility and Non-related) but poorer on the less frequent and more nuanced categories (Counter Speech, Criticism and Discussion of EA prejudice). Note that if Counter Speech and Discussion of EA prejudice are combined then there is a marked improvement in overall agreement levels, with an average Kappa of 0.5 for the combined category.

Experts adjudicated 4,478 cases (22%) where annotators did not agree. Experts tended to move tweets out of Non-related into other categories, primarily Hostility. Of the 8,956 original annotations given to the 4,478 tweets they adjudicated, 34% of them were in Non-related and yet only 29% of their adjudicated decisions were in this category. This was matched by an equivalent increase in the Hostility category, from 31.6% of the original annotations to 35% of the expert adjudications. The other three categories remained broadly stable. In 347 cases (7.7%), experts choose a category that was not selected by either annotator. Of the 694 original annotations given to these 347 cases, 18.7% were for Criticism compared with 39.4% of the expert adjudications for these entries (a similar decrease can be observed for the Non-related category). The most common decision made by experts for these 347 tweets was to label a tweet as Criticism when one annotator had selected Hostility and the other selected Non-related. These results shows the fundamental ambiguity of hate speech annotation and the need for expert adjudication. With complex and often-ambiguous content even well-trained annotators can make decisions which are inappropriate.

4.4 Secondary categories

For the Hostility and Criticism primary categories, annotators identified what East Asian entity was targeted (e.g., "Hong Kongers", "CCP", or "Chinese scientists"). Initially, annotators identified targets inductively, which resulted in several hundred unique values. We then implemented a reconciliation process in which the number of unique targets was reduced to 78, reflecting six geographical areas (China, Korea, Japan, Taiwan, Singapore and East Asia in general) and several specific entities, such as scientists, women and government, including intersectional identities. For tweets identified as Hostility annotators applied three additional flags.

- Interpersonal abuse: East Asian prejudice which is targeted against an individual. Whether the individual is East Asian was not considered. (Waseem et al., 2017).

- Use of threatening language: Content which makes a threat against an East Asian entity, which includes expressing a desire/willingness to inflict harm or inciting others (The Law Commission, 2018; Weber, 2009).

- Dehumanization: Content which describes, compares or suggests equivalences between East Asians and non-humans or sub-humans, such as insects, weeds, or actual viruses (Leader Maynard and Benesch, 2016; Musolff, 2015).

Note that our expert adjudicators did not adjudicate for these secondary categories. In cases where experts decided a tweet is Hostile but neither of the original annotators had selected that category then none of the secondary categories are available. In other cases, experts decided a tweet was Hostile and so only one annotation for the secondary flags is available (as the other annotator selected a different category and did not provide these secondary annotations). Future researchers can decide how to use these secondary categories.

5 Classification results

Due to their low prevalence and conceptual similarity, we combined the Counter Speech category

Model	Macro F1	Recall	Precision
LSTM	0.76	0.67	**0.88**
AlBERT$_{xlarge}$	0.798	0.798	0.800
BART$_{large}$	0.813	0.812	0.834
BERT$_{large}$	0.823	0.823	0.827
DistilBERT$_{base}$	0.803	0.803	0.809
ELECTRA$_{large}$	0.831	0.831	0.836
RoBERTa$_{large}$	**0.832**	**0.832**	0.848
XLNet$_{large}$	0.802	0.802	0.822

Table 4: Classification performance of models on the test set.

with Discussion of East Asian Prejudice for classification. As such, the classification task was to distinguish between four primary categories: Hostility, Criticism, Discussion of East Asian Prejudice and Non-related.

We implemented and fine-tuned several contextual embedding models as well as a one-hot LSTM model with a linear input layer, tanh activation, and a softmax output layer. We expect contextual embeddings to perform best as they take into account the context surrounding a token when generating each embedding (Vaswani et al., 2017). We compared results against a one-hot LSTM model to test this expectation.

Models were developed with a stratified 80/10/10 training, testing, and validation split (maintaining the class distribution of the whole dataset). We processed all tweets by removing URLs and usernames, lower-casing, and replacing hashtags with either a generic hashtag-token or with the appropriate thematic hashtag-token from the annotation setup. Training was conducted using the same hyper-parameter sweep identified in Liu et al. (2019) as most effective for the GLUE benchmark tasks. This included testing across learning rates $\in \{$1e-5, 2e-5, 3e-5$\}$ and batch sizes $\in \{$32, 64$\}$ with an early stopping regime. Performance was optimized using the AdamW algorithm (Loshchilov and Hutter, 2019) and a scheduler that implements linear warmup and decay. For the LSTM baseline, we conduct a hyper-parameter search over batch sizes $\in \{$16, 32, 64$\}$ and learning rates $\{10^{-i}, i \in 1, 5$ increments$\}$.

All of the contextual embedding models outperformed the baseline in terms of macro F1. RoBERTa achieved the highest F1 score of the tested models (0.832), which is a 7-point improve-

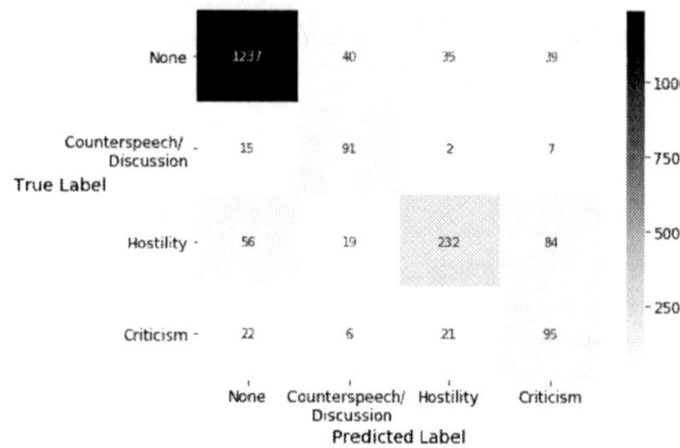

Figure 1: Confusion matrix for RoBERTa classifications on the test set.

ment over the LSTM (0.76). This model harnesses the underlying bidirectional transformer architecture of BERT (Devlin et al., 2019) but alters the training hyperparameters and objectives to improve performance. Unexpectedly, the LSTM baseline outperforms all other models in terms of precision but has far lower recall. For the best performing model (RoBERTa), misclassifications are shown in the confusion matrix. The model performs well across all categories, with strongest performance in detecting tweets in the Non-related category (Recall of 91.6% and Precision of 93%). The model has few misclassifications between the most conceptually distinct categories (e.g. Hostility versus Non-related) but has far more errors between conceptually similar categories, such as Criticism and Hostility.

6 Error analysis

To better understand classification errors, we conducted a qualitative analysis of misclassified content (from the best performing model, RoBERTa), using a grounded theory approach (Corbin and Strauss, 1990). This qualitative methodology is entirely inductive and data-driven. It involves systematically exploring themes as they emerge from the data and organizing them into a taxonomy—refining and collapsing the categories until 'saturation' is reached and the data fits neatly into a set of mutually exclusive and collectively exhaustive categories. Figure 2 shows the error categories within our sample of 340 misclassified tweets from the 2,000 (10%) validation split. The errors broadly fit within two branches: annotator errors (17%) and machine learning errors (83%). In future work, these errors could be addressed through creating

a larger and more balanced dataset, more sophisticated machine learning architectures and reannotation of data.

6.1 Annotator errors (17% of total)

Annotator errors are cases where the classification from the model better captures the tweets' content and is more consistent with our taxonomy and guidelines. In effect, we believe that the 'wrong' classification provided by the model is correct—and that a mistake may have been made in the annotation process. Approximately 17% (N=58) of the errors were due to this. Note that this does not mean that 17% of the dataset is incorrectly annotated as this sample is biased by the fact that it has been selected precisely because the model made an 'error'.

36 of the annotator errors were clear misapplications of primary categories. The other 22 were cases where annotators made detailed annotations for tweets which were incorrectly marked as East Asian relevant. These are *path dependency errors* and show the importance of annotators following the right instructions throughout the process. If an incorrect annotation is made early on then the subsequent annotations are likely to be flawed.

6.2 Prediction errors (83% of total)

83% of the total errors were due to errors from the model. We have separated these into clear errors and edge cases. Clear errors are where the model has made an error that is easily identified by humans (accounting for 29% of all errors). Edge-cases are where the misclassified content contains some ambiguity and the model misclassification has some merit (accounting for 54% of all errors).

Clear error (Lexical similarity), 16% In several cases the misclassified tweets were clearly assigned to the wrong class. This suggests possible overfitting as the tweets were often lexically similar to tweets which did belong in the category (e.g., they contained phrases such as 'Made in China' and were mistaken for Hostility). This is most likely a learned over-sensitivity and could only be addressed through using a far larger dataset.

Clear error (Target confusion), 13% The model sometimes identified tweets which were not East Asian relevant as Criticism, Hostility, or Discussion of East Asian prejudice. Aside from this, the classifications were correct, i.e. the tweets expressed hostility against another identity, such as

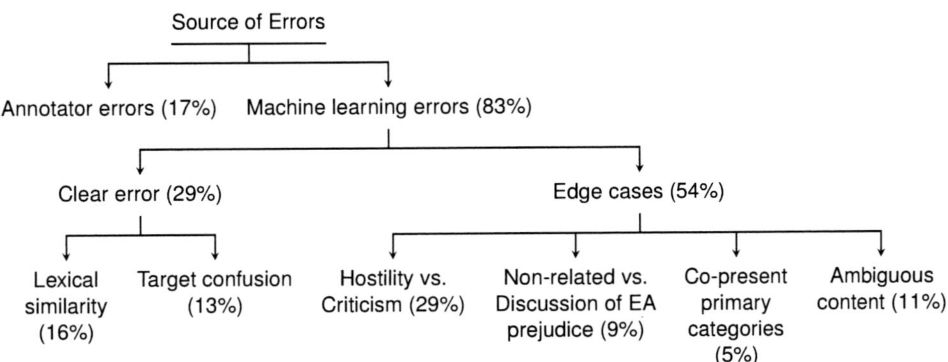

Figure 2: Sources of classification error.

women or gay people. Furthermore, in many cases, a relevant East Asian entity (e.g. China) was usually referred to but was not the object of the tweet, creating a mixed signal for the model.

Edge case (Hostility vs. Criticism), 29% Misclassifying Hostility as Criticism (and vice versa) was the largest source of error. The model particularly struggled with cases where criticism was framed normatively or expressed with nuanced linguistic expressions, e.g., "gee, china was lying to us. what a bloody shock".

Edge case (Non-related vs. Discussion of EA prejudice), 9% The model misclassified Non-related as Discussion of East Asian prejudice in several tweets. These were usually cases where the virus was named and discussed but *prejudice* was not discussed explicitly, e.g. "corona just shows why you should blame all our problems with China on Trump".

Edge case (Co-present primary categories), 5% In our taxonomy, annotators could assign each tweet to only one primary category. However, in some cases this was problematic and the model identified a co-present category rather than the primary category which had been annotated.

Edge case (Ambiguous content), 11% The model often misclassified content which was ambiguous. This is content where the true meaning is not immediately discernible to a human without careful analysis. For instance, positively framed criticism, e.g. "so glad that china official finally admits the HASHTAGEASTASIA+VIRUS outbreaks". In some tweets, complex forms of expression were used, such as innuendo or sarcasm,

e.g. "I think we owe you china, please accept our apologies to bring some virus into your great country".

6.3 Addressing Classification Errors

Classifying social media data is notoriously difficult. There are many different sources of error, each of which, in turn, require different remedies. Annotator errors, for example, illustrate the need for robust annotation processes and providing more support and training when taxonomies are applied. Removing such errors entirely is unlikely, but the number of obvious misclassifications could be minimized.

Machine learning errors are where the bulk of the errors fall (83%). Edge cases are a particularly difficult type of content for classification. They can be expected in any taxonomy that draws distinct lines between complex and non-mutually exclusive concepts, such as Hostility and Criticism. Nonetheless, larger and more balanced datasets (with more instances of content in each category) would help in reducing this source of error. Equally, the frequency of non-edge case machine learning errors (i.e. cases where the model made a very obvious mistake) could be addressed by larger datasets as well as more advanced machine learning architectures.

7 Hashtag analysis

We analysed the 20,000 tweet training dataset to understand which hashtags were associated with which primary categories. For each category, we filtered the data so only hashtags which appeared in at least ten tweets assigned to that category were included. Then, we ranked the hashtags by the percentage of their uses which were in the primary category—our goal being to understand which hashtags are most closely associated with that category. For brevity, only the twenty hashtags most closely associated with the Hostility category are shown in Table 5. This analysis is only possible because all hashtags were replaced in the tweets which were presented to annotators (either with a generic hashtag token or thematic replacement), letting us conduct meaningful analysis of the co-occurrence of hashtags with the annotated primary categories.

A small number of hashtags are highly likely to only appear in tweets that express Hostility against East Asian entities. These hashtags could be used to filter for prejudiced discourses online and, in some cases, their uses may intrinsically indicate prejudice. Surprisingly, many seemingly hostile hashtags against East Asia, such as #fuckchina and #blamechina are not always associated with hostile tweets (Hostility accounts for 67.5% and 60.5% of their total use, respectively). This shows the importance of having a purpose-built machine learning classifier for detecting East Asian hostility, rather than relying on hashtags and keywords alone.

8 Conclusion

Prejudice of all forms is a deeply concerning problem during COVID-19, reflecting the huge social costs and difficulties that the pandemic has inflicted. In this paper we have reported on development of several research artefacts that we hope will enable further research into East Asian prejudice, including a trained classifier, a training dataset (20,000 entries), annotations dataset (40,000 entries), 1,000 annotated hashtags, a list of hashtag replacements, a list of hashtags associated with hostility against East Asia, and the full codebook (with extensive guidelines, information and examples).

One concern with any model is that it will not generalize to new settings and platforms, limiting its utility for real-world applications. Our hashtag replacement method was adopted to increase the generalizability of the final model, maximizing the likelihood that it can be applied to new contexts—as it would pick up on the semantic features of hostile tweets rather than specific tokens. Nonetheless, we caution that any re-use of the model should be accompanied by additional testing to understand its performance on different data.

Hashtag	# in Hostile Tweets	% of All Uses	# of Total Uses
#rule2	20	87%	23
#rule3	17	85%	20
#rule1	22	85%	26
#makechinapay	18	72%	25
#hkgovt	22	71%	31
#fuckchina	54	68%	80
#blamechina	23	61%	38
#batsoup	15	60%	25
#hkairport	11	55%	20
#huawei	16	53%	30
#boycottchina	185	53%	350
#communismkills	14	52%	27
#communistchina	34	51%	67
#chinaisasshoe	41	51%	81
#chinapropaganda	10	50%	20
#china_is_terrorist	168	49%	345
#xijingping	17	49%	35
#chinashould apologize	14	48%	29
#madeinchina	39	48%	82
#ccp	395	47%	850

Table 5: Hashtags in Hostile tweets.

Acknowledgments

This work was supported by Wave 1 of The UKRI Strategic Priorities Fund under the EPSRC Grant EP/T001569/1, particularly the "Criminal Justice System" theme within that grant, and The Alan Turing Institute. Scott Hale was supported in part by the Volkswagen Foundation.

References

Sue Adamson, Bankole Cole, Gary Craig, Basharat Hussain, Luana Smith, Ian Law, Carmen Lau, Chak-Kwan Chan, and Tom Cheung. 2009. *Hidden from public view? Racism against the UK Chinese population.* Sheffield Hallam University.

Franck Billé. 2015. *Sinophobia: anxiety, violence, and the making of Mongolian identity.* University of Hawaii Press.

Yi-Ling Chung, Elizaveta Kuzmenko, Serra Sinem Tekiroglu, and Marco Guerini. 2019. CONAN - COunter NArratives through Nichesourcing: a Multilingual Dataset of Responses to Fight Online Hate Speech. In *Proceedings of the 57th Annual Meeting of the ACL*, pages 2819–2829.

Matteo Cinelli, Walter Quattrociocchi, Alessandro Galeazzi, Carlo Michele Valensise, Emanuele Brugnoli, Ana Lucia Schmidt, Paola Zola, Fabiana Zollo, and Antonio Scala. 2020. The COVID-19 Social Media Infodemic. *arXiv:2003.05004*.

Juliet Corbin and Anselm Strauss. 1990. Grounded Theory Research: Procedures, Canons and Evaluative Criteria. *Qualitative Research*, 13(1):3–21.

Josh Cowls, Bertie Vidgen, and Helen Margetts. 2020. Why content moderators should be key workers protecting social media as critical infrastructure during covid-19. *The Alan Turing Institute*.

Thomas Davidson, Debasmita Bhattacharya, and Ingmar Weber. 2019. Racial Bias in Hate Speech and Abusive Language Detection Datasets. In *Proceedings of the 57th Annual Meeting of the ACL*, pages 1–11.

Thomas Davidson, Dana Warmsley, Michael Macy, and Ingmar Weber. 2017. Automated Hate Speech Detection and the Problem of Offensive Language. In *Proceedings of the 11th ICWSM*, pages 1–4.

Jacob Devlin, Ming-Wei Chang, Kenton Lee, and Kristina Toutanova. 2019. Bert: Pre-training of deep bidirectional transformers for language understanding. In *Proceedings of NAACL-HLT 2019*, page 4171–4186.

Ryan Flanagan. 2020. Canada's top doctor calls out 'racism and stigmatizing comments' over coronavirus. *CTVNews*.

Sahaj Garg, Ankur Taly, Vincent Perot, Ed H. Chi, Nicole Limtiaco, and Alex Beutel. 2019. Counterfactual fairness in text classification through robustness. *Proceedings of the 2019 AAAI/ACM Conference on AI, Ethics, and Society*, pages 219–226.

Ona de Gibert, Naiara Perez, Aitor García-Pablos, and Montse Cuadros. 2018. Hate Speech Dataset from a White Supremacy Forum. In *Proceedings of the Second Workshop on Abusive Language Online (ACL)*, pages 11–20.

Tam Goossen, Jian Guan, and Ito Peng. 2004. Yellow Peril Revisited: Impact of SARS on the Chinese and Southeast Asian Canadian Communities June, 2004 Project Coordinator and Author: Carrianne Leung. *Resources for Feminist Research*, 33(1-2):135–150.

Jack Guy. 2020. East Asian student assaulted in 'racist' coronavirus attack in London. *CNN*.

Roland Imhoff and Julia Recker. 2012. Differentiating Islamophobia: Introducing a New Scale to Measure Islamoprejudice and Secular Islam Critique. *Political Psychology*, 33(6):811–824.

Jonathan Leader Maynard and Susan Benesch. 2016. Dangerous Speech and Dangerous Ideology: An Integrated Model for Monitoring and Prevention. *Genocide Studies and Prevention*, 9(3):70–95.

Yinhan Liu, Myle Ott, Naman Goyal, Jingfei Du, Mandar Joshi, Danqi Chen, Omer Levy, Mike Lewis, Luke Zettlemoyer, and Veselin Stoyanov. 2019. Roberta: A robustly optimized bert pretraining approach. *arXiv:1907.11692*.

Yuebai Liu. 2020. Coronavirus prompts 'hysterical, shameful' Sinophobia in Italy. *Al Jazeera*.

Ilya Loshchilov and Frank Hutter. 2019. Decoupled weight decay regularization. In *Proceedings of ICLR 2019*, pages 1–18.

Andreas Musolff. 2015. Dehumanizing metaphors in UK immigrant debates in press and online media. *Journal of Language Aggression and Conflict*, 3(1):41–56.

Joe Neel. 2017. Poll: Asian-Americans See Individuals' Prejudice As Big Discrimination Problem. *NPR*.

Eir Nolsoe. 2020. COVID-19: Bogus claims fool Britons. *YouGov*.

Maarten Sap, Dallas Card, Saadia Gabriel, Yejin Choi, Noah A Smith, and Paul G Allen. 2019. The Risk of Racial Bias in Hate Speech Detection. In *Proceedings of the 57th Annual Meeting of the ACL*, pages 1668–1678.

Leonard Schild, Chen Ling, Jeremy Blackburn, Gianluca Stringhini, Yang Zhang, and Savvas Zannettou. 2020. "Go eat a bat, Chang!": An Early Look on the Emergence of Sinophobic Behavior on Web Communities in the Face of COVID-19. *arXiv:2004.04046*.

Anna Schmidt and Michael Wiegand. 2017. A survey on hate speech detection using natural language processing. In *Proceedings of the Fifth International Workshop on Natural Language Processing for Social Media*. Association for Computational Linguistics.

Michael Shields. 2020. U.N. asks world to fight virus-spawned discrimination. *Reuters*.

Salem Solomon. 2020. Coronavirus Brings 'Sinophobia' to Africa. *VOA News*.

The Law Commission. 2018. *Abusive and Offensive Online Communications: A scoping report*. The Law Commission.

The New Statesman. 2020. Covid-19 has caused a major spike in anti-Chinese and anti-Semitic hate speech. *The New Statesman*.

Autumn Toney, Akshat Pandey, Wei Guo, David Broniatowski, and Aylin Caliskan. 2020. Pro-Russian Biases in Anti-Chinese Tweets about the Novel Coronavirus. *arXiv:2004.08726*.

Stefanie Ullmann and Marcus Tomalin. 2020. Quarantining online hate speech: technical and ethical perspectives. *Ethics and Information Technology*, 22(1):69–80.

Ashish Vaswani, Noam Shazeer, Niki Parmar, Jakob Uszkoreit, Llion Jones, Aidan N. Gomez, Lukasz Kaiser, and Illia Polosukhin. 2017. Attention is all you need. In *31st Conference on Neural Information Processing Systems (NIPS 2017)*, pages 1–11.

N. Velásquez, R. Leahy, N. Johnson Restrepo, Y. Lupu, R. Sear, N. Gabriel, O. Jha, B. Goldberg, and N.F. Johnson. 2020. Hate multiverse spreads malicious covid-19 content online beyond individual platform control. *arXiv:2004.00673*.

Bertie Vidgen and Leon Derczynski. 2020. Directions in Abusive Language Training Data: Garbage In, Garbage Out. *arXiv:2004.01670*, pages 1–26.

Bertie Vidgen, Alex Harris, Dong Nguyen, Rebekah Tromble, Scott Hale, and Helen Margetts. 2019. Challenges and frontiers in abusive content detection. In *Proceedings of the Third Workshop on Abusive Language Online (ACL)*, pages 80–93.

Kate Walton. 2020. Wuhan Virus Boosts Indonesian Anti-Chinese Conspiracies. *Foreign Policy*.

Zeerak Waseem, Thomas Davidson, Dana Warmsley, and Ingmar Weber. 2017. Understanding Abuse: A Typology of Abusive Language Detection Subtasks. In *Proceedings of the First Workshop on Abusive Language Online*, pages 78–84.

Zeerak Waseem and Dirk Hovy. 2016. Hateful Symbols or Hateful People? Predictive Features for Hate Speech Detection on Twitter. In *NAACL-HLT*, pages 88–93.

Anne Weber. 2009. *Manual on Hate Speech*. Council of Europe.

Tessa Wong. 2020. Sinophobia: How a virus reveals the many ways China is feared. *BBC News*.

Zhang. 2020. Pinning coronavirus on how chinese people eat plays into racist assumptions.

Caleb Ziems, Bing He, Sandeep Soni, and Srijan Kumar. 2020. Racism is a virus: Anti-asian hate and counterhate in social media during the covid-19 crisis. *arXiv:2005.12423*.

On Cross-Dataset Generalization in Automatic Detection of Online Abuse

Isar Nejadgholi

Svetlana Kiritchenko

National Research Council Canada
{isar.nejadgholi,svetlana.kiritchenko}@nrc-cnrc.gc.ca

Abstract

NLP research has attained high performances in abusive language detection as a supervised classification task. While in research settings, training and test datasets are usually obtained from similar data samples, in practice systems are often applied on data that are different from the training set in topic and class distributions. Also, the ambiguity in class definitions inherited in this task aggravates the discrepancies between source and target datasets. We explore the topic bias and the task formulation bias in cross-dataset generalization. We show that the benign examples in the Wikipedia Detox dataset are biased towards platform-specific topics. We identify these examples using unsupervised topic modeling and manual inspection of topics' keywords. Removing these topics increases cross-dataset generalization, without reducing in-domain classification performance. For a robust dataset design, we suggest applying inexpensive unsupervised methods to inspect the collected data and downsize the non-generalizable content before manually annotating for class labels.

1 Introduction

The NLP research community has devoted significant efforts to support the safety and inclusiveness of online discussion forums by developing automatic systems to detect hurtful, derogatory or obscene utterances. Most of these systems are based on supervised machine learning techniques, and require annotated data. Several publicly available datasets have been created for the task (Mishra et al., 2019; Vidgen and Derczynski, 2020). However, due to the ambiguities in the task definition and complexities of data collection, cross-dataset generalizability remains a challenging and understudied issue of online abuse detection.

Existing datasets differ in the considered types of offensive behaviour and annotation schemes, data sources and data collection methods. There is no agreed-upon definition of harmful online behaviour yet. Several terms have been used to refer to the general concept of harmful online behavior, including *toxicity* (Hosseini et al., 2017), *hate speech* (Schmidt and Wiegand, 2017), *offensive* (Zampieri et al., 2019) and *abusive* language (Waseem et al., 2017; Vidgen et al., 2019a). Still, in practice, every dataset only focuses on a narrow range of subtypes of such behaviours and a single online platform (Jurgens et al., 2019). For example, Davidson et al. (2017) annotated tweets for three categories, *Racist, Offensive but not Racist* and *Clean*, and Nobata et al. (2016) collected discussions from Yahoo! Finance news and applied a binary annotation scheme of *Abusive* versus *Clean*. Further, since pure random sampling usually results in small proportions of offensive examples (Founta et al., 2018), various sampling techniques are often employed. Zampieri et al. (2019) used words and phrases frequently found in offensive messages to search for potential abusive tweets. Founta et al. (2018) and Razavi et al. (2010) started from random sampling, then boosted the abusive part of the datasets using specific search procedures. Hosseinmardi et al. (2015) used snowballing to collect abusive posts on Instagram. Due to this variability in category definitions and data collection techniques, a system trained on a particular dataset is prone to overfitting to the specific characteristics of that dataset. As a result, although models tend to perform well in cross-validation evaluation on one dataset, the cross-dataset generalizability remains low (van Aken et al., 2018; Wiegand et al., 2019).

In this work, we investigate the impact of two types of biases originating from source data that can emerge in a cross-domain application of models: 1) task formulation bias (discrepancy in class definitions and annotation between the training and test sets) and 2) selection bias (discrepancy

Proceedings of the Fourth Workshop on Online Abuse and Harms, pages 173–183
Online, November 20, 2020. ©2020 Association for Computational Linguistics
https://doi.org/10.18653/v1/P17

in the topic and class distributions between the training and test sets). Further, we suggest topic-based dataset pruning as a method of mitigating selection bias to increase generalizability. This approach is different from domain adaptation techniques based on data selection (Ruder and Plank, 2017; Liu et al., 2019) in that we apply an unsupervised topic modeling method for topic discovery without using the class labels. We show that some topics are more generalizable than others. The topics that are specific to the training dataset lead to overfitting and, therefore, lower generalizability. Excluding or down-sampling instances associated with such topics before the expensive annotation step can substantially reduce the annotation costs.

We focus on the Wikipedia Detox or *Wiki*-dataset, (an extension of the dataset by Wulczyn et al. (2017)), collected from English Wikipedia talk pages and annotated for toxicity. To explore the generalizability of the models trained on this dataset, we create an out-of-domain test set comprising various types of abusive behaviours by combining two existing datasets, namely *Waseem*-dataset (Waseem and Hovy, 2016) and *Founta*-dataset (Founta et al., 2018), both collected from Twitter.

Our main contributions are as follows:

- We identify topics included in the *Wiki*-dataset and manually examine keywords associated with the topics to heuristically determine topics' generalizability and their potential association with toxicity.

- We assess the generalizability of the task formulations by training a classifier to detect the *Toxic* class in the *Wiki*-dataset and testing it on an out-of-domain dataset comprising various types of offensive behaviours. We find that *Wiki-Toxic* is most generalizable to *Founta-Abusive* and least generalizable to *Waseem-Sexism*.

- We show that re-sampling techniques result in a trade-off between the True Positive and True Negative rates on the out-of-domain test set. This trade-off is mainly governed by the ratio of toxic to normal instances and not the size of the dataset.

- We investigate the impact of topic distribution on generalizability and show that general and identity-related topics are more generalizable than platform-specific topics.

- We show that excluding Wikipedia-specific data instances (54% of the dataset) does not affect the results of in-domain classification, and improves both True Positive and True Negative rates on the out-of-domain test set, unlike re-sampling methods. Through unsupervised topic modeling, such topics can be identified and excluded before annotation.

2 Biases Originating from Source Data

We focus on two types of biases originated from source data: task formulation and selection bias.

Task formulation bias: In commercial applications, the definitions of offensive language heavily rely on community norms and context and, therefore, are imprecise, application-dependent, and constantly evolving (Chandrasekharan et al., 2018). Similarly in NLP research, despite having clear overlaps, offensive class definitions vary significantly from one study to another. For example, the *Toxic* class in the *Wiki*-dataset refers to aggressive or disrespectful utterances that would likely make participants leave the discussion. This definition of toxic language includes some aspects of racism, sexism and hateful behaviour. Still, as highlighted by Vidgen et al. (2019a), identity-based abuse is fundamentally different from general toxic behavior. Therefore, the *Toxic* class definition used in the *Wiki*-dataset differs in its scope from the abuse-related categories as defined in the *Waseem*-dataset and *Founta*-dataset. Wiegand et al. (2019) converted various category sets to binary (offensive vs. normal) and demonstrated that a system trained on one dataset can identify other forms of abuse to some extent. We use the same methodology and examine different offensive categories in out-of-domain test sets to explore the deviation in a system's performance caused by the differences in the task definitions.

Regardless of the task formulation, abusive language can be divided into explicit and implicit (Waseem et al., 2017). Explicit abuse refers to utterances that include obscene and offensive expressions, such as *stupid* or *scum*, even though not all utterances that include obscene expressions are considered abusive in all contexts. Implicit abuse refers to more subtle harmful behaviours, such as stereotyping and micro-aggression. Explicit abuse is usually easier to detect by human annotators and automatic systems. Also, explicit abuse is more transferable between datasets as it is part of many definitions of online abuse, including personal attacks, hate speech, and identity-based abuse. The exact definition of implicit abuse, on the other hand, can substantially vary between task formulations as it is much dependent on the context, the author and the receiver of an utterance (Wiegand et al., 2019).

Selection bias: Selection (or sampling) bias emerge when source data, on which the model is trained, is not representative of target data, on which the model is applied (Shah et al., 2020). We focus on two data characteristics affecting selection bias: topic distribution and class distribution.

In practice, every dataset covers a limited number of topics, and the **topic distributions** depend on many factors, including the source of data, the search mechanism and the timing of the data collection. For example, our source dataset, *Wiki*-dataset, consists of Wikipedia talk pages dating from 2004–2015. On the other hand, one of the sources of our target dataset, *Waseem*-dataset, consists of tweets collected using terms and references to specific entities that frequently occur in tweets expressing hate speech. As a result of its sampling strategy, *Waseem*-dataset includes many tweets on the topic of 'women in sports'. Wiegand et al. (2019) showed that different data sampling methods result in various distributions of topics, which affects the generalizability of trained classifiers, especially in the case of implicit abuse detection. Unlike explicit abuse, implicitly abusive behaviour comes in a variety of semantic and syntactic forms. To train a generalizable classifier, one requires a training dataset that covers a broad range of topics, each with a good representation of offensive examples. We continue this line of work and investigate the impact of topic bias on cross-dataset generalizability by identifying and changing the distribution of topics in controlled experiments.

The amount of online abuse on mainstream platforms varies greatly but is always very low. Founta et al. (2018) found that abusive tweets form 0.1% to 3% of randomly collected datasets. Vidgen et al. (2019b) showed that depending on the platform the prevalence of abusive language can range between 0.001% and 8%. Despite various data sampling strategies aimed at increasing the proportion of offensive instances, the **class imbalance** (the difference in class sizes) in available datasets is often severe. When trained on highly imbalanced data, most statistical machine learning methods exhibit a bias towards the majority class, and their

performance on a minority class, usually the class of interest, suffers. A number of techniques have been proposed to address class imbalance in data, including data re-sampling, cost-sensitive learning, and neural network specific learning algorithms (Branco et al., 2016; Haixiang et al., 2017; Johnson and Khoshgoftaar, 2019). In practice, simple re-sampling techniques, such as down-sampling of over-represented classes, often improve the overall performance of the classifier (Johnson and Khoshgoftaar, 2019). However, re-sampling techniques might lead to overfitting to one of the classes causing a trade-off between True Positive and True Negative rates. When aggregated in an averaged metric such as F-score, this trade-off is usually overlooked.

3 Datasets

We exploit three large-scale, publicly available English datasets frequently used for the task of online abuse detection. Our main dataset, *Wiki*-dataset (Wulczyn et al., 2017), is used as a training set. The out-of-domain test set is obtained by combining the other two datasets, *Founta*-dataset (Founta et al., 2018) and *Waseem*-dataset (Waseem and Hovy, 2016).

Training set: The *Wiki*-dataset includes 160K comments collected from English Wikipedia discussions and annotated for *Toxic* and *Normal*, through crowd-sourcing[1]. Every comment is annotated by 10 workers, and the final label is obtained through majority voting. The class *Toxic* comprises rude, hateful, aggressive, disrespectful or unreasonable comments that are likely to make a person leave a conversation[2]. The dataset consists of randomly collected comments and comments made by users blocked for violating Wikipedia's policies to augment the proportion of toxic texts. This dataset contains 15,362 instances of *Toxic* and 144,324 *Normal* texts.

Out-of-Domain test set: The toxic portion of our test set is composed of four types of offensive language: *Abusive* and *Hateful* from the *Founta*-dataset, and *Sexist* and *Racist* from the *Waseem*-dataset. For the benign examples of our test set, we use the *Normal* class of the *Founta*-dataset.

---

[1] https://meta.wikimedia.org/wiki/
Research:Detox/Data_Release

[2] https://github.com/ewulczyn/
wiki-detox/blob/master/src/modeling/
toxicity_question.png

The *Founta*-dataset is a collection of 80K tweets crowd-annotated for four classes: *Abusive, Hateful, Spam* and *Normal*. The data is randomly sampled and then boosted with tweets that are likely to belong to one or more of the minority classes by deploying an iterative data exploration technique. The *Abusive* class is defined as content with any strongly impolite, rude or hurtful language that shows a debasement of someone or something, or shows intense emotions. The *Hateful* class refers to tweets that express hatred towards a targeted individual or group, or are intended to be derogatory, to humiliate, or to insult members of a group, on the basis of attributes such as race, religion, ethnic origin, sexual orientation, disability, or gender. *Spam* refers to posts consisted of advertising/marketing, posts selling products of adult nature, links to malicious websites, phishing attempts and other unwanted information, usually sent repeatedly. Tweets that do not fall in any of the prior classes are labelled as *Normal* (Founta et al., 2018). We do not include the *Spam* class in our test set as this category does not constitute offensive language, in general. The *Founta*-dataset contains 27,150 of *Abusive*, 4,965 of *Hateful* and 53,851 of *Normal* instances.

The *Waseem*-dataset includes 16K manually annotated tweets, labeled as *Sexist, Racist* or *Neither*. The corpus is collected by searching for common slurs and terms pertaining to minority groups as well as identifying tweeters that use these terms frequently. A tweet is annotated as *Racist* or *Sexist* if it uses a racial or sexist slur, attacks, seeks to silence, unjustifiably criticizes or misrepresents a minority or defends xenophobia or sexism. Tweets that do not fall in these two classes are labeled as *Neither* (Waseem and Hovy, 2016). The *Neither* class represents a mixture of benign and abusive (but not sexist or racist) instances, and, therefore, is excluded from our test set. *Waseem*-dataset contains 3,430 of *Sexist* and 1,976 of *Racist* tweets.

4   Topic Analysis of the *Wiki*-dataset

We start by exploring the content of the *Wiki*-dataset through topic modeling. We train a topic model using the Online Latent Dirichlet Allocation (OLDA) algorithm (Hoffman et al., 2010) as implemented in the Gensim library (Řehůřek and Sojka, 2010) with the default parameters. Latent Dirichlet Allocation (LDA) (Blei et al., 2003) is a Baysian probabilistic model of a collection of texts. Each text is assumed to be generated from a multi-

Topics	Top words
Category 1	
topic 0	know, like, thank, think, want
topic 1	time, like, peopl, think, life
Category 2	
topic 2	suck, year, school, c*ck, p*ssi
topic 7	english, countri, american, nation, german
topic 8	kill, die, jewish, islam, israel
topic 9	god, christian, cast, presid, japanes
topic 12	person, editor, attack, accuse, user
topic 14	f*ck, sh*t, *ss, stupid, bastard
topic 16	team, footbal, gay, match, station
Category 3	
topic 3	redirect, talk, categori, film, episod
topic 4	page, wikipedia, edit, talk, articl
topic 5	sourc, claim, cite, wikipedia, publish
topic 6	link, list, page, inform, articl
topic 10	delet, articl, imag, tag, copyright
topic 11	univers, law, scienc, theori, definit
topic 13	page, discuss, review, talk, templat
topic 15	articl, section, discuss, refer, editor
topic 17	http, com, www, org, wiki
topic 18	edit, block, vandal, user, account
topic 19	style, align, color, background, border

Table 1: Topics identified in the *Wiki*-dataset. For each topic, five of ten top words that are most representative of the assigned category are shown.

nomial distribution over a given number of topics, and each topic is represented as a multinomial distribution over the vocabulary. We pre-process the texts by lemmatizing the words and removing the stop words. To determine the optimal number of topics, we use a coherence measure that calculates the degree of semantic similarity among the top words (Röder et al., 2015). Top words are defined as the most probable words to be seen conditioned on a topic. We experimented with a range of topic numbers between 10 and 30 and obtained the maximal average coherence with 20 topics. Each topic is represented by 10 top words. For simplicity, each text is assigned a single topic that has the highest probability. The full list of topics and their top words are available in the Appendix.

We group the 20 extracted topics into three categories based on the coherency of the top words and their potential association with offensive language. This is done through manual examination of the 10 top words in each topic. Table 1 shows five out of ten top words for each topic that are most representative of the assigned category.

Category 1: incoherent or mixture of general topics

The top words of two topics (topic 0 and topic 1) are general terms such as *think, want, time*, and *life*. This category forms 26% of the dataset. Since these topics appear incoherent, their association with offensiveness cannot be judged heuristically. Looking at the toxicity annotations we observe that 47% of the *Toxic* comments belong to these topics. These comments mostly convey personal insults, usually not tied to any identity group. The frequently used abusive terms in these *Toxic* comments include *f*ck, stupid, idiot, *ss*, etc.

Category 2: coherent, high association with offensive language

Seven of the topics can be associated with offensive language; their top words represent profanity or are related to identity groups frequently subjected to abuse. Topic 14 is the most explicitly offensive topic; nine out of ten top words are associated with insult and hatred. 97% of the instances belonging to this topic are annotated as *Toxic*, with 96% of them containing explicitly toxic words.[3] These are generic profanities with the word *f*ck* being the most frequently used word.

The top words of the other six topics (topics 2, 7, 8, 9, 12, and 16) include either offensive words or terms related to identity groups based on gender, ethnicity, or religion. On average, 16% of the comments assigned to these topics are labeled as *Toxic*. We manually analyzed these comments, and found that each topic (except topic 12) tends to concentrate around a specific identity group. Offensive comments in topic 2 mostly contain sexual slur and target female and homosexual users. In topic 7, comments often contain racial and ethnicity based abuse. Topic 8 contains physical threats, often targeting Muslims and Jewish folks (the words *die* and *kill* are the most frequently used content words in the offensive messages of this topic). Comments in topic 9 involve many terms associated with Christianity (e.g., *god, christian, Jesus*). Topic 16 has the least amount of comments (0.3% of the dataset), with the offensive messages mostly targeting gay people (the word *gay* appears in 67% of the offensive messages in this topic). Topic 12 is comprised of personal attacks in the context of Wikipedia admin–contributor relations. The most common offensive words in this topic include *f*ck, stupid, troll, ignorant, hypocrite*, etc. 20% of the whole dataset and 35% of the comments labeled as *Toxic* belong to this category.

---

[3]Following Wiegand et al. (2019), we estimate the proportion of explicitly offensive instances in a dataset as the proportion of abusive instances that contain at least one word from the lexicon of abusive words by Wiegand et al. (2018).

Dataset/Class	Cat.#1	Cat.#2	Cat.#3
Training Set			
Wiki-Toxic	48%	34%	18%
Wiki-Normal	24%	18%	58%
Test Set			
Founta-Abusive	58%	33%	8%
Founta-Hateful	54%	37%	9%
Waseem-Sexist	50%	35%	15%
Waseem-Racist	23%	67%	10%
Founta-Normal	51%	28%	21%

Table 2: Distribution of topic categories per class

Category 3: coherent, low association with offensive language

The remaining eleven topics include top words specific to Wikipedia and not directly associated with offensive language. For example, keywords of topic 4 are terms such as *page, Wikipedia, edit* and *article*, and only 0.4% of the 10,471 instances in this topic are labeled as *Toxic*. These eleven topics comprise 54% of the comments in the dataset and 18% of the *Toxic* comments.

5 Topic Distribution of the Test Set

We apply the LDA topic model trained on the *Wiki*-dataset as described in Section 4 to the Out-of-Domain test set. As before, each textual instance is assigned a single topic that has the highest probability. Table 2 summarizes the distribution of topics for all classes in the three datasets.

Observe that Category 3 is the least represented category of topics across all classes, except for the *Normal* class in the *Wiki*-dataset. Specifically, there is a significant deviation in the topic distribution between the *Wiki-Normal* and the *Founta-Normal* classes. This deviation can be explained by the difference in data sources. Normal conversations on Twitter are more likely to be about general concepts covered in Category 1 or identity-related topics covered in Category 2 than the specific topics such as *writing* and *editing* in Category 3. Other than *Waseem-Racist*, which has 67% overlap with Category 2, all types of offensive behaviour in the three datasets have more overlap with the general topics (Category 1) than identity-related topics (Category 2). For example, for the *Waseem-Sexist*, 50% of instances fall under Category 1, 35% under Category 2 and 15% under Category 3. Topic 1, which is a mixture of general topics, is the dominant topic among the *Waseem-Sexist* tweets. Out of the topics in Category 2, most of the sexist tweets are matched to topic 2 (focused on sexism and homophobia) and topic 12 (general personal insults).

Dataset/Class	Test Subset			
	All	Cat.#1	Cat.#2	Cat.#3
Out-of-Domain - Toxic				
Founta-Abusive	0.94	0.94	**0.96**	0.91
Founta-Hateful	0.62	**0.65**	0.62	0.43
Waseem-Sexist	0.26	**0.29**	0.26	0.17
Waseem-Racist	0.35	**0.37**	0.36	0.20
Out-of-domain - Normal				
Founta-Normal	0.96	0.95	0.97	**0.99**

Table 3: Accuracy per test class and topic category for a classifier trained on *Wiki*-dataset. Best results in each row are in bold.

6 Generalizability of the Model Trained on the *Wiki*-dataset

To explore how well the *Toxic* class from the *Wiki*-dataset generalizes to other types of offensive behaviour, we train a binary classifier (*Toxic* vs. *Normal*) on the *Wiki*-dataset (combining the train, development and test sets) and test it on the Out-of-Domain Test set. This classifier is expected to predict a positive (*Toxic*) label for the instances of classes *Founta-Abusive*, *Founta-Hateful*, *Waseem-Sexism* and *Waseem-Racism*, and a negative (*Normal*) label for the tweets in the *Founta-Normal* class. We fine-tune a BERT-based classifier (Devlin et al., 2019) with a linear prediction layer, the batch size of 16 and the learning rate of 2×10^{-5} for 2 epochs.

Evaluation metrics: In order to investigate the trade-off between the True Positive and True Negative rates, in the following experiments we report accuracy per test class. Accuracy per class is calculated as the rate of correctly identified instances within a class. Accuracy over the toxic classes (*Founta-Abusive*, *Founta-Hateful*, *Waseem-Sexism* and *Waseem-Racism*) indicates the True Positive rate, while accuracy of the normal class (*Founta-Normal*) measures the True Negative rate. Note that given the sizes of the positive and negative test classes, all other common metrics, such as various kinds of averaged F1-scores, can be calculated from the accuracies per class. In addition, we report macro-averaged F-score, weighted by the sizes of the negative and positive classes, to show the overall impact of the proposed method.

Results: The overall performance of the classifier on the Out-of-Domain test set is quite high: weighted macro-averaged $F_1 = 0.90$. However, when the test set is broken down into the 20 topics of the *Wiki*-dataset and the accuracy is measured within the topics, the results vary greatly. For example, for the instances that fall under topic 14, the explicitly offensive topic, the F1-score is 0.99. For topic 15, a Wikipedia-specific topic, the F1-score is 0.80. Table 3 shows the overall accuracies for each test class as well as the accuracies for each topic category (described in Section 4) within each class.

For the class *Founta-Abusive*, the classifier achieves 94% accuracy. 12% of the *Founta-Abusive* tweets fall under the explicitly offensive topic (topic 14), and those tweets are classified with a 100% accuracy. The accuracy score is highest on Category 2 and lowest on Category 3. For the *Founta-Hateful* class, the classifier recognizes 62% of the tweets correctly. The accuracy score is highest on Category 1 and lowest on Category 3. 8% of the *Founta-Hateful* tweets fall under the explicitly offensive topic (topic 14), and are classified with a 99% accuracy. For the *Founta-Normal* class, the classifier recognizes 96% of the tweets correctly. Unlike the *Founta-Abusive* and *Founta-Hateful* class, for the *Founta-Normal* class, the highest accuracy is achieved on Category 3. 0.1% of the *Founta-Normal* tweets fall under the explicitly offensive topic, and only 26% of them are classified correctly.

The accuracy of the classifier on the *Waseem-Sexist* and *Waseem-Racist* classes is 0.26 and 0.35, respectively. This indicates that the *Wiki*-dataset, annotated for toxicity, is not well suited for detecting sexist or racist tweets. This observation could be explained by the fact that none of the coherent topics extracted from the *Wiki*-dataset is associated strongly with sexism or racism. Nevertheless, the tweets that fall under the explicit abuse topic (topic 14) are recognized with a 100% accuracy. Topic 8, which contains abuse mostly directed towards Jewish and Muslim people, is the most dominant topic in the *Racist* class (32% of the class) and the accuracy score on this topic is the highest, after the explicitly offensive topic. The *Racist* class overlaps the least with Category 3 (see Table 2), and the lowest accuracy score is obtained on this category. The definitions of the *Toxic* and *Racist* classes overlap mostly in general and identity-related abuse, therefore higher accuracy scores are obtained in Categories 1 and 2. Similar to *Racist* tweets, *Sexist* tweets have the least overlap and the lowest accuracy score on Category 3. The accuracy score is the highest on the explicitly offensive topic (100%) and varies substantially across other topics.

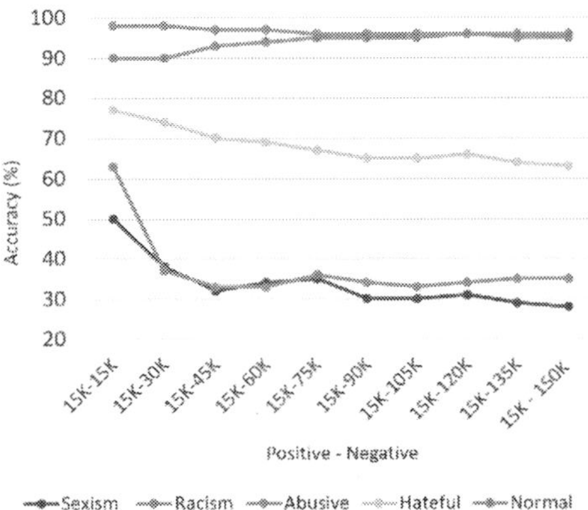

Figure 1: The classifier's performance on various classes when trained on subsets of the *Wiki*-dataset with specific class distributions.

6.1 Discussion

The generalizability of the classifier trained on the *Wiki*-dataset is affected by at least two factors: task formulation and topic distributions.

The impact of task formulation: From task formulations described in Section 3, observe that the *Wiki*-dataset defines the class *Toxic* in a general way. The class *Founta-Abusive* is also a general formulation of offensive behaviour. The similarity of these two definitions is reflected clearly in our results. The classifier trained on the *Wiki*-dataset reaches 96% accuracy on the *Founta-Abusive* class. Unlike the *Founta-Abusive* class, the other three labels included in our analysis formulate a specific type of harassment against certain targets. Our topic analysis of the *Wiki*-dataset reveals that this dataset includes profanity and hateful content directed towards minority groups but the dataset is extremely unbalanced in covering these topics. Therefore, not only is the number of useful examples for learning these classes small, but the classification models do not learn these classes effectively because of the skewness of the training dataset. This observation is in line with the fact that the trained classifier detects some of the *Waseem-Racist*, *Waseem-Sexist* and *Founta-Hateful* tweets correctly, but overall performs poorly on these classes.

The impact of topic distribution: Our analysis shows that independent of the class labels, for all the abuse-related test classes, the trained classifier performs worst when test examples fall under Category 3. Intuitively, this means that the platform-specific topics with low association with offensive language are least generalizable in terms of learn-ing offensive behaviour. Categories 1 and 2, which include a mixture of general and identity-related topics with high potential for offensiveness, have more commonalities across datasets.

7 Impact of Data Size, Class and Topic Distribution on Generalizability

Our goal is to measure the impact of various topics on generalization. However, modifying the topic distribution will impact the class distribution and data size. To control for this, we first analyze the impact of class distribution and data size on the classifier's performance. Then, we study the effect of topic distribution by limiting the training data to different topic categories.

Impact of class distribution: The class distribution in the *Wiki*-dataset is fairly imbalanced; the ratio of the size of *Wiki-Toxic* to *Wiki-Normal* is 1:10. Class imbalance can lead to poor predictive performance on minority classes, as most of the learning algorithms are developed with the assumption of the balanced class distribution. To investigate the impact of the class distribution on generalization, we keep all the *Wiki-Toxic* instances and randomly sample the *Wiki-Normal* class to build the training sets with various ratios of toxic to normal instances.

Figure 1 shows the classifier's accuracy on the test classes when trained on subsets with different class distributions. Observe that with the increase of the *Wiki-Normal* class size in the training dataset, the accuracy on all offensive test classes decreases while the accuracy on the *Founta-Normal* class increases. The classifier assigns more instances to the the *Normal* class resulting in a lower True Positive (accuracy on the offensive classes) and a higher True Negative (accuracy on the *Normal* class) rates. The drop in accuracy is significant for the *Waseem-Sexist*, *Waseem-Racist* and *Waseem-Hateful* classes and relatively minor for the *Founta-Abusive* class. Note that the impact of the class distribution is not reflected in the overall F1-score. The classifier trained on a balanced data subset (with class size ratio of 1:1) reaches 0.896 weighted-averaged F1-score, which is very close to the F1-score of 0.899 resulted from training on the full dataset with the 1:10 class size ratio. However, in practice, the designers of such systems need to decide on the preferred class distribution depending on the distribution of classes in the test environment and the significance of the consequences of the False Positive and False Negative outcomes.

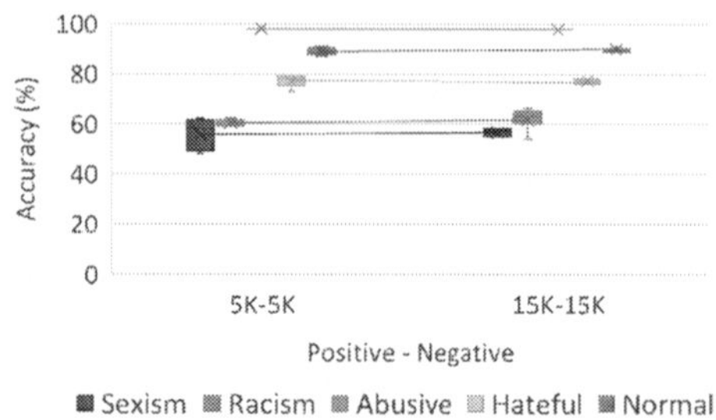

Figure 2: The classifier's average performance on various classes when trained on balanced subsets of the *Wiki*-dataset of different sizes.

Impact of dataset size: To investigate the impact of the size of the training set, we fix the class ratio at 1:1 and compare the classifier's performance when trained on data subsets of different sizes. We randomly select subsets from the *Wiki*-dataset with sizes of 10K (5K *Toxic* and 5K *Normal* instances) and 30K (15K *Toxic* and 15K *Normal* instances). Each experiment is repeated 5 times, and the averaged results are presented in Figure 2. The height of the box shows the standard deviation of accuracies. Observe that the average accuracies remain unchanged when the dataset's size triples at the same class balance ratio. This finding contrasts with the general assumption that more training data results in a higher classification performance.

Impact of topics: In order to measure the impact of topics covered in the training dataset, we compare the classifier's performance when trained on only one of the three categories of topics described in Section 4. To control for the effect of class balance and dataset size, we run the experiments for two cases of toxic-to-normal ratios, 3K-3K and 3K-27K. Each experiment is repeated 5 times, and the average accuracy per class is reported in Figure 3.

For both cases of class size ratios, shown in Figures 3a and 3b, we notice that the classifier trained on instances belonging to Category 3 reaches higher accuracies on the offensive classes, but a significantly lower accuracy on the *Founta-Normal* class. The benign part of Category 3 is overwhelmed by Wikipedia-specific examples. Therefore, utterances dissimilar to these topics are labelled as *Toxic*, leading to a high accuracy on the toxic classes and a low accuracy on the *Normal* class. This is an example of the negative impact of topic bias on the detection of offensive utterances.

In contrast, the classifiers trained on Categories 1 and 2 perform comparably across test classes. The

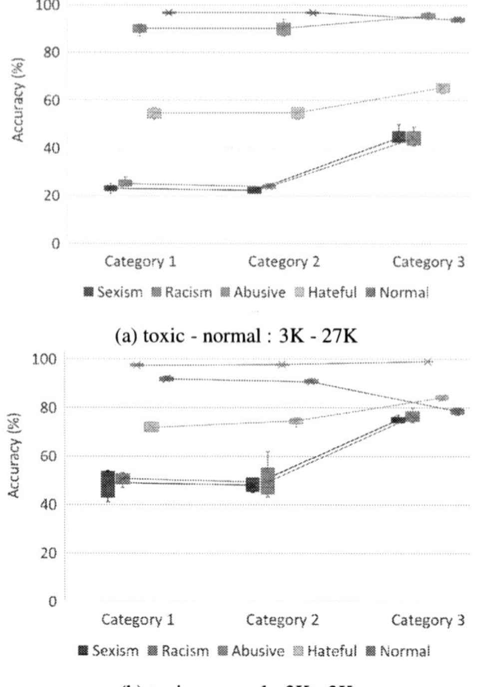

(a) toxic - normal : 3K - 27K

(b) toxic - normal : 3K - 3K

Figure 3: The classifier's performance on various classes when trained on specific topic categories.

classifier trained on Category 2 is slightly more effective in recognizing *Founta-Hateful* utterances, especially when the training set is balanced. This observation can be explained by a better representation of identity-related hatred in Category 2.

8 Removing Platform-Specific Instances from the Training Set

We showed that a classifier trained on instances from Category 3 suffers a big loss in accuracy on the *Normal* class. Here, we investigate how the performance of a classifier trained on the full *Wiki*-dataset changes when the Category 3 instances (all or the benign part only) are removed from the training set. Table 4 shows the results. Observe that removing the domain-specific benign examples, referred to as 'excl. C3 *Normal*' in Table 4, improves the accuracies for all classes. As demonstrated in the previous experiments, this improvement cannot be attributed to the changes in the class balance ratio or the size of the training set, as both these factors cause a trade-off between True Positive and True Negative rates. Removing the Wikipedia-specific topics from the *Wiki*-dataset mitigates the topic bias and leads to this improvement.

Dataset/Class	Training Set		
	Wiki	*Wiki* excl. C3 *Normal*	*Wiki* excl. C3 all
Toxic			
Founta-Abusive	0.94	0.96	0.95
Founta-Hateful	0.62	0.67	0.65
Waseem-Sexist	0.26	0.30	0.28
Waseem-Racist	0.35	0.40	0.32
Normal			
Founta-Normal	0.96	0.97	0.97

Table 4: Accuracy per Out-of-Domain test class for a classifier trained on the *Wiki*-dataset, and the *Wiki*-dataset with Category 3 instances (*Normal* only or all) excluded.

Test Set	Training Set		
	Wiki	*Wiki* excl. C3 *Normal*	*Wiki* excl. C3 all
Out-of-Domain	0.90	0.91	0.91
In-Domain	0.97	0.97	0.97

Table 5: Weighted macro-averaged F1-score for a classifier trained on portions of the *Wiki*-dataset and evaluated on the in-domain and out-of-domain test sets.

Similarly, when all the instances of Category 3 are removed from the training set ('excl. C3 all' in Table 4), the accuracy does not suffer and actually slightly improves on all classes, except *Waseem-Racist*. This is despite the fact that the training set has 58% less instances in the *Normal* class and 18% less instances in the *Toxic* class. The overall weighted-averaged F1-score on the full Out-of-Domain test set also slightly improves when the instances of Category 3 are excluded from the training data (Table 5). Removing all the instances of Category 3 is particularly interesting since it can be done only with inspection of topics and without using the class labels.

To assess the impact of removing Wikipedia-specific examples on in-domain classification, we train a model on the training set of the *Wiki*-dataset, with and without excluding Category 3 instances, and evaluate it on the full test set of the *Wiki*-dataset. We observe that the in-domain performance does not suffer from removing Category 3 from the training data (Table 5).

9 Discussion

In the task of online abuse detection, both False Positive and False Negative errors can lead to significant harm as one threatens the freedom of speech and ruins people's reputations, and the other ignores hurtful behaviour. Although balancing the class sizes has been traditionally exploited when dealing with imbalanced datasets, we showed that balanced class sizes may lead to high misclassification of normal utterances while improving the True Positive rates. This trade-off is not necessarily reflected in aggregated evaluation metrics such as F1-score but has important implications in real-life applications. We suggest evaluating each class (both positive and negative) separately taking into account the potential costs of different types of errors. Furthermore, our analysis reveals that for generalizability, the size of the dataset is not as important as the class and topic distributions.

We analyzed the impact of the topics included in the *Wiki*-dataset and showed that mitigating the topic bias improves accuracy rates across all the out-of-domain positive and negative classes. Our results suggest that the sheer amount of normal comments included in the training datasets might not be necessary and can even be harmful for generalization if the topic distribution of normal topics is skewed. When the classifier is trained on Category 3 instances only (Figure 3), the *Normal* class is attributed to the over-represented topics, leading to high misclassification of normal texts or high False Positive rates.

In general, when collecting new datasets, texts can be inspected through topic modeling using simple heuristics (e.g., keep topics related to demographic groups often subjected to abuse) in an attempt to balance the distribution of various topics and possibly sub-sample over-represented and less generalizable topics (e.g., high volumes of messages related to an incident with a celebrity figure happened during the data collection time) before the expensive annotation step.

10 Conclusion

Our work highlights the importance of heuristic scrutinizing of topics in collected datasets before performing a laborious and expensive annotation. We suggest that unsupervised topic modeling and manual assessment of extracted topics can be used to mitigate the topic bias. In the case of the *Wiki*-dataset, we showed that more than half of the dataset can be safely removed without affecting either the in-domain or the out-of-domain performance. For future work, we recommend that topic analysis, augmentation of topics associated with offensive vocabulary and targeted demographics, and filtering of non-generalizable topics should be applied iteratively during data collection.

References

Betty van Aken, Julian Risch, Ralf Krestel, and Alexander Löser. 2018. Challenges for toxic comment classification: An in-depth error analysis. In *Proceedings of the 2nd Workshop on Abusive Language Online*.

David M. Blei, Andrew Y. Ng, and Michael I. Jordan. 2003. Latent Dirichlet allocation. *Journal of Machine Learning Research*, 3(Jan):993–1022.

Paula Branco, Luís Torgo, and Rita P. Ribeiro. 2016. A survey of predictive modeling on imbalanced domains. *ACM Computing Surveys (CSUR)*, 49(2):1–50.

Eshwar Chandrasekharan, Mattia Samory, Shagun Jhaver, Hunter Charvat, Amy Bruckman, Cliff Lampe, Jacob Eisenstein, and Eric Gilbert. 2018. The Internet's hidden rules: An empirical study of Reddit norm violations at micro, meso, and macro scales. *Proceedings of the ACM on Human-Computer Interaction*, 2(CSCW):1–25.

Thomas Davidson, Dana Warmsley, Michael Macy, and Ingmar Weber. 2017. Automated hate speech detection and the problem of offensive language. In *Proceedings of the International AAAI Conference on Web and Social Media*.

Jacob Devlin, Ming-Wei Chang, Kenton Lee, and Kristina Toutanova. 2019. BERT: Pre-training of deep bidirectional transformers for language understanding. In *Proceedings of the 2019 Conference of the North American Chapter of the Association for Computational Linguistics: Human Language Technologies*, pages 4171–4186, Minneapolis, Minnesota.

Antigoni Maria Founta, Constantinos Djouvas, Despoina Chatzakou, Ilias Leontiadis, Jeremy Blackburn, Gianluca Stringhini, Athena Vakali, Michael Sirivianos, and Nicolas Kourtellis. 2018. Large scale crowdsourcing and characterization of Twitter abusive behavior. In *Proceedings of the International AAAI Conference on Web and Social Media*.

Guo Haixiang, Li Yijing, Jennifer Shang, Gu Mingyun, Huang Yuanyue, and Gong Bing. 2017. Learning from class-imbalanced data: Review of methods and applications. *Expert Systems with Applications*, 73:220–239.

Matthew Hoffman, Francis R. Bach, and David M. Blei. 2010. Online learning for latent Dirichlet allocation. In J. D. Lafferty, C. K. I. Williams, J. Shawe-Taylor, R. S. Zemel, and A. Culotta, editors, *Advances in Neural Information Processing Systems 23*, pages 856–864. Curran Associates, Inc.

Hossein Hosseini, Sreeram Kannan, Baosen Zhang, and Radha Poovendran. 2017. Deceiving Google's Perspective API built for detecting toxic comments. *arXiv preprint arXiv:1702.08138*.

Homa Hosseinmardi, Sabrina Arredondo Mattson, Rahat Ibn Rafiq, Richard Han, Qin Lv, and Shivakant Mishra. 2015. Analyzing labeled cyberbullying incidents on the Instagram social network. In *Proceedings of the International Conference on Social Informatics*, pages 49–66.

Justin M. Johnson and Taghi M. Khoshgoftaar. 2019. Survey on deep learning with class imbalance. *Journal of Big Data*, 6(1):27.

David Jurgens, Libby Hemphill, and Eshwar Chandrasekharan. 2019. A just and comprehensive strategy for using NLP to address online abuse. In *Proceedings of the 57th Annual Meeting of the Association for Computational Linguistics*, pages 3658–3666, Florence, Italy.

Miaofeng Liu, Yan Song, Hongbin Zou, and Tong Zhang. 2019. Reinforced training data selection for domain adaptation. In *Proceedings of the 57th Annual Meeting of the Association for Computational Linguistics*, pages 1957–1968, Florence, Italy.

Pushkar Mishra, Helen Yannakoudakis, and Ekaterina Shutova. 2019. Tackling online abuse: A survey of automated abuse detection methods. *arXiv preprint arXiv:1908.06024*.

Chikashi Nobata, Joel Tetreault, Achint Thomas, Yashar Mehdad, and Yi Chang. 2016. Abusive language detection in online user content. In *Proceedings of the International Conference on World Wide Web*, pages 145–153.

Amir H Razavi, Diana Inkpen, Sasha Uritsky, and Stan Matwin. 2010. Offensive language detection using multi-level classification. In *Proceedings of the Canadian Conference on Artificial Intelligence*, pages 16–27.

Radim Řehůřek and Petr Sojka. 2010. Software Framework for Topic Modelling with Large Corpora. In *Proceedings of the LREC 2010 Workshop on New Challenges for NLP Frameworks*, pages 45–50, Valletta, Malta. ELRA.

Michael Röder, Andreas Both, and Alexander Hinneburg. 2015. Exploring the space of topic coherence measures. In *Proceedings of the 8th ACM International Conference on Web Search and Data Mining*, pages 399–408.

Sebastian Ruder and Barbara Plank. 2017. Learning to select data for transfer learning with Bayesian optimization. In *Proceedings of the Conference on Empirical Methods in Natural Language Processing*, pages 372–382.

Anna Schmidt and Michael Wiegand. 2017. A survey on hate speech detection using natural language processing. In *Proceedings of the Fifth International Workshop on Natural Language Processing for Social Media*, pages 1–10.

Deven Santosh Shah, H. Andrew Schwartz, and Dirk Hovy. 2020. Predictive biases in natural language processing models: A conceptual framework and overview. In *Proceedings of the 58th Annual Meeting of the Association for Computational Linguistics*, pages 5248–5264.

Bertie Vidgen and Leon Derczynski. 2020. Directions in abusive language training data: Garbage in, garbage out. *arXiv preprint arXiv:2004.01670*.

Bertie Vidgen, Alex Harris, Dong Nguyen, Rebekah Tromble, Scott Hale, and Helen Margetts. 2019a. Challenges and frontiers in abusive content detection. In *Proceedings of the Third Workshop on Abusive Language Online*, pages 80–93, Florence, Italy.

Bertie Vidgen, Helen Margetts, and Alex Harris. 2019b. How much online abuse is there? *Alan Turing Institute. November*, 27.

Zeerak Waseem, Thomas Davidson, Dana Warmsley, and Ingmar Weber. 2017. Understanding abuse: A typology of abusive language detection subtasks. In *Proceedings of the First Workshop on Abusive Language Online*, pages 78–84, Vancouver, BC, Canada.

Zeerak Waseem and Dirk Hovy. 2016. Hateful symbols or hateful people? Predictive features for hate speech detection on Twitter. In *Proceedings of the NAACL Student Research Workshop*, pages 88–93.

Michael Wiegand, Josef Ruppenhofer, and Thomas Kleinbauer. 2019. Detection of Abusive Language: the Problem of Biased Datasets. In *Proceedings of the 2019 Conference of the North American Chapter of the Association for Computational Linguistics: Human Language Technologies*, pages 602–608, Minneapolis, Minnesota.

Michael Wiegand, Josef Ruppenhofer, Anna Schmidt, and Clayton Greenberg. 2018. Inducing a lexicon of abusive words – a feature-based approach. In *Proceedings of the 2018 Conference of the North American Chapter of the Association for Computational Linguistics: Human Language Technologies*, pages 1046–1056, New Orleans, Louisiana.

Ellery Wulczyn, Nithum Thain, and Lucas Dixon. 2017. Ex machina: Personal attacks seen at scale. In *Proceedings of the 26th International Conference on World Wide Web*, pages 1391–1399.

Marcos Zampieri, Shervin Malmasi, Preslav Nakov, Sara Rosenthal, Noura Farra, and Ritesh Kumar. 2019. Semeval-2019 Task 6: Identifying and categorizing offensive language in social media (OffensEval). In *Proceedings of the 13th International Workshop on Semantic Evaluation*, pages 75–86.

Identifying and Measuring Annotator Bias Based on Annotators' Demographic Characteristics

Hala Al Kuwatly[*]
TU Munich,
Department of Informatics,
Germany
hala.kuwatly@tum.de

Maximilian Wich[*]
TU Munich,
Department of Informatics,
Germany
maximilian.wich@tum.de

Georg Groh
TU Munich,
Department of Informatics,
Germany
grohg@in.tum.de

Abstract

Machine learning is recently used to detect hate speech and other forms of abusive language in online platforms. However, a notable weakness of machine learning models is their vulnerability to bias, which can impair their performance and fairness. One type is annotator bias caused by the subjective perception of the annotators. In this work, we investigate annotator bias using classification models trained on data from demographically distinct annotator groups. To do so, we sample balanced subsets of data that are labeled by demographically distinct annotators. We then train classifiers on these subsets, analyze their performances on similarly grouped test sets, and compare them statistically. Our findings show that the proposed approach successfully identifies bias and that demographic features, such as first language, age, and education, correlate with significant performance differences.

1 Introduction

According to the online harassment report published by Pew Research Center, "four-in-ten Americans have personally experienced online harassment, and 62% consider it a major issue." (Duggan, 2017, p.3). Online environments such as social media and discussion forums have created spaces for people to express their opinions and viewpoints, but this comes at the cost of hateful, offensive, and abusive content. Moderating this content manually requires a lot of staff and large amounts of hand-curated policies, which generated much interest in automatic content moderation systems that make use of recent advances in machine learning (Schmidt and Wiegand, 2017).

One challenge of training machine learning systems is the demand for large amounts of labeled data. Hence, many researchers use crowdsourcing platforms to annotate their data sets (Davidson et al., 2017; Founta et al., 2018; Vidgen and Derczynski, 2020), although having expert annotators has proven to improve the quality of annotations (Waseem, 2016). Such crowdsourcing approaches, however, exposes hate speech detection systems to annotator bias. Hateful behavior can take many forms (Waseem et al., 2017), making it harder to obtain a clean, common definition of hate speech, and resulting in subjective and biased annotations. Biases in the annotations are then absorbed and reinforced by the machine learning models, causing systematically unfair systems (Bender and Friedman, 2018). Therefore, it is not surprising that a large body of work has identified and mitigated this bias (Bender and Friedman, 2018; Bountouridis et al., 2019; Dixon et al., 2018).

We already know that people with particular demographic characteristics (e.g., black, disabled, or younger people) become more frequently targets of hate (Vidgen et al., 2019b). An aspect that is sparsely investigated in this context is the relation between annotators' demographic features and a potential bias in the data set. We want to fill this gap by addressing the following research question:

How do annotators' demographic features such as gender, age, education and first language impact their annotations of hateful content?

To answer this question, we conduct the following exploratory study: We sample balanced subsets of data that are labeled by demographically distinct annotators. We then train classifiers on these subsets, analyze their performances on similarly split test sets, and compare them statistically.

2 Related work

Since unintended bias in hate speech datasets can impair the model's performance (Waseem, 2016)

---

[*]These authors contributed equally to this work.

Proceedings of the Fourth Workshop on Online Abuse and Harms, pages 184–190
Online, November 20, 2020. ©2020 Association for Computational Linguistics
https://doi.org/10.18653/v1/P17

and fairness (Vidgen et al., 2019a; Dixon et al., 2018), a lot of recent work has been done to investigate this phenomenon (Wiegand et al., 2019; Kim et al., 2020).

Some work examined racial bias (Sap et al., 2019; Davidson et al., 2019; Xia et al., 2020), others explored gender bias (Gold and Zesch, 2018), aggregation bias (Balayn et al., 2018) and political bias (Wich et al., 2020b). The type of bias we are examining in this study is the annotator bias. Waseem (2016) studied the influence of annotator expertise on classification models and found that systems trained on expert annotations outperform those trained on amateur annotations, confirming and extending the results from Ross et al. (2017). Geva et al. (2019) showed that model performance improves when exposed to annotator identifiers, which suggests that annotator bias needs to be considered when creating hate speech models. Salminen et al. (2018) studied the difference between annotations of crowd workers from 50 countries and found those differences highly significant. Binns et al. (2017) examined the effect of the gender of the annotators on the performance of classifiers. Wich et al. (2020a) studied the similarities in the behaviour of the annotators to reveal biases that they bring into the data.

To the best of our knowledge, no one has developed a method to identify annotator bias based on multiple demographic characteristics of the annotators and measure its impact on the classification performance.

3 Data

We used the personal attack corpora from Wikipedia's Detox project (Wulczyn et al., 2017), which contains 115,864 labeled comments from Wikipedia on whether the comment contains a form of personal attack. The labels are the following (Wikimedia, n.d.):

- Quoting attack: Indicator for whether the annotator thought the comment is quoting or reporting a personal attack that originated in a different comment.

- Recipient attack: Indicator for whether the annotator thought the comment contains a personal attack directed at the recipient of the comment.

- Third party attack: Indicator for whether the

Feature	Trainset size	Testset size	Total size
Gender	4,401	1,100	5,501
First language	2,038	509	2,547
Age group	6,782	1,696	8,478
Education	3,174	794	3,968

Table 1: Number of comments in each demographic feature's datasets

annotator thought the comment contains a personal attack directed at a third party.

- Other attack: Indicator for whether the annotator thought the comment contains a personal attack but is not quoting attack, a recipient attack or third party attack.

- Attack: Indicator for whether the annotator thought the comment contains any form of personal attack. (Wikimedia, n.d.)

For our study, we used the attack label as the classification target label, not taking into consideration the other labels.

The comments were labeled by 4,053 crowdworkers. For 2,190 of them, we have the demographic information. For each of these annotators we have the following demographic features:

- Gender: 'male' or 'female'

- English first language: '1' or '0'; '1' = annotator's first language is English

- Age group:'Under 18', '18-30', '30-45', '45-60', 'Over 60'. Since annotators are not equally distributed across age groups (see distribution plot in the appendix), we changed the grouping to 'Under 30' and 'Over 30'.

- Education (highest obtained education level): 'none', 'some', 'hs', 'bachelors', 'masters', 'doctorate', 'professional'. 'hs' is short for high school. Since annotators are not equally distributed across education levels (see distribution plot in the appendix), we changed the grouping to 'Below hs' (includes hs) and 'Above hs'.

4 Methodology

We address the research question by training classification models on data from demographically distinct groups and comparing their performances[1].

---

[1]Code available on GitHub: https://github.com/mawic/ annotator-bias-demographic-characteristics

The hypothesis is that a statistically significant difference between the classifiers' performances indicates an annotator bias related to the studied demographic feature.

In the first step, we group the annotators by their demographic features, such as gender, age, education level, and native language. For each of those features, we create $m + 1$ datasets where m is the number of different values a demographic feature can take, e.g. for gender m could be equal to 2 if we only consider male and female annotators. All datasets have the same comments, but with different labels aggregated from annotators belonging to each different group. The additional dataset ($+1$) has labels aggregated from annotators belonging to all groups. It serves as a control group. We call this dataset the mixed dataset. We measured the inter-rater agreement within each group using Krippendorff's alpha (Hayes and Krippendorff, 2007).

In the second step, we split the datasets into train and test sets, and train 20 classifiers for each group on the group's training set and report F1 scores for all test sets. We train 20 classifiers to get multiple data points for each group's classifier and then apply the Kolmogorov-Smirnov test to examine whether they are significantly different [2]. The null hypothesis in this context is that the two samples are drawn from the same distribution. If we can reject the null hypothesis ($p < 0.05$) for a certain demographic feature, this will be evidence that annotators belonging to different groups of feature values hold different norms and are bringing in different biases into their annotations.

Concerning the classification model, we chose to make use of recent advancements in transfer learning and employ DistilBERT as a classifier due to the limited number of data points annotated by each group. DistilBERT (Sanh et al., 2019) is a smaller and faster distilled version of BERT (Devlin et al., 2018). In the context of abusive language detection, it provides a comparable performance (Vidgen et al., 2020). We used the base uncased version of DistilBERT (`distilbert-base-uncased`) with a maximum sequence length of 100, a learning rate of 5×10^{-6}, and 1cycle learning rate policy (Smith, 2018) and trained each classifier for 2 epochs.

4.1 Data split

To ensure the comparability of the classifiers, it is necessary to compile the training and test sets in the right way. Therefore, we define the following 2 conditions for selecting the comments: (1) All data sets of one feature contain the same comments. (2) At least 6 annotators from each demographic group annotated the comment. In the case of the gender group, that means a selected comment was annotated by at least 6 male and 6 female annotators.

For each demographic feature, we create 3 training and test set combinations. In the first one, the labels are taken from a random set of 6 annotators belonging to the first demographic group (e.g., males). In the second one, the labels of the comments are taken from a random set of 6 annotators belonging to the second demographic group (e.g., females). The third train and test sets are mixed: the labels of the comments are taken from a random set of 3 annotators belonging to the first demographic group and 3 annotators belonging to the second demographic group. While the subset of comments stays unchanged, for each of the 20 classifiers we sample the annotations of different random annotators. Data sets' sizes can be found in Table 1.

We also performed the same experiments without the limitation of sharing the same comments in the data sets of each feature, in order to increase the size of comments in the splits. Results were very similar to our shared comments experiments.

5   Results

In this section, we report the results of our experiments for each demographic feature. The results comprise the inter-rater agreement of the annotators in the different groups, the averaged F1 scores of the trained classifiers, the sensitivity and specificity of the classifiers as charts, and the p-values generated by the Kolmogorov-Smirnov tests.

5.1   Gender

In regards to gender, we could not find evidence of any significant difference between male and female classifiers. Although the inter-rater agreement is significantly lower for females (0.45) than for males (0.51) (Table 4), the average F1 scores of the 20 classifiers trained for each group show no significant difference (Table 2). When analyzing the sensitivity and specificity graphs in Figure 1a,

---

[2] We trained 20 classifiers only for practical constraints.

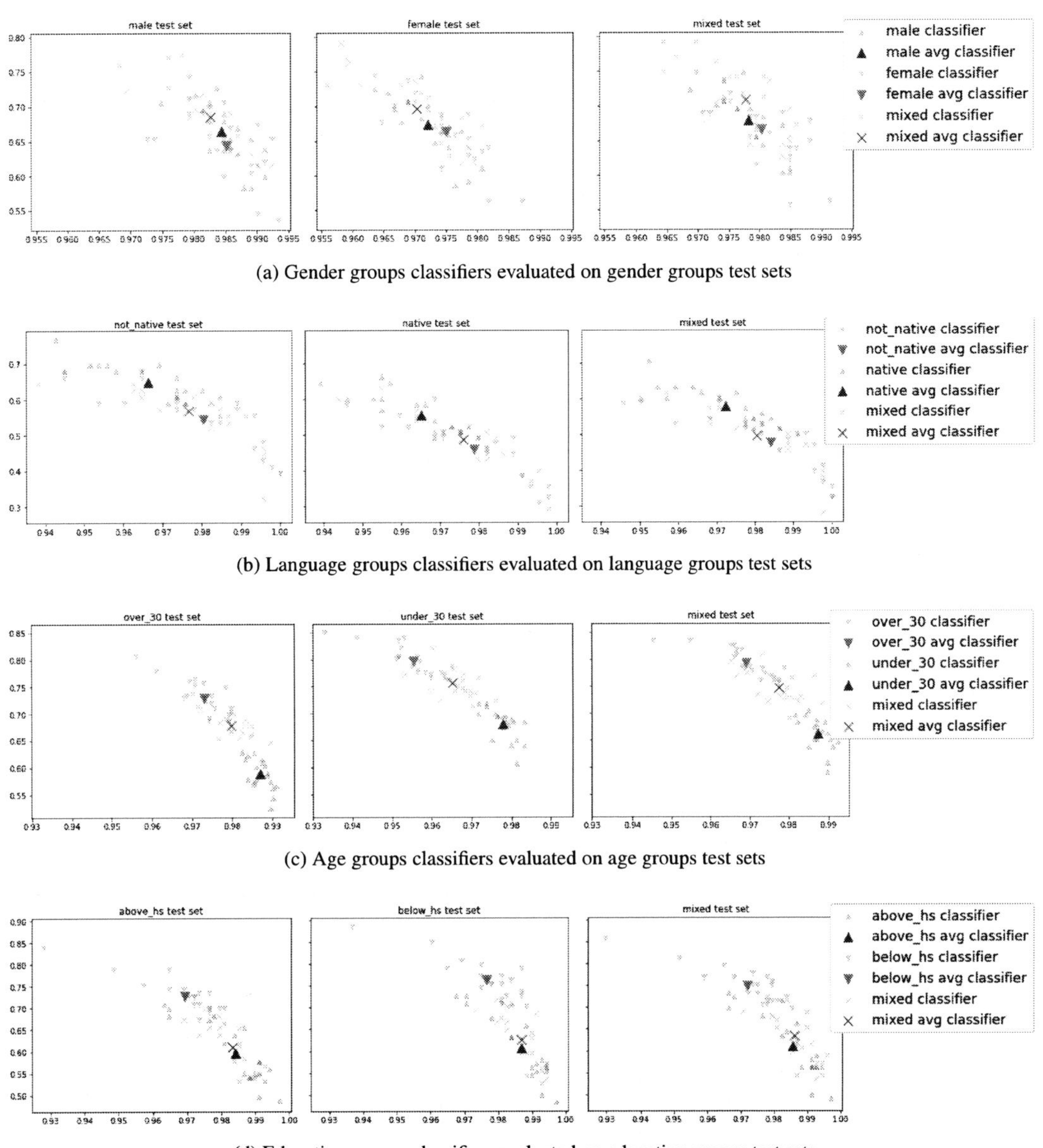

(a) Gender groups classifiers evaluated on gender groups test sets

(b) Language groups classifiers evaluated on language groups test sets

(c) Age groups classifiers evaluated on age groups test sets

(d) Education groups classifiers evaluated on education groups test sets

Figure 1: The x-axes are the specificity of the classifiers, and the y-axes are the sensitivity. Each transparent dot represents the specificity and sensitivity of each of the 20 classifiers trained for each group on the respective train set (dot marker) and evaluated on the respective test set (sub-figures). The opaque dots represent the average values.

one can also see no significant pattern or trend. The p-value resulting from the Kolmogorov-Smirnov test applied on the F1 scores of the 20 male classifiers and 20 female classifiers evaluated on the mixed test set is 0.83 (Table 3). Since it is larger than 0.05, we cannot conclude that a significant difference between the male and female classifier exists.

5.2 First Language

Our experiments on first language classifiers resulted in the following observations:

1. Classifiers trained on native-labeled data have a notably higher F1 score (Table 2) and are also more sensitive to all test sets (the blue triangles in Figure 1b), which suggests that they are particularly better at classifying comments

trainset \ testset	male	female	mixed
male	0.850	0.855	0.829
female	0.846	0.859	0.838
mixed	**0.856**	**0.862**	**0.848**
	native	not native	mixed
native	**0.814**	**0.818**	**0.816**
not native	0.768	0.786	0.764
mixed	0.783	0.778	0.772
	under 30	over 30	mixed
under 30	0.853	0.833	0.863
over 30	0.858	**0.870**	**0.883**
mixed	**0.860**	0.860	0.879
	below hs	above hs	mixed
below hs	**0.885**	**0.861**	**0.873**
above hs	0.839	0.830	0.839
mixed	0.847	0.836	0.850

Table 2: Average F1 scores of the classifiers.

Feature	p-value
Gender	8.3×10^{-1}
First Language	1.0×10^{-3}
Age group	1.1×10^{-8}
Education	1.4×10^{-7}

Table 3: Results of the Kolmogorov-Smirnov test, inputs to the tests are the F1 scores of the 20 classifiers evaluated on the mixed test set of each feature.

Feature	Group	Inter-rater Agreement
Gender	Male	0.51
	Female	0.45
	Mixed	0.48
English	Native	0.46
	Not native	0.50
	Mixed	0.48
Age group	Under 30	0.47
	Over 30	0.50
	Mixed	0.48
Education	Below hs	0.49
	Above hs	0.48
	Mixed	0.48

Table 4: Inter-rater agreement for all groups

that contain personal attack.

2. Classifiers trained on only non-native-labeled data perform almost as good as the baseline (classifier trained on mix-labeled data) (Table 2).

3. We found very minor disparities in the specificity of both classifiers (Figure 1b).

The result of the Kolmogorov-Smirnov test on native and non-native classifiers is a p-value of 1.0×10^{-3} (Table 3), thus we can reject the null hypothesis and conclude that a significant difference does exist between them.

5.3 Age group

Our experiments resulted in the following observations:

1. Classifiers trained on over-30-labeled data have higher F1 scores than classifiers trained on under-30 labeled data on all test sets. They are however comparable to the baseline (classifier trained on mix-labeled data) (Table 2).

2. All classifiers are less sensitive to over-30-labeled test set (Figure 1c), which might suggest that it contains harder examples that all classifiers failed to correctly classify.

The Kolmogorov-Smirnov test on the results of the two classifiers produces a p-value of 1.1×10^{-8} (Table 3), thus we can reject that they come from the same distribution and conclude that a significant difference does exist between them.

5.4 Education

Our experiments resulted in the following observations:

1. The F1 scores of the classifiers trained on below-hs-labeled data are higher than scores of classifiers trained on above-hs-labeled data on all test sets (Table 2).

2. Classifiers trained on below-hs-labeled data have a comparable specificity to the other classifiers but with a notably higher sensitivity on all test sets. (Figure 1d).

The Kolmogorov-Smirnov test with a p-value of 1.4×10^{-7} (Table 3) also shows that there exists a significant difference between the two groups.

6 Discussion

In light of our results, we can conclude that the gender of the annotator does not bring a significant bias in annotating personal attacks in the studied dataset. However, when Binns et al. (2017) explored the role of gender in *offensive* content annotations, they established a distinguishable difference between males and females. We think this is related to the nature of the annotation task itself. To investigate other tasks, our approach can further be applied in future work on the other data sets provided by Wikipedia's Detox project (Wulczyn et al., 2017) such as aggressiveness and toxicity to investigate the effects of gender for those tasks.

When it comes to the first language of the annotators, it seems that native English speakers are generally better at identifying personal attacks in comments. The results also suggest that non-natives could not capture attack in comments that natives found to contain attack.

In addition, age groups and education levels of the annotators also seem to play a notable role in how attacks are perceived. Training a classifier on aggregated labels from all groups, even if the data is balanced between groups, does not seem to be fair to all groups involved.

Although we have only explored the demographic features provided by the data set and grouped some of them for reasons dictated by the data size, we think other features (e.g., race, ethnicity, and political orientation), different within feature groupings and feature intersections might produce new biases. While exploring all possible demographic features prior to building models is simply infeasible, the set of studied features can be determined per task.

Our approach demonstrated how particular training sets labeled by different groups of people can be used to identify and measure bias in data sets. These biases are never constant or static even within one group, for what counts as hateful is always subjective. In consequence, having only one version of ground truth is bound to produce biased systems. It is inevitable that training models on biased datasets produces systems that amplify those biases, whether these biases are exclusionary, prejudicial, or historical. Therefore and due to the conflicting and ever-changing definitions of hate speech among communities, we urge researchers in the hate speech domain to examine their data sets closely and thoroughly in order to understand their limitations and consequences.

7 Conclusion

This work explored bias in hate speech classification models where the task is inherently controversial and annotators' demographic data might influence the labels. We demonstrate how particular demographic features might bias the models in ways that are important to look into prior to using such models in production. We explored the performance of classification models trained and tested on different training and test data splits, in order to identify the fairness of these classifiers and the biases they absorb. We hope that our proposed method for identifying and measuring annotator bias based on annotators' demographic characteristics will help to build fairer hate speech classifiers.

Acknowledgments

This research has been partially funded by a scholarship from the Hanns Seidel Foundation financed by the German Federal Ministry of Education and Research.

References

Agathe Balayn, Panagiotis Mavridis, Alessandro Bozzon, Benjamin Timmermans, and Zoltán Szlávik. 2018. Characterising and mitigating aggregation-bias in crowdsourced toxicity annotations. In *Proceedings of the 1st Workshop on Subjectivity, Ambiguity and Disagreement in Crowdsourcing, and Short Paper Proceedings of the 1st Workshop on Disentangling the Relation Between Crowdsourcing and Bias Management*, volume 2276. CEUR.

Emily M Bender and Batya Friedman. 2018. Data statements for natural language processing: Toward mitigating system bias and enabling better science. *Transactions of the Association for Computational Linguistics*, 6:587–604.

Reuben Binns, Michael Veale, Max Van Kleek, and Nigel Shadbolt. 2017. Like trainer, like bot? inheritance of bias in algorithmic content moderation. In *International conference on social informatics*, pages 405–415. Springer.

Dimitrios Bountouridis, Mykola Makhortykh, Emily Sullivan, Jaron Harambam, Nava Tintarev, and Claudia Hauff. 2019. Annotating credibility: Identifying and mitigating bias in credibility datasets.

Thomas Davidson, Debasmita Bhattacharya, and Ingmar Weber. 2019. Racial bias in hate speech and abusive language detection datasets. *arXiv preprint arXiv:1905.12516*.

Thomas Davidson, Dana Warmsley, Michael Macy, and Ingmar Weber. 2017. Automated hate speech detection and the problem of offensive language. *arXiv preprint arXiv:1703.04009*.

Jacob Devlin, Ming-Wei Chang, Kenton Lee, and Kristina Toutanova. 2018. Bert: Pre-training of deep bidirectional transformers for language understanding. *arXiv preprint arXiv:1810.04805*.

Lucas Dixon, John Li, Jeffrey Sorensen, Nithum Thain, and Lucy Vasserman. 2018. Measuring and mitigating unintended bias in text classification. In *Proceedings of the 2018 AAAI/ACM Conference on AI, Ethics, and Society*, pages 67–73.

Maeve Duggan. 2017. *Online Harassment 2017*. Pew Research Center.

Antigoni-Maria Founta, Constantinos Djouvas, Despoina Chatzakou, Ilias Leontiadis, Jeremy Blackburn, Gianluca Stringhini, Athena Vakali, Michael Sirivianos, and Nicolas Kourtellis. 2018. Large scale crowdsourcing and characterization of twitter abusive behavior. *arXiv preprint arXiv:1802.00393*.

Mor Geva, Yoav Goldberg, and Jonathan Berant. 2019. Are we modeling the task or the annotator? an investigation of annotator bias in natural language understanding datasets. *arXiv preprint arXiv:1908.07898*.

Michael Wojatzki Tobias Horsmann Darina Gold and Torsten Zesch. 2018. Do women perceive hate differently: Examining the relationship between hate speech, gender, and agreement judgments.

Andrew F Hayes and Klaus Krippendorff. 2007. Answering the call for a standard reliability measure for coding data. *Communication methods and measures*, 1(1):77–89.

Jae Yeon Kim, Carlos Ortiz, Sarah Nam, Sarah Santiago, and Vivek Datta. 2020. Intersectional bias in hate speech and abusive language datasets. *arXiv preprint arXiv:2005.05921*.

Björn Ross, Michael Rist, Guillermo Carbonell, Benjamin Cabrera, Nils Kurowsky, and Michael Wojatzki. 2017. Measuring the reliability of hate speech annotations: The case of the european refugee crisis. *arXiv preprint arXiv:1701.08118*.

Joni Salminen, Fabio Veronesi, Hind Almerekhi, Soon-Gvo Jung, and Bernard J Jansen. 2018. Online hate interpretation varies by country, but more by individual: A statistical analysis using crowdsourced ratings. In *2018 Fifth International Conference on Social Networks Analysis, Management and Security (SNAMS)*, pages 88–94. IEEE.

Victor Sanh, Lysandre Debut, Julien Chaumond, and Thomas Wolf. 2019. Distilbert, a distilled version of bert: smaller, faster, cheaper and lighter. *arXiv preprint arXiv:1910.01108*.

Maarten Sap, Dallas Card, Saadia Gabriel, Yejin Choi, and Noah A Smith. 2019. The risk of racial bias in hate speech detection. In *Proceedings of the 57th Annual Meeting of the Association for Computational Linguistics*, pages 1668–1678.

Anna Schmidt and Michael Wiegand. 2017. A survey on hate speech detection using natural language processing. In *Proceedings of the Fifth International workshop on natural language processing for social media*, pages 1–10.

Leslie N Smith. 2018. A disciplined approach to neural network hyper-parameters: Part 1–learning rate, batch size, momentum, and weight decay. *arXiv preprint arXiv:1803.09820*.

Bertie Vidgen, Austin Botelho, David Broniatowski, Ella Guest, Matthew Hall, Helen Margetts, Rebekah Tromble, Zeerak Waseem, and Scott Hale. 2020. Detecting east asian prejudice on social media.

Bertie Vidgen and Leon Derczynski. 2020. Directions in abusive language training data: Garbage in, garbage out. *arXiv preprint arXiv:2004.01670*.

Bertie Vidgen, Alex Harris, Dong Nguyen, Rebekah Tromble, Scott Hale, and Helen Margetts. 2019a. Challenges and frontiers in abusive content detection. Association for Computational Linguistics.

Bertie Vidgen, Helen Margetts, and Alex Harris. 2019b. How much online abuse is there? a systematic review of evidence for the uk. *The Alan Turing Institute*.

Zeerak Waseem. 2016. Are you a racist or am i seeing things? annotator influence on hate speech detection on twitter. In *Proc. 1st Workshop on NLP and Computational Social Science*, pages 138–142.

Zeerak Waseem, Thomas Davidson, Dana Warmsley, and Ingmar Weber. 2017. Understanding abuse: A typology of abusive language detection subtasks. *arXiv preprint arXiv:1705.09899*.

Maximilian Wich, Hala Al Kuwatly, and Georg Groh. 2020a. Investigating annotator bias with a graph-based approach. In *Proc. 4th Workshop on Online Abuse and Harms*.

Maximilian Wich, Jan Bauer, and Georg Groh. 2020b. Impact of politically biased data on hate speech classification. In *Proc. 4th Workshop on Online Abuse and Harms*.

Michael Wiegand, Josef Ruppenhofer, and Thomas Kleinbauer. 2019. Detection of abusive language: the problem of biased datasets. In *Proceedings of the 2019 Conference of the North American Chapter of the Association for Computational Linguistics: Human Language Technologies, Volume 1 (Long and Short Papers)*, pages 602–608.

Wikimedia. n.d. Research:detox/data release. `https://meta.wikimedia.org/wiki/Research:Detox/Data_Release`.

Ellery Wulczyn, Nithum Thain, and Lucas Dixon. 2017. Ex machina: Personal attacks seen at scale. In *Proceedings of the 26th International Conference on World Wide Web*, pages 1391–1399.

Mengzhou Xia, Anjalie Field, and Yulia Tsvetkov. 2020. Demoting racial bias in hate speech detection. *arXiv preprint arXiv:2005.12246*.

Investigating Annotator Bias with a Graph-Based Approach

Maximilian Wich
TU Munich,
Department of Informatics,
Germany
maximilian.wich@tum.de

Hala Al Kuwatly
TU Munich,
Department of Informatics,
Germany
hala.kuwatly@tum.de

Georg Groh
TU Munich,
Department of Informatics,
Germany
grohg@in.tum.de

Abstract

A challenge that many online platforms face is hate speech or any other form of online abuse. To cope with this, hate speech detection systems are developed based on machine learning to reduce manual work for monitoring these platforms. Unfortunately, machine learning is vulnerable to unintended bias in training data, which could have severe consequences, such as a decrease in classification performance or unfair behavior (e.g., discriminating minorities). In the scope of this study, we want to investigate annotator bias — a form of bias that annotators cause due to different knowledge in regards to the task and their subjective perception. Our goal is to identify annotation bias based on similarities in the annotation behavior from annotators. To do so, we build a graph based on the annotations from the different annotators, apply a community detection algorithm to group the annotators, and train for each group classifiers whose performances we compare. By doing so, we are able to identify annotator bias within a data set. The proposed method and collected insights can contribute to developing fairer and more reliable hate speech classification models.

1 Introduction

A massive problem that online platforms face nowadays is online abuse (e.g., hate speech against women, Muslims, or African Americans). It is a severe issue for our society because it can cause more than poisoning the platform's atmosphere. For example, Williams et al. (2020) showed a relation between online hate and physical crime.

Therefore, people have started to develop systems to automatically detect hate speech or abusive language. The advances in machine learning and deep learning have improved these systems tremendously, but there is still much space for enhancements because it is a challenging and complex task (Fortuna and Nunes, 2018; Schmidt and Wiegand, 2017).

A weakness of these systems is their vulnerability towards unintended bias that can cause an unfair behavior of the systems (e.g., discrimination of minorities) (Dixon et al., 2018; Vidgen et al., 2019). Researchers have identified different types and sources of bias that can influence the performance of hate speech detection models. Davidson et al. (2019), for example, investigated racial bias in hate speech data sets. Wiegand et al. (2019) showed that topic bias and author bias of data sets could impair the performance of hate speech classifiers. Wich et al. (2020) examined the impact of political bias within the data on the classifier's performance. To mitigate bias in training data, Dixon et al. (2018) and Borkan et al. (2019) developed an approach.

Another type of bias that caught researchers' attention is annotator bias. It is caused by the subjective perception and different knowledge levels of annotators regarding the annotation task (Ross et al., 2017; Waseem, 2016; Geva et al., 2019). Such a bias could harm the generalizability of classification models (Geva et al., 2019). Especially in the context of online abuse and hate speech, it can be a severe issue because annotating abusive language requires expert knowledge due to the vagueness of the task (Ross et al., 2017; Waseem, 2016). Nevertheless, due to the limited resources and the demand for large datasets, annotating is often outsourced to crowdsourcing platforms (Vidgen and Derczynski, 2020). Therefore, we want to investigate this phenomenon in our paper. There is already research concerning annotator bias in hate speech and online abuse detection. Ross et al. (2017) examined the relevance of instructing annotators for hate speech annotations. Waseem (2016) compared the impact of amateur and expert annotators. One of their findings was that a system trained with data

Proceedings of the Fourth Workshop on Online Abuse and Harms, pages 191–199
Online, November 20, 2020. ©2020 Association for Computational Linguistics
https://doi.org/10.18653/v1/P17

labeled by experts outperforms one trained with data labeled by amateurs. Binns et al. (2017) investigated whether there is a performance difference between classifiers trained on data labeled by males and females. Al Kuwatly et al. (2020) extended this approach and investigated the relevance of annotators' educational background, age, and mother tongue in the context of bias. Sap et al. (2019) examined racial bias in hate speech data sets and its impact on the classification performance. To the best of our knowledge, no one has investigated annotator bias by identifying patterns in the annotation behavior through an unsupervised approach. That is why we address the following research question in the paper: Is it possible to identify annotator bias purely on the annotation behavior using graphs and classification models?

Our contribution is the following:

- A novel approach for grouping annotators according to their annotations behavior through graphs and analyzing the different groups in order to identify annotator bias.

- A comparison of different weight functions for constructing the annotator graph modeling the annotator behavior.

2   Data

For our study, we use the Personal Attacks corpora from the Wikipedia Detox project (Wulczyn et al., 2017). It contains 115,864 comments from English Wikipedia that were labeled whether they comprise personal attack or not. In total, there are 1,365,217 annotations provided by 4,053 annotators from the crowdsourcing platform Crowdflower — approximately 10 annotations for each comment. Each annotation consists of 5 categories distinguishing between different types of attack: *quoting_attack*, *recipient_attack, third_party_attack, other_attack*, and *attack*. In our experiments, we only use the 5th category (*attack*) because it covers a broader range than the other labels. Its value is 1 if "the comment contains any form of personal attack" (Wikimedia, n.d.). Otherwise it is 0. The corpora also contain demographic information (e.g., gender, age, and education) of 2,190 annotators. But this data is not relevant to our study.

3   Methodology

Our approach is to group annotators according to their annotation behavior and analyze perfor-

mance of classification models trained on annotations from these groups. To do so, we firstly group the annotators according to their annotation behavior using a graph. Secondly, we split the data set by the groups and their respective annotations. Thirdly, we train classifiers for each annotator group and then compare their performances. The reader can find a detailed description of the steps in the following[1]:

Creating Annotator Graph

In the first step, we create an undirected unweighted graph to model the annotation behavior of the annotators (e.g., how similar the annotations of two annotators are). Each node represents an annotator. An edge between two nodes exists if both annotators annotate at least one same data record. Additionally, each edge has a weight that models the similarity between the annotations of the data records. To calculate the weight, we selected four functions that we will compare:

1. **Agreement Rate**: It is the percentage in which both annotators agree on the annotation for a data record:

$$a = \frac{n_{agree}}{n_{agree} + n_{disagree}}$$

   where n_{agree} is the number of data records that both annotated and assigned the same labels to and $n_{disagree}$ is the number of data records that both annotated and assigned different labels.

2. **Cohen's Kappa** (Cohen, 1960): It is often used as a measure for inter-rater reliability.

$$\kappa = \frac{p_0 - p_e}{1 - p_e}$$

   where p_0 is the "proportion of observed agreements" (Sim and Wright, 2005, p.258) among the data records annotated by both annotators and p_e is "proportion of agreements expected by chance" (Sim and Wright, 2005, p.258) among the records. The range of κ is between -1 and $+1$. $+1$ corresponds perfect agreement; ≤ 0 means agreement at chance or no agreement (Cohen, 1960). If both annotators select the same label for all records, κ is not

---

[1]Code available on GitHub: https://github.com/mawic/graph-based-method-annotator-bias

defined. In this case, we remove the edge. An alternative would be to keep the edge and assign 1. But we rejected this idea because of the following consideration. Let us assume that we have 4 annotators (A,B,C, and D). A and B assigned the same label to the same comment. C and D assigned the same labels to the same 20 comments. In both cases, κ is not defined. Assigning the same value (e.g., 1) to both edges would weigh both equally. But the edge between C and D should receive a higher weight because the agreement between A and B could be a coincidence.

3. **Krippendorff's Alpha** (Krippendorff, 2004): It is another inter-rater reliability measure, which is defined as follows:

$$\alpha = 1 - \frac{D_0}{D_e}$$

"where D_0 is the observed disagreement among values assigned to units of analysis [...] and D_e is the disagreement one would expect when the coding of units is attributable to chance rather than to the properties of these units" (Krippendorff, 2011, p.1). Further details of the calculation are provided by Krippendorff (2011). Similar to κ, α is not defined if the annotators choose the same label for all records. We handle this case in the same way as above.

4. **Heuristic**: To overcome the undefined issue, we define a heuristic weight function taking the relative agreement rate and the number of commonly annotated data records (overlap) between two annotators into account. The function is defined by four boundary points:

   - The maximum weight (1.0) is reached, if two annotators commonly annotated n data records and agree on all annotations. n is the maximal number of data records that is commonly annotated by two annotators and is defined by the data set.
   - The minimum weight (0) is reached, if two annotators commonly annotated n data records and disagree on all annotations.
   - A weight that is 20% larger than the minimum weight (0.2) is reached, if two an-

notators commonly annotated only one data record and disagree.

   - A weight that is 60% larger than the minimum weight (0.6) is reached, if two annotators commonly annotated only one data record and agree.

The transition between the four boundary points is gradually calculated. The algorithm can be found in the appendix. The purpose of the approach is to consider the overlap besides the agreement rate because the larger the overlap the more reliable is the agreement rate. Cohen's Alpha and Krippendorff's Alpha provide this, but their weakness is the undefined issue, which is a realistic scenario for our annotation task.

All weight functions are normalized between 0 and 1 to make the results comparable, if they are not already in this range.

Detecting Annotator Groups

The goal of the next step is to group the annotators according to their annotation behavior. For this purpose, we apply the Louvain method, an unsupervised algorithm for detecting communities in a graph (Blondel et al., 2008). After that, we filter the communities with at least 250 members. Otherwise, the groups do not comprise enough data records that were annotated by their members in order to train a classification model.

Splitting Data According to Groups

After detecting the groups, we split the comments and annotations according to the groups. For each weight function and the corresponding graph, we do the following: We select those comments that were annotated by at least one member of every group. For each group, we create a data set containing these comments and the annotations from the group's members. The label for each comment is the majority vote of the group's annotators. In addition, we create a further data set that serves as a baseline and is called group 0 for all experiments. The data set contains the same comments, but the labels are the results of all 4,053 annotators. After that, all data sets for a weight function are split in a training and test set in the same manner to ensure the comparability of the data sets. This is done for each of the four weight functions.

Weight function	Agreement Rate	Cohen's Kappa	Krippendorff's Alpha	Heuristic Function
Number of nodes	4,053	4,053	4,053	4,053
Number of edges	444,344	91,308	91,308	444,344
Average degree	219.3	45.1	45.1	219.3
Density	0.054	0.011	0.011	0.054
Connected components	1	1	1	1
Distribution of edge weights				

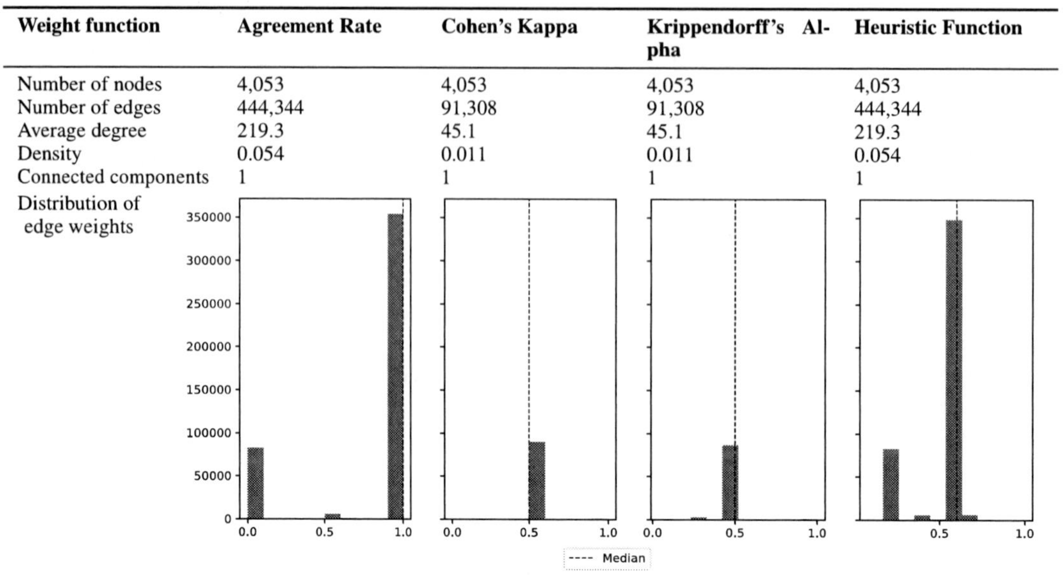

Table 1: Graph metrics

Training Classification Models for Groups and Comparing Their Performances

For the classification model, we use a pre-trained DistilBERT that we fine-tune for our task (Sanh et al., 2019). It is smaller and faster to train than classical BERT, but it provides comparable performance (Sanh et al., 2019). In the context of abusive language detection, it shows a similar performance like larger BERT models (Vidgen et al., 2020). Since we need to train several models for different weight functions and groups, we choose the lighter model.

The basis of our classification model is the pre-trained `distilbert-base-uncased`, which is the distilled version version of `bert-base-uncased`. It has 6 layers, a hidden size of 768, 12 self-attention heads, and 66M parameters. To fine-tune the model for our task, we apply the 1cycle learning rate policy suggested by Smith (2018) with a learning rate of 5e-6 for 2 epochs. The batch size is 64 and the size of the validation set is 10% of the training set. Furthermore, we limit the number of input tokens to 150. The task that DistilBERT is fine-tuned for is to distinguish between the labels "ATTACK" and "OTHER".

After training the models, we compare their performances (F1 macro). For this purpose, each model is evaluated on its own test set and the one

from the other groups including group 0, which represents all annotators. Instead of reporting the F1 score, we report them relatively to our baseline (group 0) because it allows a better comparison of the results. Additionally, the actual F1 score are not relevant for this analysis.

4 Results

The experiments show that our proposed method enables the grouping of annotators according to similar annotation behavior. Classifiers separately trained on data from the different groups and evaluated with the other groups' test data exhibit noticeable differences in classification performance, which confirms our approach. The detailed results can be found in the following:

Annotator Graph

We created one graph for each weight function. Table 1 provides the key metrics of the generated graphs. It is conspicuous that the graphs with Cohen's Kappa and Krippendorff's Alpha weight function have only 91,308 edges, while the other twos have 444,344. This difference also causes the divergence of the average degree and density. The reason for the difference is that many relations between two annotators comprise only one comment. If both agree on an annotation, Cohen's Kappa and Krippendorff's Alpha are not defined; consequently, we do not have an edge. Therefore, graphs

Weight function	Agreement Rate	Cohen's Kappa	Krippendorff's Alpha	Heuristic Function
Number of identified groups	6	13	12	6
Number of selected groups	6	6	6	6
Number of annotators	4,053	3,407	3,282	4,053
AVG(annotators/groups)	579.00	486.71	468.86	579.00
SD(annotators/groups)	266.17	239.75	224.99	258.24
Size of training set/test set	31,170 / 7,793	18,951 / 4,738	18,204 / 4,551	31,738 / 7,934
Distribution of group sizes				

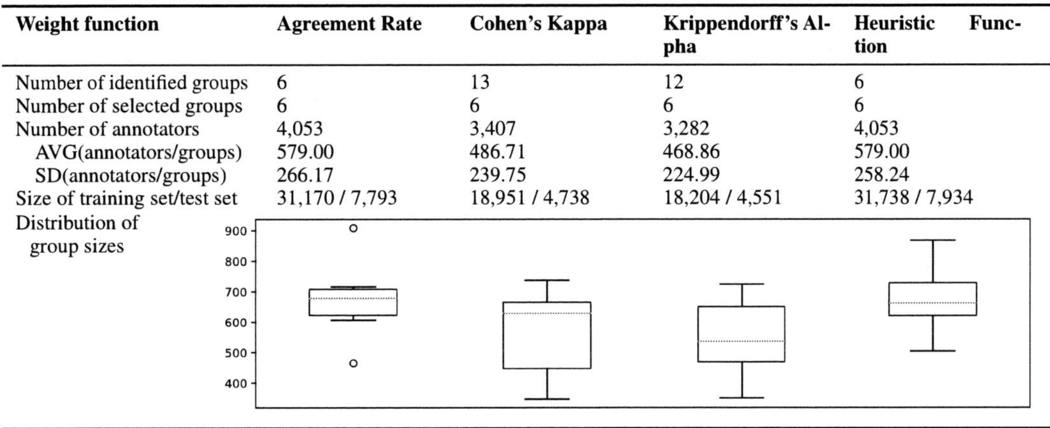

Table 2: Results of community detection

with these weight functions have fewer edges.

Community Detection

Table 2 shows the results of community detection. While the Louvain algorithm split the graphs with the Agreement Rate and Heuristic Function as weight functions in 6 groups, 13 groups in the graph with Cohen's Kappa were detected and 12 in the one with Krippendorff's Alpha. An explanation for the divergence is the difference between the number of edges of the graphs. Since the groups have various numbers of members, we select only these with at least 250 annotators due to two reasons. Firstly, we have the same number of groups for all weight functions. Secondly, we ensure that we have enough annotated comments to train the classifiers. It may be noted at this juncture that only comments were selected for the training/test set if they were annotated by the group. Therefore, groups with a small number of annotators would have reduced the size of the training/test set. The distribution of the size of the training/test set is similar to the one of the numbers of identified groups. For Agreement Rate we have 31,170 annotated comments for the training set and 7,793 for the test set, for the Heuristic Function 31,738 and 7,934, for the Cohen's Kappa 18,951 and 4,738, and for Krippendorff's Alpha 18,204 and 4,551. The smaller data sizes for the last two are related to the smaller average size of groups.

To compare the different groups, we computed the inter-rater agreement for each group and between the groups by using Krippendorff's Alpha. To calculate the rate between the groups, we compute Krippendorff's Alpha using the union of all annotations from both groups. The inter-rater agreement scores (in percent, 100% means perfect agreement) for all four weight functions are depicted in Figure 1. The first column of each subfigure shows the inter-rater agreement within each group. The 7 columns right to the line provide the inter-rater agreement between the groups, and the last column shows the average inter-rater agreement between the groups. Please note that the inter-rater agreement scores are not comparable between the different weight functions/subfigures because the groups, the comments, and the annotations are different. The scores can only be compared with scores from the same graph with the same weight function.

If we look at the inter-rater agreement within the groups (first column of each subfigure), we see that the groups exhibit varying scores and that the deviations to the baseline (group 0, data set average) also differ. If the score is higher than the baseline, the group is more coherent in regards to the annotations. If it is lower, the group is less coherent. Furthermore, the more scores are higher than the baseline, the better because it means that the algorithm is able to create more coherent groups. Considering these aspects, we can say that the Heuristic Function produces the best results. Its groups 3 (48.3%), 5 (48.3%), and 6 (48.0%) together have the largest distance to the baseline (46.5%) than the top three groups of the other groups.

The groups resulting from the graph with the Agreement Rate as weight function have less strongly varying inter-rater agreement rates than the groups of the other weight functions. In the case of Cohen's Kappa, one group with a strong inter-rater agreement is formed (49.8%) — the

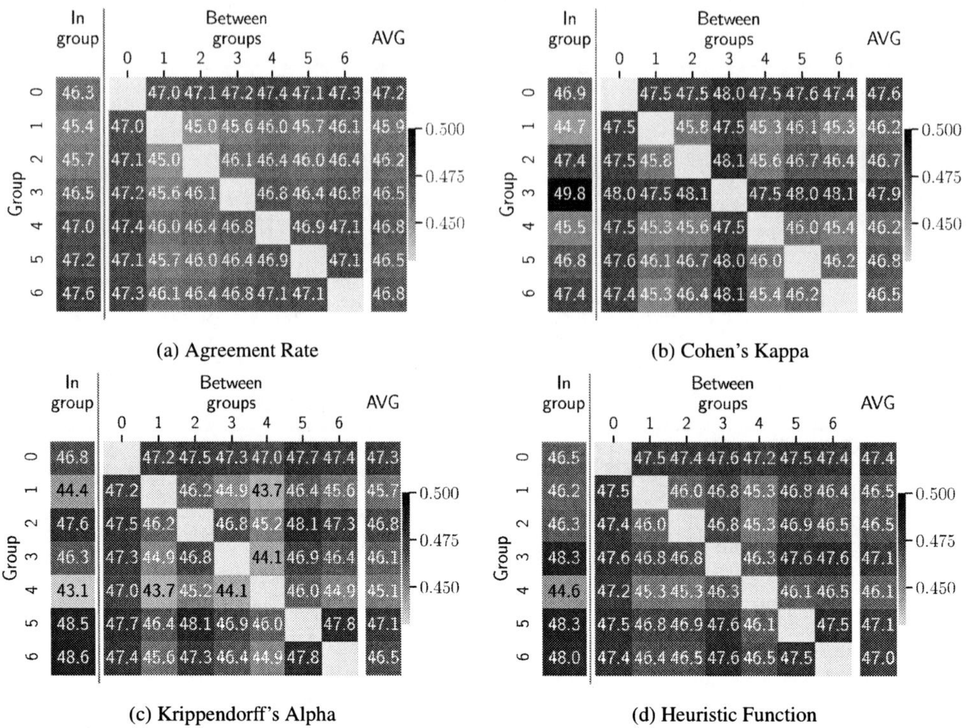

Figure 1: Inter-rater agreement within and between groups for different weight functions

highest deviation for all weight functions. But the other groups are similar to the baseline or worse. Krippendorf's Alpha as weight function produces results that are comparable to the ones from the Heuristic Function. The deviations from its top three groups, however, are smaller than the ones from the corresponding groups of Heuristic Function. Furthermore, the groups of the Heuristic Functions cover all 4,053 annotators, while the ones from Krippendorf's Alpha comprise only 3,282. Therefore, we choose the groups from the Heuristic Function for the last part of the experiment.

Classification Models and Their Performances

Instead of reporting the macro-F1 scores for the classifiers trained on the different group-specific training sets and tested on the all group-specific test sets, we report them relatively to the baseline (trained on group 0 and tested on group 0) for easier comparison. The baseline has a macro-F1 score of 87.54%. In addition to the relative scores, the figures contain an extra column and row with average values for better comparability.

It is conspicuous that the deviations reported in the first column of each matrix are lower than the rest. The reason is the following: These columns report the performances of the classifiers for the different groups on the baseline test set. Since the baseline test set has the largest number of annotations, the labels are more coherent. Consequently, classifiers perform better on the baseline test set than on their own, less coherent test sets.

The first thing that attracts our attention is column 4 because it has the largest deviations, meaning that all classifiers perform quite worse on the test set of group 4. We can explain this phenomenon with the low inter-rater agreement rate of this group (44.6%, compare Figure 1d). This is also the explanation of why row 4 has the lowest average of all rows. In this context, it is surprising that row 6 has the second-lowest average of all rows, while it has a relatively large inter-rater agreement rate (48.0%). A possible explanation can be that the annotations within the group are coherent but less coherent with respect to all other annotations. In the case of group 3 and 5 (inter-rater agreement rate of 48.3% and 48.%), the average deviations are comparable to the others. This indicate that the annotation behavior of the group members is more coherent with the overall annotation behavior.

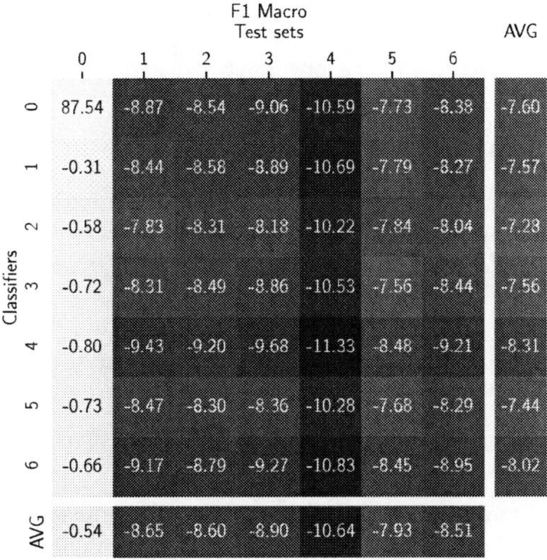

Figure 2: Macro F1 scores for the Heuristic Function

The cross-group agreement average (last column in Figure 1d) confirms this because both groups have the largest values aside from the baseline. In the case of group 5, this hypothesis is supported by the fact that all classifiers perform on average better on the test set of group 5 than on the test sets from groups 1, 2, 3, 4, and 6.

5 Discussion

The results show that the proposed method is suitable for identifying annotator groups purely based on annotation behavior. The deviations in inter-rater agreement rates of the groups and in the classifiers' performances prove this.

In regards to the weight functions, we found that the Agreement Rate is not suitable compared to the other functions. This is not surprising because there is a reason why Cohen's Kappa and Krippendorff's Alpha are used as a metric for the inter-rater agreement. An advantage of our Heuristic Function in regards to Cohen's Kappa and Krippendorff's Alpha as weight functions is that it does not have the undefined issue if two annotators assign only one type of label to the comments to be labeled. A potential improvement could be to combine Cohen's Kappa and Krippendorff's Alpha weight function with the Heuristic Function.

The results of our method can be linked to annotator bias in the following manner: An identified annotator group that has a high inter-rater agreement within the group, but poor classification performance on the other test sets indicates that it has a certain degree of bias as the group's annotation behavior differs from the rest. For such insights, we see currently two possible use cases:

- The insights can be used to mitigate annotator bias. The annotations of these groups can either be weighted differently or deleted to avoid transferring the bias to the classification model.

- The insights can be used to build classification models that model the annotator bias. This can be helpful for tasks that do not have one truth. In the case of online abuse, it is possible that one group is more tolerant towards abusive language and another one less tolerant.

The novelty of our approach is that it is unsupervised and does not require any stipulation of bias that you want to detect in advance. Existing approaches, such as Binns et al. (2017), who investigated gender bias, or Sap et al. (2019) and Davidson et al. (2019), who examined racial bias, defined in their hypothesis which kind of bias they want to uncover. Our method, however, does not require any pre-defined categories to detect bias.

6 Conclusion

In this paper, we proposed a novel graph-based method for identifying annotator bias through grouping similar annotation behavior. It differs from existing approaches by its unsupervised nature. But the method requires further research and refinement. To address our limitations, we propose the following future work:

Firstly, we used only one data set for our study. The approach, however, should be also tested and refined with other data sets. The Wikipedia Detox project, for example, provides two more data sets with the same structure, but with different tasks (toxicity and aggression). In general, data availability is a challenge of this kind of research because hate speech data sets mostly contain aggregated annotations. Therefore, we urge researchers releasing data sets to provide the unaggregated annotations as well.

Secondly, other approaches for grouping the annotators should be investigated. We used only one community detection method, the Louvain algorithm. But there are many more methods, such as the Girvan-Newman algorithm (Girvan and Newman, 2002) and the Clauset-Newman-Moore algorithm (Clauset et al., 2004).

Thirdly, our methods should be extended so that it can handle smaller groups. Our current approach requires at least 250 annotators in a group to ensure that we have enough training data. But it would be interesting to investigate smaller groups in the hope that these groups are more coherent in regards to their annotation behavior.

Acknowledgments

This research has been partially funded by a scholarship from the Hanns Seidel Foundation financed by the German Federal Ministry of Education and Research.

References

Hala Al Kuwatly, Maximilian Wich, and Georg Groh. 2020. Identifying and measuring annotator bias based on annotators' demographic characteristics. In *Proc. 4th Workshop on Online Abuse and Harms*.

Reuben Binns, Michael Veale, Max Van Kleek, and Nigel Shadbolt. 2017. Like trainer, like bot? inheritance of bias in algorithmic content moderation. In *International conference on social informatics*, pages 405–415. Springer.

Vincent D Blondel, Jean-Loup Guillaume, Renaud Lambiotte, and Etienne Lefebvre. 2008. Fast unfolding of communities in large networks. *Journal of statistical mechanics: theory and experiment*, 2008(10):P10008.

Daniel Borkan, Lucas Dixon, Jeffrey Sorensen, Nithum Thain, and Lucy Vasserman. 2019. Nuanced metrics for measuring unintended bias with real data for text classification. In *Proc. 28th WWW Conf.*, pages 491–500.

Aaron Clauset, Mark EJ Newman, and Cristopher Moore. 2004. Finding community structure in very large networks. *Physical review E*, 70(6):066111.

Jacob Cohen. 1960. A coefficient of agreement for nominal scales. *Educational and psychological measurement*, 20(1):37–46.

Thomas Davidson, Debasmita Bhattacharya, and Ingmar Weber. 2019. Racial bias in hate speech and abusive language detection datasets. *arXiv preprint arXiv:1905.12516*.

Lucas Dixon, John Li, Jeffrey Sorensen, Nithum Thain, and Lucy Vasserman. 2018. Measuring and mitigating unintended bias in text classification. In *Proceedings of the 2018 AAAI/ACM Conference on AI, Ethics, and Society*, pages 67–73.

Paula Fortuna and Sérgio Nunes. 2018. A survey on automatic detection of hate speech in text. *ACM Comput. Surv.*, 51(4).

Mor Geva, Yoav Goldberg, and Jonathan Berant. 2019. Are we modeling the task or the annotator? an investigation of annotator bias in natural language understanding datasets. In *2019 Conference on Empirical Methods in Natural Language Processing*, pages 1161–1166.

Michelle Girvan and Mark EJ Newman. 2002. Community structure in social and biological networks. *Proceedings of the national academy of sciences*, 99(12):7821–7826.

K. Krippendorff. 2004. *Content Analysis: An Introduction to Its Methodology*. Content Analysis: An Introduction to Its Methodology. Sage.

Klaus Krippendorff. 2011. Computing krippendorff's alpha-reliability.

Björn Ross, Michael Rist, Guillermo Carbonell, Benjamin Cabrera, Nils Kurowsky, and Michael Wojatzki. 2017. Measuring the reliability of hate speech annotations: The case of the european refugee crisis. *arXiv preprint arXiv:1701.08118*.

Victor Sanh, Lysandre Debut, Julien Chaumond, and Thomas Wolf. 2019. Distilbert, a distilled version of bert: smaller, faster, cheaper and lighter. *arXiv preprint arXiv:1910.01108*.

Maarten Sap, Dallas Card, Saadia Gabriel, Yejin Choi, and Noah A Smith. 2019. The risk of racial bias in hate speech detection. In *Proc. 57th ACL Conf.*, pages 1668–1678.

Anna Schmidt and Michael Wiegand. 2017. A survey on hate speech detection using natural language processing. In *Proceedings of the Fifth International Workshop on Natural Language Processing for Social Media*, pages 1–10, Valencia, Spain. Association for Computational Linguistics.

Julius Sim and Chris C Wright. 2005. The kappa statistic in reliability studies: use, interpretation, and sample size requirements. *Physical therapy*, 85(3):257–268.

Leslie N Smith. 2018. A disciplined approach to neural network hyper-parameters: Part 1–learning rate, batch size, momentum, and weight decay. *arXiv preprint arXiv:1803.09820*.

Bertie Vidgen, Austin Botelho, David Broniatowski, Ella Guest, Matthew Hall, Helen Margetts, Rebekah Tromble, Zeerak Waseem, and Scott Hale. 2020. Detecting east asian prejudice on social media.

Bertie Vidgen and Leon Derczynski. 2020. Directions in abusive language training data: Garbage in, garbage out. *arXiv preprint arXiv:2004.01670*.

Bertie Vidgen, Alex Harris, Dong Nguyen, Rebekah Tromble, Scott Hale, and Helen Margetts. 2019. Challenges and frontiers in abusive content detection. In *Proceedings of the Third Workshop on Abusive Language Online*, pages 80–93, Florence, Italy. Association for Computational Linguistics.

Zeerak Waseem. 2016. Are You a Racist or Am I Seeing Things? Annotator Influence on Hate Speech Detection on Twitter. In *Proc. First Workshop on NLP and Computational Social Science*, pages 138–142.

Maximilian Wich, Jan Bauer, and Georg Groh. 2020. Impact of politically biased data on hate speech classification. In *Proc. 4th Workshop on Online Abuse and Harms*.

Michael Wiegand, Josef Ruppenhofer, and Thomas Kleinbauer. 2019. Detection of Abusive Language: the Problem of Biased Datasets. *Proc. 2019 Conference of the North American Chapter of the Association for Computational Linguistics: Human Language Technologies, Volume 1 (Long and Short Papers)*, pages 602–608.

Wikimedia. n.d. Research:detox/data release. `https://meta.wikimedia.org/wiki/Research:Detox/Data_Release`.

Matthew L Williams, Pete Burnap, Amir Javed, Han Liu, and Sefa Ozalp. 2020. Hate in the machine: Anti-black and anti-muslim social media posts as predictors of offline racially and religiously aggravated crime. *The British Journal of Criminology*, 60(1):93–117.

Ellery Wulczyn, Nithum Thain, and Lucas Dixon. 2017. Ex machina: Personal attacks seen at scale. In *Proceedings of the 26th International Conference on World Wide Web*, pages 1391–1399.

Association for Computational Linguistics
209 N. Eighth Street
Stroudsburg, Pennsylvania 18360

ISBN 978-1-7138-2007-9